Frequencies of Deceit

Frequencies of Deceit

HOW GLOBAL PROPAGANDA WARS
SHAPED THE MIDDLE EAST

Margaret Peacock

UNIVERSITY OF CALIFORNIA PRESS

University of California Press
Oakland, California

Library of Congress Cataloging-in-Publication Data

Names: Peacock, Margaret, author.
Title: Frequencies of deceit : how global propaganda wars shaped the Middle
    East / Margaret Peacock.
Description: Oakland, California : University of California Press, [2025] |
    Includes bibliographical references and index.
Identifiers: LCCN 2024033958 (print) | LCCN 2024033959 (ebook) |
    ISBN 9780520409736 (cloth) | ISBN 9780520409743 (paperback) |
    ISBN 9780520409750 (epub)
Subjects: LCSH: Radio in propaganda—Middle East—20th century.
Classification: LCC HE8697.85.M628 P432025 (print) | LCC HE8697.85.M628
    (ebook) | DDC 384.540956—dc23/eng/20241119
LC record available at https://lccn.loc.gov/2024033958
LC ebook record available at https://lccn.loc.gov/2024033959

34   33   32   31   30   29   28   27   26   25
10   9   8   7   6   5   4   3   2   1

For my mother, Dorothy Peacock

CONTENTS

ILLUSTRATIONS

ACKNOWLEDGMENTS

I could not have written this book without the support and contributions of a remarkable group of individuals. This journey started with Safa Elnaili and Dima Ayoub, who were two of the best language professors I have ever had. In the research phase, my gratitude extends to Els Boonen and Matthew Chipping at the BBC Archive in Caversham, UK, who always ensured I had a space in front of a microfilm machine. At the Wilson Center, Liz Malinkin and the entire team supported me throughout my tenure as a Kennan Fellow. I am indebted to Mary Sadek and Djodi Deutsch at the American Research Center in Egypt, and to Alya El Marakby, Heba Sheta, and Nara Yassen at the American University in Cairo. Andrea Thal at the Contemporary Image Collective in Cairo and Elizabeth Keating, Rex Keating's wife, offered real insights. The staff of the US National Archive in College Park, Maryland, and the State Archives in Moscow provided indispensable support. Alexis Percle at the LBJ Archive at the University of Texas, along with the Moshe Dayan Center at the University of Tel Aviv, offered access to exceptional resources that significantly contributed to my project. The team at the Middle East Centre at St. Anthony's College, Oxford, especially Debbie Usher and her staff, were instrumental in facilitating this research. Re'ee Hagay, Ali Alalem, and Manasar Alharethi, my diligent research assistants, were pivotal in helping me manage over thirteen thousand sources in five languages.

When it came time to write and publish, conversations with Andrea Stanton, James Vaughan, Tony Shaw, and Nicholas Cull helped me navigate the broader academic debates. A heartfelt thanks goes to Dina Fainberg, Kristin Roth-Ey, and Victoria Phillips for inviting me to pivotal conferences in Britain at which smart people got together to talk about media and power.

Thank you to Niels Hooper, Nora Becker, and Julie Van Pelt at the University of California Press, along with Jon Dertien and Sharon Langworthy at BookComp, for setting the bar on how to publish a book. I am also appreciative to the peer reviewers who offered invaluable advice on how to make this book better. My agent, Jane Dystel, deserves a huge thank you for her unwavering support through two books and countless moments of doubt.

So much support came from friends and colleagues at the University of Alabama. Alex Boucher, head archivist, has been an essential resource, always the first person I contact when I need to find something. Erik Peterson and Lucy Kaufman, my dear friends in the History Department, were the first two people to read this book from cover to cover, when I was still too insecure to show it to anyone else. For countless hours listening to me think through problems out loud, I thank you. Waleed Hazbun in the Department of Political Science then stepped in to champion this project. He sponsored a Middle East Studies Colloquium at Alabama in 2023, bringing to Tuscaloosa key scholars—Andrea Stanton, Vivian Ibrahim, and Michelle Woodward—to give a first round of peer review to the book. Their critiques are apparent in every facet of this project. Thank you, also, to my department chair, Dr. Josh Rothman, who backed this project unquestioningly, and to the University of Alabama Leadership Board and Research Grants Council, who provided key funding for research.

My biggest gratitude goes to my husband, D. Jay Cervino, our three daughters, Amelia, Sylvia, and Mira, and my mother, Dorothy Peacock. I am a Russian historian by training. When I announced that I was going to learn Arabic, live for long stretches in Moscow, Cairo, London, and Washington, D.C., and write this book, they didn't miss a beat in saying okay. You can't do a project like this without having people around you who really love you, and I am infinitely lucky in this regard.

ABBREVIATIONS

INFORMATION AND BROADCASTING ORGANIZATIONS

BBC	British Broadcasting Corporation
CRD	Cultural Relations Department (UK)
EBS	Egyptian Broadcasting Service
IRD	Information Research Department (UK)
NEABS	Near East Arabic Broadcasting Station (UK)
PBS	Palestinian Broadcasting Service (UK/Mandate Palestine)
USIA	United States Information Agency
VOA	Voice of America

ARCHIVES

AUCA	American University Cairo Archive (Cairo, Egypt)
BBCM	BBC Monitoring, Summary of World Broadcasts (Reading, UK)
BBCWAC	BBC Written Archive Center (Reading, UK)
Cong. Rec.	US Congressional Record (Washington, DC, USA)
FBIS	Foreign Broadcast Information Service (Washington, DC, USA)

FRUS	Foreign Relations of the United States, US National Archive (Washington, DC, USA)
GARF	State Archive of the Russian Federation (Moscow, Russia)
HC	Hansard Commons, Papers of the British Parliament (London, UK)
HU OSA	Open Society Archives at Central European University (Budapest, Hungary)
LBJ	Lyndon Johnson Presidential Archive (Austin, TX, USA)
MASPERO	Egyptian National Media Authority (Cairo, Egypt)
MECA	Middle East Centre Archive (St. Anthony's College, Oxford, UK)
MDCA	Moshe Dayan Center Archive (Tel Aviv, Israel)
NARA	National Archives and Records Administration (College Park, MD, USA)
NLI	National Library of Israel (Jerusalem, Israel)
NYPL	New York Public Library (New York City, NY, USA)
SWB	Summary of World Broadcasts (London, UK)
TNA	The British National Archive (Kew, UK)

Introduction

> O Arabs, we have plenty in our bag, we have arms which we
> have saved to be used in the battle against the United States
> and Britain. We have what could guarantee the destruction of
> every house in Israel at the very same time as we are repulsing the
> aggression by the Chicago and Texas gangs. We have the battle-
> field with 100 million people. We have the oil.... We have the
> Suez Canal.... O Arabs, we have plenty in the bag!
>
> —AHMED SAID, Voice of the Arabs, June 8, 1967

ON JUNE 8, 1967, Cairo's most famous radio broadcaster, Ahmed Said,
reported to his listeners that Egyptian, Syrian, and Jordanian forces had defeated Israel's army in the Sinai, had hobbled their British and US allies, and
were liberating Palestine. It was a lie. As Arabs across the Middle East would
soon learn, Egypt's air force had been destroyed three days earlier, Jordan and
Syria had been defeated, and Palestinians were not returning home. Britain
and the United States had not intervened militarily to help the Israelis, who
had managed to emerge victorious without direct Western aid. The shock of
defeat reverberated across the Arab world. Since 1952, Gamal Abd al Nasser's
Egypt had promised liberation and redemption under the banner of Arab
nationalism. But when the war finally came, not only had the Arab armies
lost, but the Egyptian state had lied about the defeat to conceal its shame.
It was a devastating moment of betrayal and humiliation that exposed the
empty promises of the Nasserist, pan-Arab regime. To this day, Arabs of a
certain age remember where they were when they learned of the defeat. They
remember the stunned silence and the growing anger of those days, months,
and years.

Radio sat at the center of 1967's betrayal. Whether people listened on
a British-made His Master's Voice stereo box, with its walnut veneer and
polished marble knobs, or they managed to get ahold of the more modern,
Czechoslovakian Tesla model, with its rounded corners wrapped in shining

chrome, this was how most folks received their news. Hundreds of stations resided on the short- and medium-wave frequencies, with the big international channels maintaining multiple stations across the dial. Egypt's station, Radio Cairo, with its famous service, Sawt al Arab (Voice of the Arabs), were the most popular, followed by the BBC, Radio Moscow, and Voice of America (VOA). People also tuned in to Radio Jerusalem, Radio Damascus, and Radio Beirut. Many of these stations had been on the air since the 1940s. In parts of the Middle East where print media and televisions were expensive and difficult to get, or where literacy rates were low, the radio was the primary conduit to the outside world.

Many people held (and continue to hold) the radio responsible for the "Big Lie" of 1967. In particular, they blame Ahmed Said at the Voice of the Arabs, who declared victory in the face of obvious defeat, and who reported that American and British forces were involved in the invasion. But Ahmed Said was not the only broadcaster to fabricate the truth. Every international radio station had for years been telling stories and making promises that were often only tenuously connected to reality. Britain had sworn off imperial designs. The United States had promised self-determination and capitalist modernization. The Soviet Union had guaranteed the defense of Arab nationalist aspirations. All of these promises came with caveats and conditions that had become difficult to ignore by 1967. As such, that year marked not just the end of Nasser's great revolutionary dream, but also of the warrants of American, British, and Soviet modernization. It signaled the moment of eclipse, which had been long in the making, for the Cold War assurances of communist and capitalist liberation.

These massive collapses of promise played out across the airwaves. Radio, a medium that had once been an experimental space for the sharing of ideas and the breaking down of barriers across geographic and cultural boundaries, had also been a key tool in the efforts of states to build public consensus and compliance among domestic and international audiences. Over the previous two decades, it had become a space of rote messaging and half-truths. How did the audiosphere of the Middle East become so untethered from the experiences of its listeners? This book seeks to answer that question, and in the process, to better understand the role that international radio, and propaganda more generally, played in shaping the modern Middle East.

・・・

The story begins two decades earlier. In 1946, what people heard when they turned on their radios was a world in the making. The BBC, the British-run Palestinian Broadcasting Service (PBS), the covert British station Sharq al-Adna, Radio Moscow, Radio Beirut, Radio Damascus, and Radio Cairo sat just a turn away from each other on the medium- and shortwave dials.[1] All of the stations scrambled in those early years to find the words that would successfully navigate the Cold War, the decolonization process, and the rise of Arab nationalism. All of them experimented with language, looking for the key messages, phrases, and terms that would generate popular consensus.[2] They threw everything against the proverbial wall to see what would stick. They separated enemy from ally and the profane from the sacred. The British painted themselves as storied patriarchs, well intended in their remaining colonial enterprises, doing their best in a world filled with communist agitators and recalcitrant subject populations.[3] Radio Moscow blamed British and American imperial capitalist invasion for the postcolonial difficulties experienced across the Middle East and pitched itself as the great defender of a socialist, Islamic, Arab nationalism.[4] The Arab stations navigated emerging Cold War alliances, the Palestinian crisis, and internal struggles for leadership in the postcolonial world. Most of them held the West, particularly Britain, responsible for the rise of Zionism and colonial occupation.[5] It was in those first years, between the end of the Second World War and the Partition of Palestine, that the British, Soviet, and Arab radio stations laid the foundations for the massive programming that was to come.

In the twenty years that followed, propaganda in the Middle East became an enormous state business. Cairo, London, Moscow, and Washington employed thousands of people to produce hundreds of thousands of hours of broadcasts—each of them intent on constructing a specific narrative of the past, present, and future, and each shaped by its state's policies on the Cold War and the rise of Arab nationalism. What had started as relatively modest propaganda programs ballooned into a leviathan of sound, stretching across the dial, running day and night. The United States joined the fight in the 1950s, equipped with the promise of capitalist modernization and the threat of atheistic communism. The Soviets embraced the mantra of peace as a counter to American and British colonial overthrow. All the while, Cairo's

Voice of the Arabs became the beacon for pan-Arabism and nonalignment under the guidance of Egypt's Nasser.

As the years passed, the broadcasters' messages settled into self-sustaining, normalized discursive systems. Their language became increasingly circumscribed and repetitive, like a record caught on a scratch. The revolutionary language of Cairo; the rhetoric of peace and colonial liberation from Moscow; and the messages of democracy, anti-communism, and development from the United Kingdom and the United States all became mantras, repeated until they hardened into rote articulations of policies that increasingly came into conflict with the real experiences of Arab populations on the ground. The broadcasters rooted their messaging in a world that was predicated on the ideological certitudes and "common enemy intimacies" of the global Cold War.[6] Their messaging, even Nasser's Radio Cairo, was founded in a modern, secular understanding of how social progress and development could happen. When those promises and threats failed to materialize again and again, despite the constancy of the state mantras, the underlying capacity for official language to provide guidance for public action and belief became suspect as well. The ability of development and modernization to both liberate and subjugate became undeniable, as did the ideological emptiness of the Cold War divide.[7] State broadcasters were compelled to pitch the narratives of promise and peace into a violent landscape.

This was the double bind that leaders and propagandists faced in the "Arab Cold War."[8] The audiospace itself, that ephemeral world of waves and sound, helped to create the calcified soundscape of state-run broadcasting. Because it was such a costly and massive enterprise, it was slow to change and prone to habit. Bureaucratic inertia took its toll. When the stations did alter their language or their argumentation by adding new phrases or omitting subject matter, they changed by borrowing from each other. They listened almost as much as they spoke, responding to and repurposing the arguments made by their opponents up and down the dial. These armies of international propagandists created a "dialogized" world, where their messages continuously shaped each other and the language of the public sphere in a constant cycle of reentrenchment both in their own messages and in their responses to others' messages (which were often one and the same thing). They were never "self-enclosed or deaf to one another."[9] Their narratives become interwoven inside a geography of sound.

Over time, the messages of the state-run broadcasters increasingly settled into a shared vocabulary, learned from each other over decades. The promises of peace, development, safety, liberation, and threat—the staples of the Middle Eastern audiosphere—took on the same descriptive qualities across the dial, even if their protagonists were different, and even if they were trying to achieve very different goals with that language. Ironically, in their attempts to stay attuned to each other and create unique messaging that would separate them from their competitors as more authentic and resonant, they regressed to one language that ultimately failed most profoundly in its ability to be unique. From the beginning, these grand state narratives set themselves up for their own collapse. The ideological messaging produced by the British, Soviets, Egyptians, and Americans was always insufficient in its attempts to describe a "truth" that would sustain popular consensus and belief.[10] This inherent contradiction, wherein the very language intended to manufacture consensus was no longer able to describe the complex world it inhabited, ultimately undermined the legitimacy of the state-run audiosphere and the power it supported.

In the last twenty years, scholars have turned their attention to the unique history of Western propaganda in the Middle East.[11] In particular, James Vaughan, Tony Shaw, Gary Rawnsley, Susan Carruthers, Andrea Stanton, and Melani McAlister have laid much of the theoretical groundwork and asked many of the critical questions that this book seeks to answer.[12] In their examinations of American and British propaganda in the Middle East, they have exposed the damaging role that Orientalism and the Cold War played in shaping the "politics of representation" and the exercising of state power.[13] In their studies of UK and US propaganda during the Palestinian Mandate period and the Suez Crisis, they have unearthed many of the organizational causes for the failure of the British and Americans to gain the allegiances of Arab listeners. They have moved beyond the recounting of institutional histories to examine the activities and operations that broadcasters undertook on the ground in these critical years. Stanton, in particular, has taken the critical step of uncovering the soundscapes that defined the radio space of Palestine and the Middle East in the 1930s and 1940s.

This book is a history of a single, dialogic space made up of many voices all speaking at the same time. It weaves together the sounds, ideas, and messages of the four major state-sponsored, Arabic-language broadcasting nations, focusing on what the broadcasters had to say over the air and to each other, not just the behind-the-scenes activities of their respective organizations.[14] By reading across the British, Russian, Egyptian, and American archives, we can put those voices in conversation with each other. Critically, this story includes the voices of the Soviet Union and Egypt, which, despite being powerhouses in the production of radio propaganda, have too often been relegated to the footnotes of this history.[15] *Frequencies of Deceit* also spans twenty years, from 1947 to 1967, offering a sweeping view of the medium and its messages. As such, it is concerned with deciphering the larger structural and linguistic shifts that shaped the Middle Eastern audiosphere.

Getting at these voices has been no easy task. Only the BBC and Radio Moscow archives have extensive copies of their programming transcripts. A fire wiped out many of the records of the VOA in 1978, and Egyptian officers destroyed the transcripts of Voice of the Arabs after Nasser's death.[16] The difficult conditions of the varying state archives made research for this project no easier.[17] There are cases when all we have are stacks of broadcast program titles or half-faded mimeographs of handwritten transcript ideas. As such, this book can only offer an incomplete glimpse into an echo chamber, a partial picture into a corner of a thing.

Nonetheless, it is possible to resurrect many of the vanished conversations that happened over the air, day after day. The British, US, Russian, Egyptian, and Israeli national archives are filled with people responding to what they were hearing over the air, mostly in Arabic and sometimes in English. The well-known BBC Monitoring Service and US Foreign Broadcast Information Service (FBIS; run by the Central Intelligence Agency [CIA]) have been digitized, offering the opportunity to put their massive records in conversation with each other. The Soviet State Television and Radio Bureau (Gostelradio) kept careful tabs on what everyone else was saying up and down the dial in Russian and Arabic. The British and American state archives hold the transcripts of the Soviet and Egyptian radio services, while the Russian archives hold the transcripts of the British and Americans. From this, one can triangulate the sources and reassemble the broadcasts, even if at times they more closely resemble Swiss cheese than a tapestry. Smaller organizational archives help to fill in the gaps. Recent memoirs from Arab broadcasters and letters from listeners make it possible to give life to the experience of the radio in these years. This reconstructed audiosphere is imperfect and problematic; we can only see the material that listeners chose to collect, and often those who were doing the collecting were not listening favorably to those they were hearing. And yet the tens of thousands of available transcripts do still tell a compelling story about the proficiency and incapacity of language and propaganda as tools of power.

Like a Rube Goldberg machine, one can see how one message spurred another, and then another. An idea, issue, or phrase that started on a Radio Moscow broadcast would appear the next day on Sharq al-Adna, the covert British station in Cyprus. Two hours later, it would make an appearance on Voice of the Arabs in Cairo. Over time, those messaging structures became a part of the scaffolding of the audiosphere and the ontological space that populations inhabited. This project pays attention to that conversation, which included Arab speakers and broadcasters as much as it did those of the foreign powers.

These mantras *did things*. They were key tools in the construction of state power. They attempted to provide a conceptual universe that would explain everything a listener might need to navigate the world and their role in it.[18] These mantras marshaled populations to solidarity and defined the obligations of the listener. They were at times quite successful. Standard histories of Voice of the Arabs argue that the station was a juggernaut in the construction of Nasser's Egyptian-led, pan-Arab identity and nationalism.[19] Indeed, Nasser, and his radio leviathan, "represented an entire Arab generation mesmerized by similar problems."[20]

At the same time, the failures and contradictions of those messaging structures led subject populations to doubt not just whether they were hearing the truth, but whether the truth could be known at all. These mantras by the 1960s had become sacred and static, permitting little change to the fundamental rhetorical framing that undergirded them.[21] They had great power over their audiences, but that power was nonetheless tenuous. If ever that messaging came into question, the power it helped to construct would become "a dead thing, a relic."[22] Against the radio's promises of liberation, peace, defense, and development sat the realities of neocolonial interference and invasion, collusion, war, displacement, and defeat. Such revelations engendered deep skepticism from Arabs across the Middle East toward state-led structures of power in the Arab world, first toward the West and eventually toward Nasser and the promise of secular pan-Arabism. Without question, subject populations frequently moved through their days acting in sincere and earnest compliance with the hegemonic messaging coming from the state. But there were other times, particularly as the 1960s waned, when listeners merely performed their fealty, behaving "as if," not because they believed in the various state mantras, but because it was safe or profitable.[23] This lasted until the sociocultural and economic costs of those performances became too high. In other words, the messages of the international propagandists were productive only as long as they matched the circumstances in which they were delivered.

The reason these messages stopped working was that they were not able to do the work of building public consensus on their own; they relied on the conventions, experiences, realities, and contexts that surrounded them to give them life. As Pierre Bourdieu put it, the power that comes from language "resides in the institutional conditions of their production and reception."[24] By 1967, those conditions were not easy for any of the propagandists working in the Middle East. Britain and the United States had shown themselves, multiple times over, willing to undermine democratic movements in the defense of their own economic, colonial, and Cold War interests. The Soviet Union by then had become more of a reluctant debtor to the Middle East than a crusader for anti-imperial liberation. Nasser's United Arab Republic (UAR), once the paragon of revolutionary Pan-Arabism, found itself isolated, locked in unpopular conflicts, facing internal dissent and bankruptcy. And yet none of these realities made their way into the great narratives of the state broadcasting programs. Instead, the language of the state-led broadcasters became a rote exercise, and the echo chamber they had built got smaller, more brittle, and less able to see or speak outside of the confines of its own nomenclature. Just as political rhetoric mapped onto and created the political landscape of the Middle East, so too did it undermine those spaces.

Aspirational master narratives are powerful. In the Cold War Middle East, these narratives provided simple solutions to complex problems based on an increasingly calcified message that defined what could and could not be said and understood. This powerful language did not just reside in the propaganda world; it reverberated in the discourse of diplomats, politicians, and subject populations. As such, it limited the possibilities of language as a tool for building the kind of nuanced interconnectedness that it should have made possible. Limitations in language create and reinforce limitations in perception. In other words, we are only able to understand a thing if we have the language to articulate what it is. If the shared vocabulary that one needs to find reconciliation with one's adversary is lost, then all one is left with is a dry, tired heuristic that is defined by what it cannot say. Even more tragically, once those words are lost, entire societies forget that they were ever available. This is why the combined catastrophes of Orientalism, the Cold War, and the Arab-Israeli conflict were so damaging for the Middle East; they were, and are, limiters of language. This language defined what could and could not be said, eventually shaping how propagandists, politicians, and populations understood and articulated the world they saw around them. This is a reality that has persisted to this day, continuing to limit the possibilities of language, peace, and reconciliation for millions of people. It is reflected in the desiccated language of the Middle East peace process and in the rhetoric of the region's continuing wars.

The first two chapters of this book explore the efforts of the British, Soviet, and Middle Eastern broadcasters of the late 1940s to find a unique language upon which their messaging could rest. They constructed an audioworld that was both deeply divided and profoundly interconnected.[25] They struggled to steer the development of Arab nationalism down paths that were increasingly shaped by the Cold War. They worked to develop master narratives for a great Arab future that were both hopeful and under threat—made possible by British or Soviet patronage. The first real test of these narratives came in 1947, when the UN Special Committee on Palestine (UNSCOP) recommended the creation of an Israeli state, and everyone had to take sides. The United Nations vote and the 1947–48 war that followed exposed the emptiness of British, Soviet, and American promises of modernity and peace to the Arab world.

Then, in 1954, the Voice of the Arabs shifted the radio world on its axis—the subject of chapter 3. Voice of the Arabs and its broadcasting director, Ahmed Said, became the standard that had to be copied if one wanted to be heard. Said, whose voice was known across the Middle East, developed a new form of colloquial Arabic for the airwaves. His use of irony, metaphor, and sarcasm offered indicting critiques of the West. He posited alternatives to the British, American, and at times Soviet versions of Middle Eastern history, viewing Israel as a product of Western imperialism and placing Egypt and the Arab-speaking world in a place of agency where it could shape its own fate. It was revolutionary, both in form and content. And yet even in its early years, it was in constant dialogue with its neighbors on the radio dial, sometimes borrowing the arguments made there, often functioning under the same Cold War and nationalist assumptions that defined Western broadcasting.

At the same time, an explosion of Western radio happened across the dial, the subject of chapters 4, 5, and 6. While the US Information Agency (USIA) joined the struggle with a message of anti-Soviet capitalist development, Radio Moscow doubled down on the mantra of peace. Meanwhile, the British posited themselves as a viable, experienced alternative to US and Soviet meddling. Whether coming from Washington, Moscow, or London, these stations posited elementary explanations for complex problems and shallow caricatures of populations in conflict whose needs and desires could only be met through the perpetuation of that conflict. They returned to the same, shared messages: that the Middle East was backward and in need of help; that an ideal future would embrace Arab and Jewish nationalism while also looking surprisingly Western, liberal, and secular; that this future could only be made possible through outside aid; that this aid was dependent on Cold War fealty; that peace was possible only through ideological adherence; that foreign and domestic enemies posed an existential threat to that peaceful future; and that the defeat of those enemies would solve all of the other socioeconomic and religious issues that plagued people's lives. As such, these years solidified the foundation for a radio space in which words and tropes could be emptied of their original intent and refilled with new significance, in which language became an all-purpose tool for conveying belief more than reality. Words like *freedom*, *liberty*, *modernization*, *progress*, and *peace* stopped carrying any real meaning, because they could mean anything.

The second great test of the broadcasters and their messaging happened during the Suez Crisis of 1956, which is the subject of chapters 7 and 8. Many historians have endeavored to give clarity to the events that shaped those months. These chapters attempt to do the opposite by focusing on the many versions of what was going on that swirled simultaneously through the airwaves. They trace the deeper rhetorical currents that had, by 1956, come to shape and circumscribe the broadcasters' linguistic regimes. They reveal the widening chasm that lay between propaganda's vision of the world and the lived experiences that Arab-speaking populations were having. By the time the Suez Crisis ended, Western radio's claims to truth had begun to collapse, and Radio Cairo seemed to have become the undisputed representative of pan-Arab unity. Cairo actively tuned out not just the West but also Islamic Arab voices that pursued political alternatives to Nasser's secular promises. Meanwhile, in place of the humbled British broadcasting juggernaut, the United States and Soviet Union stepped in to fill the void, attempting to make the goal of Arab nationalism contingent upon Cold War fealty.

By the mid-1960s, all the broadcasting services had settled into a shared set of tropes, reified into established heuristics over years of use (the subject of chapter 9). The revolutionary, anti-imperial rhetoric of Radio Cairo now justified Nasser's dictatorial hold on power. Britain struggled to retool itself as a moderate socialist advocate for Arab development, all while increasing its anti-communist programs and its renewed brinkmanship with

Nasser. The VOA continued to pitch itself as the defender of democracy and freedom in the world at the same time that the US government orchestrated armed interventions in Syria and Lebanon. All the while, Radio Moscow's professed support for Cairo concealed growing crises in Yemen and elsewhere.

By the time Ahmed Said claimed Arab victory over Israel in the summer of 1967, international radio had a long record of abrogating its responsibility to tell the truth. As chapter 10 recounts, there were lots of occasions when sincere broadcasters did attempt to speak honestly over the air, particularly at the BBC, but also in Moscow, Washington, and Cairo. But occasions for dissimilitude and diversion were frequent enough to put all of it in question. As such, that summer provided a backdrop for the collapse of international radio's legitimacy. The very weapons that had once been so powerful in shaping Arab opinion exposed a falsity that shook the Arab world.

Across the dial, the state-led promises of development and peace became emptied of meaning. As a consequence, populations across the Arab-speaking world no longer looked to these stations and the states they represented to understand the political landscape and themselves in it. *Frequencies of Deceit* seeks to explain how that collapse happened. Language could not exist outside the struggle for power. But living in a world where language was always first loyal to power and then only secondarily to the truth (what we now call the "post-truth" world) had an impact on people. In their search for veracity, many turned their hopes away from the grand secular promises of Western development toward social and political systems based on faith and tradition. This was the case in the Middle East in the 1950s and 1960s. It arguably is the case in much of the world today.

ONE

The Rise of a "Radioyazik"

BRITISH AND SOVIET RADIO
IN THE POSTWAR MIDDLE EAST

BEFORE THEY KNEW that they were fighting a Cold War, Britain and the Soviet Union battled over the airwaves of the Middle East, with Palestine in the center. Many of their broadcasters had worked during the war. They carried with them messages and methods borrowed from the empire, the collective farms, and the battlefront. They saw Palestine and the Middle East as an emerging market and an opportunity to create new alliances in the evolving geopolitical landscape.

In 1946, the future of the postcolonial Middle East still had many potential outcomes. Yishuv and Arab leaders still spoke sincerely about a peaceful future. The opportunity for Arab Palestinian independence seemed very real. The world was still addressing the terrible plight of Europe's displaced Jewish Holocaust survivors. The terms of the Cold War were still being formed. Colonialism still struggled to hold fast, and the identity of the postcolonial Arab world seemed to be under construction. Utopian visions of an Arab Palestinian state, free of the British Mandate, mingled with equally aspirational plans for an independent Israeli state, which in turn met the evolving Cold War and imperial desires of Great Britain and the Soviet Union to build spheres of influence—all happening alongside the development of new technologies that brought the people of the world into closer contact than ever before. The radio carried all of this history, confusion, anger, anticipation, and hope. This period was marked by the simultaneous mobilization of older propaganda practices mixed with experimentation and new initiatives meant to capture a growing, modern, radio audience. It was here, in these years, that the rhetorical groundwork for the modern Middle Eastern audioscape was shaped and contested.

Britain's broadcasters were unsure about how to do their jobs in the early years. They knew that the radio could function as a "tool of empire."[1] But the Palestinian Mandate was infinitely complex and overwhelming.[2] The broadcasters struggled to understand their Middle Eastern audiences, often conflating the "Arab question" with the "Irish question."[3] Such misconceptions limited their ability to combat counterinsurgency.[4] The local and international British stations often could not agree internally on how to tackle the threat of communism or the attacks on their imperial history. In response, they spent much of their time highlighting the cultural and technological gifts that Britain had given the world, promising law and order in exchange for popular consensus. This promise of the Western imperial "gift," which would, in the decades to come, transform into the promise of capitalist modernization, found its early language here. Here too lay the foundations for how the West would understand, and misunderstand, the Arab nationalist cause.

Like the British stations, Radio Moscow worked to build a grand message, a belief system, that would support state-directed policies and construct a consensus among Middle Eastern audiences.[5] Unlike its British counterparts, however, Radio Moscow harbored no uncertainty about its messaging. Radio Moscow pitched a story that hinged on the refashioning of Middle Eastern history as a narrative of revolution and class conflict, the rejection of Western colonialism, the promise of Soviet-led happiness and economic modernization without the inherent exploitation of capitalism, and the embracing of religious diversity.[6] Moscow offered a "grand narrative," a march from a heroic, anti-colonial past to a Soviet-led "radiant future."[7] This narrative sustained "the myth of the Soviet Union as an anticolonial power," even as it expanded its empire.[8] At the same time, Radio Moscow tackled problems and contradictions in its messaging that were not unlike those faced by the British. Key among them was the question of religion and the rise of Islamic nationalism. While promising a revolutionary, pan-Arab future, it could not extricate that promise from the prerequisite of a Soviet-led socialism. Like its Western counterparts, Radio Moscow suffered from a Cold War Orientalism that framed Arab liberation as a Soviet-supported, socialist project.

All of these contradictions continued to shape British and Soviet propaganda in the Middle East. These propaganda projects established many of the rhetorical and linguistic boundaries that defined the Middle Eastern audiosphere for decades to come. Most crucially, they helped to build a network of voices that intertwined and shaped each other.

· · ·

When Rex Keating, the assistant director at the British Mandate's PBS, spoke over the airwaves one afternoon in the late summer of 1946, he painted an image of a happy Jerusalem: "There is a tide of life that flows through the narrow lanes of Jerusalem in an endless stream of picturesque humanity." Keating's voice was slow and easy like a doting English father telling a bedtime story. "Here a lemonade seller pours a cooling drink for a thirsty customer. . . . An elderly Jew passes by. . . . Now a Christian priest. . . . And close by, an Arab Sheikh. . . . A dignified Arab, full of years, rubs shoulders with a young Jewish farmer from the hills." Keating paused, the resonant lilt of his high-English diction and years of training as a broadcaster hanging in the air. "Beside them, among them, a highly efficient British police force protects this bewildering variety of people. The policemen have a reputation for courtesy and helpfulness, with a profound understanding of the populations they serve."[9] It was a lovely vision of a bustling Jerusalem, made vibrant by its diversity and gentility, policed benevolently by a doting British Empire.

These were inspiring words, but even Keating did not believe them. "Palestine is a heartless and humorless place," he scrawled privately in his journal that same night.[10] He hated the violence and anger of Jerusalem. Two months earlier, he had asked a friend to go in his stead to a meeting at the headquarters of the British Mandate, located in the King David hotel. Zionist terrorists from the Irgun group had bombed an entire wing of the hotel that night, killing his friend and ninety other people. "It had an ambience of evil," Keating later remembered of the city, "three thousand years and more of hatred, revenge, and violence, all fueled by religious intolerance."[11] Keating dreamed a few months later that he was in a broadcasting studio standing before a wall, studded with thousands of tiny lights. When he started his broadcast, all the lights were burning brightly. As he talked, they began to go out—one by one at first and then by the dozens.[12] None of the work they were doing seemed to be having any effect. Jerusalem was no haven, and British broadcasters like Keating were pretty sure no one was listening.

In 1946 there were several English radio programs dotting the frequencies of the medium and shortwaves, reaching local and international audiences, most notably the British Broadcasting Corporation (BBC), the Near

FIGURE 1. Caricature of Rex Keating smoking his pipe. *Source: Radio Week* 1, no. 7 (March 1, 1946): 3, St. Anthony's College, Oxford, Middle East Centre Archive, GB165-0361, Keating Box 2, 2/5/2.

East Arabic Broadcasting Station (NEABS), and the PBS. The BBC, which ran on shortwave frequencies across the Middle East, had the largest listenership of any radio station in the world. Its first regular foreign-language broadcasts in 1938 were in Arabic. The organization was ostensibly independent from the British government.[13] In 1945 the BBC broadcast twelve to eighteen hours a day to populations in Egypt, Palestine, Syria, the Lebanon, Iraq, and South Persia—a much larger time-share on the air than its competitors.

The NEABS, also on the shortwave, was responsible for the covert station Sharq al-Adna. "Sharq," as many called it, had begun broadcasting from its nondescript building in Jaffa sometime in 1941. The former Sharq al-Adna building now sits nestled around the corner from Jaffa's famed shakshuka restaurants, its roof loaded with a tangle of antennas and its balconies situated perfectly in the afternoon sun for the leisure needs of the city's cats. Back in 1946, the building was English owned and operated. The programming was full of Arab entertainment shows, while British officers supervised the writing and translation of the news.[14] Many people knew that Sharq was secretly sponsored by the British. Even so, by most accounts it was the most popular radio station for entertainment in the Middle East.[15]

Then there were the smaller British-run regional stations, most notably the PBS, which began in 1936 and was the official radio station of the British Mandate, running on the medium wave. The PBS only reached populations in Palestine and the Levant, but it was nonetheless a critical part of the story because of its links to the British Foreign Office and the BBC and the outsized role it played in shaping language and strategy for the region. From its studio in Jerusalem, the PBS aired over four hours of content each day in English (in the program, *Jerusalem Calling*), in Hebrew (as *Kol Yerushalayim*), and in Arabic (as *Iza'at al Quds*).[16] Its mission, according to the British Foreign Office, was to keep out of politics and promote a positive vision of the British Mandate in Palestine.[17] For a decade the PBS had produced a steady stream of stories about the region and the loving protection, culture, and wealth that Britain offered.

The two men in charge of shaping British broadcasting in the Middle East after the Second World War were Ivone Kirkpatrick, the Foreign Office undersecretary in charge of information activities, which oversaw the PBS and Sharq al-Adna, and Cyril Conner, the head of the BBC Overseas Service.[18] In the fall of 1946 they traveled to Jerusalem to assess the strength of the British radio service and to make recommendations on how to "solidify the British position in Palestine."[19] They awoke each morning within the fortified walls of the British compound, sometimes referred to as "Bevingrad," in reference to its history as an imperial Russian enclave.[20] Conner and Kirkpatrick read the summaries of world broadcasts from the BBC Monitoring Service. They flipped through the most popular Arab Palestinian paper,

Falastin, which railed against the Mandate, reminding its readers that after the British had gone, "the Jews of Palestine will have no choice but to live among us."[21] They also read the *Palestine Post*, which was run by the Jewish Agency. It declared, amid advertisements for Bush radios and invitations to eat hot dogs and burgers at the new Brooklyn Ice Cream Bar on Allenby Road, that everyone was "angrier and more frustrated with the British than ever."[22] The radio stayed on all morning. Conner and Kirkpatrick spent the afternoons in meetings and dinners with ambassadors and politicians, followed by long evenings writing reports back to London.

According to Conner and Kirkpatrick's assessment, the source of the Arab world's bad feelings toward the British was not the legacy of empire, but international communism, carried on the back of the Soviet propaganda machine. Conner wrote back to the main office that the Soviets were disseminating "untrue reports," all of which were gaining traction among students and workers.[23] "The time has come," Kirkpatrick declared, "to counter the infiltration of communist propaganda."[24] It was, in the end, far easier to blame the Soviet Union for anti-British sentiment in the empire than it was to acknowledge legitimate Arab frustration with British occupation.

To address the burgeoning communist threat, Conner and Kirkpatrick sent out a new directive to the BBC, NEABS, and PBS offices in Jerusalem, Cairo, Baghdad, Tehran, Beirut, Damascus, and Jeddah. The communists were following a deliberate, "savage" anti-British propaganda campaign, and there was no sign that they were planning on letting up soon. The information offices couldn't afford to ignore the attacks, the memo argued, if Britain's "legitimate interests" in the Middle East were to be defended.[25] Their suggestions on how to tackle the communist menace were myriad, including the use of images of Moscow's impoverished suburbs and the barren pantries of the Soviet countryside, with long lines for basic necessities and citizens quaking in fear.[26] "We should give publicity to the real state of affairs in Russia," a subsequent British Foreign Office memo harangued: "the [Soviet] system of government, their oppression of the workers, their inequality between the government classes and the masses, their low standard of living, their tyranny of the police," along with "publicity about Russia's own activity and intentions in Middle Eastern countries."[27] Soviet domestic politics would become truncheons in the British effort to push listeners into reconciling with the British presence in the Middle East.

The Soviet threat seemed clear enough, but knowing how to attack it was not. The Sharq al-Adna, PBS, and BBC radio transcripts from these years show how difficult it was for broadcasters to follow this directive. Sharq al-Adna, the covert Arab station, found itself stuck in the double bind of needing to attack the Soviets, defend the British, and yet still appear to be an authentic Arab station. The result was that its attacks remained vague and tepid. For instance, on March 4, 1946, when the news broke that Stalin had decided to keep troops in Iran, Sharq simply reported, "The Soviet Union's decision is a direct challenge to the Western countries." Three weeks later, it tersely noted that the Soviets would be withdrawing from Iran "to save face," with no discussion of the pressure that had been placed by the West on the Kremlin to withdraw.[28] Despite Conner's direction, nowhere on the station could one hear stories about the lives of anti-Soviet activists in Eastern Europe or the plight of Russian mothers looking for meat to feed their families. Nowhere was there a conversation about Soviet meddling in the Middle East or stories on the ideological dangers of communism. Sharq's Arab staff understood that it was no easy task to criticize the Soviet colonial danger while also insisting on the continued need for the British Empire in Palestine, Egypt, Sudan, Cyrenaica, Tripolitania, Kuwait, Qatar, Transjordan, and Aden.

The PBS broadcasters in Jerusalem met the anti-communist directives coming from London with similar uncertainty, preoccupied as they were with internal divisions and other broadcasting plans that had been in the works for years. Diaries and memoires from the era show how the new demands of the Cold War often got lost amid larger disagreements among the staff over how to deal with Zionism and the Arab Palestinian cause.[29] The director of the PBS, Edwin Samuel, was simultaneously a defender of the British Empire and an avid Zionist. In his memoir, Samuel recounted proudly how he had overseen a "closely welded department, with the minimal of personal friction."[30] But the documents tell a different story. He was the son of Sir Herbert Samuel, who had been the first high commissioner of Palestine in 1920–25. Everyone knew that he was a supporter of Israel, and many questioned his political loyalties to the Mandate.[31]

Personal conflicts over the direction of the station made unified, anti-Soviet programming difficult to execute. Rex Keating, the broadcaster who had painted that bucolic image of a happy Jerusalem just days before the King David hotel bombing, believed his boss to be "the worst possible person to be in charge of the British Mandate's propaganda program, with a consequent bias against all things British, a softness towards the Soviets, [and] a neglect of the Arab side of its activities."[32] Proof of this seemingly came when Samuel ordered his broadcasters to stop calling the Zionist Irgun group "terrorists" on the air.[33] More critically, the broadcasts coming out of the PBS seemed to lean heavily toward the Jewish cause. On any given day, one could expect to hear around ten hours of shows from transmitter II directed to Yishuv listeners in Hebrew and English, with morning prayers at 7:00 a.m., a biblical play "Elijah and the Prophet" at 8:00, and a review of the films showing in the Tel Aviv theaters at 13:00, followed by afternoon performances of *The Scarlet Pimpernel*, Hebrew lessons for immigrants, lectures on the Talmud, and music until 22:30. All these programs were advertised in detail each day in the early morning papers and in the magazine *HaGalal*.[34] The PBS aired farming shows for members of Palestine's kibbutzim and daily readings from the Torah.[35] It gave airspace to Ben Gurion in early 1947, who spoke uncensored about the desired liberation of the Jewish people in Palestine.[36] In contrast, Arabic programming ran for only five hours daily, with the PBS giving no details in the newspapers on the particular shows planned for the day.[37] There were no farming shows or Arabic readings of *The Scarlet Pimpernel*.[38] By May 1947, 74 percent of PBS employees were Jewish. The station even aired incendiary stories like one that was broadcast on February 22, 1947, which likened the Jewish people immigrating into Palestine to the persecuted English who had left Britain and colonized North America, comparing the Arabs of Palestine to the Native Americans, all in need of civilizing.[39]

Instead of tackling the threat of communism directly, the bulk of the stories coming from the PBS worked to reinforce the great civilizing power of the British Mandate. Starting in May 1947, the BBC and the PBS decided to address the "virulent flood of Anti-British propaganda" by initiating what they called, "The Second Programme." For eight and a half hours weekly, the PBS broadcast Western classical music, directed "uncompromisingly, to a discriminating minority . . . with a disregard for so-called popular taste."[40] It aired dramatic plays and music ranging from chamber ensembles to "off the beaten path" music like Beethoven's Overture Leonore No. 1. There were weekly programs, such as *This is London* (about the great features of the city: the parks and palaces, the Tube, and the East End), *Whom the Gods Love* (about great British men who died young: Percy Bysshe Shelley and General James Wolfe, "the hero of Quebec"), and *Experiment in Humour*, described as "an elegant anthology with music, containing many learned and unwanted facts." The broadcasters were excited by the plan to play all of Haydn's Piano Trios, from No. 1 to No. 45.[41] Keating announced the new

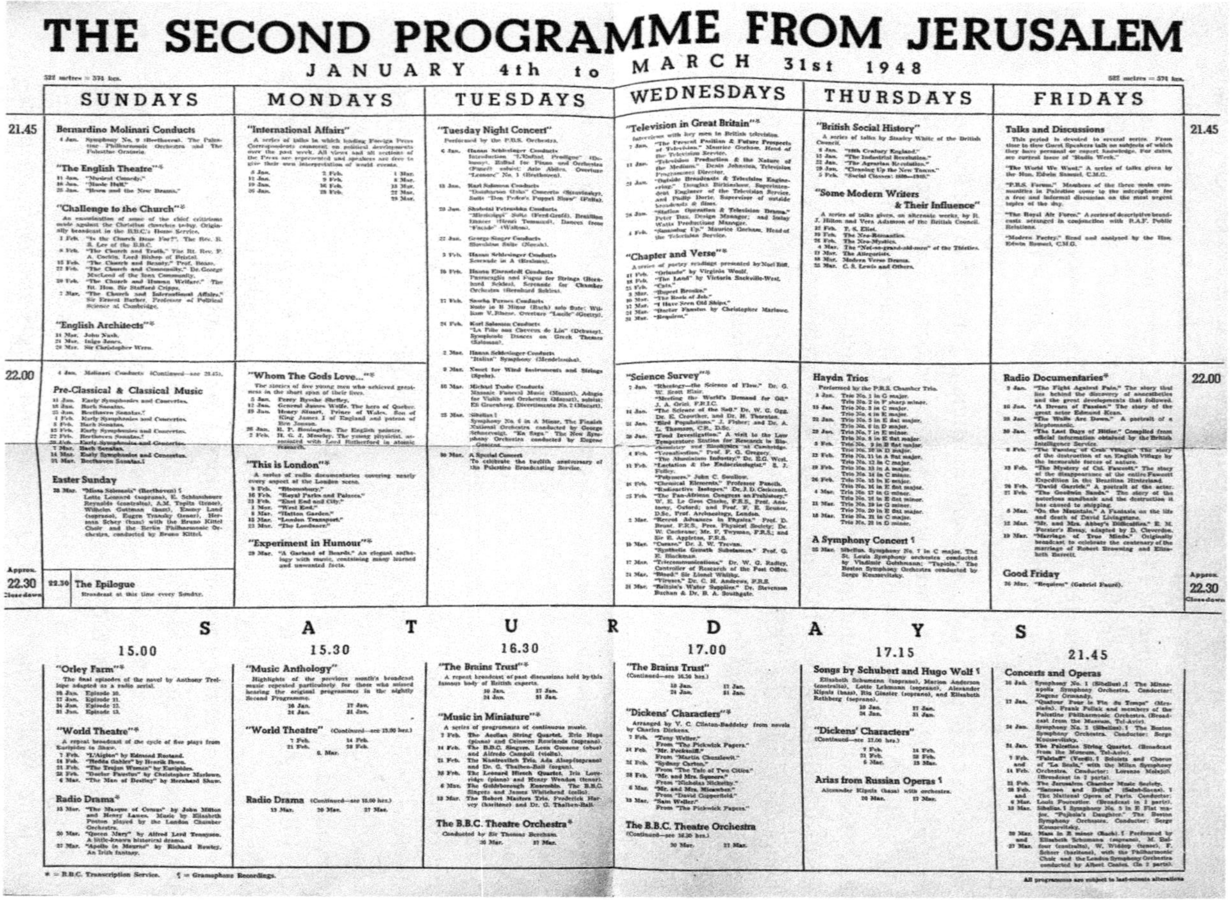

THE SECOND PROGRAMME FROM JERUSALEM

JANUARY 4th to MARCH 31st 1948

SUNDAYS	MONDAYS	TUESDAYS	WEDNESDAYS	THURSDAYS	FRIDAYS

FIGURE 2. PBS program showing its extensive plans to air classical music and high-brow stories. *Source:* Second Programme from Jerusalem, January 4 to March 31, 1948, Rex Keating Collection, box 1, GB165-0361, Keating Box 2/4/.

program to his listeners in an article in the local newsletter *Radio Week* with the inauspicious title of "Caviar for Highbrows." In a later broadcast, he told his listeners to expect a typical evening's fare to include "a Sophocles play, an appraisal of Russian Foreign Policy, a complete opera and a recital of Tudor church music."[42] Such was the plan to combat communism and defend Britain's occupation of Palestine.

All these plans reflected the belief that high Western culture could build bridges between people who only days earlier had driven trucks filled with bombs into each other's Saturday morning markets. Perhaps somewhere in the melancholy adagio of Haydn's 28th piano trio, Yishuv and Arab listeners would catch a glimpse of their shared humanity and acknowledge the gifts that the West still had to offer. "There is no reason why . . . Jews should not live happily in Palestine with Arab acquiescence and in harmony with their neighbours a generation hence," the PBS argued in May 1947. This would not be possible, it argued, if Britain failed to "keep faith and hold the scales fairly between Jew and Arab."[43] Here, the PBS played a critical role in shaping the early language of progress in the audiosphere. Long before the Americans picked up the mantle of promised development and modernization under the protection of a Western gaze, the British were positioning themselves and their culture as the conduits for Arab and Jewish advancement.

Further up the dial, the BBC frequencies echoed these promises and inconsistencies. Like every broadcaster in Palestine, the BBC Arabic workers believed that they were mandated to tell the truth. And yet they were restricted in what that truth should look like because of administrative directives, uncertainty about how to tackle the Soviet "menace," and a worry that real coverage of the events happening on the streets of Palestine would only do more damage. Since before the Second World War, the BBC's larger goal had been the "projection of Britain" to subject populations, meant to show the nation's strength, pride, and "pluck."[44] On a standard day in 1946 and 1947, BBC Arabic ran sports stories; variety shows; a half-hour of Welsh or Irish music; children's shows; stories on bird watching; a steady stream of music by Elgar, Dvorzak, Brahms, and Beethoven; recordings of Vera Lynn; and one comedic show, *Ignorance Is Bliss*.[45] Exposés on the trim housing estates of Manchester were mingled with assurances from Arab émigrés living in Britain that every worker did, in fact, have a garden. Stories went out daily on British democracy, local government, the efficiency of the English transportation system, education, trade unions, and childcare. The station aired stories by Humphrey Bowman, the director of education in Palestine, who attested to the "strong affinity between the average Englishman and the average Arab."[46]

Often the BBC delivered the news of violence on the streets of Palestine in the tersest of terms. In the BBC archives in Reading, UK, lie hundreds of folders of dry news reports that broadcasters once read into microphones in small sound rooms from their desks in Wooferton and London. "A new curfew was enforced today," the BBC reported on New Year's Day 1947, "in the Jewish settlement of Rishon le Siyon, south of Tel Aviv, as troops of the 6th Airborne Division began a house-to-house hunt for the Jewish terrorists who flogged a British officer and three British N.C.O's on Sunday."[47] The broadcaster made no mention of the twenty-five hundred people whom British soldiers had examined and the forty-nine Yishuv people who were detained during the investigation into that unseemly flogging. After a pause (which is notated in the transcript), "British casualties in Palestine from terrorist action during 1946 were as follows: In the Police, 28 killed and 35 wounded; in the Army and R.A.F., 45 killed and 93 wounded. In addition, 300 civilians— British, Arabs, and Jews—were killed or wounded by terrorists."[48] That was the entire broadcast. After a shuffling of papers and a quiet clearing of the voice, the reporter moved on to announce an upcoming performance of the BBC Northern Orchestra and a special story on the history of forestry in Britain.[49] From the transcripts that we have, there is no evidence that explicit talk about the dead ever made its way onto the BBC airwaves; numbers had to suffice. It was perhaps all the broadcasters could do to report on these unsavory events with the barest amount of attention that the news allowed. And, as one broadcaster put it, "Arabs (and still less Jews and Armenians) do not have the British temperament to tolerate too much bad news. They cannot handle unpalatable prophesies of serious crisis."[50]

If the British broadcasters were unclear on how to articulate a Cold War strategy over the air, they were even more uncertain about how to deal with Arab nationalism—a difficulty that was made pronounced by a palpable reticence to acknowledge the desires, rights, and abilities of Arabs in particular to lead themselves.[51] It was common for British information specialists to argue that the majority of the Arab population of the Middle East could be pacified simply by offering, "free enterprise and agriculture."[52] As the BBC correspondent (and soon to be Middle East director) Edward Living commented, "What is necessary to keep always in mind is the fact that there is a large proportion of the population whose only interest is self-interest." This large population would accept peace in exchange for the "lowest price."

Living believed that as long as the English paid to develop business and agriculture in the Middle East, Arab listeners would accept British control.[53] In 1946 and 1947, the BBC argued regularly that the Arabs of the world would prefer to have Palestine run by the British than to be left to their own devices.[54] Indeed, in the transcripts and organizational documents from this era, one cannot find an instance in which the BBC or the PBS acknowledged the potential for Arab leadership free of British mentoring. While Arab musicians frequented the stations, expressions from native Arabic speakers about national sovereignty or self-determination were very rare. Messages to Arab listeners consistently framed Arab safety and well-being as something that was only attainable through British patronage.

Even the British departure from Palestine, which was announced in January 1947, functioned as an opportunity to exhibit British benevolence and maturity when dealing with a recalcitrant and childish subject population. "If, in the end," the BBC intoned on the day after the announcement, "a satisfactory settlement can be reached by this method, and enforced with the full authority of the United Nations, the precedent may become a milestone in the development of international government."[55] By withdrawing from Palestine, where conflict between Arabs and Jews had become a "fact of life," and by allowing the UN to become the arbiter of the "quagmire" in their stead, the British, the BBC argued, would be taking a noble first step in initiating and legitimizing the UN and its ability to solve international problems.[56] Walking away from the Mandate would be a great sacrifice, a willing relinquishment of power for the betterment of Palestine and the world. Also, as one commentator argued, even if Britain could maintain the thousands of troops needed in Palestine, "a country so divided and so disloyal as Palestine must be a source of weakness rather than of strength."[57] Ungrateful and disloyal subjects would only, in the end, pose a liability.

But were the Soviet broadcasters as dangerous as Conner and Kirkpatrick believed? The Russian State Archive is filled with boxes of broadcasting transcripts to the Middle East, typed first in Russian (often covered with handwritten edits), then translated into Arabic. Each broadcast had a proscribed life. Writers of the Soviet Radio and Film Union wrote their scripts and handed them to the censors, who then delivered them to trusted, Arabic-speaking employees for translation. They then gave the translations to native Egyptian or Jordanian speakers to read as they sat behind a microphone at the State House of Radio Broadcasting and Sound Recording on Malaya Nikitskaya Street, not far from embassy row in Moscow. From there, the recording traveled to a shortwave transmitter in Baku, then on to radio listeners all over the Middle East.

Radio Moscow was, from its inception, a state-controlled enterprise. Since the nineteenth century, socialist revolutionaries of all stripes had agreed that independent journalism was a synonym for the bourgeois press, run by and for the wealthy to keep the poor under foot. The radio was too powerful to be left in the hands of people who might not be sufficiently educated to wield it responsibly. The only way to ensure that the needs of the workers would be met in the media was to put the radio (and the press and film) under the control of the centralized workers' state. In Lenin's words, the radio was a "newspaper without paper or distance."[58] The microphone was the greatest of printing machines, producing thousands of copies instantly through the simple act of tuning in.[59] It would carry revolution on its invisible waves. It would liberate and awaken.

In the 1930s the state's strict control over radio continued, becoming a critical tool for the promotion of mass industrialization and collectivization, a vehicle for Stalin's hagiographic rise to power, and a medium for conveying the constant public performances of gratitude toward the state that were expected of the general population.[60] Soviet international broadcasting began in 1929, with its first transmission directed at Germany.[61] Another sixteen years and a brutal world war would pass before the Soviet Union started transmitting in Arabic to the Middle East and North Africa. At first there were two national stations—Radio Peace and Progress and Radio Moscow—and three regional stations: Radio Baku, Radio Tashkent, and Radio Yerevan.[62] The bulk of the state's energy went to developing Radio Moscow, recruiting the best university graduates and journalists to work and write for the program.[63] By 1946 Soviet propaganda in the Middle East was well developed, if small.

The Soviet argument that so scared Conner and Kirkpatrick in the late 1940s hinged on a message that was familiar to everyone in the Soviet Union: happiness.[64] That term, which revolutionaries and reactionaries have used ubiquitously since the Enlightenment as a catchall justification for any imaginable policy, found itself in great demand in Palestine in 1947. The British promised the happiness that comes when everyone agrees to put down their bombs, follow the rules, embrace Western culture, and accept their situation. Radio Moscow's version of happiness was defined by the promise of material contentment, industrial development, and education for the average citizen. This was not a promise of happiness like the one made by the

Americans or the British, Radio Moscow argued. This was a kind of joy that could only exist in the communist world, under centralized management, led by a workers' state. The capitalists might know how to make money, Radio Moscow claimed, but they did it through exploitation while the rest of the world continued to suffer.

While the BBC and PBS aired stories nightly on the achievements of Britain's colonial modernization projects, Radio Moscow broadcast series on the joys of collective farming for populations sitting under Soviet protection, particularly in Kazakhstan and Azerbaijan.[65] Radio Moscow painted a picture of Muslim countries in the Russian Far East as once backward places, illiterate, dark, and lawless, now literally and figuratively electrified by the influx of Soviet investment and concern. At least four times a week, one could tune in to hear a story about the construction of electrical stations in Kazakhstan and the development of the textile industry.[66] These stories always highlighted the work done by Kazakh and Azeri scientists and workers. Unlike on the BBC, which highlighted British achievements in science, invention, and art, it was rare to hear an explicit mention of ethnically Russian engineers, architects, or agronomists in these massive projects. Radio Moscow understood the power of telling stories about local populations shaping their worlds on their own, with the supportive, Soviet "adviser" standing in the wings with a full pocketbook of expert experience and funding to offer.[67]

All this achievement was made possible, Radio Moscow argued, through the Soviet sponsorship of vast education programs across the Soviet empire. Radio Moscow broadcast shows with titles like, *State Investments in Education in the Soviet Union and in Capitalist Countries*, which slowly, almost tortuously, recited a long list of foreign aid amounts given by the East and West to the developing world. When the station put on a half-hour show about the opening of Azerbaijan State University in March 1946, it did so to send a message that the Soviet Union offered access to education for populations that had, for at least the last century, been denied it as a part of state colonial policy.[68] Here was seeming proof that the Soviet system worked.

The speed of Soviet postwar recovery provided additional proof of the communist ability to provide happiness to subject populations. "Only in the Soviet Union do workers strive every day to rebuild and remake a better world. In Ukraine, once ravaged by fascists, life has returned to normal. The shops are open and children go to school," one broadcast declared in June 1947.[69] That any country could recover at this speed was a marvel and a clear testament to the success of the communist system and the commanding heights economy, they argued. For populations that were themselves looking for paths to modernity, self-sufficiency, and a chance to extricate themselves from the colonial albatross, the promise of swift economic modernization could not be overestimated.

In return for these gifts, Radio Moscow's broadcasts conveyed a clear expectation of gratitude from its listeners in the Middle East. Since the 1930s, performances of appreciation toward Stalin had become a prerequisite for public life in the Soviet Union. Posters of children thanking Stalin for their "happy childhood" dotted the civic landscape. The "economy of the gift" required that populations participate in a spectacle of appreciation and dependency that confirmed their loyalty to Stalin and the state and modeled patriotism for the rest of the community.[70] In the postwar period, the figure of Stalin became even more deified as he assumed the role of savior of Europe against the Nazi menace. By 1947 the cult of personality was in full swing in the Soviet Union, with tests and performances of gratitude determining the relative fealty of Eastern Europeans who had recently entered the Soviet sphere. The Poles, the Czechs, the Yugoslavs, and the Romanians were grateful and free by Radio Moscow's reckoning, setting an example of how Arab populations could evolve if only they took hold of the hand being offered. These stories represented a full recasting of the Eastern European narrative as one of liberation from poverty under the friendly parenting of the Soviet victors.

Radio Moscow intermingled stories about these leaps forward (a positive argument rooted in aspiration and desire) with exclusives on the abject poverty experienced by populations in the West (a negative argument rooted in threat and fear). "West Germany is being turned into a paradise for speculators," broadcasters argued one evening, the purpose being the "enslavement of West Germany by American and British monopoly capital."[71] On August 18, 1947, they reported that Britain was only complaining about Zionist terrorists in Palestine in order to cover up the "wave of Jewish pogroms" happening in Britain.[72] In Greece, where a communist revolution was being thwarted by a coordinated CIA operation, "all the funds liberally paid out by the monarchist-fascists in accordance with the Truman doctrine [were] being spent upon a war against the Greek people." Moscow reported that Americans had recently shipped a massive cargo container to Austria, filled with mosquito nets, brassieres, canned codfish, fish heads, and liver paste made from soy—all of which the Austrians either didn't need or refused to eat. Even worse was the shipment to Latin America filled with canned pork "made from pigs which had died of dysentery."[73] The Western world was particularly brutal, Radio Moscow declared, for people who were not white. "After 1946," Radio Moscow declared on New Year's Day 1947, "there can be no return to a state in which the white third of mankind rules the world. Whatever the tricks and ruses used, color-bar oppressed nations have no intention of being political martyrs."[74] This kind of story became a staple of Soviet broadcasting by the 1950s.

Perhaps the worst conditions were in the United States, Radio Moscow reported, where two-thirds of all farmers had become paupers and workers had lost their democratic freedoms. It didn't matter if one voted Democrat or Republican in America; both parties exploited workers and trade unions. Here was the idea of the "Two Americas": the exploitative rulers taking advantage of the decent American workers, who were by nature communists. Whether or not Arab populations bought the Soviet claim that there was still something redeeming about regular, working-class Americans is unclear, given the predominant belief at the time that the American public was dominated by Yishuv groups lobbying in New York for partition and the creation of the state of Israel. This perhaps explains why the "Two Americas" argument did not survive the 1950s and was gone from Soviet rhetoric directed at the Middle East within a decade.

These broadcasts created a vocabulary for talking about Western aid that persisted. *Speculators, monopoly capital, monarchist-fascists,* and *billionaires* became the standard nomenclature used to identify Western leaders in Soviet broadcasting to the Middle East until the 1990s. In a standard day, one hour of stories included titles like, "Imperialist Intrigues in the Arab East" and "The Palestinian Question and the United States."[75] "Feudal Arab circles and reactionary Jews" remained the tools of Americo-British meddling.[76] It was, in Radio Moscow's opinion, the fault of the imperialists that the entire Palestinian crisis existed.[77] These tried and tested metaphors had become handy, oversimplified but still resonant, signifiers for capitalist structures of power. They provided a clear and nonnegotiable dialectic that, ironically, became a critical part of Radio Cairo's vocabulary in the years to come.

From the beginning, both Radio Moscow and the BBC spent time proclaiming their own commitment to the truth while attesting to their enemies' slanderous lies. The BBC repeated its mission to deliver "straightforward news, good or bad, told simply but with a punch."[78] "They [British radio] have created their own language and terminology," Radio Moscow declared in response in the summer of 1947. "When they use the word independence, they mean colony; [w]hen they say help for economic rehabilitation, they mean enslavement and the destruction of economic and therefore political independence." In its own broadcasts, however, the station argued that there was no such solecism. "The people of the Soviet Union," Radio Moscow declared, "are plain speaking."[79] By 1956 Arab broadcasters like Ahmed Said were lodging the same criticisms of Britain, France, Israel, the United States, and sometimes even the Soviet Union.

Conner and Kirkpatrick did not know it, but Radio Moscow's problems were not unlike their own. Behind the scenes, Moscow scrambled daily to face issues with limited transmission capacities, a small Arabic-speaking staff, constant problems with sound quality, and the need for more programming.[80] Even more problematic, as Sergei Kaverin, the director of Radio Moscow to the Near and Far East, put it, was "finding a language" that could carry its intended message in the scripted discursive environment of the high Stalinist period. Finding an accessible, working-class language for public communication had actually been a part of the early Bolshevik project. Soviet broadcasters had worked in the 1920s to develop what they called a "Radioyazik" (a radio language) that would be more flexible and relatable for audiences. By the 1930s, however, official state language had become carefully manicured, with a heavy, often pedantic vocabulary and particular phrases used over and over again as a kind of identity signaling that every good Bolshevik was expected to use.[81] This language created a script for public discourse that facilitated Stalin's consolidation of power and the demonization of internal enemies. The destruction of peasants who resisted collectivization in the early 1930s became the "liquidation of the kulak as a class," for instance. Similarly, the extermination of the old Bolshevik guard during the Stalinist Terror became the "rooting out of wreckers and saboteurs." Language's first obligation was not to describe reality but to articulate power. Some freedoms in language and expression were allowed during the Great Patriotic War (the Second World War), most famously over the radio during the siege of Leningrad, but that did not last. After 1945 it again became dangerous to communicate "off script" in public.

Those rhetorical rules might have been useful domestically, but they were a hinderance abroad. Kaverin and his colleagues knew that the administrative and often officious language of the Bolshevik regime did not work well over the air.[82] It sounded censored, with marshaling undertones that reflected the militarization of public life. Radio Moscow needed to convey a positive, liberationist, adaptive, communist alternative to the officiousness of colonial messaging. It had to meet Arab listeners' nationalist and religious expectations, counter accusations of brutality and depravity coming from the West, and address the threat of Western imperialism—all without sounding predictable or rote. In the Middle East division of Radio Moscow, staff even talked longingly of creating a pan-Arabic radio dialect that would become the broadcasting standard from Morocco to Iraq.

To these ends, while the PBS and the BBC were embracing the Second Programme, Radio Moscow resolved to shorten the brain-numbing tirades of the standard domestic radio show and embrace what was, for them, a relatively revolutionary commitment to avoiding vague and convoluted forms of speech. The Russian language actually translated relatively well into Arabic, with their shared practice of putting the subject in the place usually reserved for the predicate or placing the subject as the last word in the sentence and the verb at the beginning in order to shift emphasis. Nonetheless, the transformation of the Bolshevik Party's stodgy Russian nomenclature into a looser and more expressive Arabic was less easy.[83] Broadcast transcripts in the archives show how frequently original Russian stories had to be entirely altered to "work" in Arabic, the editor's red ink running off the margins (creating no shortage of difficulties for later historians). Most of all, they desperately needed to be less boring.

Soviet broadcasting in the late 1940s also struggled to gain command over certain topics, particularly when they had to do with religion. The region now covered by the Soviet Union was historically Christian, with Islam only appearing among populations that fell under its colonial domain. More critically, it was now an atheist state with a history of religious suppression that nonetheless claimed to support Islam in the Middle East.[84] The Soviets walked a tightrope of condemning the reticent capitalism inherent in religion while simultaneously trying to convince Islamic listeners that the Soviet Union was not planning on tearing down their mosques. To this end, Radio Moscow spent significant time countering the stereotype of the Soviet Union as militantly godless, with stories showing its openness and tolerance of Islam in the Caucasus and the Far East. A series entitled *Religious Life in the Soviet Union* aired every week, focusing almost exclusively on Kazakh and Azeri families, showing how workers integrated their lives in the factories and communal farms with their daily prayers.[85] The station also strove to show the similarities between the Soviet and Arab people by airing stories on religious life in Russia. At the end of July 1947, for instance, the Soviet press began a massive radio campaign in the Middle East to talk about celebrations happening in the Russian Orthodox Church. Melodic sounds of the liturgy followed detailed descriptions of Moscow's most beautiful churches and stories about common people stopping by for a quick prayer on their way home from work. The programs explained the role of the patriarch and his connection to Russian government going back to Peter the Great (under whom the state controlled the church). They coupled these stories with reports on the dangers of Western religion, particularly Roman Catholicism.[86] All of this the Soviet broadcasters did while crackdowns against religious activity were happening across the Soviet Union—a point that the BBC made regularly. As the British Foreign Office in Cairo noted, Stalin's government was again shutting down churches and arresting parents who baptized their children, all the while promoting a vision of a tolerant state to Arabic-speaking listeners.[87]

Radio Moscow understood perhaps better than anyone that the key to undermining British (and eventually American) credibility among Arab listeners would be the instrumentalization of history. "Remember your history!" Radio Moscow declared again and again.[88] In the years and decades to come, Radio Moscow ran hour-long history lessons with titles like, *British Colonial Imperialism in the Nineteenth and Twentieth Centuries*, *The Historical Intrigues of the Imperialists in the Arab East*, *The American and British Historical Fight for Oil*, and *The First Colonial Captures of Great Britain*.[89] Cumbersome titles to be sure, but they reflected an acute understanding of the extent to which the Arab world saw the presence of the British and French as a product of historical currents, rooted in imperialism, that went back decades. In particular, Arab-Soviet émigrés repeated the mantra that the United States and Britain were inflaming old religious and nationalist enmities because they objected to the "Arab national feeling" and the Middle East's rejection of foreign subjugation.[90]

In 1947 the British Mandate in Palestine sat at the center of that historical argument. "The history of Palestine during the last thirty years is another clear example to show that the settlement of a national problem through a policy of colonial imperialism is impossible."[91] Radio Moscow had a point. "History has shown that the British will remain where they are," they declared one evening.[92] "There is only one reason why Arab and Jew cannot live together. They have been forced into this antagonism by imperialist powers who do not care if they live or die."[93] In the Soviet rendering, Yishuv-Arab antagonism was a product of continued British and Western European meddling in the region since the nineteenth century. The British were to blame for the settlement that left Palestine under Mandate control, for the failure to manage Yishuv immigration, for using the Zionist cause to enflame the class- and race-based Arab revolts of the 1920s, for using Arab and Yishuv populations as slave labor in the pursuit of natural resources, for signing the Balfour declaration, and for allowing Yishuv immigration to continue in the postwar era in order to salve their guilt over the Holocaust. "Jew and Arab lived in peace in Palestine for centuries," Radio Moscow claimed. "It was only when the British imperialists arrived on her shores that the hatred began."[94] This truth, it argued, was the root cause of Britain's hatred of the Soviet Union, because the Soviet Union was not afraid to recount a history that the queen's government would rather their Arab listeners forget.

Radio Moscow's history lessons worked daily to show how anti-colonialism, pan-Arab nationalism, and Islamic nationalism were, by their nature, socialist. In one broadcast, *Islam and Socialism*, the station recast the history of the Arab golden age (eighth to thirteenth centuries) as a story of rising class consciousness, wrapped up in a Marxist-Leninist dialectic that, despite the toxic imprint of colonialism, had led inevitably to the rise of a revolutionary proletariat in the Arab world in the twentieth century. *Islam and Socialism* came originally from a story published by the Soviet-funded Cairo press Propaganda and Publicity House, which was known for carrying scandalous reports pulled from the newspapers about exploitative bosses and the daily perils faced by the poor. In the hands of the Soviet propagandists working in Moscow, these shocking stories became saucy object lessons for inciting the workers of the city to action.

Islam and Socialism was a typical story. It told a Soviet version of the life story of Abou Far Al-Ghafari (also spelled Abu Dharr Al-Ghifari), who was the Prophet Muhammed's trusted companion. He was famous for his orthodox adherence to the prophet's teachings, even in the face of censorship and abuse from the Arab Caliphs who established a non-Muslim monarchy in the seventh century. The radio told a story that most workers would know. Abu Dharr was a favorite of the Prophet's and the fourth or fifth person to convert to Islam. He was a pious man from an early age and fought alongside Muhammad at the Battle of Badr. He rejected the rising worldliness of his peers after Muhammad's death and was eventually exiled to Damascus.

For the Soviet broadcasters who retold this story over the airwaves in 1947, the epic of Abu Dharr became a history lesson in social justice and class warfare, about a man who had only two sets of clothing and gave one set away. For the Soviets, and certainly for later Muslim philosophers like Ali Shariati, early acts of sharing wealth, combined with the proscriptions of the Quran to be kind and merciful to the poor and downtrodden, seemed to create a clear connection between the Prophet and his caliphate and the importance of worker solidarity. For Shariati, Islam was by its nature a revolutionary ideology, capable of overthrowing imperialism first and exploitation, capitalism, and poverty second.[95] For the Soviet broadcasters, imperialism functioned more as a symptom of capitalist degradation than as a cause. Capitalism was the ideology that enabled the vagaries of colonialism and slavery, Radio Moscow argued. In order to free itself of colonialism, the Muslim world would first have to reject the socioeconomic system that made colonialism possible. There was plenty of common ground between these groups, which Radio Moscow believed could be used to create solidarity and mobilization.

This steady, contested casting of Middle Eastern history had a lasting impact. History defines group and individual identities for both perpetrators and victims. It shapes the nature of current and future antagonisms as well as the path to reconciliation.[96] On the one hand, Radio Moscow's telling of history offered a profound indictment of the West. It held Britain responsible for the chaos and violence in Palestine. In turn, it rid Arab and Yishuv populations of responsibility for the current terror at home, rendering them all victims of Western historical exploitation. On the other hand, it offered Arab populations a sense of agency in its vision of anti-colonial revolt. It was here, in these Marxist readings of the stories of the Arab golden age and of the Arab revolts of the 1920s, that Arabs could understand and build upon their own historic legacy. The rejection of Britain was, of course, a prerequisite.

. . .

By 1947 the boundaries of the audiosphere being created by international radio in the Middle East were starting to take shape. While Britain offered continuity, stability, and capitalist colonial development, the Soviet Union promised a liberating vision of anti-colonial revolution with its modernizing support. Radio Moscow established a vocabulary for thinking about Western imperialism and articulated a socialist version of Islamic nationalism that would resonate for decades to come.

British and Soviet broadcasters brought their history with them when they set out to build compliance and allegiance. For the BBC and the PBS, the legacy of empire dictated that they remain silent on many of the key messages that were available to their counterparts at Radio Moscow. It was difficult to criticize the Soviet Union for its imperial aggression or its false claims of proletarian fidelity. To conjure such images invited comparison. Instead, they relied on the promise of English development and culture as a balm for the inconvenience of military occupation. The British would fight both communism and Arab independence through the pledge of benevolent care and happiness. The violence that ensued in those last years of the Mandate is evidence enough of their failure.

For Radio Moscow, the messaging of socialist revolution was the cornerstone for a narrative of Arab, proletarian uprising. In many ways, it was the Soviets who set the terms for the great debates that shaped the soundscape of the Middle East, at least in the 1940s. In the years to come, the British, American, and Egyptian broadcasting programs were compelled to address the working class as a socioeconomic entity. The language of Arab revolution bore unmistakable resemblances to the rhetoric that first emerged from Radio Moscow in the postwar years.

Beneath these differences ran similarities. Both sides promised modernization and development to those who remained loyal. Both promises were rooted in an assumption about the Arab colonial world: that leaps forward could only happen with outside help. Each constructed the other as an existential threat to that promised modernization and independence. Both also assumed the revolutionary character of the Arab world, seeing it either as an asset or a threat. Both saw potential use from these assumptions in the burgeoning Cold War, where the promise of modernization, the threat of outside invasion, and the revolutionary nature of Arab identity could be mobilized as a tool in the fight for hegemony and global consensus.

TWO

The Resonance Machine Is Born

THE FIGHT FOR PALESTINE,
THE BATTLE FOR ISRAEL

ON FEBRUARY 18, 1947, Foreign Secretary Ernest Bevin announced over the airwaves of the BBC that Britain would soon be handing over the fate of Palestine to the UN. The violence from Zionist and Arab nationalist groups had rendered the place ungovernable, he said, even by the British. "We have reached the conclusion that the only course now open to us is to submit the problem to the judgment of the United Nations."[1] The UN announced its plan to send its Special Committee on Palestine (UNSCOP) to assess the problem and come up with a solution that would end the violence. This was the latest in a long line of attempts made by governments, individuals, and international groups to solve the "Palestinian Question" in the twentieth century. The UNSCOP, like so many committees before it, would attempt to assess the nature of the crisis by visiting the region and then making recommendations that would eventually be brought before the UN General Assembly for a vote.[2]

That night, and in the many months that followed, the news of the UN's investigation into Palestine became the central story for every radio station from Tiberias to Asluj. From the way that international broadcasters framed the UNSCOP's tour through Palestine, to their coverage of the *Exodus* crisis, to their discussions of the UN deliberations and final vote, each broadcasting station created a framework for understanding the situation that was embedded in intertwining debates surrounding the future of Jewish and Arab national sovereignty, the legacy of the British Empire, the rise of Soviet and American global power, and the burgeoning Cold War. All sides argued that they were working to unveil the truth in the face of dissimilitude. All swore themselves to the highest of ethics. All worked to build unanimity among their listeners, to limit the boundaries of discussion, to exclude contradiction, and to delegitimize the alternative voices that swirled through the airwaves. They omitted certain stories and emphasized others. They struggled to find the words that would cultivate the support of their Middle Eastern and North African listeners. They usually matched their reporting with their own nations' agendas, whether it was the British attempting to extricate themselves gracefully from Palestine and stop the spread of global communism while still protecting their investments and trade routes, or the Soviets working to attract a new population of allies in the Middle East while stopping the spread of global capitalism. Adding to the soundscape were the many Arab radio stations, which railed against Western imperialism while using the Palestinian question as a locus for the development of a pan-Arab national identity.

While each station attempted to follow its own, specific national agenda, each was forced again and again to answer the other voices churning through the airwaves. As such, the stations began to generate a "resonance machine."[3] They infiltrated each other, metabolizing into a moving complex, morphing into "energized complexities of mutual imbrication," creating a unified assemblage of messages that set the stage for the evolution of radio's discursive framework.

. . .

Any mapping of the Arabic-language soundscape would be incomplete without considering the medium-wave broadcasts that came predominantly from Lebanon (Radio Beirut), Syria (Radio Damascus), and Egypt (Radio Cairo) in the late 1940s. All of these stations were newly separated from imperial oversight. Radio Beirut had been founded by the British in 1936 and taken over by the Lebanese government in 1946. Radio Damascus had a similar story, coming into existence in 1946 with the founding of the Syrian Broadcasting Organization shortly after the French evacuation.[4] Radio Cairo had been under British control until the Egyptian government canceled the contract on March 4, 1947, and took over.[5] All of the Arab stations sought to differentiate themselves from the West. They argued to the Arabic-speaking world that exploitation and trickery defined their relationship with white Europe and the United States, including the United Nations. They frequently stood in opposition to all of the Western-funded programs around them, opposing colonial intervention, protesting Jewish immigration, and refusing to negotiate with nations that they believed had no right to arbitrate terms in Palestine.[6] Fear of Cold War ideological infiltration took second stage to the larger worry over continued colonial occupation and internal civil war.

At the same time, all of these stations carried heavy British or French influences even as they rejected Western presence in the Middle East. Many of their broadcasters had been trained by the West, particularly at Sharq al-Adna. By 1947 these workers had moved on to take over the leadership of Radio Beirut, Radio Cairo, and Radio Damascus. This transfer of personnel, ownership, and training carried with it a transfer of language and methodology. It meant that while Radio Beirut, Radio Cairo, and Radio Damascus railed against Anglo-American empire building in Palestine and elsewhere, they often did it in the language of the occupier, at least in the early years. This was supplemented by the presence of Radio Moscow, whose anti-imperial mantra provided ample ammunition to the newly sprouted voices of Arab independence.

This intermingling manifested in the Arab and European coverage of the UNSCOP's visit to Palestine in the summer of 1947. Rumors became statements as one station made a claim that was then picked up and repeated by another. Radio Beirut repeated Radio Moscow's claims that the Jewish Agency was spreading falsehoods about the Arab League.[7] Some Arabic broadcasts could be traced back to Jewish or British sources. In the spring of 1947, the Palestinian Jewish newspaper *Haboker* reported that Bevin and George Marshall had secretly agreed to divvy up Palestine, with a Jewish home under American supervision and an Arab home remaining under the British Mandate (a falsehood). Two days later, Radio Egypt picked up the story and broadcast it in Arabic to the Middle East. Four hundred thousand Jews would be admitted to the United States, the broadcasters reported, with the rest heading to Palestine under American supervision.[8] Radio Cairo repeated interviews done by Rex Keating's PBS with the prime ministers of Iraq and Lebanon, especially when they spoke of their belief that the UNSCOP would rule in favor of Palestine's Arab community.[9] Every Arab station had carried the words of the Syrian premier, Jamil Mardam Bey, when he seemed to encourage the UN visit based on the Soviet argument that the countries of the world would inevitably be convinced of the "justness of Arab Palestinian claims."[10] Radio Moscow aired the speech three times in two days.

The Arab radio stations, including Sharq al-Adna, quickly came to a consensus in their condemnation of the UN visit. They protested the UN's refusal to simply declare the end of the British Mandate and the independence of Palestine. They opposed its failure to separate the Jewish refugee crisis from the Palestinian right to sovereignty. And they argued that religious interests could not supersede the interests of Palestine's majority inhabitants. It was inconceivable to many that a country with an 80 percent Arab majority could be forced to accept a settlement that the majority did not want. Hussain Khalidi, the secretary of the Arab Higher Committee for Palestine, put it succinctly. Seated at his desk, he lifted up a stack of papers, all listing the commissions that had come to Palestine since 1918 to solve the crisis. "There are no facts which can be found by any fact-finding commission," he said. Only two issues mattered: what to do about the incoming Jewish refugees and how to deal with the British Mandate.[11] Radio Morocco argued that just as the League of Nations had once betrayed its ideals, so too "should it not be expected that the UN will adopt the course dictated by justice."[12] Similarly, Radio Tunis argued that the British were collaborating secretly with the Zionists: "If the Big Powers send a new inquiry commission, this only means they are trying to gain time in order to help Britain strengthen the situation of the Jews in Palestine."[13] If a discerning listener had, at that same moment, switched to the British stations, particularly Rex Keating's PBS, they would have heard broadcasts that were surprisingly quiet about Jewish immigration and Zionist terrorism in Palestine.[14] For the Arab stations, all of this smacked of duplicity. When Radio Tunis announced that the UN investigation was a "waste of time," it was because, for that station, the complicity of the UN in undermining Arab interests was already assumed.[15] As Radio Cairo put it, "To rely on these international organizations is like depending on a broken leg."[16]

One thing the Arab stations agreed on was that the threat of outside invasion had to be managed. This included Jewish immigration, which was another manifestation of Western attack, brought on by Western guilt over the Holocaust. When the UNSCOP announced its fact-finding mission in early 1947, Arab radio reported with dismay that UNSCOP was also going to be visiting a European concentration camp. Again and again, the Arab radio stations expressed sorrow for the Shoah.[17] At the same time, they argued vehemently that the Holocaust could not be a factor in deciding the Palestinian Question, that Palestine was not a "dumping ground for displaced persons, nor a sanctuary for criminals, nor a solution for Anglo-American political problems."[18] Arab radio declared regularly that the unfortunate Jewish immigrants who were appearing on the shores of Palestine were merely "pawns in a propaganda game."[19]

All of the broadcasts that came from the Arab countries reflected a sense that the Arabs of Palestine were struggling to get people in the European and American world to listen to their story and were consistently encountering the willful deafness of latent, paternalist Orientalism. They reported back to their listeners that the Arab delegates at the UN faced an untenable situation in which a "well-prepared" British government had secured American support in the steering committees and plenary sessions. Everyone knew that President Harry S. Truman supported the Jewish cause, and no one trusted the British to defend Arab interests. The Soviets were equally untrustworthy. As Hussein Khalidi noted, "Russian policy in connection with Palestine has never, not even for a day, been clear."[20]

For Arab broadcasters and their governments, the act of coming together to resist UN intervention functioned as a building block in the formation of a public language for talking about Arab national identity, at least in the public sphere. One could hear the common mantra from almost any station, that "relations between the Arab countries [were] very friendly" and that all were adhering to the Arab League Charter and its principles.[21] Support of the Palestinian Arabs provided (and still provides) a powerful cause behind which Arab nationalism could rally. For instance, when Shukri Al-Kuwatly, the Syrian president, gave a speech in Homs that May, Radio Damascus carried the message that it would celebrate Syrian independence "with support for our Palestinian neighbors with the spirit of cooperation with all our neighbors."[22] For Radio Beirut and Radio Damascus, it was critical to show continued solidarity with the Arabs of Palestine while also projecting to Palestine's Jews, and everyone else, that the Arab world was united and strong.

At the same time, rejection of the UN was also a critical part of the complex internal struggles that were ongoing between the Arab nations in 1947. Egypt, Iraq, Jordan, Lebanon, Saudi Arabia, Syria, and Yemen were all members of the Arab League, and all expressed differing levels of support for the decision to boycott the UN's visit to Palestine. Each national broadcasting station argued that it was working the hardest to defend the interests of the Palestinian Arabs around the world, while also pursuing its own geostrategic interests. Amin Al-Husseini (the mufti of Jerusalem who had collaborated with the Nazis during the war, escaped in disguise from Europe, and was only recently out of hiding in Egypt) had been at odds with other members of the Arab Higher Committee and King Abdullah of Jordan for some time over who should be entitled to speak for Palestine's Arabs.[23]

Old divides played out on the Palestinian audioscape. Radio Beirut and Radio Baghdad levied criticism at the Egyptian government for failing to offer sufficient backing to the Palestinian cause. "We have all hoped that Egypt would relieve their sufferings and heal their wounds." But Egypt wasn't boycotting Zionist goods, Radio Beirut claimed, and was failing to see how its "younger brother suffer[ed] under the weight of imperialism and economic foreign monopoly."[24] Radio Cairo responded, "Egypt is [Palestine's] elder sister." It argued that Egypt was intent on "relieving their suffering and healing their wounds" (using exactly the same words that Radio Beirut had used). Radio Cairo created an image of Palestine and Egypt locked together in their shared plight as nations occupied by the British. "Like in Palestine, The British Government is fully aware that the presence of soldiers in our country is against our will!" it declared that May.[25]

Underlying this rhetoric was the ongoing struggle between Iraq and Egypt for leadership of the Arab world. For everyone, Palestine symbolized the survival of the Arab world in the face of continued outside pressure. "Join Iraq in the struggle against Zionist greed in Palestine!" Iraq's pro-British prime minister, Nuri Es-Said, declared in the spring of 1947.[26] "If we accept to lose Palestine, we lose everything," Es-Said bellowed to an attentive listening audience.[27] Meanwhile, Radio Cairo reported daily on the various conferences it was sponsoring to find a solution to the "Palestinian Problem." These assurances stood in contrast to Egypt's actual policy toward the Palestinian Question, which was characterized by ambivalence and reluctance to intervene.[28] Central to all of these projects was the rewriting of Palestine's, and their own, histories, so that in the case of partition, it would appear as though they were not responsible for the loss of Palestine.

The UNSCOP tour began on June 15, 1947. The English, Soviet, and various Middle Eastern broadcasting stations had laid out the basic lines, and the basic vocabulary, of the Palestinian divide. While the English struggled to orchestrate an honorable departure based on arguments of colonial benevolence and promised Western development, the Soviets became the great harbingers of impending doom, arguing to anyone who would listen that the leadership of the West offered only more poisoned imperialism. At the same time, the Arab and Jewish worlds struggled to navigate a path between the latent imperial desires of the outside world and their own immutable visions of a self-determined future.

The broadcasts from these days recount the adventures of the delegates who came ostensibly to examine the lives and needs of Palestine's inhabitants. UNSCOP delegates visited the sacred sites of Jerusalem, walking in the searing heat from the Haram esh Sharif and the Al Aqsa mosque through the bustling tunnels and open air markets of Jerusalem's old city, to the Wailing Wall, and then back to the Church of the Holy Sepulcher, with its Christian tourists crowding around the Stone of Unction, jostling to touch a rosary or a scarf to its worn surface. In Haifa, they toured an Arab-owned cigarette factory and a Jewish-owned textile factory. They visited a kibbutz near the Dead Sea and the ruins of old Jericho. They inspected schools in Gaza and Hebron before heading north to meet doctors in Jaffa and Ramle. In neighboring Tel Aviv, they were impressed by the Jewish-owned modern laboratories, where skilled workers were making precision optical instruments. They enjoyed the museums and the chocolate factory, all before visiting the People and Its Land exhibition of the Jewish National Fund. They visited Hebrew University in Jerusalem, teachers' schools in Ramallah, six Jewish settlements, numerous factories and laboratories, and one Jewish children's home.[29]

Meanwhile, on June 16, one day after the UNSCOP delegates had arrived in Palestine, the mufti of Jerusalem took to the radio, calling upon "all Arabs to protect the Holy Land."[30] Arabs prepared for a mass commercial strike of all factories and businesses to show the UNSCOP what power they could wield. The Arab Higher Committee announced that it was going on a world tour to convince the great powers that they had a cause worth defending at the UN. While all of this was happening, British Mandate authorities sentenced four members of the Zionist terrorist organization, Irgun, to death for the famous Acre prison break "to defend the Holy Land." For centuries, defending the Holy Land had been a justification for mobilization and violence. By 1947 that call to arms was not new. Irgun backtracked on its cease-fire and promised "blood for blood" retaliation against the British in defense of its homeland.[31]

All of the radio stations followed the UNSCOP tour closely. Radio Moscow worked to thread the needle of support for both Arab and Jewish listeners while condemning the West at every opportunity. The station maintained its ongoing commentary on "the representatives of Britain and America at the UNO . . . who look to the aspirations of Jews and Arabs in light of their imperialist aims in the Middle East."[32] "The British will remain where they are," Radio Moscow declared one evening, making sure to point out the hypocrisy of Britain's promises to give a homeland to both the Jews and Arabs in decades past. Radio Moscow claimed that Britain had become a lackey of the United States, declaring that Bevin had "acted as a servant to U.S. monopoly capitalism, especially in connection with Near Eastern affairs."[33] The station argued that Anglo-American forces had created a puppet regime of the Arab ruling class (who were long known for their relations with Europe and fascists), which only made "reactionary Jews" even more intractable. The broadcasters criticized Jamal Mardam Bey for refusing to consider the creation of a Jewish national home. They simultaneously argued that it was "equally natural that one should not agree" with Jewish newspapers that wanted to establish a "Jewish state dominant over all the land of Palestine."[34]

Soviet criticisms of Anglo-American duplicity and those countries' claims to support both Jewish and Arab interests, quickly rang hollow for Arab listeners. Radio Damascus responded to Radio Moscow that same day with the airing of a speech by Azzam Pasha, the general secretary of the Arab League, in which he quipped, "All the great powers were staging maneuvers for their own interests." The very next day, Radio Moscow replied that it was "astonishing" that the Arab League would react so negatively to its "clear and just" approach.

The historian Elad Ben-Dror has observed that the Arab Higher Committee forbade the Palestinian press to talk about the UNSCOP visit.[35] This may have been the case, but there was no dearth of news about the tour on the radios of Palestine and the larger Middle East. Radio Damascus regularly reminded its listeners to the south that the "Arab Governments reserved the right of action to realize Palestine independence by any means they consider suitable."[36] It railed until the last minute against the possibility that the UNSCOP might visit European concentration camps on its tour.[37] Radio Beirut reported weekly on the Palestinian strike and the Arab boycott, even covering the decision to boycott Polish goods in the wake of Poland's seemingly pro-Jewish stance during the discussions on Palestine at the UN.[38] Radio Cairo meanwhile reported daily on the "strong popular sentiment among all of the Arabs of Palestine demanding national unity."[39] The BBC could be counted on to trace the steps of the UNSCOP. It reported on the twelve UNSCOP public hearings that took place in Jerusalem between July 4 and 17, in which thirty-one Jewish witnesses and seventeen Jewish organizations gave testimony on their experiences during the war and their plans "to bring water to the desert" of Palestine.[40] No Arabs spoke at the hearings.

Then, on Friday, July 18, *Exodus* arrived. The Jewish paramilitary organization Haganah had secretly bought the refurbished American warship and had sailed from France earlier that week with 4,554 Jewish immigrants, most of them survivors of the war. As the ship neared the shore, Haganah representatives broadcast in Hebrew, English, and French from transmitters aboard the ship. "Listen world," the broadcasters bellowed, "this is the Haganah ship, Exodus 1947." They repeated these words again and again for the next hour. "We are approaching the shores of Palestine." The BBC announcer described how the ship had departed from Philadelphia on March 29 and had been delayed on its trip to Europe because the British had refused to allow it needed oil. After reaching France, the ship had picked up its human cargo and "slipped out of a French port" that Friday night. British warships spotted it within a couple of hours and took turns shadowing the *Exodus* as it moved south. "At the present moment we have an escort of one cruiser and two destroyers," the Haganah broadcaster announced.[41] The transmission, which lasted for exactly one hour, ended with a children's choir singing the Hebrew fight song of the Palmach, which was the elite fighting force of the Haganah. The British navy boarded the ship after it arrived on Palestine's shores, but not without coming up against significant, sometimes violent, resistance from the passengers onboard. The BBC reported that three British sailors had been injured in their efforts to board, and that the British warships had been damaged when the *Exodus* had "taken evasive action."[42]

Two of the UNSCOP delegates were there when the *Exodus* landed at the port in Haifa that evening. They watched as British soldiers forcibly removed the unfortunate refugees from the boat and put them on deportation ships headed back to Cyprus. On Sunday, May 23, the radio announced that the "Jews of Palestine" would be going on strike at 4:00 that afternoon. It was an explosive international story, picked up and retold by the BBC, the PBS, and eventually on radio stations and newspapers around the world.[43] That Monday, the BBC reported in Arabic and English that the deportation ships were heading back to France. From that day on, *Exodus* was on the front page of every international newspaper and in every radio broadcast, from CBS to the BBC. Heartrending reports told of Jewish Holocaust survivors being held prisoner on board increasingly unsanitary British ships, facing the prospect of having to return to Europe. In awe, the world press spoke of the unwavering commitment of the Jewish passengers to stay on the boats, regardless of their suffering. Images of dirty children in the arms of desperate but resolute Jewish mothers standing up to British colonizers made for compelling copy. The saga of the *Exodus* refugees did not end until they were made to leave France and were eventually forced off the ships on

September 9, into camps in Hamburg, Germany, that were lined with barbed wire and manned by dogs. The stories coming from the increasingly squalid ships, filled with refugees who refused to disembark, were so disturbing that the US maritime workers' union appealed to the sailors of the British navy to mutiny against the orders of their government.

The radio story of the *Exodus* leaves more questions than answers. There are some perhaps not so surprising voids in the historical record where the Arabic-language broadcasts about *Exodus* should be. Not once does the *Exodus* appear in the FBIS radio transcript archive, which was maintained by the CIA and was famously thorough when it came to listening to Radio Moscow, Sharq al-Adna, the PBS, and Radio Beirut. One transcript appears that only vaguely references the *Exodus*, when, months later, Radio Beirut broadcast that the Jewish Agency had decided to "sever relations with the Palestine Government because the Palestine Government has returned immigrants to France."[44] One cannot know whether this relative absence of stories about the *Exodus* has occurred because the CIA monitors at the FBIS were ordered to keep stories about it out of the record, or if there were simply no broadcasts to transcribe. The former answer seems likely, given that the Arab newspapers carried daily stories on the events happening on the ship. The other archival sources offer little clarity. The BBC archives, which keep a full daily transcript of the covert British broadcasts of Sharq al-Adna, are equally bare. In the months of July, August, and September Sharq broadcast stories on the Arab leaders' work with the UN, the continuing Zionist terrorist violence in Palestine, and the Arab world's anger after the release of the UNSCOP report on September 8. Not once does the *Exodus* appear. In the case of the Soviet state archives, one cannot currently access the Radio Moscow programming records for the month of July through August 1947. There are many possible reasons that folder does not appear to exist in the record, the most likely being that it reveals the Soviet Union's troubled inconsistency when it came to courting the Arabs of the world as anti-imperial compatriots. All this is to say that there were ample reasons not to keep a record of how everyone had talked about the *Exodus*.[45]

Regardless, the *Exodus* episode was an international public relations disaster for the British, a step backward for the Arab cause, and a victory for Haganah and the Jewish Agency, albeit at great cost. The struggle and suffering of the displaced people on the *Exodus* were critical to the Jewish propaganda program in Palestine and around the world. With each ship loaded full of enfeebled, starving Jewish Holocaust survivors that the British army turned away from Palestine's shores, the level of embarrassment and discomfort for the British government increased geometrically. The literature seems to show that illegal immigration of Jewish immigrants in 1946 and 1947 was not very successful, if gauged by the numbers of people who actually arrived that way. And yet as a propaganda tool meant to horrify and enrage the world, "the show," in the words of Avigdor Lieberman, Israel's defense minister, "paid off!"[46]

As far as the Arab radio stations were concerned, the Jewish immigration crisis was a Machiavellian stunt orchestrated by Zionists to cultivate world sympathy on the backs of their own suffering children. Arabs, Jews, and Christians were capable of living together, they argued in the weeks that followed, but not Zionists, who were, in their words, defined by "savagery, cruelty, and murder."[47] In response to the stories of the horrible conditions that Jewish refugees were experiencing as they waited for immigration in ships offshore (*Exodus* was only the most famous of these ships; they arrived weekly through the summer and fall of 1947.), stations like Radio Damascus called the whole process a "farce," not because the refugees were farcical but because the entire public exhibition of arriving on Palestine's shores only to be shuttled away by the British navy under the gaze of international observers represented a "tragic staging by Zionists to win mercy and compassion."[48] Such claims of Zionist duplicity, characterized by seeming savagery, became staples of Arab broadcasting.

That September, after the UNSCOP finished its twenty-two-hundred-mile, two-and-one-half month tour—a tour of misery and hope, of destruction and rebuilding, and of significant chaos—the committee concluded that the only viable solution to the Palestinian Question was partition. The UNSCOP declared that the area must become a constitutional democracy with rights guaranteed, that a system should be established for the settling of disputes peacefully, and that the economic unity of Palestine had to be preserved. A majority report recommended the partition of Palestine with an internationalized Jerusalem, followed by a minority report that recommended no partition, with local self-government and the international arbitration of Jerusalem. To the dismay of the Arab world, the United States and the Soviet Union expressed their support for the partition plan.

The news of the UNSCOP decision spread quickly over the radios of Palestine and the Middle East. All of the radio stations, regardless of their source, described the Arab world's collective shock, anger, and rejection of the UNSCOP's proposals. The PBS broadcast Abdullah of Transjordan's declaration that the "Arab countries will categorically reject the partition plan of UNSCOP" (which was itself duplicitous, as Abdullah supported partition in the hope that the Arab areas of Palestine would be annexed into Transjordan).[49] Reports came in from Syrian tribes who were meeting in Tudmor to announce that Palestine would be "defended with blood if necessary." Kamel Jaderji, the leader of the Iraqi Democratic Party and a renowned photographer, announced on the radio: "The Arab countries should proclaim that they are not bound by the [UNSCOP] decision.... If the UN agrees to the UNSCOP recommendations, the Arab countries should leave that organization." Pausing for effect, he spoke clearly and slowly: "Confidential decisions have been made by the Arab countries."[50] Four days later, Salih Jabr, the Iraqi premier, called upon the Arab countries to "prepare Arab youth for the undertaking awaiting them to save Palestine.... The Arab countries are moved by one desire and towards one common objective." He spoke resoundingly over the airwaves as millions listened in: "If the UN approves the partition plan, it will provoke disturbance in the Middle East."[51] It was a clear message meant for every Arab listener across the Middle East and North Africa: war would come if the UN voted for partition. As would happen again in the coming decades, a vision of an overwhelming, unified Arab force took shape on the airwaves. More than this, this speech and the others like it helped to create a vocabulary for understanding the coming catastrophe.

Whether one tuned in to Radio Beirut, Radio Damascus, or Radio Cairo, they all made it clear that how the UN voted on Palestine would be a barometer for separating friend from foe. It would also be a testing of the metal of the United Nations. As far as the Arab stations were concerned, if the UN chose partition, it would mean that it was choosing against its own original charter. It had sworn to "save succeeding generations from the scourge of war" and to "reaffirm faith in the equal rights of nations large and small."[52] To choose partition would, in their eyes, nullify the legitimacy of the organization altogether.

The Arab countries also threatened to withhold oil. As it would do in years to come, the Egyptian Home Service reminded its listeners that the control of oil could wield great power in the coming negotiations. "British businessmen are interested in the Arab league threat of cancelling the Middle East oil concessions ... if they accept the partition of Palestine," one broadcaster declared. "Oil prices are still inclined to rise in the United States and may continue because of the threat announced by the Arabs."[53] From

Jerusalem (and perhaps unbeknownst to Edwin Samuel and Rex Keating), the Arab Section of the PBS told its Palestinian listeners that the entire Arab world was prepared to use its oil to teach America a lesson in return for its support of partition. "It will be a great pride for the Arab countries to be shortly able to give America a lesson which will terminate U.S. boastfulness and will help it to return to its senses."[54]

While all the Arab radio stations decried the UNSCOP recommendation for partition, their emerging Cold War alliances determined where they laid the blame. The pro-American Radio Beirut reported to listeners across the Levant and North Africa that the Soviets were using their new support for the Jewish cause as a pretext for interfering in the affairs of the Middle East. They argued that the Soviet Union only backed partition because it would give the Soviets "the opportunity of sending troops to Palestine under the pretext of helping to implement the partition plan."[55] For other Arab stations, the blame lay squarely at the feet of the United States. Back in August 1945, following mass rallies for the Jewish cause in New York and under increasing pressure from his staff, President Truman had asked Clement Atlee to grant one hundred thousand Jews admission into Palestine immediately. By 1947, for many Arabs in the Middle East the rise of Zionism in Palestine was inextricably tied to Truman's policies, which they believed he had adopted in order to win Jewish votes back in America. The Arab press continuously noted that Truman had pressured Palestine to take 100,000 Jewish refugees, while the United States had only admitted 4,767 Jews to its shores during the Second World War.[56] The pro-Soviet Radio Damascus declared that Arabs could not allow themselves to be the "catspaw" of American politicians who were desperate to safeguard their electoral successes through the securing of Zionist votes. "Arabs do not want to be sacrificed for the sake of Presidential elections," Radio Damascus argued.[57] Even the Zionist organizations were quietly skeptical of American intentions; the Irgun secret radio station contended that the American proposal (which required the British to stay in Palestine until the following May) had been proposed as an underhanded trick to convert Palestine into another US military base.[58]

Critically, the US information services offered little in the way of response. Many in the State Department believed it would be better to remain silent over the airwaves than to risk highlighting their own allegiance with the Zionist program. American leaders and diplomats frequently dismissed Arab desires for independence as "politically primitive, economically suspect and ideologically absurd."[59] And as the historian Heonik Kwon has noted, US policy makers were hobbled by racism, Orientalism, emergent Cold War antagonisms, and the tendency to oversimplify complex issues when it came to the postcolonial world.[60] American state officials knew that the United States was facing increasing Arab acrimony in the Middle East.[61] As a consequence, the USIA and the Office of Information and Cultural Affairs remained "paralyzed" and "rudderless," with little plan and even less action for what they should do to win the allegiance of listeners.[62] This perhaps explains why the Russian Federation and the BBC have so little in their archives by way of American, Arabic-language radio transcripts for the Middle East and North Africa in 1947. US broadcasters knew that Truman had soured Arab opinion toward the United States and that if they launched cultural activities in Palestine, only Jewish populations would agree to participate. This would only make them look worse. So they chose to do nothing. Many professional American diplomats disagreed with Truman's policies toward Palestine but could only respond with silence.[63]

Meanwhile, Sharq al-Adna, the covert British station pretending to be an Arab station, attempted to shape the news about the UNSCOP recommendation into a narrative that would salvage Britain's record and show its support for the Arab cause. The broadcasters were quick to report on the findings of the UNSCOP's second subcommittee, which unlike the first had a large Arab membership. They railed against the idea that a Jewish state could be carved from a place that had a majority Arab population.[64] They also issued subtle warnings to their listeners that, in the end, Ernest Bevin would make the final call on whether or not to follow the UN's recommendations. "It must not be forgotten that UNSCOP is only an advisory committee not only for the [UN] Security Council, but for Britain too."[65] And they mocked the conclusions of the UNSCOP as being ill-informed and naïve. "One cannot help feeling that a person like Bevin who for several years has been studying the Palestinian question will be just as qualified to give an opinion on the Palestine question as the Guatemala representative" (a representative from Guatemala sat on the UNSCOP).[66] The sourness of the English at not being given more of a say in deciding the shape of Palestine's new management was palpable, even on a radio station that was pretending to not be British.

A steady barrage of broadcasts from Sharq al-Adna and occasionally the PBS carried the unmistakable tone of bitterness at Britain not being asked to choose its own successor. Britain's withdrawal from Palestine was a shameful episode, a blight on Britain's self-perceived stellar record of creating happy and modern peoples under its dominion. The "you don't know how good you have it" calls for gratitude were common. On October 14, 1946, Sharq al-Adna told Arab listeners that they should expect to have to handle their problems alone once the British had departed, without support from either of the superpowers.[67] "Neither the Soviets nor the Americans have any interest in defending you," a broadcaster intoned. Later that day, Sharq declared to its listeners that the Soviets and Americans were only able to criticize the British because they did not have to deal with the logistical nightmare that Palestine presented.[68] Such statements carried many inflections. They laid blame for the situation squarely at the feet of the Jewish and Arab people of Palestine. They lashed out at the Americans, who had so easily sat in judgment of Britain's efforts over the years. They worked hard to show British solidarity for the Arab cause and to stir up fears about the end of the Mandate. They also took care to lay responsibility for the chaos on the Soviets. "Soviet authorities in Germany are behind attempts by Jews to reach Palestine," the BBC declared at the end of September. It reported that Soviet authorities in Eastern Europe were encouraging Jewish immigration to the Anglo-American zones of Germany "as the quickest and surest route to Palestine."[69]

Only slightly further up the dial, Radio Moscow mobilized the mantra of peace to articulate its response to the UN decision. "This war of nerves which has broken out in connection with the Palestine problem cannot in the least contribute to peace." Not surprisingly, Radio Moscow connected British imperialism to American intervention in the Middle East. "This duplicity in politics continues," the broadcasters declared, "with the United States acting on behalf of Rockefeller, Morgan, and Mellon in its pursuit of the Middle East's oil reserves."[70] Radio Moscow reported that US "expansionists" were making every effort to turn Iran and Turkey into military strategic bases on the southern borders of the Soviet Union. They argued that American monopolists were drawing huge dividends from the sale of arms, atomic blackmail, and in preparation for another war. "They are already coining into hard cash the blood of the millions to be shed in the new world war they are plotting. . . . [B]lood is already flowing in Palestine." Meanwhile, the British had acquiesced at every turn, they said, with "America's imperialist policy." "Masters of the art of deceiving the masses," even the British labor leaders had become "representatives of monopolistic American capital."[71]

Then, in a feat of impressive linguistic gymnastics, Radio Moscow set out to explain to Arab listeners why partition was actually in their best interests. They argued that through partition, Jews and Arabs would be able to build a peaceful future that would "not be hampered by the monopolists."[72] The enmity would disappear, they argued, as soon as British and American interference was gone. The partition plan, in this Soviet rendering, offered the best way to rid Palestine of Western exploitation, thereby offering an ideological justification for Moscow's "yea" vote for partition at the UN. Only the Soviets could speak about Palestine without bias, they claimed. And only the Soviets saw how the problems between the Arabs and Jews could be solved. The Soviets had chosen to support partition, but they had justification, they argued, that differed fundamentally from the American support of it. Not to mention that their support for partition paled in comparison to the decades of lies and exploitation that the Arab world had endured because of British imperial folly.

The weather was stormy and cold in Manhattan on November 12, 1947. A record 2.4 inches of rain poured down, adding to the 8 inches that had fallen in the last fifteen days.[73] Members of the UN huddled under umbrellas held by eager aides as they climbed out of taxis and hurried into the Assembly Hall at Lake Success for the day's debates. At the helm of the UN sat the Norwegian Trygve Halvdan Lie, who had served as a foreign minister for the Norwegian government in exile during the war and had chaired the Norwegian delegation at the first session of the UN General Assembly when it met in London in 1946. The delegates were there to debate and vote on the future of Palestine.

Over the last several decades, historians have spilled much ink unpacking the machinations that occurred in the days before the final UN vote on November 28. When the news broke on November 12 that the Soviet Union and the United States would both be voting to support the partition, Jamal al-Husseini, the chairman of the Arab Higher Committee, declared, "The Russian-American agreements are part of the maneuvers staged by Washington in the interests of the Jews, especially since the date of the U.S. elections is approaching."[74] American diplomats fanned out among the varying delegations, promising the carrot and stick to make sure they had the two-thirds majority needed to pass the proposal for partition. Just before the vote was taken, the Arab nations put forward a last-minute compromise plan for an independent federal state of Palestine, which was turned down after speeches against it by the delegates of the United States and Soviet Union. Prince Faisal led the procession of Arab delegates down to the rostrum, where one by one they declared in rousing and bitter language that they were not bound by the UN's decision. They viewed the entire vote as contrary to the spirit of the UN Charter and said that from now on they held themselves free to act as they saw fit. They put the responsibility for what was to come at the feet of those who had rigged the voting: the Soviet Union and the United States.

The radios of the world were tuned in. In the day before the vote, the PBS played dramatic performances of *Jane Eyre* and of the famous correspondence between Charles Dickens and William Makepeace Thackery (in which, a hundred years earlier, they had pondered the hubris of the wealthy and the seething anger of the poor).[75] "Expecting decision on Partition Plan," Rex Keating scrawled on a dog-eared page of his diary marked Friday, November 28.[76] Everyone listened in to the final vote. "You all know . . . how . . . to vote!" Trygve Halvdan Lie said to the UN Assembly, his halting words crackling across the airwaves. "Those . . . who are in favor will say yes. . . . Those who are against it will say no. . . . And the abstainers . . . always this, they know what to say." The room laughed. "We will start it now." The voting was certainly peculiar. Two of the states that had declared themselves against partition earlier that week—Haiti and the Philippines—voted for it, as did several countries that had thus far abstained, including France, Liberia, Paraguay, and Luxembourg, despite the large Muslim populations of their colonial empires.[77] At the end, the result was thirty-three votes for partition, thirteen votes against partition, ten abstentions, and one absence. Of the thirty-three that voted for Partition, thirteen were from Latin America. In fact, Cuba was the only Latin American country to vote against it. A great roar of celebration broke out in the General Assembly Hall.

That night, in a voice of mixed resignation and sadness, a BBC correspondent at the UN reported that "many people, according to our correspondent, consider it an unsatisfactory ending for a most important political decision was taken with nearly half the membership of the United Nations against it, and with many of its supporters doubtful about is success."[78] The announcer then shuffled his papers, cleared his throat, and moved on to say that it had been the coldest day in November in London since 1940; it was Winston Churchill's seventy-third birthday; and King Michael of Romania, who had come to Britain for the royal wedding of his cousins Queen Elizabeth II and Prince Phillip of Greece, was able to go home now that the bad weather had passed, "piloting his own plane."[79] It was clear that partition meant war. In the BBC transcripts from that night, an editor ran a line through the phrase, "Arabs will never accept the settling of a Jewish State in the Holy Land." The words are difficult to read on the old, hand-reeled microfilm readers of the BBC archives, now quietly nestled away in the green woods outside Caversham, England. This was the line that the BBC couldn't bring itself to say on November 30. It was true, but perhaps it was just too scary for the 8:00 a.m. news.[80]

The great outburst of rejoicing from Israel's Jewish population that had overtaken Jerusalem the previous night gave way the next day to sobering conversations about the "dangers of peace" and the West's betrayal of the Arab world. Jewish reports emerged that Arab ambushes near Jerusalem had led to casualties.[81] Azzam Pasha, the secretary-general of the Arab League in Cairo, told his listeners that while the Arab people did not want to fight, they would nonetheless resist any forces that tried to implement partition, including the UN and any American oil operations. Pasha's voice rang out across the airwaves: "The United Nations decision will set fire to the Middle East."[82] The Arab Higher Committee ordered a general strike for Tuesday and a complete boycott of Jewish businesses. Meanwhile, the radio announced that Arab offices in New York and Washington had closed in response to the American use of intimidation and blackmail to coerce the small nations into voting for partition. Accusations weren't reserved for the United States. The Arab stations also charged Britain with responsibility for the partition because of its "attitude of pusillanimous passivity."[83] Britain had abstained from the vote, failing to take a stand either way. That night the BBC sent the following broadcast out over the airwaves:

> The Jewish Agency in London put out a statement welcoming the Assembly's decision which it described as "this just solution." The Jewish Agency, it said, "was confident that the new Jewish State would bring peace to the Jewish people and progress to the Middle East and would worthily bear its responsibilities in the community of nations."

> PAUSE

> "Five Jews were killed and eleven wounded when Arabs ambushed Jewish buses near Ten Aviv during the night. In Jerusalem tonight it was officially stated that Arab prisoners in Acre Central Prison had attacked Jewish prisoners while they were exercising. The prison warder used tear gas before opening fire. Several Arabs were wounded."[84]

Claims that partition would create peace were upended before the broadcaster could take a breath.

Back in Palestine, in the two days after the UN made its announcement, the PBS in Jerusalem stayed closed.[85] It had trouble with its drivers, who were increasingly jittery on the roads.[86] When Rex Keating finally wrote in his diary on November 30, all he could say was that "news of Palestine partition came through. Shocking!" He had tea that night with friends. All were speechless, except for one American, who was "disgusted with the chicanery of his country."[87] Keating was particularly frustrated with Edwin Samuel, his boss, who seemed obviously pleased but was "pretending to be against it."[88] Samuel spent significant time assuring everyone that there would be work for them in the years to come, after the PBS had departed. Some he asked to come work for the new Jewish broadcasting agency. Meanwhile, the PBS cut back on its Arab-language programs and encouraged its Arab broadcasters to start seeking alternative employment. By the end of the year, all of the Jewish and Yishuv workers were gone from the PBS. The Second Program cut back its hours, and the PBS hired guards to protect its workers.

Keating had the inglorious job of closing up the Palestine office that winter and spring. By all measures, it was an unpleasant departure. Christmas was upon them, and Keating and his wife Leslie decided to take a well-earned vacation in Cairo. They found the place "ridden with cholera and Anglophobia" and set out a day earlier than planned for the drive back across Sinai to Palestine. Soon they were lost on the open roads that cross the desert, searching for the quarantine station near Lydda. Darkness fell. Eventually they found an isolated house on the edge of town. A single light emanated from the front room, its curtains drawn. Rex knocked on the door. A group of Arabs answered. They welcomed them in and invited them to sit in a back room while they found the quarantine manager. It was Leslie who noticed the quiet sound of the door being locked behind them after they had gone in. Twice they carefully checked the door, realizing that they were in serious trouble. After ten minutes of pacing the room, waiting to be handed over to what they assumed would be terrorists or kidnappers, Leslie noticed that a high window had been left unlocked. Removing their shoes to avoid making a sound, the two quietly escaped and scrambled to their car, skipping the quarantine station altogether and not stopping until they had reached the outskirts of Jerusalem.[89]

After sleeping and bathing, Rex penned a letter to Cyril Conner of the BBC back in London. "In forty-eight hours' time it will be Christmas Day," he wrote, "and I feel that I cannot let the season pass without sending you greetings from the Holy Land. Here, this year, there will be very little peace and certainly no good will towards men. Thousands of decent law-abiding people face untold misery in the coming year and all because of the machinations of a group of unscrupulous politicians. It is a shocking business and one which, I fear, the world will have cause to remember for a long time." After recounting the harrowing tale of their return to the city, Rex hurriedly wrote, "Believe me, I shan't be at all sorry when I see Palestine disappearing over the back end of a ship for the last time."[90]

At some point in February or March 1948, Keating got on the microphone to tell his listeners that despite what the Soviets were saying, the British really were leaving Palestine. "My Palestinian friends just don't believe that we, the British, are leaving this country," he blurted out over the air. "That is why I'm talking to you tonight—to try to clear up any misapprehensions of this kind concerning the future position of Britain in Palestine." And then Keating explained in careful words that the British were a "peculiar people"—filled with caution and "Elizabethan daring," easygoing acceptance and a "stubborn unity of action." He reminded his listeners that the British had carried the "burden of war for six years" and were now "bracing themselves to make greater sacrifices than ever before." Then he shifted to the language of a parent, bitter toward his child for lack of gratitude: "The British people have determined that the thankless burden of governing this country must be lifted from their shoulders, that the continued waste of effort and resources in Palestine must stop."[91]

At the end of April the PBS held a "pitiful" farewell party for its Arabic staff, filled with sad conversations about the lost opportunity for peace and equal rights and the only alternative of war. Edwin Samuel wrote sad farewells to the Arab staff. "You never let me down. . . . I only wish that we could do more for you. . . . Arab listeners have much to thank you for. . . . I am certain that you have a great future."[92] Then he left Keating in charge and moved back to his London house on Porchester Terrace. As Keating took over, the chaos escalated. He sold his car and sent Leslie back to England. War settled in. On April 25, 1948, Keating ordered the partial evacuation of the PBS studios to Ramallah, as shells fell in the garden. "We are powerless," Keating wrote in his diary that day, "[a] shocking black mark against England." Two days later, Keating and his English staff left Jerusalem amid an eerie atmosphere of doom. "Terror walks the streets and death whispers on every breeze," he wrote in his diary, a shocking juxtaposition to the bucolic description of Jerusalem that he had recounted a little more than a year earlier. The evacuation was desperate. Keating was one of two thousand people waiting on the ground in Jaffa for boats that never came, during three days of Jewish shelling. "This is our Dunkirk," he scribbled in his tattered diary under the gloomy skies of the late spring day.[93] He eventually made his way to Cyprus via Cairo. On May 14, 1948, the PBS played "God Save the King" and went off the air. In the next year, Jewish workers from the PBS would join with Haganah's underground radio station to become Kol Israel (The Voice of Israel) in Jerusalem.[94] The PBS materials that were left in Ramallah helped to create Radio Jordan.

In the coming years, whether the broadcast came from Radio Moscow or the BBC, each of the Western stations argued that it was blameless in causing the brutal war that ensued. Radio Moscow, which had assured the population that peace would soon be at hand, pretended its government had had nothing to do with the partition outcome. "We cannot express our regret that because the U.N. took the decision to partition Palestine, the number of clashes between Arabs and Jews in Palestine has increased," it said that January.[95] It argued that "international reactionary quarters" were to blame. The culprits were Arab leaders like Azzam Pasha, who had once sided with the fascists and were now pushing for war. All of the fighting, all of the Arab calls to resistance, Radio Moscow argued, were a cover-up to distract Arabs from the predations of Anglo-American imperialists.[96] Meanwhile, negotiations continued for Czechoslovakia to sell Soviet arms to the Jewish Agency.

The same story applied to the BBC, which did not once give airtime to the legacy of colonialism that had brought the people of Palestine to this situation. The PBS and the BBC may have tried to make their departure a smooth one, but it was far from graceful and dignified. It created a "poisonous legacy" that impacted how the British would respond to future events in the Middle East and to uprisings under their domain around the world.[97] This legacy did not just stoke the fires of anger among Britain's subjects; it also helped to radicalize some British in their understandings of their subject peoples. Based on centuries of Orientalist assumptions about the people of the Middle East and Britain's role in civilizing them, conservative British leaders found in the chaos of Palestine (a chaos they had helped create) seemingly more evidence that "the Arabs" (and "the Jews") could not be trusted to act as rational actors and that the only viable way to deal with the Middle East was through force.

The international radio coverage of the Nakhba that followed reflected the growing political, racial, and ethnic divides that characterized those terrible months. The number of Western radio stories highlighting Arab violence during the war overwhelmingly exceeded any recounting of Jewish assaults on Palestinian villages. On November 30, 1947, the night after the partition was announced, the BBC announced that London "welcomed" the UN Assembly's "just solution." It then went on to describe the eleven Jews wounded in fighting in Jerusalem, the Arab ambush of a bus, and an attack on Jewish prisoners by Arabs at Acre Central prison.[98] On January 11, 1948, Radio Moscow reported in Arabic that British agents were behind the Arab revolt.[99] It made no mention of Haganah's bombing of the Semiramis Hotel six days earlier. Nor do the records show that the BBC, Radio Moscow, or the PBS ever mentioned the ethnic cleansing of the Arab village of Qisarya near Haifa in February 1948 or the Stern and Irgun massacre of Arab women, children, and elderly in the village of Dayr Yassin in April. The only broadcast about Dayr Yassin came from Haganah Radio, which declared in Arabic over its clandestine station on April 12, 1948, that there had been no massacre of unarmed Arab women and children by Jewish forces. In the same broadcast in which Haganah repudiated the slaughter, the reporters argued that the Arabs had reached "such a standard of slyness" that they had forgotten the "humanitarian rules of war."[100]

The real plight of the displaced Arab populations of Tiberias, Haifa, and the Galilee was of little interest to the Western broadcasters. A pall of silence fell over the terrifying predicament of Arab Palestinians living in territories that had suddenly become a part of the Jewish state. Historians have fought for decades over the question of what led the Arabs of Palestine to leave their villages. Zionist nationalists argue that they left voluntarily, but the standard interpretation now is that they were forced out, either from fear induced by psychological warfare or at the point of a gun. Either way, there is nothing in the broadcasting record—not in the CIA, BBC, or Radio Moscow archives—about the seven hundred thousand Arab women, children, and elderly who fled their homes in fear with nothing but the clothes on their backs, and whose homes quickly became occupied by Jewish populations intent on creating a homeland. If Radio Beirut, Radio Damascus, or Radio Cairo spoke of the exodus, the Western monitors chose not to keep records of it.

· · ·

Regardless of how each side sought to fashion its role in the partition, few can claim that the outcome was a successful one. A bloody civil war ensued that left hundreds of thousands dead and set the stage for a conflict that continues to rage today. In the preceding years, the British and Soviets had endeavored to establish themselves as the great protectors of the Middle

East from the vagaries of communism and capitalism. They had attached themselves to promises of aid and expectations of gratitude. They had begun to establish the language of the Cold War, with the existence of the post-colonial Arab world in the balance. They had also established a dialogue over the air that was joined in the late 1940s by the voices of Arab radio stations. Those stations walked a fine line between expressing independent national interests, supporting the cause of pan-Arabism, and navigating inter-Arab tensions that were themselves wrapped up in the global fight for Cold War alliances. In the coming years, those powers came into closer and even more contentious contact with each other, as the politics of the Cold War continued to make its way into the scaffolding of sound that defined the radio world of the Middle East.

THREE

"Imagine, O Arabs!"

VOICE OF THE ARABS AND
THE RISE OF EGYPTIAN RADIO

IN THE HISTORY of international radio, 1953 was a big year. The United States Information Agency came into existence, taking under its wing the previously underfunded and much-derided Voice of America. Britain's Information Research Department (IRD), which had been secretly created in 1948 to promote a semisocialist alternative to brutal Soviet communism and rapacious American capitalism, doubled its staff and adopted an explicitly British-led, anti-communist message.[1] Radio Moscow tripled its foreign-language output in the promotion of its new "Peace Offensive."

Most critically, Sawt al Arab, Voice of the Arabs, came on the air, supported by Egypt's new revolutionary leader, Gamal Abd al Nasser, and its famous broadcaster, Ahmed Said. The audiosphere shifted on its axis when this service hit the airwaves in 1953. It established a non-Western vocabulary and voice for the Arab world, complete with the development of an Arabic "radio language" that became the standard for all to follow. Millions of people tuned in every day to hear Ahmed Said deliver his pronouncements on the news, to chuckle at his sharp humor, and to hear the great music that was produced during this golden era of Egyptian songwriting. Voice of the Arabs and its parent station, Radio Cairo, functioned as a center for anti-colonialism and Arab nationalism, a nexus for the playing out of inter-Arab conflicts, and a mouthpiece for Nasser's leadership.

The original transcripts of Voice of the Arabs were infamously destroyed after Nasser's death in 1970.[2] Our records are limited to various memoirs written by Radio Cairo broadcasters and the transcripts that BBC, CIA, and Soviet radio monitors wrote down as they listened from their dusty offices in Reading, Cyprus, and Baku. These recordings tell us as much about the people who were listening as they do about the broadcasters who were talking. When British monitors wrote that the Voice of the Arabs was courting Soviet aid, they were building a particular vision of a world under threat that they believed they could still manipulate. American monitors recorded stories that attested to the seeming volatility of the region and the need for a steadying American hand. They looked for evidence of communist influence in Egypt, with each pro-Soviet utterance seeming to confirm their worst fears.[3] For US monitors, Egypt's largely Western orientation was overshadowed by the preoccupation to detect signs of underlying communism. When Soviet monitors tuned in, they heard American and British imperial meddling and an opportunity for the promotion of the Soviet Union as a country committed to Arab nationalism. All the monitors paid equally close attention to the moments when Voice of the Arabs made them look bad. There can be no doubt that, to some extent at least, monitors chose to record these particular broadcasts (and not to record others) because they reinforced implicit ideas about the region and justified policies there. This compendium of gathered broadcasts, collected from four countries, ten archives, and three languages, is a constructed archive, as most are.

At the same time, the Americans, British, and Soviets actually wrote down almost every word that Ahmed Said spoke. These sources offer a glimpse into the evolving, revolutionary radio form that defined much of the Middle Eastern audiosphere and shaped Arabic-speaking people's perceptions of events happening around the world for fifteen years. These transcripts track the rise of postwar, Egyptian-led Arab nationalism and its intersection with the Cold War. They tell a story of an Arab world under attack from Israel, Britain, France, eventually the United States, and sometimes the Soviet Union. They reveal the tensions that arose in these years between the Baghdad Pact nations (Turkey, Iraq, Iran, Pakistan, and the United Kingdom, with Lebanon never joining but remaining a British ally) and the rest of the Arab world, led by Egypt. They tell the story of Nasser's domestic consensus-building project and his gradual movement away from a revolutionary identity to one that used the language of revolution to defend state power. They give a peek into the linguistic underpinnings of Middle Eastern propaganda and speak to the priorities and grievances that dominated Arab culture. When taken in their entirety, these many thousands of available transcripts provide a view of an Egyptian propaganda program that was defined by its ironies. They project a vision of a secular, Arab, revolutionary regime, intent on expanding Egyptian power while promoting pan-Arab identity. They give agency to the masses while promoting the vision of one man as the savior of the Middle East. They utilize the tools of the West in order to undermine it.

Numerous Arab and Western scholars have noted the importance of Voice of the Arabs in shaping the soundscape of the 1950s and 1960s.[4] Few have devoted attention to what that shaping really looked like. It was here that Ahmed Said developed his iconic approach to broadcasting, with his use of metaphor and imagery and his merging of modern, highly emotional, propaganda techniques with older Quranic themes and the secular revolutionary promise of an Egyptian-led, pan-Arab liberation for the Middle East. It was here that professional journalism also developed, characterized by measured, rational arguments; journalistic integrity; and a careful approach to broadcasting.

While Egyptian radio became the standard against which the other services would measure themselves in the coming decade, it was not free of its neighbors' influence up and down the dial. Not only did Radio Cairo and Voice of the Arabs reply to the BBC, the VOA, and Radio Moscow regularly over the air, but they also borrowed themes and language from them. It was not uncommon to hear Ahmed Rashad Ali offer assessments on Radio Cairo of geostrategic issues that borrowed entirely from BBC nomenclature.[5] At the same time, the similarities between the polemical broadcasts of Ahmed Said and Radio Moscow were impossible to ignore, especially when it came to their shared critiques of imperialism. "We will continue to unmask, resist, and defeat imperialism and its agents," Said said in May 1956.[6] A day later, Radio Moscow reported, "The Soviet Union and the people of the Middle East will continue to unmask, resist, and defeat imperialism and its agents."[7] Similarly, the prevalence of language about peace, crafted as an ideal that at times required war, was a narrative trope conjured in response to similar Soviet, and later American and British, programming.

Like their European and American counterparts, Radio Cairo and Voice of the Arabs sought to control the language of Arab nationalism, increasingly moving away from versions of that nationalism that might support workers' collective action, the Ba'athist socialist movement, or conservative Islamic agendas coming from groups like the Muslim Brotherhood. Similarly, Radio Cairo's promises of modernization for the Arab world, contingent upon the adoption of Egyptian-led technologies and methods of mass production, bore a close resemblance to Cold War stories told by the United States and the Soviet Union that promised a better material life in return for ideological fealty. There were ways in which Egyptian radio was profoundly new, yet it could not be separated from the echo chamber in which it resided.

. . .

Standard histories of modern Egyptian radio start in the wake of the 1952 Revolution. One of the first acts of Nasser's Revolutionary Command Council was to create the Ministry of National Guidance, under which the Egyptian Broadcasting Service (EBS) system resided. The EBS offered more than double the coverage and radio time as any other Arab country. It opened with broadcasts in Arabic, Turkish, and Hebrew. By the end of the year it had added Indonesian and Urdu, offering twenty-eight hours of coverage each week.[8] Histories of the EBS's inception vary greatly. The Maspero archive in Cairo notes humbly that back then it couldn't broadcast over shortwave at all and only had 72 kilowatts of power at the medium wave.[9] In contrast, the BBC journalist and historian of Suez Keith Kyle has written that the station had, by 1953, a propaganda program that "even Dr. Goebbels would have envied."[10] Radios from the late 1940s have "Radio Cairo" printed directly on their prescribed frequency on the physical shortwave dial, which means that it must have been large enough to merit being a part of the labeling that was reserved for the big international radio stations.

However relatively modest its beginnings, Radio Cairo quickly grew into the primary conduit for the promotion of a particular vision of a revolutionary Egypt. "We want our voice to be heard by the Western world, and we want to speak to them in their own languages so that they may understand our problems and know our intentions," Raif Abu al-Lam'a, the assistant secretary-general of the Arab League, declared in August 1952 to a room of crowded broadcasters at a radio conference sponsored by the Arab League. "We will fight our enemies with the same weapon that they have used against us."[11] After much applause, Egypt's new revolutionary president, Mohamed Naguib, took the podium. It had been less than two months since he had taken office in the wake of King Farouk's deposition. With some of his first public words, which were broadcast across Egypt and Syria, he gave a history lesson. He told the crowd that the Arabs had been the "first people in the world to propagate and transmit ideas." From the very spot upon which he now stood, their ancestors had "spread the religion of Moses, then of Jesus, and then of Mohammed." Radio would be the conduit for a sacred Arab renaissance. "Any failure or reluctance in the question of broad-casting amounts almost to betrayal of the holy cause," he intoned to steady applause. Central to that plan was the need for all the broadcasting stations in the Arab countries to "become one whole, complementary to each other, until each one becomes an echo of the other."[12] Delegates from Syria, Jordan, Iraq, Saudi Arabia, Lebanon, and even Libya (which did not have a broad-casting station yet) agreed, championing unified broadcasting as the key to international recognition. Such aspirations concealed internal differences, particularly between Nasser and the Hashemite kingdoms, and overlooked domestic subaltern voices that had alternative ideas about what the future of the Arab world should look like.

It was Naguib's successor, Nasser, who turned the radio into a medium of vital national significance. By the end of 1953 Radio Cairo could be heard for eleven hours a day. It added broadcasts in Persian and Swahili in 1954, with the station's weekly output growing to sixty-four hours.[13] It also extended the service to one hundred hours per week in 1955, adding Malayan and Am-haric, with a service to Latin America and North America in Arabic, Portu-guese, and Spanish. The station also started new shows aimed at Palestinian refugees. To put this in perspective, in 1955 the Soviets and Americans were broadcasting for thirty-three and fourteen hours a week, respectively.[14] By the time the crisis in Suez had begun, Radio Cairo's signal was reaching from Algeria to Iran. It could even be picked up in Yugoslavia when the weather was good.[15] The EBS had an Arabic Service, a foreign-language service, an engineering division, a Political Department, a Talks Division, and a moni-toring service responsible for listening to foreign broadcasts.[16] On a normal day, the Voice of the Arabs ran four hours of news, alongside shows for chil-dren, the army, students, workers, and villagers, with a *Sudan Corner*, a *Pal-estine Corner*, and a history lesson.[17]

This was a medium that mattered. Egyptian state television would not appear until 1960, and even then, not everyone had a television or access to a TV signal. Every village had a radio. As Nasser told the American am-bassador to Egypt, Raymond Hare, war in the future would be "psycho-logical rather than military, and radio is a weapon." While the prospect of nuclear war had immobilized armies, "great latitude" still existed "in the bat-tle of ideas."[18] (He also told his shocked guest that the Soviets were better at propaganda than the Americans and that he himself had a "gift" when it came to the craft. Both claims were arguably true.) Nasser famously refused Anglo-American requests that Voice of the Arabs tone down its language by arguing that to do so would be like putting down one's best weapon. "Disarming the radio," he said, "would . . . mean complete disarmament."[19]

Ahmed Said's radio show *Voice of the Arabs* was the tip of the spear, there to explain and give meaning to the world through the repeated mantras of revolutionary independence, unity, and anti-imperialism. The station had many jobs, the first of which was to solidify the power of the Egyptian state and Nasser's leadership.[20] On the air, Nasser represented the revolution's response to the old regime—down to earth, incorruptible, energetic, honorable, committed to helping the poor—the historical culmination of a victory long awaited. The station argued that as a result of Nasser's revolution, Egypt was poised to become the center of academic and political work in Islamic affairs and in the teaching of history and Arabic. It presented Egypt as teaming with modern potential and hope, focusing on the accomplishments of Egyptians in medicine, engineering, hydrology, and agriculture and on the developmental gifts that Egypt could give the region. It also highlighted Egypt's continued cultural and athletic power, its sporting exchanges, musicians, artists, writers, spiritual leaders, and student missions.

This positive message ran alongside a second message, which was the threat coming from the imperial West and its allies—a threat against which ostensibly only Egypt could defend the Arab people. The transcripts of the Voice of the Arabs broadcasts tell the story of Nasser's tumultuous relationship with the United Kingdom, the United States, and the Soviet Union from 1953 to 1967. In the early years, Voice of the Arabs maintained a relatively positive rapport with the VOA and Radio Moscow. This changed in 1956 with the creation of the Baghdad Pact and the American withdrawal from the Aswan Dam project. From that point on, the Anglo-American enemy became ever present on the air.

The third key message that Voice of the Arabs reinforced was that of Arab unity. It was "Arab unity," according to Said, "that would not permit foreign forces ever to show their noses again."[21] Critical from its inception was the argument that a unified Arab world stood together against the colonial West. This made it possible to argue that any person or state that opposed Nasser also opposed Arab nationalism. Through its silence, Voice of the Arabs also worked to determine what Arab nationalism did *not* look like—making no mention in any of the extant transcripts of the Muslim Brotherhood and Ba'athist movements that represented alternative ideas about anti-imperial state building. The very year that Radio Cairo embraced the message of Arab unity, 1954, was also the year of the *minha* in

Egypt, when more than twenty thousand Egyptian members of the Muslim Brotherhood were either arrested or exiled for treason against the state.[22] No mention of this ever appeared on the radio. Instead, Voice of the Arabs told the story of gross imperialist meddling that could be combated only by a unified embrace of a Nasserist Pan-Arabism. Similarly, it was Voice of the Arabs that led the crusade against Iraq as a British-sponsored center of corrupt power in the Middle East. For Nasser and for Voice of the Arabs, it was critical that Iraq's leader, Nuri al-Said, be painted as an Anglo-American stooge. As Nasser claimed, "the banner of nationalism" was his and his alone.[23]

These narratives performed key functions for the Egyptian state. Said, alongside the efforts of Muhammad Haykal, who was the powerful editor of the newspaper *Al Ahram*, established the language for how to talk about anti-imperialism in mainstream secular Arab society, creating the parameters for what that revolution should look like in Nasser's regime. They also created a specific rhetoric of aggrievedness that claimed state ownership of the colonial experience: to legitimize the state based on how it defined the nature of colonial victimization. The threat of colonial invasion set the parameters not just for what defined the outside enemy, but for what qualified as Arab national patriotism. Said and Haykal determined the criteria for domestic compliance with the state, establishing a performative script and rhetoric about what acceptable and expected revolutionary anti-imperialism looked like. They taught their listeners a revolutionary heuristic that simultaneously defended the state, maintained order, and enforced discipline. They also explicitly tied the Cold War to the cause of Arab nationalism. Partnership with Britain and the United States would be impossible so long as the West endeavored to "convince the Arab people of the Communist menace without also acknowledging Arab national identity," Nasser famously declared.[24] Such language functioned as a qualification of the Cold War that problematized the ideological arguments being made by the Western powers, the Soviet Union included.

More than anyone else, Ahmed Said was the architect of this new identity and the master narrative that accompanied it. Born in Cairo in 1925, Said grew up amid the anti-Zionist and anti-colonial uprisings of the 1930s. He graduated from Cairo University in 1946 and joined many of the young professional men in those years who rallied to the call for Egyptian independence. He started working in broadcasting as a technical secretary for Egyptian Radio, and then in Egypt's foreign relations radio program in 1950.

FIGURE 3. Ahmed Said at height of his power, 1965. *Source:* Associated News.

Said built his methodological toolbox and discovered his style in those early years, traveling with the Fedayeen to Port Said and broadcasting about their guerrilla operations against the British from the frontlines. After Nasser came to power in 1953, he hired Said to be the director of Sawt al Arab, where he stayed until 1967.

On Said's watch, Voice of the Arabs was profoundly modern in its methods. It mobilized powerful imagery and argumentation that blended classic Quranic Arabic with colloquial Egyptian to build a language that carried the official imprimatur of formal journalism while still sounding familiar and intimate. Irony and satire sat at the center of Said's programming. Whole broadcasts could include a sarcastic re-reading of an anti-Nasser broadcast from Britain, only then to refute it as lies or to characterize the British critiques not as weaknesses but as points of pride. As other broadcasters noted at the time, this was unique to this radio station.[25] By the end of the decade, the Soviet, British, and American programming offices were all attempting to adopt Said's new radio language.

What did Said sound like? One of Said's most powerful rhetorical devices was to fill entire broadcasts with loaded questions. For instance, in 1954 he asked the following questions in a piece entitled, "Who Has Set Up Israel?"

> Who has promised the Jews [indistinct word]? Why did Britain betray the Arabs with the Balfour Declaration? Why has imperialism sent us Israel in a way unknown to history before? Why did Britain give up her mandate and withdraw quietly? Did Britain leave Palestine to the people of Palestine and the Arabs of Palestine? Or was Britain aware of the fact that she was withdrawing from Palestine and leaving it to the armed Zionist gangs and the army of the Haganah? Did Britain know that the Arabs of Palestine were to be left to their inevitable destiny?[26]

This broadcast offered an all-encompassing answer for the causes of the Palestinian refugee crisis and the conflict with Israel: Britain. It took as assumed fact that the British had betrayed the Palestinians, were responsible for the existence of Israel, and had withdrawn in May 1948 as part of a deeper plan to support the Jewish state. Voice of the Arabs was able to position Nasser's Egypt as a source for revealing the sophisticated secret plans of British officials and bureaucrats. Karl Popper famously argued that it is much easier to believe events have a singular cause as a part of a larger master narrative than it is to acknowledge how complex political and social currents can inadvertently cause events to happen.[27] This was what Said provided. Such arguments offered up a clear enemy around which a pan-Arab group identity could form (made more powerful by the fact that parts of the explanation were true). They helped to spread distrust not just of Her Majesty's government but also of Britain's emissaries on the radio dial. They established the Voice of the Arabs as the only venue capable of providing such critical revelations. In the end, Voice of the Arabs, like its counterparts up and down the dial, demanded from its listeners the acceptance of a specific, assumed reality that, once established, could be used to question the other master narratives swirling around them.

Said was a master in what communication theorists call *echoic irony*, the echoing of thoughts and utterances attributed to someone else in order to reveal those utterances as empty.[28] Rich with insincerity, Said inverted the very arguments made by the British to expose their seeming hypocrisies. He regularly spoke of the "honorable" British claim that Her Majesty's government was in the Middle East to defend the Arab populace, only to spend five minutes listing the abuses happening at the hands of the British, each time commenting sardonically that of course all of it was done for the "defense" of the Arab populace. "By killing us, colonizing us, stifling our economy, plundering our homeland, making the soil of our Christ and our Islam Jewish, by making the Arabs of Palestine homeless—the West is doing all of this to defend you."[29] Said spent long stretches of time discussing why the Arab world deserved to be disrespected—all for the purpose of hammering home the sheer level of disrespect the Arab world could no longer tolerate. An illustrative example occurred in May 1956, after Nasser had signed a deal to buy Soviet-made arms from Czechoslovakia. This had prompted British broadcasters to claim that Egypt had become a communist puppet. In his "This Is Your Enemy" broadcast, Said delivered his response, offered as a piece of anaphoric prose. His voice started quietly, building to a crescendo by the end:

> Imagine, O Arabs! that the power which was given to you by the arms deals concluded by your free leaders with certain Eastern states [meaning the arms deal that Egypt had made with Czechoslovakia] was an evil which befell you, not the imperialists or even the Zionists! This is what imperialist propaganda hopes to convince you of now, while it calls on you to be weak, to surrender to imperialism and to succumb to Israeli aggression.
>
> Imagine, O Arabs! that the strengthening of your armies and defenses to protect the dignity of your countries is an abominable action which must rouse you against your leaders!
>
> Imagine yourselves, O Arabs, as seekers of disunity, supporters of imperialism and prisoners of Egypt whose walls stand between you and alliance with the imperialists, surrender to the Zionists in Palestine, and silence about the despotism of the renegade rulers, as if you did not want the freedom which Egypt is forcing you to achieve, as if you were not working for the unity which Egypt wants to impose, as if you would shun the strength with which Egypt is trying to equip you and as if you have not been, since the dawn of Arabism and religion, calling, struggling, and dying for freedom, unity, and Arab dignity.
>
> Imagine, O Arabs! that your revolt against the renegades is primitive, your wrath against the imperialists is communist and your zeal to install free Arabs as the leaders of your countries is backwardness, disintegration, and reaction, which requires the imperialist Powers of the international organizations to occupy your countries.[30]

"Imagine, O Arabs" was a powerful phrase. It was a cue to listeners that Said was switching to the first-person plural. It implied the existence of a "we," putting Said in a place of personal solidarity with his Arab listeners that no British, Soviet, or American broadcaster could assume on the air. The phrase was usually accompanied by the juxtaposing of one possible reality with another and often signaled that Said was switching from using formal Arabic (*fuṣḥá*) to colloquial Egyptian (*ʿāmmīyah*)—a practice that Nasser and Said pioneered, which could only happen in the spoken word over the air, and which had the immediate effect of inviting listeners to assume a place of familiarity and proximity. In broadcasts like the preceding one, Said asked his listeners to imagine a first possible reality that painted the Arab world as backward, duplicitous, and easily manipulated. This was the reality that the pro-Zionist West wanted them to believe. He then pitched a second reality that envisioned an honorable, strong Arab populace, free of colonial interference. "Imagine, O Arabs! Imagine that your revolution and your support for the Free Arabs and the cleansing of your countries. . . . [A]ll this is referred to as retrogression, dissolution, and savagery."[31] Out of these dueling realities Said offered his listeners only two possible futures: a revolutionary cleansing made possible by the Free Arab movement of Egypt or the continued colonial yoke that saw Arab freedom as retrogressive and savage.

There were other times when Said was perfectly blunt, such as when he provided a commentary on the Baghdad Pact and its Western sponsorship:

> You are aware of the colonization of the West: You know of the exploitation of the West: You know of the Domination of the West: You are aware of the plots being planned against you by the West: You know of the obstacles being put in your way by the West: You know of the arms and equipment provided to your enemies by the West. This Western alliance is working and acting for the colonization of all mankind.
>
> [pause]
>
> This is the truth we have learned from the West. It is a picture impressed on our minds through tens of years of bitter experience, false promises, military occupation, economic stifling, and killing of thousands and thousands of martyrs.[32]

Said understood the power of repetition, anaphora, and meter. Each sentence, punctuated by the phrase "the West," progressed logically from the one before it to argue that the colonial past of the West was undeniable and that the Baghdad Pact was evidence of its persistence. Just as critically, each sentence followed a rhythm, structured with a shared meter so that one sentence came after its predecessor intuitively.

Like the Soviets and the English, Said's master narrative was embedded in a carefully crafted historical narrative. He had a famous saying that would, for many, come to define his and others' particular way of understanding the Arab world, its relationship to the Middle East's colonial past, and the possibility of its independent future:

هكذا كان أجدادنا في الماضي، وهكذا يجب أن يكون العرب في المستقبل

As were our ancestors in the past, so must be the Arabs in the future.[33]

For Said, the fight for Arab independence was both very old and very modern. It was a story rooted in an ancient call to past glory, particularly to the greatness of the Egyptian empire. The general historical narrative held that until the Egyptian Revolution, even after the end of the British Mandate, Britain had dictated the fate of the Middle East. They had offered the Jewish people a slice of the Sinai Peninsula, which had been taken from Egypt before the First World War, but when the Jewish populace had refused, as the story went, Britain gave them a slice of Palestine. He argued that Britain sold arms to the Arabs, not to bolster Arab security, honor, or dignity, but to make profit and foster war. Ultimately, Britain used these arms to impose its imperialist plans, Said contended, as was evidenced in its creation and arming of the Baghdad Pact. *Imperialism* became a synonym for Britain. In one broadcast in 1956, in one paragraph Said declared that "imperialism" had announced its alliance with Israel, "imperialism" had declared its alliances against the Arab world, and "imperialism . . . would not be bound by its past actions in the UN and would reserve the right to interfere."[34] It was as though "imperialism" had been interviewed and had made some statements on the record. Voice of the Arabs then presented Nasser as the leader of a modern, revolutionary Middle East, born from a commitment to Arab freedom and independence that dated back many millennia. One regular segment on Voice of the Arabs, entitled "Egypt, the Grave of her Invaders," offered a daily history of Egypt since ancient times, showing the nation's long opposition to occupation.[35] This was a tale of a great people subjected for centuries to violent colonial conquest, now awakened to revolutionary consciousness.

Other broadcasters on Radio Cairo gave history lessons as well, such as when Ahmad Shawkat recounted to his listeners the Allied betrayal of Palestinians after the First World War, made more acute after the "Palestine tragedy" of 1947, and the continued Allied support of Israel. "It is only natural that the Arab peoples should regain their consciousness and become nationalists against the imperialists."[36] On another occasion, the broadcaster Ahmed Rashad Ali gave an insightful lesson on the growth of the British Empire at the end of the nineteenth century and the emergence of neo-colonialism. As he framed it, the English bilked Asia, Africa, and Central America of their raw materials and used those materials to produce a large surplus of manufactured goods, which they then sold back to those same foreign lands at great profit. In the process, they built railways, harbors, canals, bridges, dams, "and anything else they needed that would help them make money."[37] He spoke of how the colonized countries were not allowed to build industries for themselves, trade with each other, or gain education, and so were not able to progress while under British control. The British pretended, he said, to care about the countries under their charge: "But alas, the British were only working for their own good."[38]

Music was a big draw for every station and should be the subject of its own book. At the BBC, light music, dance music, and jazz consistently ranked just below the news as the reason people tuned in.[39] At Radio Moscow, broadcasters hoped that the beautiful, peerless works of the great Russian composers would mobilize Arab listeners. Perhaps not surprisingly, the station's favorite was Rimsky-Korsakov, who, ironically, was (and is) famous for his use of foreign melodies, rhythms, and harmonies, a practice known as "musical orientalism." His most famous piece, *Scheherazade*, which is a retelling of *Arabian Nights*, played on heavy rotation. Moscow also periodically broadcast traditional Russian songs like "Vesnoi Volga razol'etsia" (In the spring the Volga will spill), "O' Gazel'" (O, gazelle), and "Zachem tebia ia mil'yi uznala" (I learned why you are my love).[40] All of these songs harkened to the shared identity of the peasant across time and space, connected to the land and the basic joys of life.

Radio Cairo's choice of music helped to highlight the Arab world's revolutionary future and the hypocrisies it saw in Europe's treatment of the Arab world. Resistance songs written for the *simsimiyya* played alongside the modernist musical form of *musiqa al-tarab* and the popular tunes of the stars Umm Kulthum, Muhammad Abd al-Wahhāb, Farid al-Atrash, and 'Abd al-Halim Hafiz. Egyptian radio had supported Arab musicians since its inception in the 1930s. They all became hugely popular, literally accompanying Nasser's consolidation of power and the rise of Arab nationalism.[41] On Radio Cairo, if you waited long enough, you could be guaranteed to hear a song praising Nasser that harkened to older musical roots in the Arab tradition.

Radio Cairo also understood the value of Western music, such as when it played Beethoven's famously anti-Napoleonic *Fidelio* for three straight days after the French announced that they would be selling arms to the Israelis in 1956, or when it played Chopin's Polonaise in A flat major (written in 1842 in support of Polish independence) in the early summer of 1956 on the eve of the Suez Crisis and when it looked as though the Soviet Union might invade Poland.[42] These were songs of nationalism and revolution, written by Europeans who at some point in the past had rejected outside occupation, as the Egyptian broadcasters knew well.[43] The playing of Beethoven and Chopin was arguably done not just for Arab audiences, but for listeners at the CIA, TASS, the IRD, and the BBC.

Said's broadcasts, in particular, borrowed from numerous older Muslim and European rhetorical traditions. For instance, he gave consistent attention to the image of the martyr, sacrificed for the survival of the pan-Arab and Palestinian cause. The language of martyrs was (and is) resistant to definition.[44] The martyr functions as an embodiment of a belief system and sets a standard by which all other believers can be judged. While martyrdom promises everlasting life after death to the martyr (either in heaven or in the rational-humanist footprint of posterity), for those left behind it helps to beatify a canon of witnesses whose ultimate sacrifice demands recognition. Religious martyrdom functions as a physical, violent articulation of injury for persecuted groups.[45] It implies a struggle for the truth and a submission to the will of a higher ideal, whether that be God, a grand revolutionary cause, or the survival of one's community under siege. Under Said's watch, martyrdom was a fully developed propaganda tool. In early 1956, for instance, following the news of the deaths of Palestinians in Gaza, Said gave the following speech. Note the repetition and cadence: "We honour the martyrs who fell. We honour these martyrs since martyrdom is the supreme human virtue. Wherever it is found it is always coupled with the virtues of sacrifice and contribution. Fathers sacrifice their lives to help their sons. This is the first biological sacrifice imposed by God on mankind, and it indicates the great law of life, the law of the sacrifice of the individual to maintain the group." Then Said paused, lowering his voice a few notes. "As for the treacherous aggressor, we tell him to give us more of his treachery and meanness. The more he increases his aggression against peaceful inhabitants, the more the flame of hatred in our hearts is fanned and the nearer draws the end of his evil, sin, and aggression."[46] This speech mobilized the language of the religious martyr to substantiate a secular one—a person who dies not for God, but for the Arab cause.

Radio Cairo also summoned the image of the young as both victims and warriors in the fight to come, in need of defense and mobilization. As scholars have shown, by the twentieth century the modern construction of "childhood" as innocent, beleaguered, and in need of protection had become a justification for popular mobilization and a symbol of the nation-state itself, equally endangered and in need of protection.[47] Just as any ethical population should feel obliged to safeguard its young, so too should it feel compelled to protect its country. As such, the image of the child became a tool in the construction of popular consensus and compliance, particularly during the Cold War. This was a global phenomenon. The Egyptian call to Arab youth to fight for the Palestinian cause in 1956 was indistinguishable from the language that the United States and Soviet Union were using at the same time to enliven their own young for the Cold War struggle. For example, in one broadcast, Radio Cairo brought a teenage girl to the microphone to recite the following speech: "Our present Arab generation is not born for luxury and comfort, because it is a generation committed to great responsibilities, the responsibility of the hoped-for unity of the Arabs and the formation of the greater Arab fatherland, the responsibility of the restoration of Palestine and the purging of the Arab fatherland of every foreign influence and every intruder."[48] Youth served as a call to arms for the rest of their nation, functioning similarly to the famous British First World War enlistment posters on which children shamed their fathers into going to war by asking them what they had done for the effort. "I am longing for the day when I shall have the opportunity to march forward in the front ranks," the young woman said. "Either life with the restoration of the Holy Land, or death with the satisfaction that I have done my duty." If the children were obliged to defend their nation, then so too were the adults.

Animal imagery was also central to Said's rhetoric. Perhaps no animal received worse treatment than the dog in twentieth-century propaganda, with its once admirable characteristic of blind loyalty becoming a symbol for groveling beggary and weakness in enemy populations and in the self. "The Arabs are no longer dogs," Said declared in early 1956. "For the first time, they have become lions.... That is why the British are angry; they let themselves sleep because they lived with dogs and they have suddenly awakened to find themselves among lions."[49] Britain, whose traditional personification was the lion, was now reduced to something lesser, its national symbol usurped. Two weeks later, amid a discussion of the infamous expulsion of English ambassador Glubb from Jordan, Said declared that Glubb had been expelled, "in the way a dog is expelled."[50] Said was tapping into an old tradition when he referenced the dog in his rhetoric. The British had used dog imagery to describe the Germans in the First World War. The Soviets had arguably perfected it during the Stalinist show trials, with their demand that the regime "shoot the dirty dogs" of the counterrevolution.[51] Joseph Goebbels used similar language during the Second World War to describe Jewish populations slated for extermination, seen as dogs and as eaters of dogs.[52] Even the Americans had used the image of a dog in military uniform to conjure guilt among young American men who were reluctant to enroll in the war effort. Later, the dog became a symbol for Soviet dissenters like Vasily Grossman, who sought to describe the sycophantic, conformist nature of Soviet society through the image of the dog that loves her master even though he beats her.[53] Said reappropriated the image to emphasize the transformation that had occurred in the character of the Arab world, made possible by the Egyptian Revolution. He presented a vision of an earlier Arab passivity and subservience, now turned on its head to describe a "lionized" Arab populace standing before a desperate British Empire that refused to leave.

Equally prevalent in Voice of the Arabs broadcasting was the metaphor of light and the promise of illumination and liberation that the motif of light instantiated:

> O Arabs, toilers, workmen, receive your smiling day with golden beams of sun which are shining to pierce the darkness. Be like those beams and dispel the darkness of imperialism in every place.... Yes, O Arabs in every place, receive your day with faith. Struggle and strive to fight this nightmare known as the English.[54]

And again:

> The rays of light of the dawn of a new epoch have shone.[55]

And again:

> The sun of unity has begun to rise in the far distance. The masses of the conscious Arabs are removing from themselves the darkness of imperialism. They are heading towards the sun and towards light. The first rays of unity fell on Syria and Egypt. The Arabs of Syria and Egypt were able to see in the bright light the weakness and the stupidity of the powers that separated the two countries. The second ray of light fell on Saudi Arabia and Egypt. Through the true and bright light the Arabs of the Peninsula

and Egypt saw that their power and strength had been reduced because of their disunity. The bright lights that shone forth as a result showed Jordan which way to go. Yemen too saw the light. The light feel on the Eastern Arab world and its powerful beams shows the Arabs the way to Unity, Glory, Peace, and Prosperity. The beams have blinded the enemies of the Arabs.[56]

Light has historically functioned as a symbol for God, who is both apophatic and unfathomable, while also being physical and present in the lived world (like God, light is both visible and at the same time ephemeral and unknowable).[57] The Quran speaks of the Prophet Muhammed as an "illuminating lamp" (*siraj munir*, 33:46), while the Apostles' Creed describes the Prophet Jesus as "light from light." Said similarly spoke of a rising, unifying, independent, secular, Arab identity—a thing that could be seen in the real world through revolution, but that was also an intangible force, willed into being, impossible to define, and capable of great power. The idea that the light of Arab nationalism would shine through the darkness of colonial exploitation was clear enough.

Not coincidentally, light also sat at the center of a vision of the world to come, both for Islamic eschatology and for modern secular state builders of the twentieth century.[58] Whether one was envisioning finally seeing God or seeing one's own nation free itself from colonial control, the scenery was always filled with light.[59] While for Alexander Pope this final state of lighted being would lead to an "eternity of the spotless mind," for Said and Radio Cairo it promised "Unity, Glory, Peace, and Prosperity" in the Middle East, under Egyptian leadership, for generations to come.[60]

Light was not just a metaphor for revelation; it was also at the center of debates over modernization and development in the 1950s. Since the late nineteenth century, electrification had become the global symbol of modernity—the sign of a nation's movement into the modern world, made possible by bringing light into the literal darkness of night, a man-made alternative to the light of the hereafter promised by God that stood as evidence of humankind's capacity for progress and growth. This was also a central theme in Soviet and particularly American broadcasting in the 1950s. Electrification and light became the prize for Cold War fealty. The propaganda of modernization and its promise of a brighter future were a defining feature of the postwar era at least in part because it "operated under the façade of an apolitical campaign," that could normalize capitalist or socialist tropes.[61] Development could justify capitalism or communism, not as an ideological argument, but simply as the best way to get the lights on. It was a profoundly materialist argument, regardless of where it came from.

Voice of the Arabs promised this to the Arab world, using much of the same language that was coming from the West. The difference was that this modernization promised to be free of colonial obligations. "Those who think it possible for the great Powers to buy smaller countries with gifts over well-lit dinner tables at lovely banquets miss the truth of the miracle which has occurred in the Middle East," Said stated in early 1956. "They fail to appreciate that the jinn which emerged brilliantly from the bottle [in 1952] performed that miracle unaided and without outside help."[62] Notice the centrality of light, both as a conduit for modern development and as a spiritual force. Such statements constituted a refutation of the indebtedness that the West had attached to *its* promises of electrification and modernization.

Voice of the Arabs also introduced oil into the audiosphere, forcing the other international broadcasting services to reckon with it. For Said, oil was integral to sloughing off imperialism. "Oil is the pivot on which plots and political manipulations in the Middle East revolve," Said reported. "How Naïve we are! Imperialism is divesting us of the strongest weapon in our land.... Remember the oil which flows from your land is seized by your enemy.... We are the owner of the house. We, the Arabs, now fully realize our strength and potential."[63] The potential for oil to change the Middle East created a new space for the future to unfold, brought about by the passage from older forms of economic production to this new one.[64] Thanks to oil, old seaside towns across the Middle East would now be transformed into shining cityscapes, symbols of newfound prosperity and evidence of good political leadership.

Such arguments arrived alongside a rejection of the idea that the Arab world could only survive with the arms and other gifts that the Soviet Union and the West promised, or that receiving those gifts represented ideological fealty on the part of the Egyptians. Arms may have come from the Soviets or the Czechs, Said argued, but the Egyptian people would be the ones wielding those guns. The sale of those arms did not mean the Arabs were willing to convert to communism. It was merely a transaction, Said argued, executed rationally for the defense of the Arab world by Arab leaders. It was the West that was using the sale of arms as an excuse to justify aggression and the removal of aid—all as a cover-up for deeper imperialist motivations. As Anwar Sadat said over the air, "Today and tomorrow, as yesterday, imperialism will repeat to the world that Egypt will become a Communist zone of influence and that the arms deal marks only the beginning of this influence. . . . They know perfectly well that Gamal will not replace one influence with another."[65]

In the 1950s it was a common practice to envision Israel both as a manipulator and puppet of Western Europe and the United States. Said made the argument daily that the British had been bribed by Zionists to support Israel. "I accuse British democracy," he said, "and demand that the British Government announce the names of the companies in which those defending lawyers of Israel work. Then, and only then, the world will learn of the depths to which democracy in Britain has sunk, tempted by Zionist wealth and Zionist bribery."[66] This paralleled British accusations that the Egyptians were bribing the Arab world into backing the cause of Arab nationalism. "Nasser works to buy his way into the hearts of his listeners," Sharq al-Adna claimed in April 1956. In response, Said asked scoffingly, "Is it possible to bribe 100,000,000 Arabs from the Atlantic Ocean to the Arab Gulf?"[67] The image of Israel as the briber of the West would shift as the years wore on into a portrayal of Israel as a vassal of Western imperial designs. It was useful to argue in 1955 that Israel was attempting to buy favor (and arms) from its Western allies. Such claims made Israel appear insidious, desperate, and small. By the 1960s, however, it was vital that Israel's military power be only explainable through the intervention of the West. That way, when the Israelis won on the battlefield, Ahmed Said could argue that the Arabs had lost to the US and British juggernauts, not to their "little neighbor to the North."

It wasn't always obvious, but Voice of the Arabs actually showed ambiguity to the West writ large, the Soviet Union included. It was common to hear a report that Soviet Muslim troops were being trained against Israel. Radio Damascus might tell its listeners in its morning broadcasts that Egyptian officers were undergoing a special training course in the Soviet Union or that Soviet Muslim veterans of the Second World War were volunteering for combat brigades in readiness for war.[68] Such broadcasts articulated a level of gratitude to the Soviet leadership that was clearly needed in order to continue the supply of aid. But even this vision of Soviet benevolence was not without complication. While many appreciated Soviet aid, there were those who made the argument that communism was the "offspring of Jewry." While one commentator might report on the persistent loyalty of the Soviets, others reminded these same listeners that "thousands of Jewish volunteers from Communist Europe [had] rushed to fight the Arabs in Israel" during the 1948 war.[69]

The Arab broadcasting stations arguably saw the situation with the Soviets more clearly than any of the Western information services could have imagined. "The Russians supported us and offered us aid in recent months for two reasons," a broadcaster on Radio Cairo grumbled in late April, 1956. "First, to strengthen our determination to frustrate the Baghdad Pact, which is primarily directed against themselves. And second, to open for themselves an outlet to the Middle East."[70] All of this happened against the backdrop of Anglo-Soviet talks happening in London that spring and summer about the fate of the Baghdad Pact and the sale of Czech arms to Egypt. These recordings attest to the fact that even the Soviets were held at a distance.

The biggest and most common message to come out of Voice of the Arabs was that Egypt and the rest of the postcolonial world had the ability to save themselves by uniting. This is what the Bandung Conference, the nonalignment movement, and Nasser's policy of "positive neutralism" represented. "Every day, the Bandung Conference faces a new field where it acts sincerely and faithfully," Said told his listeners. "It cannot fail to defeat the enemies of freedom. It raises its banner after suffering at the hands of the West the bitterness of enslavement."[71] Radio Cairo's and Voice of the Arabs's attention to Bandung was, in the words of USIA researchers, "lavish."[72] Bandung played a critical role in the Egyptian propaganda program, presenting Nasser as a "world statesman" who had successfully steered the conference along an anti-Israel and pro–North African independence line. Notably, Voice of the Arabs shied away from the arguments made by early Arab nationalist philosophers Zaki al-Arzuzi and Sari al-Husri, who argued for a united Islamic nationalism that paid no attention to geographic distinctions. The great unification would have to come not from these thinkers, but from Nasser and the Egyptian state.

Ironically, Radio Cairo's rejection of obligation to the West in return for aid did not necessarily preclude it from arguing that the rest of the Arab world had obligations to Egypt. An example is how Radio Cairo talked about Palestinians and their role in the project of building and reinforcing the pan-Arab cause. Far from promoting a unique, Palestinian identity, Voice of the Arabs encouraged Palestinians to think of themselves first as Arabs, with their loyalties not to Palestine but to a larger, transnational destiny, led from Cairo. Egypt reminded its listeners that it was a Palestinian's duty to assume major obligations toward their new homeland in diaspora, and "that a Palestinian's devotion to Egypt" should be the same as their devotion to their own land. "We must do our duty to the land that gives us refuge."[73] The show *Palestine Corner* was in many ways indistinguishable from the rhetoric that had been imparted from colonizer to colonized for centuries. The ideal Palestinian would be dutiful and civilized, would understand their indebtedness to the larger powers that protected them, and would always remember that "each son of Palestine is an ambassador of his country. . . . Catastrophes and adversities should be no reason for the loss of dignity and honour. . . . Gratitude should be our most prominent characteristic in any country we live in.[74] This demand, not just for compliance but for appreciation, was by 1956 a vital part of all the propaganda programs in the Middle East.

. . .

Voice of the Arabs was both a pioneer and an echo. Whether or not Said was the first broadcaster to use these methods in the Middle Eastern audiosphere, we know that they were the standard by the mid-1950s. Said's attention to the cause of Arab nationalism and its intersection with colonialism and the Cold War defined the issues that the Soviets, British, and Americans would have to tackle from this point on. They also eventually set the standard for how to communicate popular grievance and solidarity. Voice of the Arabs created "performative utterances"—language that doesn't just propose, but actually does things and changes social reality, whether it is felicitous or not.[75] This was programming that demanded response, that moved populations and shaped worldviews. Like the British, Soviets, and Americans, this programming offered up a language that sought to create a hegemonic world—a language whose structures were shaped by hierarchically organized binary oppositions ("us" versus "them"), which in turn linked signs (like "freedom" and "peace") to other nationally inflected signifiers (like the image of a strong liberationist Egyptian leadership).[76]

And yet despite the power of Said's arguments, Voice of the Arabs and Ahmed Said could not extricate their messaging from the space that it inhabited. Their words and methods had long historical roots from the Middle East and Europe, reflecting the extent to which the meanings of words are shaped by relational structures of language. Said's words functioned in a mutually defining and historically inflected audiosphere that was eternally impossible to control. As the philosopher Ernesto Laclau put it, "Neither absolute fixity nor absolute non-fixity is possible."[77] In the years to come, that carefully constructed world came under increasing fire, not just from the Occident, but from Arab voices unwilling to tolerate the performative spectacle that Said's words had created.

FOUR

The Power of Peace

RADIO MOSCOW AND THE SHAPING
OF THE AUDIO LANDSCAPE

"PEACE" WAS AT THE CENTER of the soundscape of the Middle East in the 1950s. What had been a steady part of Radio Moscow's rhetoric for years became the central topic of conversation and debate for everyone by 1955. Questions of how peace could be achieved, what it should look like, and what Carthaginian bargains might be needed to reach it were woven into the fabric of every crisis that marked the post–World War II era. Whether it was the US overthrow of Iran's leader Mohammed Mossadeq in 1953 or the British and Soviet invasions of Egypt and Hungary in 1956, all of it was done ostensibly in defense of peace. The ability to bring peace became a part of the larger promise of modernization and development, all in pursuit of Cold War alliances and favorable economic conditions.

People often associate the rhetoric of peace with the late 1960s, but before it became a mantra for the counterculture, it was a weapon of the state, wrapped up in the promise of economic well-being. Since the end of the First World War, peacefulness had become synonymous in the West with the Keynesian argument that economic well-being enabled peace, which in turn enabled more economic well-being.[1] This argument had further ideological underpinnings, connoting peace with living in either the capitalist or communist camp of the burgeoning Cold War. By 1950, when mutually assured destruction had rendered direct conflict between the two superpowers impossible, peace became a key weapon in the cultural Cold War struggle, turning each side's ability to provide economic well-being and peacefulness into an explicit means by which the relative victory of each side could be measured. At the core of the promise of peace was the idea that it was an intrinsically materialist state of being—equating peace with the acquisition of goods. From tractors to corn to schools, hospitals, factories, and dams, peace was tied inextricably to the acquisition of the stuff that made life happy and peaceful. It meant having a nice kitchen, a good school for one's children, and an affluent, "civilized" neighborhood to live in.

In the world of Cold War propaganda, the giving and receiving of aid and guidance offered seeming proof of the desire by the donor state to end the suffering of its loyal citizenry. As evidence, state broadcasters in the 1950s created a whole category of stories that focused on the happy, peaceful, well-off lives of domestic and colonial subjects who were prospering under the state's steady care. By portraying visions of domestic peace and economic well-being, whether it was American housewives getting a college education over the television or Soviet Muslims building a new mosque in Uzbekistan, there was a promise that the state could provide happiness, security, meaningfulness, and peace for its people. The Cold War vision of peace (which included the Soviet Union), which really meant the "giving" of gifts and the promise of domestic bliss, could be a powerful tool.

There was always a cost to this peace, however. Soviet, American, British, and eventually Egyptian broadcasters framed peace as a thing that could be bequeathed or taken away. It was something for which Arab populations could barter in exchange for allegiance, exhibitions of gratitude, trading relationships, and the rejection of the enemy's gifts. It was based on the assumption that only outside supervision, efficiency, invention, and secular development could create peace and domestic bliss. It was an invitation to come together in shared humanity and to find middle ground and understanding, but always in return for something. This was the modern phenomenon of the "economy of the gift," which historian Jeffrey Brooks has deftly explored.[2] International giving and the pursuit of peace were never free. The "peace" that the Soviet Union, the United States, the British, and the Egyptians offered was based on the precondition of Cold War/imperial/Nasserist victory and was predicated on the gratefulness of the receiver.

While the idea of peace may be benign, *persuading* for peace for the purposes of mobilizing a population to action always serves the "interests of power."[3] Peace served the "interests of power" for the state-run radio stations of the Middle East in the 1950s. For the Soviets, who arguably mobilized the politics of peace to the greatest effect, peace was a metonym, carrying with it an array of meanings that could be triggered through its use. It hearkened to the Soviet sacrifices of the Great Patriotic War, legitimizing and authenticating the ostensible Soviet desire for peace around the world. It attested to the ability of the Soviet Union to bring material comforts to its subject populations and its resolute solidarity with Arab populations who wished to stand in defiance against American and British warmongering. Just up the dial, the Americans, whose radio foray into the Middle East was only now beginning, responded in kind, harnessing the idea of peace and the economy of the gift to do the heavy lifting that the cultural Cold War demanded. They, like their Soviet and British counterparts, positioned themselves as the best able to provide a peaceful life to allied Arab listeners while thwarting the manipulative designs of Soviet communism. Despite their frantic attempts to separate themselves from the Soviet promises of peace and to expose the purported duplicity of those promises, the Americans nonetheless mobilized the same language and the same arguments in the same ways as the Soviets, fundamentally for the same reasons.

In the end, peace became a reified word, "degraded," in the words of Edward Said, "by slothful association" and overuse.[4] Those "associations" turned peace into a commodity that could be bought and sold. Although all of the broadcasting programs gave lip service to the idea that peace represented an objective good worth pursuing on its own, in reality, peace was always contingent, always provisional. It was also profoundly contestable, used to define policies that frequently seemed to undermine the very experience that peace was supposed to provide. By the end of the decade, "peace," at least when it was talked about over the air, had become an ambiguous ontological state, in which being at peace often looked a lot like war.

. . .

The story of peace in mid-century Cold War propaganda begins in the Soviet Union. In 1949 the Cominform launched its World Peace Campaign, arguing that "Anglo-American imperialists" were intent on resolving their own "internal contradictions" and stopping the "march of historical development by means of a war."[5] Over the following years, the Soviet Peace Campaign became a full-blown international movement that included cultural and educational exchanges; sporting and youth events; village-level peace rallies across the Soviet Union; and the signing of thousands of petitions in Soviet schools, offices, and factories denouncing Anglo-American warmongering. The Peace Campaign ran alongside the Berlin blockade, the Cominform's expulsion of Yugoslavia in 1948, and the Soviets' detonation of their first atomic bomb, seemingly without contradiction.[6] By the time Stalin died in March 1953, peace was a staple on Soviet radio around the world.

Soviet support for Arab peace and its rejection of American and British warmongering were the defining features of Radio Moscow broadcasting to the Middle East in the 1950s. Here is a sample of one evening's programming itinerary from 1954:

18.30 "Speech by NS Khrushchev at a rally dedicated to friendship between the Soviet Union and Yugoslavia"
20.30 "The love of peace in the countries of socialism"
21.30 "Who is exacerbating tensions and opposing peace in the Near East?"[7]

When the Soviet minister of foreign affairs, Dmitri Shepilov, visited Cairo on June 18, 1955, on the eve of the Bandung Conference and the anniversary of Egyptian Independence Day, Radio Moscow ran a three-day program on Soviet solidarity with Pan-Arabism and peace.[8] Broadcasts reinforced the idea that the Soviet desire for peace motivated its domestic and foreign policies. It was, in the words of one radio broadcaster, "the deciding factor" in Moscow's "continuing support of Eastern Europe and the many ethnicities that inhabit the Soviet Union."[9] Peace was to be the hook that would legitimize the Soviet mission in the world and at home, and every policy could be framed in terms of its relative proximity to the cause of peace.

In the hands of Radio Moscow, peace functioned as a powerful vision of all that was under threat from capitalist and imperialist intervention. There was ample evidence of Western imperial meddling by the 1950s, whether it was US intervention in Korea in 1950, the CIA overthrow of Mohammed Mossadegh in 1953, the Iranian spy trials of 1954, the formation of the Baghdad Pact in 1955 and the subsequent US declaration of the Eisenhower Doctrine, or the Suez Crisis in 1956. It was common to hear programs with titles such as "American 'Help' Is a Means of Imperialist Warmongering, Where War Masquerades as Peace."[10] Arab listeners heard about the race riots happening in the United States on a daily basis. On March 15, 1956, it became world news when the Egyptian Ministry of Education offered Autherine Lucy admission to Cairo University after she was turned away from the University of Alabama because of the color of her skin.[11] All of these moments seemed to attest to the threat posed by the West to the cause of peace.

Tied to this was the argument that the imperialist powers were to blame for the continuing Arab-Israeli conflict. "In whose interest does tension in the Middle East survive?" Radio Moscow asked its listeners. "These circles wish to employ the dispute between the Arabs and Israel to promote their plans for armed interference in the Near East. . . . They nourish the dispute between the Arabs and Israel in the hope to drag the Arab countries into the aggressive bloc and to impose a new yoke of imperialist opposition and domination on the necks of the Arab peoples." This was an argument that Radio Moscow had been making since the 1940s, that there was no inherent cause for the Arab-Israeli conflict and that the United States and Britain were responsible for maintaining it in pursuit of their own agendas. As proof, they harkened back to the West's interference in the Russian Revolution in 1919, reminding their listeners, much as Ahmed Said did in his historical discussions of British colonial interference, that war profited the colonizer at the cost of the colonized. Perhaps not surprisingly, never did Radio Moscow mention the 1948 UN vote to create the state of Israel.

In the hands of Radio Moscow, peace served as a vehicle for the establishment of solidarity between the Middle East and the people of the Soviet Union. "The Soviet Union has always fully understood and sympathized with the aspirations of the colonial and dependent peoples for their national liberation," the speaker declared during a New Year's broadcast on January 1, 1956.[12] In particular, Radio Moscow argued that the desire for peace tied together the working class, who rebuked war as a tool of capitalist monopolies. "Worker and trade unions are fighting shoulder to shoulder against the imperialists," Moscow declared. "This is how peace will be achieved."[13] In their desire for peace, and based on their profound feelings of solidarity with the anti-imperialist struggle, the people of the Soviet Union seemed to promise aid with no strings attached. Soviet aid to the Middle East, including the financing of the Aswan Dam, the sending of medical and agricultural experts, the shipment of food, and the training of soldiers, functioned simultaneously as evidence of the Soviet promotion of peace and the Soviet commitment to anti-imperialism and anti-Zionism.

History continued to serve as the best proof of American and British perfidy. When Nasser nationalized the Suez Canal in 1956, Radio Moscow aired a ten-minute broadcast that began, "The whole world knows that the purchase by Britain of the Suez Canal Company's shares was the opening for British occupation of Egypt in 1882."[14] For Radio Moscow, Suez was not an exceptional event but part of a pattern. Similarly, when the rumors swirled that September that the British were preparing for an armed intervention to regain control of the Canal, Radio Moscow declared that this "gunboat diplomacy" was a classic tactic of the English past—a policy to be denounced as a remnant of Egypt's colonial suffering and a deterrent to the cause of peace. Then, when the not so covertly-funded British station Sharq al-Adna declared over the air that British army reservists would be entering the Sinai as peacekeeping forces, Radio Moscow responded that this was but a ruse for renewed occupation—a ruse made evident by Britain's long history of invasion. "Such statements recall to one's mind the dark ages of imperialism," Radio Moscow warned.[15]

This vision of peace in turn became a justification for violence and a call to action. Borrowing from arguments made by Lenin four decades earlier, Moscow declared that the struggle for peace could require violent measures. As one Soviet dignitary put it, "He who wants a stable and democratic peace must favor civil war against governments and the bourgeoisie."[16] The deliveries of arms from the Eastern Bloc to Egypt became actions carried out in the interests of world peace, "intended to break the British-American alliance, which is also directed against the Soviet Union in the Middle East."[17] That people would take up arms to fight for peace was not as paradoxical as one might think in the wake of the Second World War, when such arguments had been tied to the Allied cause. Soviet broadcasters understood this perhaps better than anyone.

Radio Moscow was in fact participating in a larger, transnational, on-air conversation about the shape of the past and the meanings of peace and democracy. When Radio Moscow narrated the stories of the British and US empires in the Middle East, the BBC replied with tales of Britain's steadfast movement toward democracy and peace since the Magna Carta. They focused on the positive aspects of the British Empire. Meanwhile, the VOA countered with its own liberal revolutionary story, rooted in the 1776 promise of a capitalist democracy and peace, combined with an explicit ahistoricity that privileged the possibilities of a modern future over debates concerning who was to blame for problems in the past. Voice of the Arabs utilized many of these historical tropes to construct a powerful version of Egyptian and Arab identity. For Ahmed Said and his colleagues, the Middle East was a place defined by its historical revolutionary spirit and its colonial past that simultaneously rejected that past and embraced a vision of an Egyptian-led, Arab nationalist, peaceful future untethered from the confines of imperialism.

These differing visions of the past had much in common. They were all predicated on a positivist belief in the historical capacity of humans to mobilize rational and secular problem solving to make the world a better place. They all had similar understandings of what was at stake in the fight over the telling of history; each was committed to molding the past into a singular,

FIGURE 4. Joseph Stalin perched at top of viewing colonnade as dove of peace flies overhead. "Peace can only be preserved and strengthened if the peoples take the cause of its preservation in their own hands and defend it until the end." *Source:* Soviet/Lebanese cover of *Altariq*, May 1953.

profoundly determinist narrative that, if followed to its conclusion, would lead to an inevitable, bright, peaceful, future. They all viewed the past as something inscribed by the march of modernity, progress, and the movement to more democracy. Each posited an objective past, described by objective language. And yet underlying these shared understandings of history was a central tension. Listeners were presented with a wide variety of different positivist histories on the radio, all of them promising the culmination of the past in a happy future. If one agreed with the premise that the world was destined for one, peaceful, Hegelian future, then how could one reconcile the myriad versions of that past and future being presented on the radio? Which one of those positivist histories being told on the radio was real? How could one choose between them, or was it possible that all of them, or none of them, were speaking the truth? All of this inevitably brought the conversation back to conflicting understandings of what "peace" might actually look like for the Arab world.

Such questions hovered like ghosts in the propaganda machine, not just when it came to debates over the past, but in economic and social disputes as well. Take, for instance, Radio Moscow's explanations for the material hardship being experienced by Arab populations in the 1950s. Labor movements continued to organize throughout the era (much to Nasser's chagrin), largely in response to ongoing conflicts between labor and capital.[18] But as was the case for Voice of the Arabs, Radio Moscow found no use in reporting on the domestic causes of Egypt's economic woes. Instead, it reported daily that the United States and Britain were sending aid in bad faith, and that such "gifts" were causing incalculable damage to the people of the Middle East. Such claims sought to absolve the Nasser state from responsibility for continuing shortages and labor unrest, along with any sense of obligation that Arabs might feel for US care, and to replace it with anger and humiliation.

A classic example of Radio Moscow's claims regarding American bad faith aired in 1953. This short drama, called *Mister Johnson in Trouble*, highlighted the malevolence that undergirded American aid and peace. Recorded on a Foley sound stage, the radio play presented a vision of a malicious and incompetent American propaganda and aid program unable to conceal its manipulations. As Ahmed Said was doing at Voice of the Arabs, it seemed to offer a secret glimpse into the underhanded lives of the colonialists, establishing the Soviet Union as the bearer of those secrets and a friend that could be trusted to speak the truth.[19]

The Soviet, Arabic-language play is set in the opulent office of the director of a radio station called Voice of the USA. As the scene begins, the station director, named Mr. Johnson, summons his one specialist on the Middle East, Mr. Strenly, to his office. After instructing Strenly to never express his opinions and "God forbid, never interrupt," Mr. Johnson gets to the point. "Strenly," he says, the squeaking of his leather armchair accompanying him as he flips through a program of upcoming radio broadcasts on his desk (the transcript in the Soviet archive is complete with instructions on how loud to make the sounds of the creaking chair and the ruffling papers). "I am sure you are aware that recently, in the Arab countries, we Americans have clearly ceased to be loved," Mr. Johnson opines. "We must write a radio show. In it, praise our products, find examples. At the very least, embellish a little. . . . I remember not so long ago we sold first-class American tractors to the Syrians." In the opening lines, the perfidious action of American propagandists selling goods to Arabs is clear. In this radio show about a radio show, Moscow was taking on the USIA as much as it was the US State Department.

Johnson continues: "The program should show the civilizing role of America. Describe the nakedness and poverty, the ignorance and darkness of the people of the Middle East. Then . . . American tractors appeared, and everything changed!" The stage directions instruct the actor to swell his voice. "The deserts turn into flowering fields, gardens turn green, the unfortunate fellah does not moan, but smiles, happy and joyful!" Such seeming Orientalism from the American Mr. Johnson stood in stark contrast to a story that had aired just before the play on Soviet respect for Syrian workers.

Strenly replies (stage directions say he should be almost screaming). "I can't, Mr. Johnson! I cannot write about the tractors." Strenly goes on to tell Mr. Johnson that there was a scandal with the American tractors in Syria, that they were unusable and fell apart after a few weeks of operation. He tells Mr. Johnson that the news of the faulty tractors was mentioned in international magazines published in ten different languages. "What a shame," Johnson replies. "It is inappropriate to remind the Arabs of this misunderstanding." Strenly, the working-class clerk, then asks Mr. Johnson how those tractors ever got into Syria. "You are a naïve man, Strenly," Mr. Johnson replies, laughing. "If these tractors had not ended up in Syria, then they would have been abandoned in Egypt, if not in Egypt, then in India, or even in Europe—our guys need to sell all that rubbish somewhere. Here in America, no one would give even a broken penny for these tractors, but there, across the ocean, they pay the price that we set." Radio Moscow was now making the claim that American goods were of poor quality, only being sent to vulnerable populations outside the United States; that the director of American broadcasting was such a fool that he did not remember the scandal; and that he was also a spin doctor who had no intention of reminding his listeners of, or apologizing for, such a mishap.

After a moment, Mr. Johnson lands on a new idea: they could do a show on the US shipment of cottonseed to the Middle East. Strenly reluctantly explains that "the same happened with the cottonseeds." The Syrian farmers planted the cottonseed, but it did not grow. The seed was unsuitable for sowing, and the newspapers reported that the Americans had sold the farmers garbage seed, "which should have been thrown into the sea long ago." Strenly then tells Johnson a similar story about an American pesticide that did not work, leading to blight for Syrian farmers. At the end of the scene, Johnson tells Strenly to leave, declaring that he is tired, leaving the show unwritten. In the epilogue, the Radio Moscow broadcaster tells his listeners that this scene was based on a true story—that Americans did sell faulty tractors, garbage seed, and blight-inducing pesticide to the Syrian people. As for Mr. Johnson and his clerk Strenly, "it is enough to say that such proto-types exist in today's America."

Dramatizations like this served many functions. Radio Moscow's story seemed to confer insider knowledge, ostensibly providing a secret view into the offices of US propagandists. In stories about American aid, which appeared at least once a week from 1951 to 1956, not only did American giving appear to be dishonest and poorly executed, but any problems with Soviet aid also seemed to be explained away. If Soviet aid was not forthcoming, it could only be because the Americans prevented it. This play also carried particular significance in the Syrian context, given that it aired two months after the overthrow of Colonel Adib Shishakli by members of the Syrian Communist Party, Druze officers, and Ba'ath Party members. While there is no clear evidence that the United States sold Syria faulty tractors, bad cottonseed, and harmful pesticides, it *was*, by 1955, planning to orchestrate a CIA- and MI5-led coup in Syria (a plan that failed). The best stories usually have a kernel of truth in them.

Food was a key weapon in the Soviet and American fight over peace and the cultural capital of giving. In 1951 the United States established the Point IV program to provide "international development"—an initiative that became a part of American foreign policy with the passing of Public Law 480 to sell US agricultural surplus for local currency around the world, and then later with the Food for Peace program. Meanwhile, in the Soviet Union, Nikita Khrushchev promoted the promises of the Virgin Lands project and the creation of trading regimes with anti-capitalist nations around the world. Agriculture also dominated Egyptian domestic policy and became a defining feature of the Free Officers' revolutionary project. In 1952 Naguib and Nasser passed Law Number 178, which sought to redistribute the nation's arable land to its peasantry, most of which was owned by a small number of large landowners. Nasser's agricultural policies were motivated largely by a desire to foster Egyptian and Middle Eastern agricultural self-sufficiency. The feeding of the population could not be held hostage by large landowners or international lenders, who might use the threat of starvation to gain access to miliary bases and oil fields.[20] Postcolonial independence could never be achieved as long as the Middle East was beholden to other powers for calories.

It was no coincidence then that tractors were at the center of *Mr. Johnson in Trouble*. Perhaps no other object carried so much significance as a symbol of modernity and national power. Since the 1930s, the tractor and the intrepid tractor driver had been the subject of countless Soviet novels and films attesting to the transformative and modernizing power of the Revolution. State-run tractor stations dotted the Soviet landscape, testaments to the success of collectivized agriculture and the promise of peace. The Soviet tractor represented the power of the commanding heights economy, the success of Soviet engineering and education, and the value of shared ownership of the means of production.

Similarly, the John Deere tractor became in the late 1930s the symbol of the intrepid independent farmer in the American Midwest, made stronger by the trials of the Great Depression, now more efficient than ever, the most self-sufficient and patriotic of its citizens. This image of the American tractor as the savior of civilization came to the fore during and after the Second World War, as Movietone newsreels attested to the American grain being exported through the Marshall Plan to a beleaguered Europe, as well as to the joy of Italian farmers upon receiving their tractors.[21] By far the most popular image in American publications, films, and radio programs transmitted to the Middle East and North Africa were American cows or tractors being given to grateful Arab and Persian populations. For the propagandists at the VOA and the USIA, the giving of the tractor stood in contrast to the image of the Soviet Union as a giver of weapons.

In the end, these debates returned to the larger fight over who could carry the mantle of peace by being the greater giver of goods in the Middle East. While both sides sold arms, it was the four-wheeled thresher that seemed to hold more traction in the struggle to prove one's repudiation of war. This was the context for Radio Moscow's interchange between Mr.'s Johnson and Strenly. Not surprisingly, VOA responded to the performance two weeks later. "The United States is the greatest manufacturer of tractors in the world," the VOA reported that March. "Ask your neighbors. They will tell you how good an American tractor is." With the sound of a tractor running in the background, the broadcaster declared, "We have sent thousands of tractors to Syria, Jordan, and Iran. These are the same tractors that our farmers use to grow grain for the world."[22]

For all of the broadcasting programs, the antecedent to peace was not just war; it was being lied to. Just like the VOA, Radio Cairo, and Sharq al-Adna, Radio Moscow regularly claimed that the other stations were lying about their desire for peace. Accusations of lying became a common trope, spoken of explicitly and regularly, a thread woven into the fabric of the

FIGURE 5. Dwight Eisenhower and Georgy Malenkov standing before a tank and a tractor. On the tank are the words "Communist and Soviet actions in Korea, Indochina, and elsewhere." By the tractor are the words "U.S. Peace Plan." Underneath, Eisenhower says, "I recommend this model." *Source:* "US Peace Plan," *'akhbar alwilayat almutahida* [*USA News Review*], May 28, 1953, Records of the USIA, Publications about the United States, 1953–1999, *USA News Review* (English/Arabic) 1951–1961, NARA, RG 306, entry 1053, box 502, folder 1953, 2 of 3.

audiosphere so much that listeners frequently wrote in to the various radio stations expressing deep worry that nothing could be believed anymore. When Khrushchev spoke in support of a détente between Egypt and Israel, the VOA reported that the Soviet Union was lying and had no desire for détente or peace. Radio Moscow's response came quickly: "We should like to say frankly that the Western propaganda is a lie . . . for the Soviet Union is simply interested in safeguarding and consolidating peace in the Middle and Near East."[23] When the VOA declared in 1956 that the Soviet Union had refused to offer funding for the Suez Canal, Radio Moscow responded that "many lies are appearing about the Soviet Union's policy and its readiness to continue to offer economic and technical aid." It warned its listeners not to heed the "fabrications of the Western propagandists," reminding them that the Soviet Union "offers aid backed by experience," while asking for nothing in return.[24] Accusations of mendacious treachery flew in every direction, every day.

What is perhaps most apparent in the Soviet, American, British, and Egyptian broadcasting transcripts is the distrust and anger that characterized much of the spoken audiospace in the 1950s. Take, for instance, a poem that was read over Radio Moscow in December 1951, entitled "Notorious Defense," by V. Bunni. The archival copy of the poem is littered with edits, presumably made by Radio Moscow editors who, in their words, were searching for "just the right tone." Everyone agreed on the opening line, however:

> What they talk and write is a lie!
> Aggression—that's what this "defense" means!
> Who are they?—These Wall Street tycoons, war-hungry predators
> Ask their victims in Egypt and Morocco
> And listen to what your ears cannot hear
> Ask Palestine how many people shed their blood on her hills,
> How many wandered and starved?[25]

Such language was not exclusive to Radio Moscow. Everyone argued that they were exposing a lie, particularly the lie of peace. Further up the dial, the materials provided by the British IRD and the USIA made similar claims about the Soviet Union and Egypt. All called upon Arab populations to "listen to what their ears could not hear" and to understand the duplicity of enemy narratives. And given the centrality of agriculture and aid in the audiosphere of the 1950s, it is not surprising that the poem should end with a vision of precarity and starvation.

Juxtaposed with the specter of the Western threat to peace was the vision of a peaceful life that the Soviet Union offered. Radio Moscow's claims invariably focused on the image of the happy child and their mother, allowed to live in a safe world thanks to the gifts given them by the benevolent Soviet state. As in the West, the 1950s was an era of demographic boom in much of Soviet Asia, the Middle East, and North Africa. Uzbekistan's growth rate rose from 2.58 percent in 1950 to 3.98 percent in 1962 (an increase of about nine million people), while Egypt's population famously grew by nearly 3 percent throughout most of the decade.[26] Such demographic explosions, which were caused by improved standards of living, widespread disease control, and improved sanitation efforts, led to longer life spans and lower infant mortality rates. This trend caused a myriad of new challenges across the Middle East, from housing and food shortages to insufficient schools and declining employment opportunities.[27] It was in response to these concerns that Radio Moscow offered up the image of the happy family made better by the peace and economic stability provided by the Soviet regime. Unfailingly, Uzbek and Kazakh families offered a handy metonym for all the benefits that the Soviet Union offered its most vulnerable populations.

Take a typical 1952 broadcast, *The Peace of an Uzbek Mother*, which told the story of a widowed Muslim woman named Risolet who had seven children. It described her hard work at the local factory, raising her children and pursuing her education when possible. The focus of the program was her children, whose lives had improved remarkably in just one generation. "Looking upon her daughters and sons, her heart fills with pride," the broadcaster intoned. One son was writing his thesis at the university on the construction of a new power plant in the Fergana valley. Another was a tractor engineer (yes, another tractor) studying the problem of using the Fergana's natural resources. Her oldest daughter, also an engineer, was the director of Tashkent's city planning.[28] All of her children, along with the other eight thousand young specialists studying engineering, agronomy, husbandry, and education in Moscow, would return to Uzbekistan to bring electrification and science to the region. This was what the Soviet Union offered its people, argued Radio Moscow, regardless of the relative backwardness from whence they came. In the final swelling segment of the broadcast, the narrator hammered home the lesson: "There is no more pleasant thought for a mother than her children. The whole life of old Risolet, the widow of a farm laborer, who never had his own piece of land, lies in her children. The Soviet authorities raised her children. The Soviet state created for her children, as well as for all Soviet boys and girls, excellent conditions for studying at a higher school. The Soviet state gives her a peaceful world in which her children can thrive."[29] And if the Soviet Union could save her, it could save anyone.

The story of the widow Risolet, whose greatest fulfillment came from her role as a proud mother, is reflective of the specifically gendered vision of Middle Eastern peace that Radio Moscow constructed in the 1950s—a vision that was in explicit conversation with Egyptian revolutionary visions of womanhood. Soviet imagery frequently included female university students or engineers as emblems of the shared Soviet and Egyptian embrace of the emancipated woman. In its stories of young women finding success as enfranchised citizens in the Soviet postrevolutionary moment, Radio Moscow harkened to the similar promises of liberation and inclusion promised by the Nasser regime. This "state feminism" seemingly bound together the two revolutionary projects in their shared commitment to solving the "women question," ushering in a new kind of socioeconomic liberation for the 50 percent of the population whose needs had been largely ignored by a capitalist or colonialist system that profited from their subjugation.[30]

At the same time, it was not uncommon to encounter stories in Radio Moscow's Arabic broadcasts that positioned women in traditional roles. As mothers, they became the surrogates for a nation and its concern for the preservation of the home and family. They were conduits for outrage in the face of colonial and capitalist exploitation who, like their innocent children, functioned as immutable indictments of the imperial world. They could also be vehicles of revolution, both as craven images calling men to war and eventually as revolutionaries themselves, driven to violence by fury over their family and home torn asunder. As icons for peace, traditional images of women in the home embodied the vision of a particular kind of bright future that Radio Moscow argued it shared with the Arab world. This was not the peaceful future of personal autonomy and power in the public sphere that early Soviet feminist leaders like Alexandra Kollontai and Nadezhda Krupskaia had envisioned during the Russian Revolution. Alongside promises of women's emancipation through the success of the Soviet-supported pan-Arab movement, Radio Moscow also attested to a shared belief with the Arab world in the ideal of the peaceful woman as a domestic and private being, surrounded by her children and unthreatened by the invasions of the outside world.

The VOA did its best to respond to the Soviet peace campaign. It told its listeners that there was no reason to believe that the Soviet Union desired anything other than "the destruction of freedom everywhere and a life of hardship for women and families."[31] The VOA argued frequently to listeners that the Soviet Union "concealed itself as the camp of peace and democracy," all while portraying the United States as the "camp of imperialism" in its plan to create a communist world order.[32] As Eisenhower put it in 1953, if the Soviets were serious about peace, they would seek an armistice in Korea, would stop "attacking" Indochina and Malaya, would withdraw from Austria and advocate for a united Germany, and would give Eastern Europe its independence and allow it to enter the "European Community." Based on these terms, "disarmament [would] be possible," and the money saved by disarming could be used to "develop the undeveloped world, to stimulate profitable and fair world trade, to assist all peoples to know the blessings of productive freedom."[33] The VOA argued that the Soviet peace offensive, if successful, reduced the Soviet military costs of achieving world domination because it "brainwashed" populations with the promise of a peaceful future.[34]

The VOA translated and read aloud the most sensational of the anti-communist stories printed in the US media, including Nicholas Nyardi's "I Saw Russia Preparing for World War III"; Paul Ruedemann's "I Learned about Communism the Hard Way"; Donald Knode's "Escape from Tyranny"; and Werner Knop's "I Prowled Russia's Forbidden Zone," in which he declared, "The people were both more shabbily dressed and more irritable than those in the Western zones."[35] Knop told a story of standing in one of the ubiquitous queues outside a shop in Moscow, waiting to see if goods would become available, only to be pushed aside by a "little fat man, who bore all the earmarks of being a police agent." The little man tried to push his way forward through the line. "At this, [the crowd's] ugly mood flared up, and several women denounced the fat man furiously for trying to get ahead of them. One woman became so incensed she took her wicker basket and began to pummel him, screaming that people like him waxed fat while the ordinary people were being bossed and starved." At the end, after visiting the famous Eliseevsky grocery store on Tversakaia Ulitsa in Moscow, which was reserved only for the elite of the Bolshevik leadership, Knop concluded, "Food is so scarce it has become a means of rewarding political service." When conveyed over the radio in Arabic, this message took on new meaning as a harbinger of the kinds of meager rewards the Soviet offer of giving really held.

In response, Radio Moscow claimed that Eisenhower was "fanatically interested" in propaganda as he attempted to "inspire nations with the fear of "Soviet aggression" and to frighten them with the threat of an atomic war—all of it concealed by "peace-loving phraseology."[36] The Soviets estimated that the Americans were spending $1 billion annually on propaganda, while the Americans estimated the Soviet expenditures at over $3 billion—though they were the first to admit that these were just estimates.[37]

Confessional anti-communist stories like Werner Knop's continued to be a staple on the VOA throughout the 1950s. On one day in 1954, the VOA announcer read excerpts from a *Life* magazine story, "I Escaped to Speak for the Enslaved," followed by readings from William Faulkner's famous commencement speech, "Faith or Fear."[38] The first story painted a picture of the hopelessness borne by people on the other side of the Iron Curtain. The second called on the next generation to seek "liberty, freedom of the body and

« حمامة السلام
الجديدة للرسام
بيكاسو »

كاندبدو ، ميلانو ، ايطاليا .

FIGURE 6. Soviet dove of peace carrying weapons under its wings. *Source:* "Dove of Peace," *'akhbar alwilayat almutahida* [*USA News Review*], February 21, 1954, Records of the USIA, Publications about the United States, 1953–1999, *USA News Review* (English/Arabic) 1951–1961, NARA, RG 306, entry 1053, box 502, folder 1953, 1 of 3.

spirit both, security for the weak and helpless, and peace for all."[39] The VOA aired stories about East Germans in Leipzig rising up against "Red Rule." It broadcast reports on Albanians refusing to pay their taxes, Czech workers striking in the factories, Romanians plundering state warehouses containing food destined for the USSR, Hungarian workers being intentionally lazy on the job, and Bulgarian workers organizing guerrilla bands in the mountains near Sophia.[40] The VOA reported all of these stories on one day, July 16, 1953, five days after Eisenhower had given his approval for the plan to overthrow the democratically elected leader of Iran.

Not to be overlooked, the British Middle Eastern Information Service also scrambled to respond to the Soviet peace campaign. It could not help but acknowledge the power in the Soviet "exploitation of a) the widespread desire for peace, b) anti-imperialism, and c) neutralism."[41] As the broadcasters admitted, it was a potent message that contributed to the growing tensions between "extreme Arab nationalism and the Western Powers, with Egypt as the prime target. The BBC argued that the Soviet Union could not claim to want peace, oppose imperialism, support neutrality, crusade for Palestinian rights, or defend the pan-Arab cause while it also maintained an iron fist on

- سانت لويس (مسوري) غلوب - ديمقراط

لا تزال افو الرهم بدوه افعال

FIGURE 7. Soviet dove of peace looking despairingly over Kremlin wall. *Source:* "Still All Words and No Deeds," *'akhbar alwilayat almutahida* [*USA News Review*], July 9, 1953, 5, Records of the USIA, Publications about the United States, 1953–1999, *USA News Review* (English/Arabic) 1951–1961, NARA, RG 306, entry 1053, box 502, folder 1953, 2 of 3.

Eastern Europe and kept the world hostage with the threat of nuclear attack. Perhaps not surprisingly, the British message came in the form of warnings not to believe in the Soviet messages of peace and anti-imperialism, which were too good to be true.[42] Repeatedly, the BBC expressed the belief that anti-imperialism only opened the door for communists to take positions of power in the name of national self-determination. This threat was, in turn, tied to the "spectre of peace," which ironically represented a threat to democracy and peace.[43] Peace—a movement rooted in a desire for security and freedom—nonetheless created a chaos that communists could use to generate a Moscow-led revolution. These threats seemed to exist in a relationship of infinite regress, in which each was both the cause and consequence of the other.

. . .

While all the broadcasters talked about peace in the 1950s, it was Radio Moscow that forced everyone to reckon with peace as a defining feature of the audiosphere. In the hands of Radio Moscow, a nation's ability to pursue and defend peace constituted a key piece of cultural capital in the Cold War and the struggle for popular consensus. Peace became a shorthand for the promise of aid, the promotion of Arab independence, and the Soviet Union's powerful ability to defend the Middle East from the violence of Western colonialism.

By the mid-1950s, these arguments could be heard up and down the dial. Sharq al-Adna, the VOA, and Radio Cairo all promised peace. All positioned themselves as the only force capable of ensuring peace. All provided examples of innocent women and children flourishing thanks to the gifts on offer from their peaceful governments. All made it clear that such joys were available to those whose fealty remained constant, who embraced the socioeconomic system and friendship on offer, and who rejected the beguiling but nonetheless dangerous temptations of the enemy.

The language of peace coming from Radio Moscow, the VOA, and the BBC simultaneously applauded and infantilized its Arab listeners. On the one hand, the broadcasters frequently painted a picture of the Egyptian people as newly invigorated by their independent status. As Radio Moscow declared in 1956, "Those whom imperialism formerly prevented from assembling, which considered them as no more than cotton producers, have proven that they have enough resolve and vigor to proceed on the path of national independence."[44] That August, Radio Moscow repeated again and again the phrase, "The Egyptian people are the masters of their home."[45] And yet it made clear that resolve and vigor would not be enough. After Nasser nationalized the Suez Canal and the Western powers gathered in London to decide what to do, Radio Moscow took to the air to reassure the Arab world that the Soviet Union would be taking care of the situation. "Without the USSR, nothing of consequence will be decided in London," it declared.[46] The Arab desire for independence was worthwhile, but insufficient without the backing of a larger power.

As a consequence, Western rhetoric about colonial benevolence and the promise of peace came to signify manipulation and violence for many Middle Eastern listeners, eliciting skepticism instead of allegiance. Ahmed Said at the Voice of the Arabs constantly took note of the word's duplicity and increasing meaninglessness. Aid, which was the mechanism for the achievement of peace, became synonymous with neocolonial dominance. In the process, *peace*, or at least the Western and Soviet versions of it, was rendered increasingly meaningless. For decades, diplomats, politicians, activists, and pundits would continue to struggle to guide the "Middle East peace process" with accords and agreements. But the process was always hindered by the fact that peace seldom meant shaking hands and finding middle ground in the Middle East. It was, instead, instrumentalized—a political tool. This explains why *peace* has largely become a dead word in the modern era, bereft of meaning. As Tolstoy noted a hundred years earlier, the line between war and peace was not always clear. Like war, peace could be used to mobilize populations and define the conditions for its achievement. Indeed, much of the purpose of propaganda is to establish those conditions, to show the state as a defender of peace who is more than willing to go to war.

FIVE

The Echo Chamber

THE AMERICANS ENTER THE FIGHT

IT WAS BECAUSE OF THE COLD WAR that the USIA was born in 1953.[1] While American legislators had been generally reticent about the use of propaganda in the years immediately following the Second World War, their opinions changed quickly as the realities of the Cold War conflict and the need for economic and cultural alliances around the world came into sharper focus.[2] The US response to Soviet propaganda began with the Truman Doctrine, Marshall Plan, Point IV aid program, and founding of the CIA in 1947. It was not until Dwight Eisenhower became president, however, that the State Department decided it would need to respond on a grand scale to Soviet propaganda with some of its own. Eisenhower called for a "total Cold War" that would operate in the world of culture and propaganda to fight against the contagion of communism and to make a clearer path for the pursuit of US foreign policy.[3] When the Korean War broke out in 1950, followed the next year by the Iranian oil crisis, Eisenhower embraced a "New Look" on the Middle East, based on the argument that the region was susceptible to Soviet penetration.[4] The US propaganda program would have to get serious, carving a space for itself amid the cacophony of messages appearing in print and on the radio dial.

Into this new, urgent world, the VOA was reborn. The VOA took as its task the job of softening the image of the United States in the Middle East and around the world. It would show US support for Arab economic and political independence, exhibit an even hand when dealing with the Arab-Israeli conflict, cultivate Arab backing for a US-driven promise of capitalist happiness, and reveal the "Big Lie" that sat behind Soviet promises of peace and aid. Like the Soviets, Egyptians, and British, the American broadcasters based their messaging on the creation of a bargain with the listening public, offering gifted, secular development and modernization in return for fealty. Everyone offered freedom, for what it was worth.

The single-mindedness of the American program to counter communism around the world meant that its effectiveness was often restricted by a Cold War mentality that assessed all crises by the same restricted criterion.[5] That criterion was defined at least in part by the audiosphere that shaped how people talked about and understood the Cold War. At the center was the endless mantra of the United States as an agent of material comfort and modernization, capable of making the lives of subject populations happy and wealthy while protecting them from communist invasion. It relied on the triumphal promise of American consumer society as a beacon of what defined the "good life."[6] Much like in the Soviet Union, in return for such happiness, the state expected popular loyalty and indebtedness, which sometimes ironically demanded a call to arms.

In the end, whatever honorable intentions undergirded American perspectives on the Middle East, they were lost in the great tidal wave of contradictory and condemnatory information coming from other places on the dial that matched the VOA at every turn. From its inception, the VOA struggled to control the parameters of the propaganda debate, frequently functioning more as a repeater of messaging than as a generator of it. It was, in the words of Mikhail Bakhtin, increasingly locked into a particular "discursive framework" that had been developing for years and that exercised a force on every word it uttered.[7] This cacophony would only grow louder in the decades to come. American propagandists were unable to extricate themselves from the shrinking confines of the discursive world they inhabited—a world whose parameters were impossible to see and yet shaped their path at every turn. They also faced the profoundly difficult task of pitching a narrative of happiness that again and again clashed with the realities of American foreign (and domestic) policy—a policy that frequently ignored the happiness of the very people whose approval they were trying to cultivate.

· · ·

By most measures, the United States arrived late and unprepared to the Middle Eastern propaganda battle. The VOA had developed during the first months of 1942, broadcasting in English, German, French, and Italian. Like so many inventions, it was born from war and the need to reach domestic and international audiences with a unified and compelling message. The

VOA added Arabic in 1944, with two hours of airtime in the Middle East and North Africa. Most US politicians assumed that once the war was over, the VOA would pack up and go home. As far as they were concerned, propaganda was a tool used by authoritarian regimes to brainwash and control populations.[8] Because it required the employment of people who spoke foreign languages, it also smacked of outside infiltration and seemed difficult to control.[9]

The Americans got serious about propaganda when the Cold War became a reality. In 1947 the US Senate Foreign Relations Committee concluded that America was losing serious ground in its fight to be the defender of freedom in the world and to counter Soviet influence. "Hundreds of millions are being expended by the Soviets," Secretary of State George Marshall told Congress that year, "and the United Kingdom, although heavily in debt, supports a program employing some 8700 people as against our less than 1400 and costing three times ours. Even little Holland is spending nearly a quarter of a million dollars a year and spent half a million last year in the United States alone to defend and explain her policies."[10] As Chester Bowles, the US ambassador to India from 1951 to 1953, wrote, American policies still rested largely on martialized concepts of power: "An inflexible diplomacy in Asia and in Africa still ties us to an outmoded, despised and doomed status quo."[11] Given that mutually assured destruction now precluded the real possibility of military war, Bowles argued that the United States was failing to heed the "political, economic, and ideological forces which are now writing history," and which provided an easy target for Soviet soft power tactics. Even the famous statesman George Kennan noted as late as 1948 that the propaganda strategies being pursued by US competitors and allies were "ahead of anything the U.S. had to offer."[12] The American propaganda program would have to change, the nation's leaders concluded. They reconciled themselves to the necessity for the "dirty business" by arguing that there were two kinds of propaganda: the good kind, undertaken by good people to tell the truth, and the bad kind, told by evil people to lie. Theirs would be the good kind. When the US Congress passed the Education and Exchange Act in 1948, it did so with the understanding that US propaganda would constitute a noble pursuit. It would promote "mutual understanding" that would serve the cause of peace, a peace that was endangered by the weapons of false propaganda and misinformation.[13]

In the decade that followed, the United States doubled down on the use of propaganda in the fight for soft power in the Cold War. In 1950 President

Harry Truman called for a "Campaign of Truth" against the Soviet Union's "Big Lie." The VOA set out to launch an information blitz about the positive aspects of American culture. That November it launched a new radio program in Arabic, with Truman giving the inaugural broadcast, stating his commitment "to promote peace and economic betterment."[14] Its sole purpose was to combat the spread of communism abroad. Like the British in Palestine, the VOA believed that its first job was to counter the Soviet propaganda juggernaut by exposing communist perfidy and uniting the free world behind US leadership.

Then, in 1952, Joseph McCarthy dealt a blow to the VOA as part of his "relentless assault on the State Department."[15] Everyone fell under suspicion of being a Soviet agent or for insufficiently showing their fealty to the American Cold War cause. American broadcasters worked to muster their anti-Soviet mettle on the air as a defense against attacks and suspicions at home. Despite their best efforts to appear loyal, staffing cutbacks nonetheless hit the VOA like a cold blanket, with Arabic broadcasting dropping to one hour per day by the middle of 1953.[16] Even the CIA's FBIS, which kept transcripts of foreign broadcasts, saw cuts in personnel. The BBC archives are filled with thankful letters from the CIA to the BBC's Monitoring Service for its tracking and translation of critical events that aired on the radio around the world—because its own teams were too understaffed to handle the task.[17]

The development of the American propaganda program did not cease, however, and in 1953 President Eisenhower authorized the creation of the USIA, which would centralize overseas information activities. This was what "total Cold War" would mean in the Eisenhower era.[18] Now there would be a unified voice for America's "empire of ideas," filled with a single, positive vision for what it meant to be an American.[19] Like Radio Moscow, the BBC, and Voice of the Arabs, the USIA struggled to reconcile its desired ends with the means employed to get there. Should it report on information that was unfavorable to the United States? Should it attempt to justify and explain the aspects of American life that the rest of the world might find unappealing? What did it mean to "define America to the world"? These questions became particularly thorny when they spread out into the ether of the Middle East and North Africa.[20]

By December 1954, just as Joseph McCarthy was being censured for his lack of decency on the US Senate floor, the VOA's new director, Leonard Marks, implemented his plan to transmit fourteen hours of Arabic broadcasting a week to North Africa and the Middle East. The signal would travel from the VOA studio in Washington, D.C., over eight shortwave transmitters in Tangier, Rhodes, and Salonica, Greece, to millions of Arabic-speaking listeners.[21] The VOA staff ceased outsourcing the research for their stories, instead employing local officers who were responsible for being aware of communist propaganda activity on the ground in their various regional offices.[22] Heard on the shortwave in Beirut, Damascus, Amman, Cairo, and Baghdad, the first hour was filled with music, cultural stories, and news. They aired programs with titles such as *Echo of the News*, *Health Program*, *University Forum*, *Woman and Child in Society*, and on Sundays, *Arabs in America*. The second hour (which came from the VOA's relay ship, *The Courier*), followed what it described as "a lighter pattern." It included Arabic poetry readings, a quiz show, and an attempt at humor, *Arabic Anecdotes and American Novelties*.[23]

What did the American promise to the Middle East of happiness and peace look like in the 1950s? In so many ways, it was a sponge for the language being used on other points of the dial. When the VOA set out to talk about the material happiness of the American population, it often sounded like a Radio Moscow program. "All America pays homage to the dignity of labor. . . . America's 64 million workers have grown to an awareness of their bond with the working men and women of the free countries of the world as they play a vital, constructive and responsible part to win peace and security for all free peoples."[24] It was a line that could have been written in Russian, clearly meant to resonate with the growth of socialist movements in the Middle East and hopefully steal listeners from Radio Moscow. The broadcaster went on to explain how powerful unions like the AFL-CIO participated in the political process in the United States, ensuring that the economy avoided inflation, that workers had affordable housing, that state-funded education was growing, that a national health insurance program was being planned, and that social security benefits could be secured. The VOA contrasted this to the slave labor of the East, both in China and in the Soviet Union. "These are the differences between the lives of workers in the free nations of the world and those of workers in the Soviet slave world," the broadcaster warned. "Reform through labor"—a phrase used heavily in the early years after the Chinese Communist revolution—appeared as a pejorative term again and again in American parlance. And as the VOA reminded its listeners, whereas an American worker needed to work for thirteen minutes to buy a loaf of bread, a Russian worker had to work for

العمل من اجل الحياة ــ اميركا وروسيا

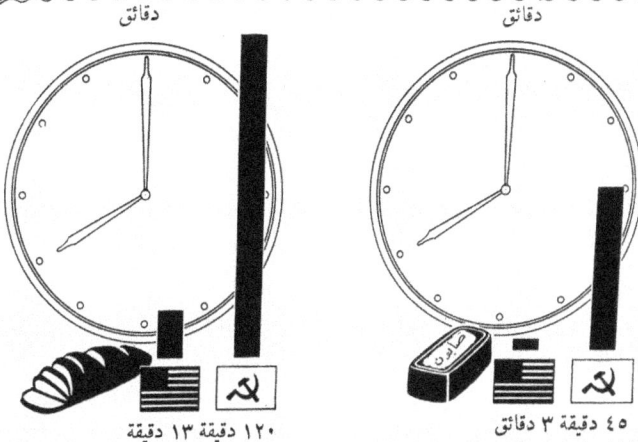

دقائق   دقائق

٤٥ دقيقة ٣ دقائق   ١٢٠ دقيقة ١٣ دقيقة

نظرًا لارتفاع الاسعار وانخفاض الاجر في الاتحاد السوفياتي ، فان على العامل ان يشتغل مدة ساعتين كاملتين قبل ان يتمكن من الحصول على رغيف من الخبز الابيض . (انظر الرسم اعلاه) . اما في الولايات المتحدة كما يشير الرسم نفسه فان العامل العادي لا ينفق الا ١٣ دقيقة من يومه العملي للحصول على نفس المادة . وكذلك يحتاج العامل في روسيا ان يشتغل ثلاثة ارباع الساعة لكي يحصل على قطعة صابون بينما لا يحتاج ذلك الا ٣ دقائق في الولايات المتحدة . ولكي يحصل العامل في الاتحاد السوفياتي على بدلة يجب عليه ان يعمل ٣٩ يوماً (انظر الرسم تحت) في حين لا يتطلب ذلك في اميركا اكثر من ٣ ايام . وبدل الرسم في اسفل ايضاً ، على ان العمل من اجل شراء حذاء يكلف ٦٦ ساعة ونصف في روسيا بينما لا يكلف ذلك في الولايات المتحدة سوى ٣ ساعات من العمل .

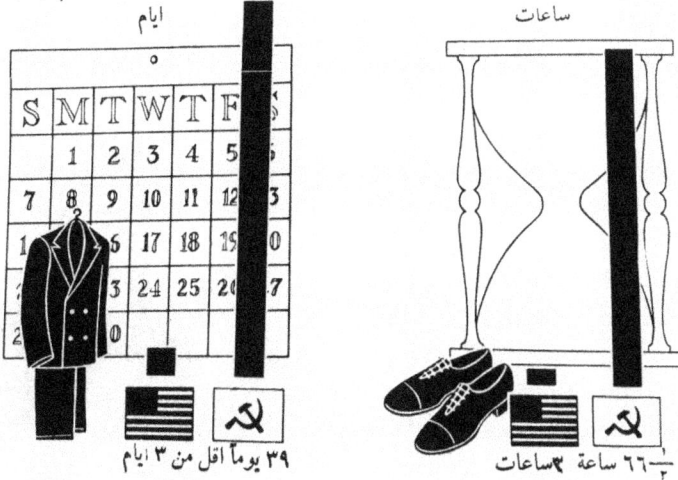

ايام   ساعات

٣٩ يوماً اقل من ٣ ايام   ٦٦- ساعة ٣ساعات

FIGURE 8. Pictures showing that US workers have to work less time than Soviet workers to purchase necessities like bread, soap, clothes, and shoes. *Source:* "Celebrating Labor Day in the United States," *[USA] News Review*, August 19, 1953, Records of the USIA, Publications about the United States, 1953–1999, *USA News Review* (English/Arabic) 1951–1961, NARA, RG 306, entry 1053, box 502, folder 1952, 2 of 2, 3.

two hours. In a hypnotic voice, the broadcaster listed a variety of consumer items and the relative work required to acquire them: for a bar of soap, three American minutes of work and forty-five Soviet minutes of work; for a man's suit, 2.7 American days versus 38.8 Soviet days; and for a pair of work shoes, 3 American hours versus 66.5 Soviet hours.

As on Radio Moscow, such arguments, which were articulated on the air and in USIA publications, quantified happiness. They took an explicitly materialist approach in arguing for the capitalist alternative to worker success, turning Marx's famous critique of the working day and the quantification of wage labor on its head.[25] Instead of labor losing its value in the antagonistic struggle between capitalist and worker, capital allowed labor to be more efficient, creating a greater return on worker investment and ultimately a better quality of life. It was the Keynesian promise spelled out in suits and shoes. At their core, however, broadcasts and publications like this bought into the deeper assumption that the wage labor of the worker was tied inextricably to happiness, peace, and meaning in life.

Indeed, it was a clear program of the USIA to promote a kinder, gentler image of capitalism that had evolved from the older, nineteenth-century stereotypes of wealthy monopolies and rapacious robber barons. In the 1950s the USIA pitched capitalism to Middle Eastern audiences as a freer form of socialism, with workers functioning as stockholders and American capitalism "affording each person the right to take part in all phases of the country's economy." And while management helped to make plans and policies, they represented millions of workers, working more as team captains than as bosses. In one 1953 broadcast, the VOA used the phrase "from each worker according to their talents" to describe the running and "group ownership" of corporations.[26] If someone had only listened to the VOA in Arabic in 1954, the United States would have sounded like a place where the proletariat was in control.

Ironically, just as VOA messaging highlighted stories about American workers whose lives were made happier by the success of capitalism, Radio Moscow stopped using explicit Marxist language in its discussions of worker happiness under the Soviet program. Even at events like the 1952 Arab Workers Congress, which Radio Moscow broadcast on all of its frequencies, one was hard pressed to find staple words like *proletariat, bourgeoisie, formalist,* and *reactionary*—words that were in heavy use domestically in the Soviet Union in 1952.[27] Also, nowhere in the Radio Moscow arsenal could the word *capitalist* be heard, although conversations about American and

English imperial exploitation continued unabated. It seemed Moscow was shying away from the use of ideological language just as the VOA was picking it up.

By the 1960s the VOA had shifted away from explicitly ideological language as well, telling steady stories about the happiness and peacefulness of US families without harkening to the explicit promises of "capitalism." While all of these messages were materialist by definition, what was missing from them by 1956 was any explicit conversation about the economic systems that made such physical and educational improvements possible. The United States, it would seem, had finally learned the lesson that the Soviets had realized earlier: that there was a risk in making explicitly capitalist and communist ideological cases over the air. Such arguments could fly in the face of the nonalignment and pan-Arab movements. They had the potential to seem dogmatic amid Nasser's nationalist project and his tentative approaches to Egyptian socialist reform. For Radio Moscow, they ran the risk of encouraging radical communist movements in the Middle East that the Soviet Union was loathe to support. Most critically, there was real worry among the broadcasters that such language would smack of colonialism. The USIA continued to speak of the evils of communism, but only in terms of how it squelched human freedom, not as a flawed economic system that offered the working class a raw deal. Behind the scenes, the ideological underpinnings of the US, Soviet, and British propaganda programs were explicit, but over the air they were invariably couched in terms of the possible happiness and peace that each nation had to offer its populations.

Also like Radio Moscow, the USIA regularly chose one Arab American to stand in as an ideal example of how successful Arabs could be in America. Instead of living in Uzbekistan, these Arab Americans lived in Cleveland, Ohio, or Albany, New York. In the early 1950s the USIA wrote and broadcast no fewer than seventeen stories on Major James Jabara, "the world's first jet ace in the Korean war," who was from Wichita, Kansas, and was of Lebanese decent. Stories spoke of Jabara's lovely wife and two children, James and Carol Ann. In an interview, Jabara declared that he thought of communism "as something like an octopus with long arms reaching out to grab off land and snuff out people's freedom. . . . If ordinary guys like myself, who like their freedom and love their families enough to fight for them, don't go out and face it wherever it appears—even on the other side of the world— there may be more Koreas closer to home."[28] Jabara, as the stories went, had come from Lebanon with his family as immigrants, seeking, as millions had before them, a better life filled with opportunity in America. His father had worked in the coal mines, and his mother was a seamstress. Jabara had not come from wealth, but just like the children of the widow Risolet, he had been given a great education by a nation that supported his dreams. Jabara presented an image of happy assimilation, complete with a boy and girl whose names evoked white, middle-class comfort and afternoon barbecues. This was the future that American patronage could make possible.

The USIA regularly weaponized religion as a freedom that could be endowed or denied depending on the ideological system that presided over it. While Radio Moscow aired features on the beauty of Tashkent, with its thirty mosques "open for all who wish to pray," the VOA aired stories like, "Islam is Dying in the Soviet Union," which argued that in Alma-Ata, "not a single mosque is in sight."[29] Radio Moscow conjured images of Muslim workers making important discoveries in institutes of science, engineering, and technology, surrounded by people speaking many languages, especially Arabic. In response, the VOA declared that "the era of the great theistic religions is coming to an end in the Soviet Union. They are on the threshold of a new era of Godlessness. There is a new religion, the religion of Lenin and Stalin. And as for Islam, it is in its last dying throes." A standard part of the VOA narrative included quoting Muslim leaders who denounced communism. When the Muslim Brotherhood's Hassan El Hodeibi told a reporter at the Cairo newspaper, *Al Misri*, that "Communism is a materialistic doctrine which denies all religions," the VOA and the USIA publishing houses were quick to put it into copy and on the air.[30] In November 1954, when the Central Committee of the Communist Party of the Soviet Union announced its Anti-Religion Decree, the VOA cautioned its listeners not to be hoodwinked. "Yes," one announcer declared, "Khrushchev has enjoined the Soviet people not to offend the religious sentiment of believers or ministers of cults. This is supposed to be a response to the crude mistakes that have been made in the course of what they call their scientific-atheist propaganda among the population." "But do not be mistaken," he continued, "the Soviet Union believes that you should be freed from the influence of your religious prejudices."

Just as Radio Moscow had told stories about Abu Darr to show the socialist tendencies of the Muslim faith, the VOA took on the project of aligning Islam as closely to American ideals as possible. It broadcast stories about the unity of American Muslims with their counterparts around the world—bound together by their shared commitment to "freedom of the individual, the rights of private capital, and democracy."[31] The VOA also took shots at Soviet racism, or "Great Russian chauvinism," in which the best positions in industries and universities went to Western Russians while Uzbek and Kazakh students were left with little access to the basics needed to succeed.[32]

The USIA used the seeming legacy of the benevolent British Empire to argue that there was a difference between civilized Western colonialism and brutal Russian imperialism. In a 1953 broadcast, it told its listeners:

> The policy of the colonial powers who have been ruling over these lands has been elastic all along. Besides allowing their subjects self-rule stage by stage, [the British and French] never interfered with their religion and culture, and did not prevent them from having contact with the outside world. Inside the Russian border, however, the Moslem lands appear to have passed into the oblivion. . . . A systematic effort, it is said, is made to turn the entire Moslem population into a godless people. . . . They plan for elimination of religious leaders followed by a suppression of religious teachings and Moslem culture, the detachment of children from their parents, and the introduction of godless education. . . . The ray of hope we generally come across among the subjected races of colonial powers, we find completely absent among the Moslems in Russia. . . . What will befall those nations that cease to be alert to the dangers that undermine their very foundations?[33]

Broadcasts like this one reinforced classic racist perspectives of the European West on the unkempt and Asiatic Soviet East, all while arguing that the Soviet Union had the capacity to rid the Middle East of Islam. It also gave explicit support to Islamic nationalism, if only because such movements presented a potential thorn in the Soviet side. The Soviets were the great empire builders. In a story entitled, "Soviet Imperialism," the VOA described the governments of Eastern Europe as puppets who "move only when Moscow pulls the strings."[34] It argued repeatedly that after the war, the Soviet Union "looted Manchurian industry," shipping entire Chinese factories to the USSR, ultimately orchestrating the downfall of Chiang Kai-shek's nationalist government, and placing its puppet, Mao Tse-tung, in charge. Steady stories ran on the "88 million non-Russian peoples inhabiting the Soviet Union who are robbed of their nationalities and of the heritages handed down by their forefathers."[35]

Just as Radio Moscow warned Arab listeners to be wary of American aid, so VOA echoed back the same alarm. In February 1956, only months before the US withdrawal of funds for the Aswan Dam and the joint British-French-Israeli invasion of Suez, America's Dwight Eisenhower and Britain's

Anthony Eden signed the Declaration of Washington, the text of which the VOA and the BBC read in their daily broadcasts. After presenting a balance sheet showing how many people around the globe the United States and the United Kingdom had aided, and how many people the Soviet Union had imprisoned, the VOA declared that it would henceforth take "action, jointly with France, in the defense of peace in the Middle East," that they would endorse the Baghdad Pact, "as a bulwark against Soviet aggression."[36] The VOA issued reports that the Poles had been forced to turn down the request by Egypt for coal to build a bunker base in Suez because they themselves had simply run out. "Why did they run out? Because Polish coal is going to the [Soviet Union] in large quantities."[37] Other stories highlighted the efforts that the United States was making to give aid to starving East Germans, who were unable to receive the aid because the Soviet Union would not allow it.

There were many problems with the US information program in the Middle East that few could ignore. Listeners' surveys reported again and again that the VOA broadcasts were heavy handed, poorly composed, and often downright terrible. The station continued to struggle with the quality of the signal and the fact that the cafés where its broadcasts played were often too noisy for anyone to listen. Sometimes the broadcaster's dialect was incomprehensible to listeners—a problem exacerbated by the USIA's need for loyalty checks from its Arabic-speaking employees and a deep reticence toward hiring non-US citizens. "A commentator has to demonstrate with every breath he takes that he is familiar with the listener's present life," Ralph White, a USIA researcher wrote in a memo in 1952. Not many Americans lived abroad or even traveled. As a result, listeners told USIA researchers that the VOA reminded them mostly of Soviet propaganda. It was too "energetic and vigorous." And "for God's sake," White wrote, "we can't keep calling Stalin a liar. People can turn the dial and listen to the Soviets calling Eisenhower a liar, . . . and the whole thing sounds fake." Surveys even reported evenings when a music record was allowed to play to the end and then was not picked up for minutes, leaving only the droning crack of the needle against the vinyl's paper center, scratching again and again over the air.[38]

Similarly, when handling what the USIA called the "liberation issue" (referring to still-colonized populations in the Middle East and North Africa), USIA researchers knew as early as 1952 that they had to stop telling colonized populations that the Americans were going to save them. "Like the British, we [must] give them sympathy but not promises," Ralph White wrote. "We [must] avoid the word 'liberation' almost completely. . . . We [should] talk about peace, but we should not be so blunt as to say 'We won't start a war even to liberate you.'"[39] It was a difficult tightrope to walk, and of course, Radio Moscow had no qualms about using the word.

All of these issues were exacerbated by the steady news of race violence in America. Stories of Black men in Alabama receiving death sentences for the theft of $1.95 forced many around the world to question the US ostensible commitment to its own ideals.[40] For the US State Department, it certainly was problematic that opera houses across the world were selling out tickets for *Porgy and Bess* while Radio Moscow continued to label the United States a "race of racist materialists" who measured their successes in terms of automobile purchases and segregated neighborhoods instead of cultural achievements and the pursuit of racial equality.[41] Eisenhower, who oversaw the resegregation of the White House after the relative openness of Truman's presidency, nonetheless recognized the damage that America's race relations were having on the image of the United States abroad. As a result, he tasked the USIA with rewriting the race narrative as a problem that no longer plagued American culture.

The USIA's tack on managing its race messaging underwent a transformation from the 1950s to the 1960s. In the early years it offered a sanitized, largely ahistorical narrative of a nation committed to equality, with steady stories of "Negro" athletes and musicians like Jackie Robinson and Louis Armstrong representing the unique freedom and diversity of American culture. Performers like the famous jazz trumpeter Dizzy Gilespie and his integrated band toured the Middle East, Africa, and Asia, functioning as representatives of a color-blind democracy that belied the realities of Jim Crow America.[42] By the 1960s the USIA had recognized the need for a more nuanced approach that tacitly recognized the nation's troubled past, arguing that America still had its problems but was working hard to get better.

Radio Moscow countered these assurances at every turn. "Racism is in the blood of capitalist America, like guns and poverty. You need look no further than the rising popularity of George Rockwell, whose Nazi party has attracted thousands of members not just in Alabama but in Kansas City and Washington, DC."[43] Rockwell, who had demonstrated in front of the White House in protest against the 1958 US invasion of Lebanon because he believed it to be coordinated by Israel, was a perfect foil for the USIA's claims of racial reconciliation. Before he was assassinated in 1966, Radio Moscow reported periodically on Rockwell's demonstrations against Martin Luther King Jr. and his organizing of a "Hate Bus" in response to the Freedom

Riders who campaigned for the desegregation of the American South in the 1960s. The USIA may have produced many earnest broadcasts presenting a post-racial version of American democracy, but other voices in the audiosphere made that message far muddier than the USIA broadcasters wanted.

Then there was the problem of oil. By 1956 there were ample examples of American and British meddling in Middle Eastern affairs in the pursuit of oil. As Radio Moscow put it, "American and British agents organized and carried out in 1949 three coup d'états in Syria, through which the oil pipeline was supposed to pass."[44] "The struggle for oil is extremely fierce. Penetrating into the oil industry of the countries of the Middle East, the American and British imperialists will not hesitate to subjugate the largest oil regions in the world." The Soviet broadcaster reminded his listeners that in 1950, the profit of Standard Oil of California was more than $150 million, the profit of Texas Oil was $149 million, and the net profit of the Anglo-Iranian Oil Company reached £81 million. "The plunder of natural resources and the merciless exploitation of the working people of the countries of the Near and Middle East by the American-British imperialists caused ever greater indignation among the peoples of this part of the globe," leading to an upsurge of the anti-imperialist movement. As far as Radio Moscow was concerned, this was the reason that Iran nationalized its oil industry in 1951 and that the United States orchestrated Mossadeq's overthrow.

Long before the Soviet Union's empty promises of peace and support for national sovereignty came to the fore in Hungary in 1956, they became explicit for the United States in Iran in 1953. Since the early 1950s, the US government and its propaganda arms had concealed American oil interests behind the specter of the communist threat. Throughout 1951, they ran exposés on the rise in communist activity in Iran, arguing that this was preventing the United States from extending aid to the nation. They blamed communist agitators for popular riots against the Shah of Iran and for his eventual flight from the country. US politicians and propagandists justified the overthrow of Mossadeq as a necessary measure to mitigate the spread of communist ideology in the Middle East.

While the Mossadeq coup itself received almost no attention from the USIA, it framed the Shah's triumphal return as a manifestation of popular will and a referendum on socialism in Iran. On September 3, 1951, the VOA broadcast a reading of Eisenhower's congratulatory letter to the Shah: "I offer you my sincere felicitations on the occasion of your happy return to your country."[45] Audaciously, in the USIA publication of Eisenhower's message in the journal *U.S. News Review,* which ran in Arabic as "akhbar alwilayat almutahida," a full-page banner entitled "A Message for Free Men" was printed with the Eisenhower quote, "Only courage and sacrifice can keep freedom alive on the earth."

The outlawing of the socialist Tudeh Party after the Shah's return to power also became a subject for continued heroic narratives by the USIA. One VOA broadcast in the fall of 1954 told a breathtaking story of the Shah's catching and shutting down of a secret Tudeh printing press, complete with the discovery of a secret tunnel that communist revolutionaries had been accessing through a toilet.[46] The VOA announced that the Shah had "smashed a Communist spy network" within the Iranian armed forces and civil service. "A list of the spies, all of whom were members of the Tudeh Party, were found in the home of a former officer, all of whom were Iranian spies being paid by the Soviets, caught betraying their own country." When the Shah's executions of communists in 1954 and 1955 did not meet with more public approval in Iran, researchers at the USIA were surprised to learn that the executions had "caused shock and distaste rather than a feeling of satisfaction that justice had been done." This public display of shock and distaste was tinged, too, by "a widespread pity for the families of the condemned."[47] As the USIA admitted internally, there did not seem to be widespread anger at the Soviets among the general population after the Shah's return or a sense that the Russians had outstayed their welcome after the war.

For Radio Moscow, it was clear that this mass arrest was yet more evidence of American colonial meddling—all done to clean the government of Mossadeq's allies to ensure access to oil. The Soviet critique of the United States came in all shapes and sizes, from claiming that Iran was becoming an American colony, to holding the United States responsible for the Iranian famine of 1949, to stories about how the Shah had to check in to a hospital in Washington, D.C., because he ruined his health on prostitutes, to reports that the United States and Britain had bred locusts in their laboratories and turned them loose on the wheat fields of Iran in 1951.[48] Radio Moscow adamantly denied any Soviet connection to the Tudeh Party men who had been arrested and executed after the Shah's return, instead providing steady evidence that this arrest, the overthrow of Mossadeq, and the VOA's coverage of it were part of a "hostile conspiracy by Iran, being used as an excuse to cool relations with the Soviet Union." Soviet broadcasts argued that the entire affair was an "American plot" against patriotic, anti-colonial, and anti-fascist citizens, done for the purpose of seizing Iran's oil resources as a first step in the creation of "an aggressive Middle Eastern military bloc." In fact, many news outlets made note of the fact that the Shah's "discovery" of the spy ring happened just on the eve of parliamentary approval for the Iranian-American oil agreement. When the Iranian government executed the accused spies, only the Americans and the British held back from criticizing the killings. Everyone else could only ponder the implications of returning to a world where "political opposition is treated with bullets."[49]

Internally, many in the USIA worried that the Iranian coup had damaged America's reputation in the Middle East, especially given the poor reception it had unexpectedly received and the negative press coming from Radio Moscow. They were nonetheless comforted by the knowledge that overt, anti-American protest had stopped in Iran, even if this had been accomplished through violence and intimidation.[50] Fewer workers were striking, the USIA reported with relief, although internally it conceded that the corruption, low pay, late pay, mismanagement, and miserable working conditions were still there. The USIA was also pleased to learn that the nation's teachers, who had been a center for communist activity and support of Mossadeq, had gone silent, despite the continued low pay and low living standards. "Look," one USIA reaction report claimed, "at the number of people in Iran who have renounced their earlier allegiance to the Tudeh Party and have made oaths on the Koran that they will not engage in Communist activities!"[51] Some Iranians went so far as to advertise their renunciations in local newspapers. Anti-American language had stopped in the Iranian press, and Iranians seemed to appreciate the monetary gifts the United States was sending (even if they also believed that it was not enough). And yes, as the USIA noted, it did appear that the execution of the "Soviet spies" had acted "more than any other factor as a deterrent to Communist activity."[52]

By all accounts, the USIA took this silence as evidence of success and popular consensus building, not as proof of intimidation. It excitedly devised a new plan for propaganda to Iran, applying the same formula as in other parts of the Middle East. The staff lit upon the idea of developing a series of "Horatio Alger type stories about Iranians who were honest, industrious, started out with little, and made good." They also explored showing commonalities between American and Iranian workers, and the two nation's "fight against venality in public office." Thanks to the coup, they could now reopen their embassy library, which had been closed in 1952. The USIA also agreed to tell its English-language broadcasters to slow down their speech because they spoke so fast that English-speaking Iranians could not understand them.[53]

Amid the ongoing struggle to create popular consensus in Iran, the VOA also had to deal with its increasingly troubled relationship with Egypt. In the early 1950s, the USIA had maintained close ties with the Egyptian Broadcasting Service, even after the Egyptian revolution. The CIA had been instrumental in 1952 in setting up the Voice of the Arabs radio station as well as Egypt's intelligence and military services. In 1954 the director of the EBS, Yaya Abu Bakr, took a trip to the United States to see the USIA facilities. The USIA maintained the Cairo Packaging Center, which gave out material for the VOA and the Middle Eastern Stations that wanted to air its programs. The USIA estimated that it was giving the Egyptians more than half of their foreign-language material in 1954.[54]

This all changed when the relationship started to sour in the summer and fall of 1955, when the Egyptian-Czech arms deal happened, and Nasser gave diplomatic recognition to China. It was no coincidence that the USIA began sending its materials to Iraq, Jordan, Syria, Lebanon, and the Sudan just as the United States withdrew its offer to fund the Aswan Dam. Almost overnight, the VOA began to attack the Voice of the Arabs as a tool of militant Arab nationalism that was prey to communist influence. As one confidential source in Vienna at Radio Free Europe/Radio Liberty reported in November 1955, the "Soviets are using Egypt as a base for penetration, under the guise of developing 'cultural' relations into other parts of Africa. . . . The Soviet Embassy in CAIRO is said to have recently set up a central office, from which the activities of the Communist agents in Egypt, and especially in South Africa, Kenya, the Congo, and other European-controlled areas of Africa, are to be guided and closely monitored."[55] Two weeks later the same confidential contact reported to RFE/RL that small arms were being shipped from Bratislava to Egypt as "gravel."[56] When the new prime minister of Jordan, Samir al-Rifai, promised not to participate in the Baghdad Pact when he came to power in early 1956, the United States blamed the Voice of the Arabs for influencing him.[57]

By 1956 the USIA was listening to, and worrying about, how Radio Moscow talked about Arab nationalism. It took particularly careful notes on the occasions when the Soviets positioned Nasser as a leader who would redistribute the land and the wealth of Egypt while successfully fighting US and British imperialism. It sent internal memos when Radio Moscow claimed that Ben Gurion's "fascist" government in Israel was a stronghold of American imperialism and the "seed-bed for an anti-Soviet Russian block in the Middle East." It reeled at the reports that Radio Moscow was pitching the

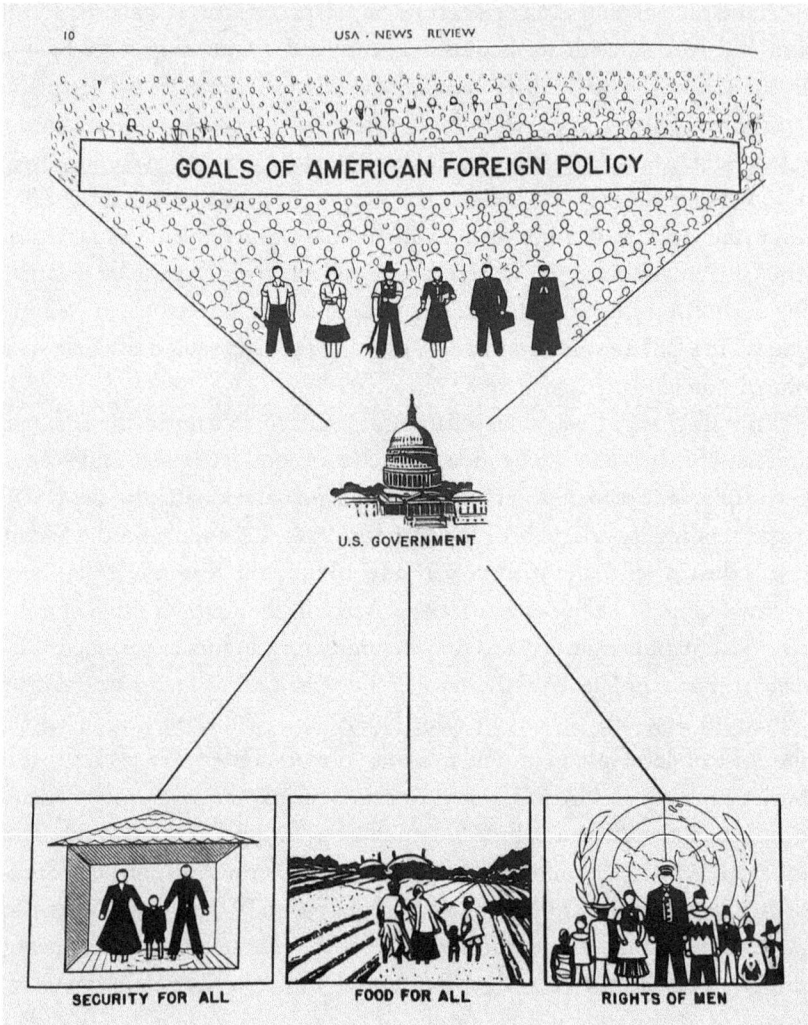

GOALS OF AMERICAN FOREIGN POLICY

U.S. GOVERNMENT

SECURITY FOR ALL   FOOD FOR ALL   RIGHTS OF MEN

FIGURE 9. The USIA presents a visual guide for understanding US foreign policy. *Source:* "Goals of American Foreign Policy," *[USA] News Review*, October 12, 1953, Records of the US Information Agency, Publications about the United States, 1953–1999, *USA News Review* (English/Arabic) 1951–1961, NARA, RG 306, entry 1053, box 502, folder 1952, 2 of 2.

Soviet sale of arms through the Eastern Bloc as an action "done in the interests of world peace . . . intended to break the British-American alliance."[58] Beginning in January 1956 and lasting until the end of the year, in a set of confidential RFE/RL memos that made their way back to the VOA (in a folder stamped "Read and Destroy"), the Americans worried deeply about radio reports that Poland was recruiting workers to construct a railway in Egypt (March 8), that Soviet technicians were heading to Egypt (April 21), that the Poles were sending jets to Egypt (May 29), that a new trade agreement between Romania and Egypt was being signed (July 12), that Czechoslovakia was the chief purchaser of raw materials from Egypt in the first quarter of 1956 (June 5), that the Soviets had sold two destroyers to Egypt (July 5), that the Poles were selling metal sheet boxcars to Egypt (August 7), that Soviet ships were sailing under Polish flags to Egypt (August 8), and that Polish pilots had been recruited to run the ships through the Suez Canal in Port Said (October 22).[59] According to one USIA report, the Soviet Union was "pressing ahead with an economic offensive unequalled since the Second World War," using economic aid to "find outlets for their goods" and to gain "political capital."[60]

As had been the case with the BBC, Sharq al-Adna, and even Radio Moscow, behind closed doors, workers at the USIA lamented their inability to sway the Arab mind through rational argumentation, believing that only through emotion could Arabs be brought to one side or the other.[61] As Eisenhower's special adviser for psychological warfare, C. D. Jackson, told the president, "All our speeches and proposals are made as if we are talking to Anglo-Saxons. They are based on reason with no emotion. The Arabs don't give a damn about that." He argued that the Arab people had convinced themselves that they were victims of a "nonexistent imperialism" as a result of their irrationality.[62]

On August 19, 1953, the USIA newspaper *U.S. News Review* published in English and Arabic an inspiring explanation of why America did what it did in the world. The full-page image bore the title "The Goals of American Foreign Policy." In the center sat the White House with three lines jutting from it leading to three pictures of a white family in a home, another white family looking out at its farm, and a group of people in varying national costumes standing before a background of a globe, lined in laurels. Beneath the three images were the words "Security for All," "Food for All," and "The Rights of Men." These were the promised intentions of American foreign policy. In the text below the images, the USIA assured its Middle Eastern readers that all Americans believed in the "dignity of the individual and his right to security and well being."

Here was the economy of the American gift on full display, presenting a vision of the worker as independent but also protected under the patronage of the US government. The presence of the world's population in the

"Rights of Man" drawing spoke to the power of American might in protecting its allies and subjects. The last sentence of the text declared that the American people wanted "these rights extended to everyone. When fully informed on the issues, the American people can be expected to act along these lines." Here was the justification for US involvement in the Middle East—an extension of human rights to people everywhere that sometimes required US intervention. Here, too, was an explanation for the lingering racism that still appeared in some of America's white populace, whose only problem was that they were ill-informed on the issues.

This piece was published on the same day that the coup in Iran occurred, hitting the stacks of USIA libraries and being accompanied by bulletins on the radio. It touted the US support for individual and national self-determination across the Middle East, all while the CIA was orchestrating the overthrow of Iran's democratically elected president.

Such were the contradictions reflected in the US information program. Like its peers, it was committed to the conveyance of a noble message that held the hearts and minds and fates of the world at stake. It sought to present a vision of a bright future, protected by American support and ideological fortitude. The information program faced two profound problems, however, in executing this mission. First, it was incapable of functioning outside of the shaping force of the Cold War. National self-determination *was* an ideal, but only insofar as it also met the global needs of the grand Cold War struggle. Second, it had already, by 1953, a puny vocabulary from which to choose its messaging. That language had already been defined by the British and the Soviet Union, who had molded the audiosphere around the mantras of peace, aid, and ideological dogma—all wrapped up in a language of brinksmanship that made compromise and legitimate connection between people increasingly difficult to cultivate. These were the same constraints that would eventually overwhelm Radio Cairo and the promise of secular pan-Arab nationalism.

SIX

Britain's Struggle for Air

THE SOUNDS OF A DWINDLING EMPIRE

THE BRITISH PROJECT in the Middle East failed in the 1950s because it could not see past its Cold War and postcolonial-colored glasses to the real problems being experienced by populations on the ground.[1] How did the British language and propaganda fit into the larger puzzle of the Middle Eastern audiosphere? On the one hand, there was a direct line from the efforts of the BBC, Sharq al-Adna, and the PBS in the 1940s to the explosion of messaging that came from British broadcasters in the 1950s. Much of the language of the late 1940s persisted into this new era, from the belief that "expert opinion" would sway listening populations to the conviction that Arab peoples would follow the Union Jack if they understood the generous gifts on offer from their former colonial benefactor. On the other hand, much of what British broadcasters put out over the airwaves was defined and limited by the linguistic regimes that swirled around them in these years. As for their peers, peace and the economy of the gift became cultural capital to be wielded in war. More than any of the other broadcasting services, British radio in the Middle East in the 1950s was dominated by the intermingled dangers of communism and Arab nationalism. What started in the early 1950s as a full assault on Soviet influence in the region by 1955 had become an attack on Nasser and the Voice of the Arabs. These two hazards were not mutually exclusive, each seeming likely to exacerbate the other and both a clear threat to British sovereignty.

The consequence of this was that the Cold War became inextricably wound up in the British (and Soviet and American) approach to Nasserism and his version of pan-Arab nationalism. The varying British stations seemingly combined Radio Moscow and Radio Cairo into one enemy whose dangerous message threatened to seduce populations into a specifically Soviet version of Arab nationalism. British broadcasters were frequently unable to disaggregate communist anti-Westernism from nationalist anti-Westernism. Thus, in 1953 the Foreign Office argued that "communism, neutralism, nationalism, and peace are working in closer alliances."[2] And again in 1954, it declared that "bitterness over Palestine and general "anti-Imperialist," and anti-Western emotional prejudices among "sensitive Arab nationalists" were being constantly exploited by communist propaganda. Whether the British broadcasters recognized it or not, their messaging and language was often dictated by the arguments set forth by their perceived enemies. Seldom were they able to set the terms of debate.

· · ·

The British radio service in the Middle East in the 1950s was formidable. At any point of the day or night, an English-sponsored station could be found playing music, news, children's programs, readings of the Koran, and special interest stories delivered in multiple Arabic dialects. Numerous organizations, all of them connected in varying degrees to Her Majesty's government, operated offices in Britain, Cyprus, and the many legations across the region. At its cornerstone sat the newly formed Information Research Department (IRD) and the BBC. The IRD had been created by the British Foreign Office in 1948. It was formed, according to James Vaughan, "to prosecute a vigorous set of anti-Communist and anti-Soviet Cold War propaganda campaigns."[3] It was financed with the same discretionary funds as MI5 and MI6.

The IRD, in turn, financed and provided material to the NEABS, better known as Sharq al-Adna, with a staff of seventy people. Sharq broadcasted from its four shortwave transmitters in Limasol, Cyprus, and then from a medium-wave transmitter that went on the air in 1952. Sharq was one of the most popular stations in the Middle East and North Africa. It played great music, sprinkled with news and entertainment programs. In 1954 it moved into commercial broadcasting in order to generate additional operating funds and attract listeners.[4] Sharq made every effort to appear as though it was a legitimate, Arab radio station, although it was common knowledge among people in the radio business that the station received support from Whitehall.[5] Sharq periodically caused significant consternation for the Foreign Office, as it often suppressed pro-British commentary to keep up the ruse.[6] In late 1955 Sharq ran programs about the French desecration of mosques and even about the rediscovery of the "Protocols of the Elders of Zion."[7] On the few occasions when the station did express some open support for British policies or the Baghdad Pact, its director had to spend a week in Cairo apologizing to Egyptian officials in order to avoid losing his Arab broadcasting personalities, who threatened to walk out.[8]

Further up the dial on the short and medium waves was the BBC, which was not covert, and which expanded exponentially in the 1950s to meet increasing demand, even when it didn't have the staff. In 1950 the BBC had a staff of nineteen and was producing 19.25 hours of Arabic material weekly. By 1954 it was broadcasting 28 hours weekly with a staff of sixteen, with the added pressure to produce more creative features that could compete with the other stations. In 1955 the number of people listening in their cars grew large enough to merit traffic reports in the big cities.[9] The BBC struggled mightily in these years to walk the tightrope between offering objective news and supporting British foreign interests. Often broadcasters found themselves in the unenviable position of seeming too beholden to the Foreign Office for the liking of listeners and too independent for the liking of the Foreign Office.

The British radio world took the communist threat seriously. As Ralph Stevenson, a director at the British Middle East Office, put it, "If the depressed masses in the Middle East once get the idea that they have a choice for the betterment of their lot between immediate communism and success 'in the long run' with Britain, they might be tempted to choose the former."[10] The Russians would, in the words of one official, use "any organization, whatever its ideology, if it will serve their own ends of creating national or international disorder," their aim being to "create conditions in which Communist terrorism can gain control."[11] In July 1953 Lord Drogheda gave his now famous report to the Cabinet Committee on Information Services on the state of British broadcasting. The report suggested increased funding for broadcasting, instead of the cuts that the committee and the House of Commons had expected, especially for the developing world. "A great war is being fought in the air," the report declared.[12] "Unless more is done to counter this propaganda and expose the hypocrisy of the Communist position," the Foreign Office replied, "there is a danger of the Western case going by default."[13]

As numerous scholars have noted, the IRD represented one of the primary ways that the British thought they could stand against the Soviet Union in the nuclear age.[14] They set out to portray Moscow not as a champion of peace but as an imperial aggressor. They would attack the notion of neutralism as a Soviet strategy intended to distract the Arab world from recognizing the "real" Soviet enemy. Over the next seven years, the IRD produced a full complement of anti-communist radio programs.[15] Nightly talks featured a distinguished author or lecturer offering an analysis of a communist doctrine. This could include refutations of Marxism (which, by this point, Radio Moscow was no longer talking about), discussions of the communist desire to dissolve the family (also something Radio Moscow denied), or the incompatibility of communism with religion and the ownership of property (Radio Moscow also refuted this, as we have seen). The speakers were an illustrious bunch, including famous Egyptian philosophers and poets like Abbas Mahmoud El Akkad and Ibrahim Abdel Kader El Mazni; the once presumptive heir to the Egyptian throne, Mohammed Ali Tewfik; and the journalist Fekry Abaza.[16] The IRD brought in experts who would affirm the current status quo in the Middle East and the dangers of communism to Islam. This included a lesson from Sheikh Abdel Rahman Hassan on how "the teachings of the Koran uphold the current social system" and another from Sheikh Abdel Wahab Khallaf Bey, "Islamic Legislation Refutes the Pretenses of Communism." Other talks included "Communism and the Dissemination of Immorality and Nihilistic Ideas" and "Communism Saps the Foundations of Society."[17]

History lessons played a central role in these talks, with discussions of how Islamic history provided a better path to social equity and the "presentation of historical evidence that Communism limits individual effort, is based on Despotism, is a return to the savage state, and is contrary to positive laws." The IRD eventually developed an entire program that offered a historical survey of "the traces of Communism in the unsettled state of world politics."[18] It did the same with a show on the economic destruction wrought by communism and an additional morning talk show that dealt with issues of religion and communism. The IRD produced stories intended to "train" listeners to recognize and resist the appeal of local communist parties that focused on "radical anti-imperialism and land reform."[19] Echoing this, the BBC aired regular stories on the dangers of land redistribution in the Arab world, summoning Arab scholars from universities in Britain, Syria, and Sudan to attest to the dangers of communism in agriculture.[20]

The IRD also launched a full radio drama program featuring plays based on stories from Viktor Kravchenko's bestselling book *I Chose Freedom*. Published in 1947, the book told the story of a Soviet defector who witnessed the horrors of the Ukrainian famine and the Stalinist Terror. Testimonials like Kravchenko's marked the emergence of a literary genre in the 1950s, defined by the publication of confessional autobiographies by former communists who had since seen the error of their ways.[21] These testimonials became necessary acts of contrition for ex-communists who sought reentry into American and British public politics and culture during the height of the Red Scare. They also provided seemingly firsthand evidence of Soviet perfidy. The IRD did not just translate the book; it launched a full program of original dramatic plays based on the "spirit of Kravchenko," written by some of the era's most famous playwrights. It sent copies of the book to the famous authors Mahmoud Teymour Bey and Mahmoud Kamel, tasking them to tell stories like Kravchenko's but with Arab protagonists. One tale told the story of a young Uzbek man who managed to escape a workers' camp and religious persecution by escaping to Iraq, but whose heart was broken because he had to leave his mother behind. The similarities to the Soviet story of the proud Uzbek mother, Risolet, which aired one year later, are difficult to ignore, as though this were one of her sons, living in a different reality than the one described by Radio Moscow. The BBC adopted a gargantuan Kravchenko program involving over ninety-three guest lecturers, writers, and composers. Every participant received a free copy of *I Chose Freedom* to use as inspiration for their work.[22] The BBC recruited popular songwriters to write a new "anti-communist song" each week and even roped in five comedians to produce "humorous, anti-communist monologues" for the light entertainment portions of its programs. Six months later the British Information Legation printed a cheap copy of Kravchenko's book for mass distribution.[23] Just as *I Chose Freedom* hit the press, the USIA broadcasted a full reading of the book in Arabic translation.[24] In the wake of Kravchenko's famous victory in his libel suit against a French newspaper (the paper had claimed he was too ignorant to have written the book), the autobiography became a hot commodity around the globe. Well into the 1950s, the various legations of the British Information Services continued to offer the book in their libraries.

And this was just one of many such books that made their way over the air and into the libraries of the British and America legations. Famously, George Orwell contributed on his deathbed to the IRD by recommending his favorite authors to be tapped for further anti-communist publications (and by secretly sharing notebooks filled with the names of suspected communists whom he believed should not be trusted by the IRD or the BBC). For a man who had once been a beacon for bringing awareness to the world of the plight of the poor, this was, in the words of one critic, "a shabby end to a crowded life."[25] As with the work of Kravchenko and many of the other authors that found airtime through the IRD, what mattered most was that the stories be "short, lurid, and pungent . . . dramatized and overdrawn."[26] The IRD, like Orwell, was convinced that such tactics would "ensure wider currency, stronger credibility, and greater efficiency," particularly in comparison to the "heavy-handed" Americans.[27]

The IRD's assault on communism matched Radio Moscow's messaging note for note. While Radio Moscow ran stories on May Day celebrations about the happiness of Soviet workers, Sharq al-Adna ran messages that same day expressing sympathy and solidarity for workers behind the Iron Curtain (directed ostensibly at Soviet workers, they were nonetheless in Arabic). When Radio Moscow aired interviews with African students studying in Moscow, Sharq aired interviews with African students condemning racist communist youth organizations in the Soviet Union, levying accusations of Soviet racism against Muslim students in Moscow and Leningrad. Each week Sharq listed the latest corrections that had been issued by the Soviet government to the *Soviet Encyclopedia* (which had become infamous in the West for wiping from the historical record important people who had been purged by Stalin, like Nikolai Bukharin and Nikolai Vavilov). One program, *Communist Words Contradict Facts*, existed for the sole purpose of exposing Soviet fallacies. To bolster this, Sharq ran investigative stories on the propaganda techniques used by the Soviet Union on domestic and foreign audiences. "They offer choice, force choice, then reinforce choice," one commentator claimed in a story entitled "Propaganda Textbooks for Armenians." Ironically, this was a standard phrase used in the IRD to describe how British propaganda tactics should operate and was a staple of the classic "black and white fallacy" used by all modern propagandists.[28] To counter the Soviet claims of women finding a happier life under Soviet protection, Sharq ran exposés on "overworked Russian mothers" and the general exploitation of women.[29] Regular stories also aired on Russian religious persecution, Soviet and Chinese imperialism, how no one in Russia could afford to go on holiday, and the low industrial output of Eastern Europe. Internal memos repeated the demand that more broadcasts be aired on "facts about life in the Soviet Union."[30]

The British also ran stories on the combined mediocrity and danger of the Soviet military. In 1953 the BBC aired two concurrent stories, "No Relaxation of Defense" and "Glimpse at the Soviet Navy," in which it noted that the new Soviet heavy cruiser, the *Sverdlov*, looked surprisingly like a German ship from 1940, with "little originality in her design."[31] Borrowing from the language of Radio Moscow, the narrator went on to describe the "warmongering and expansionism" that seemed to characterize the Soviet program in the Middle East. "To ask whether we may not relax our defense efforts is just as reasonable as to ask wither the first fine day does not offer the occasion for giving away our raincoats and umbrellas," the narrator scoffed.[32] They then turned to the next story, "Britain Building Most Ships," describing how Britain had 323 ships under construction, retaining its status as the ruler of the waves.[33] All of this language matched what was being said over Radio Moscow, accusing the East of warmongering and equating Western militarization with the preservation and defense of peace.

Implicit in the British propaganda program was the belief by the 1950s that communism had to be stopped, not just because it enslaved populations behind the Iron Curtain, but because it promoted pan-Arab nationalism as part of its larger plan to dominate the Middle East. Soviet propaganda was offering a powerful message, the British argued, that contributed to the growing tensions between "extreme Arab nationalism and the Western Powers, with Egypt as the prime target" of Soviet propaganda.[34] Arab independence—a movement rooted in a desire for self-determination and reform—created chaos that communists could use to generate a Moscow-led revolution. Broadcasters argued internally and on the air that Nasser was merely a Soviet puppet and that Arab nationalism was just a manifestation of communist chicanery.

Such duplicity seemed most evident in the "Big Lie" of the Soviet peace offensive, which was also tied inextricably in the eyes of the British Foreign Office to the rise of Arab nationalism and anti-colonialism. "Does Russia really want peace?," Sharq al-Adna asked over the air, arguing that the Soviet Union could not make claims to peace as long as it occupied Eastern Europe and kept the world under the threat of nuclear attack.[35] Perhaps not surprisingly, the British response to the Soviet Union's seeming simulacrum of peace was to do exactly as the Soviets had done. They levied constant warnings not to believe in the Soviet messages of peace and anti-imperialism, which were too good to be true and only concealed the Soviet Union's more nefarious designs.[36]

This belief in the dangerous connection between Arab nationalism and Soviet communism was manifested in the BBC's meticulous monitoring of the relationship between Cairo and Moscow. The BBC included in every report that it issued on the state of Arab broadcasting a section entitled "Relations with the Communist Bloc," which covered any broadcast having anything to do with the Arab world and its relations with Eastern Europe. When the Moscow dance troupe Berezka visited Lebanon, the BBC monitors recorded it. When a member of the Polish Lenin iron and steel combine visited Iraq to submit tenders for the building of a bridge over the Euphrates, the BBC reported internally on it. When the Romanian ambassador presented his credentials to the president of Turkey, the BBC recorded it.[37] When the United States pulled out of the promise to help fund the Aswan Dam, the BBC recorded that Voice of the Arabs had declared the Soviets as the great helpers who were willing to give aid. The BBC took note when Radio Cairo told its listeners that Soviet Muslim veterans of the Second World War had been called upon to form a volunteer combat brigade that would be in readiness in the event of a conflict between the Arab countries and Israel. And later, the BBC kept a transcript of a radio broadcast out of Syria telling its listeners that the USSR had offered the Arab governments "arms and unconditional aid."[38]

Britain's official stand against the communist and Nasserist threats came in 1955 with the creation of the Baghdad Pact. Organized explicitly to prevent Soviet expansion into the Middle East and to provide a counterweight to Nasser's rising star, it brought together Iran, Iraq, Pakistan, Turkey, and the United Kingdom in a loosely bound defensive alliance (with great hopes that Jordan would soon join). As ordered, all of the British broadcasting programs, overt and otherwise, worked to promote the pact—a bulwark against rising Egyptian pan-Arab nationalism, a counter to Soviet communist expansion in the Middle East, and a vestigial remnant of British imperial power.

The British broadcasters promoted a vision of the Baghdad Pact as an alliance that would offer the kind of development and modernization that only the West could provide. Such was the promise of British care meant to counter the promises being made in Moscow, Cairo, and even the United States. Stories attested to the educational programs being founded in the Iraqi countryside through British support. The British aired programs on British-founded factories employing thousands of workers who enjoyed decent working conditions and a living wage. They ran stories with titles like "Britain Spends 70 Millions for Colonies," "Development and Welfare," "Medical and Health Services," and "Water Supplies, Agriculture, Roads and Civil Aviation."[39] Gripping titles, all. Sharq aired stories on the Owen Falls Dam in Uganda, the Central Development Board in Iraq, various medical programs, the UNRWA, and the seven-year plan in Iran. One memorable broadcast asked hypothetically, "What does the British Government gain from all this apparent free service? It is due in large measure to the British Government's belief that highly developed countries have a moral duty to extend help to less advanced areas."[40] A steady stream of broadcasts accompanied the General Electric Company's lighting of the Grand Mosque in Mecca with fluorescent lights in 1953 (the theme of light was used by all). The task was all the more impressive given that British engineers had designed the lighting based solely on pictures, schematics, and pilgrim's maps, since they were not Muslim and not allowed to travel to the mosque in person.[41] There were stories about British scientists who were preparing to photograph the sun at eighty-thousand feet, held aloft in the sky by a giant plastic balloon.[42] The stories spoke of British experts in agriculture, forestry, soil conservation, animal husbandry, cooperatives, land tenure, statistics, health, locust mitigation, and labor—all working inside the Baghdad Pact to makes people's lives better.[43] The BBC also gave sizeable attention to the creation of "cultural ties," leaning on the metaphor of a relationship, like a tapestry, simply needing mending in order to be of use again.[44] Whether it was the six hundred Middle Eastern visitors at the British Industries Fair in Birmingham or the Moslem Festival in Cardiff, with its green and white banners fluttering in the streets, the vision of a tightly connected Britain and Middle East was there to make the Baghdad Pact feel almost like a comfortable part of the Commonwealth.[45]

Behind closed doors, the Foreign Office, the BBC, the VOA, and their allies in Iraq, Saudi Arabia, and Lebanon knew that they were at a disadvantage when it came to selling the Baghdad Pact to Arab listeners. The British embassies complained that the propaganda materials being sent to them by the IRD were "dull," with few Arab listeners interested in "whether people behind the Iron Curtain enjoy good or bad living conditions."[46] They got this feedback directly from listeners as well. As one listener wrote to the BBC, "I make allowances for your attacks on Egypt, Syria, Saudi Arabia . . . because you of imperialist Britain still believe that the Arabs understand nothing and are like ostriches ready to follow you wherever you pull them. The Baghdad Pact is known to be a purely imperialist device and was not intended to combat communism in the Middle East. Anyway, the Arabs are not so much interested in that as in saving their Palestinian brothers."[47] Broadcasters on the ground admitted that most listeners "had not the slightest idea what the Baghdad Pact was for, how it had come about and what advantages Jordan might get from joining."[48] The BBC frequently wrote in its internal memos that its news items dealing with the Pact "provoked hostile comments in 'Voice of the Arabs' transmissions."[49]

At the same time, the BBC held on, like much of Her Majesty's government, to the idea that the Egyptian people continued to support and believe in the English mission in the Middle East. As one report declared, "Despite superficial political quarrels, there does seem to exist between the Brit and the Arab a peculiar sympathy which facilitates understanding on both sides."[50] When Egyptian radio attacked the BBC for its support of the British government's decision to suspend shipment of tanks to Egypt following the Egyptian request that Britain withdraw from the Suez, the BBC's representatives confidently wrote back to the home office that these attacks had come not from "real" Egyptians, but from disaffected Arabs abroad. "They are more likely to originate in London than in this country," John Whitehead, the BBC's director in the Middle East, wrote to his superiors.[51]

By 1955 the BBC, the VOA, and a number of British and American diplomats and politicians had come to see Radio Cairo as a major barrier standing in the way of the Baghdad Pact's policies in the Middle East.[52] The BBC Monitors and the CIA called Ahmed Said "The Sphinx" in their transcripts of Voice of the Arabs broadcasts.[53] The CIA worried in typical fashion that Voice of the Arabs had achieved the effect of hypnosis upon its listeners.[54] The French blamed Voice of the Arabs for the rise in anti-colonial violence in Algeria, Tunisia, and Morocco and for the widespread protests against their continued imprisonment of Front de Libération Nationale (FLN) freedom fighters. The British and French also held the Voice of the Arabs responsible for Swahili broadcasts supporting anti-colonialist efforts in Somaliland. These broadcasts reached as far as Zanzibar and Pemba, both British protectorates, as well as Kenya, Uganda, and Tanganyika, and even, occasionally, to the Portuguese colony of Angola. They noted with chagrin that Voice of the Arabs broadcast programs to Mau Mau activists in Kenya opposing white rule.[55]

Tracing the effects of radio campaigns is like tracing the erosion of a stream against rock; the change, if it happens at all, is imperceptible at any one point. If there was any moment when the impact of radio was visible, it was in the fight over Jordanian membership in the Baghdad Pact that unfolded in the months before the Suez Crisis. The British, French, Iraqi, and Jordanian governments all blamed Radio Cairo for the spontaneous riots that broke out across Jordan, in 1955 when news hit that Jordanian premier Samir el Rifai was considering joining the Baghdad Pact. The famous *New York Times* reporter Osgood Carruthers argued in these heady days that Voice of the Arabs was responsible for spreading anti-Western messages to small towns across Jordan that had little physical access to the outside world. People heard of the riots in Amman over the radio and followed suit.[56] They might not have been able to read or have had access to newspapers, but it only took one radio for everyone to hear the news.

Then in early 1956, General John Glubb, who was the British envoy in Jordan, was forced to leave the country by Jordanian king Hussein bin Talal after being accused of trying to take over the Jordanian government and for generally behaving like an imperious bully. Glubb was known for his public expositions on the childishness and immaturity of "the Arabs," who, in his words, showed "all the instability and emotionalism of the adolescent. . . . Like children they will sometimes be rude, and sometimes plunged in despair and self-deprecation. Like big schoolboys they glory in their new freedom."[57] The story promoted in British circles was that Egyptian propaganda against Glubb was ultimately responsible for convincing Hussein to fire the British emissary.

In response to these accusations, Ahmed Said (who knew that Sharq al-Adna was British run) declared that he was proud that his condemnations of Glubb had gotten the man expelled.[58] When Sharq blamed Glubb's dismissal at least in part on the Egyptians and their encouragement of the riots, Said replied by calling Sharq al-Adna a "dangerous imperialist agitator."[59] Said declared in March that Britain's outcry against Voice of the Arabs was "the roar of a decrepit giant who hopes to recover some of the prestige which he lost by oppression and brutality during the period of his youth and power."[60] Three days later, Said explicitly tied Glubb to the Palestinian tragedy: "[Glubb] directed with his own hand the poisonous dagger with which the imperialists stabbed Palestine, rendering its people homeless." And the next day he said, "the Arabs refuse to take filthy hands, hands stained with our blood, hands which killed and continue to kill our sons, hands which worked and continue to work to immortalize colonialism. . . . Glubb is the one who organizes plots against the Arabs. Glubb is the one who imposes fines on you. . . . It is a question of your freedom and your unity." And again, the day after that, he said, "[Glubb] is the little god who sends some people to their deaths and resurrects others."[61]

Glubb himself certainly was convinced that Egyptian propaganda had been responsible for his ouster. He wrote in March, "Britain is being driven from the Middle East by words—words to which with British impassivity she refuses to reply."[62] After he left Jordan, he threw whatever weight he still had into the cause of British information political warfare, writing increasingly concerned letters to members of Parliament about the Egyptian propaganda threat.[63] Years later Glubb said that he believed his dismissal was "entirely due to Egyptian propaganda."[64] The question of whether or not Egyptian propaganda was actually responsible for Glubb's firing remains a point of debate to this day.[65] He certainly provided the ammunition that Voice of the Arabs needed to call for his discharge. It may have been partially accurate to lay blame for Glubb's expulsion and the failure of the British project in Jordan at the feet of Egypt, but it was also very convenient for the British broadcasters who sought a narrative that would absolve Her Majesty's government of responsibility.

Convenient, too, was the communist threat as an explanatory cause for failing British preeminence in the Middle East. By 1956 Nasser and his relationship with the Soviet Union had become the scapegoat for understanding the decline in British influence.[66] It was Nasser, the *Daily Mail* and subsequently the IRD argued, who kept ex-Nazi propagandists on staff, flirted with communists, and exploited the mantra of peace and national sovereignty to accumulate personal power.[67] This scenario supported a whole series of larger beliefs about the Middle East that were rooted in older colonial thinking—such that imperialist and racist views on the Middle East and the ideological underpinnings of the Cold War became complementary beliefs.

Indeed, when Radio Cairo, Egypt, and the Cold War failed to work as foils for the failures of the British broadcasting program, there was always racism to help explain away the rise of Arab nationalism and the lack of popular consensus. On the issue of Arab nationalism, for instance, the IRD argued that there was a distinction between the kind of nationalism that sought to promote the interests of the Middle East peoples and extreme nationalism, "which is blinded by the Arab's emotional and anachronistic obsession with 'Western imperialism.'" And in any case, the "ill-organized and dissension-ridden" nationalists, having "whistled up the wind," would not be able to ride the "whirlwind of social revolution," which would eventually enable the communists to seize power.[68] This was a particular crisis in Egypt, the IRD believed, where, again, "the emotional obsession with 'Western imperialism'" brought the country to a state of chaos, with the Wafd and the Muslim Brotherhood "seeking Soviet support."[69] Nowhere in its assessments of Arab animosities did the IRD acknowledge the radicalizing damage done by the Arab-Israeli dispute.[70] The IRD distributed this memo in early July 1952, two weeks before the Egyptian revolution. Sadly, this created a situation in which, for the next two decades, conversations about national self-determination, the tragedy of colonialism, and even peace would be problematic for the West. When, eventually, the Western countries realized that they had to engage in these conversations if they hoped to gain credibility among their audiences, too much time and violence had passed for them to be believed. As Gordon Waterfield wrote in 1953, it was exceedingly difficult to present "logical and rational arguments to peoples . . . who are, for a great part of the time, in a high state of emotion."[71] Similarly, Chapman Andrews, the ambassador to Beirut, claimed that they were handicapped by the fact that they were "dealing with people who for the most part are incapable of appreciating close argumentation. Logic never convinces the Oriental. It's hearts not heads we need to win out here."[72] This was typical of the thinking prevalent among Western propagandists and diplomats operating in the Middle East in the 1950s.[73] When the Egyptian government began to press hard in the early 1950s for British withdrawal from the Suez Canal, the standard British response (both in state media and in the BBC) was that the Egyptians were not able to handle such a large responsibility. They argued that the Egyptian "slave mentality" rendered Egyptians incapable of running a modern state.[74] They even went so far as to argue over the air in 1950 that the Egyptians were being uncivilized and rude by asking the British to leave the canal while Whitehall was busy managing the crisis of the Korean War.[75]

· · ·

It is clear that the broadcasters were listening to each other, and any movement from one affected the functioning of the others.[76] Take, for example, the topic of the Soviet Union's training of Arab soldiers. On April 5, 1956, Radio Damascus described to its listeners how the Soviets were providing special training to Egyptian officers in Czechoslovakia.[77] At the time it was rumored that the Czechs and the Soviets were negotiating to sell upward of $250 million in arms to the Egyptians, based at least in part on the argument that the sale would provide equilibrium against the US sale of arms to Israel. Suddenly the Soviet training of Egyptian officers became a feature on every other radio station. The next day Radio Moscow broadcast a story entitled, "About the Life in the USSR of the Repatriated Armies of Syria and Egypt," in which it argued that the training of Arab soldiers in the Soviet Union and

Czechoslovakia represented a clear and consistent commitment to the ending of colonial tyranny.[78] That night the transcripts of Radio Damascus and Radio Moscow made their way through the channels of the BBC broadcast monitoring service and into the hands of the IRD. The next morning Sharq al-Adna carried a story chronicling how British Royal Air Force experts were training Jordanian pilots.[79] This was less than one month after King Hussein had expelled Glubb.[80] Kol Israel then reported on April 18 that the Soviet Union was orchestrating a "one-sided training of the Arab states for war" and was failing to restore "equilibrium between Israel and her neighbors."[81] Ahmed Said then responded to the British broadcasts in his classic style, asking his listeners to "imagine, O Arabs, a world where British officers are justified in receiving the best training, but Egyptian officers are forbidden!"

Over time, each of the broadcasting services found itself needing to escalate its outrage toward the others for their seemingly open disregard for common decency. The British and American monitoring services created a feedback loop, in which what they recorded became a catalyst for the decisions they made in their own broadcasting, which led to particular responses from the Arab press, which they recorded, and so forth. They paid attention to what they wanted or expected to hear, whether good or bad, and then crafted their broadcasts in response. The Arab broadcasting companies then wrote their reports at least in part in response to Sharq al-Adna and VOA. In the end, they heard exactly what they expected to hear, finding confirmation for their own arguments and justifications for their responses and policies. The same tropes appeared again and again on each station, each arguing for its own honest intentions, each providing a clear set of enemies, made venal by their willingness to exploit for their own gain the noble impulses of postcolonial populations for peace and national independence. These attestations of peace and accusations of falsity created profound contradictions as they resounded through the echo chamber of the audiosphere. Perhaps one side was lying. Perhaps everyone was.

SEVEN

The Eleventh Hour

THE AUDIOSPHERE PREPARES FOR WAR

THE PERIOD BETWEEN 1956 AND 1967 marked the first major clash of international broadcasting in the Middle East. It was the task of the British propagandists to orchestrate acceptance of Britain's claim over the Suez Canal, a planned coup in Syria, and Britain's continued presence in Aden, all while warding off the communist threat coming from Radio Moscow. American broadcasters had the job of establishing Arab approval for the United States and the Eisenhower Doctrine amid Soviet accusations of collusion and warmongering, all while mollifying angry Arab populations who protested the military interventions and assassinations that President Eisenhower authorized as a part of his doctrine. Further up the dial, Radio Moscow took on the mission of shifting the Soviet message to adapt to the rise of Arab nationalism and nonalignment. Meanwhile, Radio Cairo set out to develop a language of outrage and injury, of victory and unity, that would establish Egypt and Nasser as the leader of the Arab world.

All of the broadcasting services approached these tasks with the rhetorical tools that they had been developing since the 1940s. They would pitch the mantra of peace, the narrative of soft development and self-determination, and the message of threat. They would conjure images of endangered and mobilized youth, of enemies as dogs, of heroic martyrs committed to liberty and the ever-present promise of light and peace.

But it was difficult to sell the promise of peace at the point of a gun, challenging to pitch the commitment to liberty amid mass arrests and orchestrated coups. For millions of Arabs, the collapse of Western promises became unavoidable in 1956. By 1967 that collapse had come home, encompassing all of the radio services that found themselves relying on language that fewer and fewer people spoke any longer, making promises that were increasingly difficult to believe.

The story of the Suez Crisis is well known. By the summer of 1956, Whitehall, Paris, Washington, and Jerusalem were all angry with Nasser. Britain's prime minister, Anthony Eden, blamed Nasser and his propaganda machine for the mass anti-British riots in Jordan earlier that year.[1] He was furious at Nasser's public claim that the Baghdad Pact represented a new kind of "veiled colonialism." He was angry at Nasser's decision to sign an arms deal with Czechoslovakia and accept a Soviet loan, signed in June, that would finance the construction of the Aswan High Dam.[2] France's prime minister, Guy Mollet, was livid at Nasser's support for the Front de Libération Nationale (FLN) in Algeria. The Israelis, led by Prime Minister David Ben-Gurion, were furious at the closure of the Straits of Tiran and the Suez Canal to their shipping. The CIA, which was busy planning a coup in Syria—a plan that would be delayed by the Suez Crisis but not canceled—had also concluded it could no longer work with Nasser. President Eisenhower and Secretary of State John Foster Dulles were dismayed to see Nasser turning to the Soviets after the US withdrawal of aid. Everyone except the Americans was willing, in Eden's words, "to use force to bring Nasser to his senses."[3]

For his part, Nasser was also furious. He railed against the British for supporting the Baghdad Pact. He was livid at the French for selling arms to the Israelis and their insistence on staying in Algeria. He was incensed at Israel for its persecution of Palestinians.[4] He was angry at the United States for backing out of its promise to finance the Aswan Dam, for its support of the Baghdad Pact, its refusal to sell arms, its threat to dump surplus cotton on the world market, its equivocation over the fate of Algeria, its affinity for Israel, and its perceived efforts to prevent the unification of Sudan and Egypt.[5]

And so, at the end of July 1956 Nasser announced that Egypt would be nationalizing the British-owned Suez Canal Company. He demanded that the British withdraw from the region and declared that Egyptians would now be responsible for piloting the nearly fifteen thousand ships that passed through the canal every year.[6] Overnight, the British-owned Suez Canal Company saw its assets frozen. The Soviet Union sent engineers and pilots to train Egyptian technicians in the running of the canal. Over the next few months, Anthony Eden's government argued that the nationalization of the canal represented a direct threat to British interests. A conference of maritime countries who used the canal met in London that August, followed by a visit of international representatives to Cairo in September. For

Eisenhower and Dulles, these meetings, and the months of working through diplomatic channels that followed, represented a desperate effort to find a peaceful solution. As Dulles insisted, "We do not intend to shoot our way through the canal."[7] For the British, French, and Israelis, however, the use of force was always an option. The conferences, which were unsuccessful, provided a useful delay while Eden, Mollet, and Ben-Gurion weighed their options and prepared for invasion. On October 22–24 they secretly signed the Sévres Protocol, agreeing that in five days' time the Israelis would invade the Sinai. Britain and France would then step in as a peacekeeping force and order both sides to withdraw from the canal. Egypt would lose control of the canal, Israel would regain shipping access, and Britain and France would come out of the situation looking like peacekeepers.

The war itself was quick and brutal. Israel invaded on October 29, moving across the Sinai Peninsula, taking the Gaza Strip, and occupying Sharm el-Sheikh by November 5. The Israelis and the British used napalm against Egyptian soldiers to wreak havoc and encourage surrender, while the Israeli Defense Force was responsible for the massacre of an estimated 275 refugees and residents in Khan Yunis.[8] At the same time, the British and French began their bombing campaigns. Nasser mobilized the Egyptian army and closed all shipping through the canal. As the Royal Marines came ashore at Port Said on November 6 and French paratroopers dropped near Port Faud, Nasser declared the crisis a "people's war." Egyptian soldiers would now dress as civilians, becoming guerrilla fighters, forcing the British, French, and Israelis to fire on people in plain clothes with the high likelihood that they would kill noncombatants. Egyptian vans equipped with loudspeakers roamed the streets, informing listeners that the Soviet Union had bombed Britain and that World War III had begun.[9]

The British, French, and Israelis may have been winning on the battlefield, but they were losing terribly in the court of international public opinion. As soon as the war began, mass public protests broke out across Britain. The Soviet invasion of Hungary had occurred a week earlier, and the parallels between the Soviet and Western use of force to retain colonial power were unmistakable. Britain's allies levied strong criticisms at Whitehall, while hundreds of thousands of people from Pakistan to Syria to Saudi Arabia rallied in support of Egypt. On November 2 Eisenhower, Khrushchev, and Jawaharlal Nehru uncharacteristically found common cause in their renunciation of the British, French, and Israeli invasions, resulting in the Soviet Union and the United States voting together on the floor of the United

Nations to demand an immediate ceasefire, the withdrawal of all forces, and the reopening of the canal. For his part, Eisenhower used the International Monetary Fund to deny Britain needed loans and threatened to sell part of US sterling bond holdings to devalue the British pound. Meanwhile, Khrushchev and the Soviet premier, Nikolai Bulganin, threatened to send troops to aid the Egyptian army. Britain faced an oil shortage when Saudi Arabia instituted an oil embargo—a problem that was made worse when North Atlantic Treaty Organization (NATO) members refused to sell oil to the United Kingdom to make up the difference. Under this pressure, Eden, who was ill, agreed to a ceasefire on November 6, informing neither the French nor the Israelis ahead of time, just as British troops were on the verge of taking Port Said. Eden hoped that a UN occupation (that would include British troops) would prevent Egypt from regaining control of the canal and would maintain a British presence in the region. While Mollet agreed to the ceasefire, Ben-Gurion refused. He proclaimed a great victory. He renounced the 1949 armistice lines with Egypt, declared that Israel would never accept a UN occupation of the region, and hinted at a plan to annex the Sinai Peninsula. In the end, the British and French were compelled to leave Egypt, disgraced for their aggression, and were replaced by UN units from Denmark and Columbia. The Israelis, under international pressure, eventually withdrew from the Sinai the following March, systematically destroying the infrastructure of the Sinai on their way out.[10]

Scholars and journalists have written thousands of pages debating the details and points of contention that shaped this crisis and its legacy. All of them have declared their goal to bring clarity to a befuddling set of events whose causes, details, and meanings are still opaque. This is also the case regarding the history of broadcasting during the Suez Crisis.[11] Much of the literature focuses on the internal debates happening inside the various broadcasting services. All are interested primarily in showing was what really going on inside the fog of war.

That is not the intention here. The chaotic months surrounding the Suez Crisis were not characterized by lucidity and precision. Voices dropped and swirled across the radio dial in 1956, including the BBC, Sharq al-Adna, Radio Moscow, the VOA, Voice of the Arabs, Kol Israel, Radio Paris, and Radio Damascus. In the midst of this, the various radio services tried to sculpt the audiosphere into a shape that would encompass the policies of their leaders and solicit Arab consensus. Each propaganda program attempted to frame its policies using long-standing, increasingly problematic, rhetorical tropes, leading to the collapse of the British rhetorical regime. The varying Western promises of peace, development, and freedom came crashing up against reality in those fateful months. These were months of turmoil and confusion, when listeners were unable to know what to believe because the conduits that delivered information had become so profoundly dissociative and contradictory.

This confusion was made worse by the discursive regime that now defined and shaped the possibilities for communication inside the varying broadcasting programs. All of them leaned on the older rhetorical practices that they had been developing since the 1940s to position themselves as truthful and their enemies as false in the ensuing maelstrom. Attestations of peace, freedom, and the economy of the gift, which were founded in Cold War imperialist mentalities, conjured simulacrums of national policies, all seemingly motivated by altruistic desires. The language that the Western services had at their disposal had by 1956 become unsinewed and insufficient, hemmed in by its own outrage, its repetitive mantras increasingly tired and empty, its duplicity revealed. This was the moment when the Western message collapsed. After the dust settled, only Voice of the Arabs remained standing.

. . .

On July 26, 1956, Nasser got on the radio and gave the order to nationalize the Suez Canal. He would pay for the Aswan High Dam, he said, with the revenue generated by the canal, and he would assert Egyptian national sovereignty. That day, Radio Cairo announced that the "first and last vestiges of imperialism have been erased!" Nasser declared that the country would now build "two dams": the High Dam and the "great dam of prosperity and dignity." He thanked the Soviets for their support and reiterated his commitment to peace. He commanded his listeners to "direct [their] attention to the future, feeling that we shall, God willing, score one triumph after another. Imperialism attempted to shake our nationalism, weaken our Arabism, and separate us by every means. Thus it created Israel, the stooge of imperialism."[12] He went on to conjure the image of Bandung and the plan for a unified, nonaligned center of power away from the United States and the Soviet Union, committed to the cause of anti-imperialism.

Kol Israel was the first state broadcasting program to reply. "Israel . . . does not want to dominate and wipe out the Arabs. . . . If anyone wants to dominate the Arabs, it is Nasser himself. . . . Nasser has transferred to Israel his own expansionist megalomania." The broadcasters noted again and again that the Western powers had stood idly by for the last eight years while the Egyptians closed the canal and the Straits of Tiran to Israeli shipping.[13] They claimed that attacks on Israel were always a harbinger of larger Arab aggression. It was the West's fault, they contended, for not heeding Israel's warnings and stopping Egypt eight years earlier. "Discrimination against Israel today means discrimination against other countries tomorrow."[14]

The British and French radio responses to the nationalization were marked by shock and dismay. "It hit like a bombshell," John Rae at the Cairo office of the BBC wrote to Gordon Waterfield.[15] "The Suez Canal is a key waterway for world trade and is an important source of revenue for Britain," a BBC broadcaster reported during the lunchtime news report.[16] Meanwhile, Sharq al-Adna ran stories on the opening of Khartoum University, "the first university between South Africa and Egypt."[17] The British conservative domestic press lambasted Nasser for orchestrating the "theft" of British property. Not surprisingly, the BBC and Sharq al-Adna did not convey these sentiments to their Arab listeners.

Thanks to the broadcasters at Radio Moscow, Arab populations *did* hear the British domestic press, however. Moscow translated and read the London and Paris newspapers over the air in the days that followed. "The British paper, *The Daily Mail,* openly demands that British troops be sent to the Canal," Moscow reported on July 28 in Arabic.[18] "The *Daily Mail* is calling the Canal's nationalization an act of robbery. Would it be out of place to ask on what grounds the nationalization of assets belonging to a nation could be called an act of robbery?" Radio Moscow asked incredulously. "The British are the ones who have been doing the robbing for the last ninety years . . . 120,000 Egyptians lost their lives in the construction of the Suez Canal, while the colonial powers made enormous profits out of it. Now the Egyptian government has decided to use these sums for its own economic projects. In what way is this illegal or illegitimate?" Radio Moscow pointed out that the Anglo-American West's seeming anger over the illegality of the nationalization was just a ruse to cover up their fury over lost profits and the repudiation of their imperial power.[19]

Radio Moscow worked quickly to spread blame for Nasser's nationalization to the United States and its rescinding of funding for the Aswan Dam. Notably, in a move that Otto von Bismarck would have respected, Moscow altered Nasser's nationalization speech slightly when it was read out in Arabic over the air, translating Nasser as saying the following:[20]

> The United States demanded that Egypt should conclude a mutual security agreement. That implied the dispatch of American military missions to Egypt, which would establish their control over the Egyptian Army. They were out to exploit our desire for arms to make slaves of us. We turned this down. We bought arms in Russia without any terms whatever. The West made a lot of fuss about it. They declared that they were Communist arms. But these declarations do not worry us. They are ours.[21]

Nasser did not say this. In the original speech, he made no mention of the United States:

> We asked for arms from Britain, which they agreed to on the condition that Egypt back down at the Bandung Conference and stop attacking Britain in the press and radio. This was not a business transaction, but the use of arms for domination and arbitrary rule.... Afterwards, we were able to buy arms from Russia. I say from Russia and not Czechoslovakia.... Russia agreed to supply us with arms. Then there was a big hullabaloo. What was the object of this uproar? They say these are Communist arms. I really do not know whether they are "Communist arms" or "non-Communist arms. If they are in Egypt, these arms are Egyptian arms.[22]

For Radio Moscow, Suez became an anti-Western issue writ large. "Nationalization of the Suez Canal is a link in the chain of anti-imperialist liberation movements which have included the Near East and North Africa, and for this reason all progressive peaceful mankind supports Egypt's equitable decision."[23] Stories aired every day on the solidarity of India, Vietnam, Burma, Afghanistan, Pakistan, and others in supporting the anti-imperialist cause—of which Suez was a manifestation.[24] Such was the role of peace in again separating East from West.

Voice of the Arabs joined in on July 30. Ahmed Said declared in his resounding, booming voice that the British were "floundering," with no guiding principle except "exploitation, plotting, and tyranny."[25] For Said, nationalization of the canal symbolized nothing less than the culmination of Arab destiny. "Oh Arabs!" he proclaimed, "Arab nationality has come into being. Yes, Arab nationality has burst forth, a shining light in the darkness of imperialism."[26] Light again played a central role in the imagery of historically determined liberation. Nationalization and nationality had become the same thing. They represented nothing less than the culmination of the Arab dream of modernization and self-sustainability.

The American response to the nationalization of the canal was true to form in its delays and ambiguity. The USIA spent the first few days listening with increasing dismay, internally noting that Radio Moscow was delivering many of its stories in Arabic at a slowed speed with the clear intent that they be copied and reprinted in the Egyptian newspapers the next day.[27] As the USIA knew, the issue was lack of uniform messaging from the US media. The VOA dutifully aired steady reassurances from Eisenhower that he and Dulles were seeking a peaceful diplomatic solution to the crisis and were distancing themselves from Eden, Mollet, and Christian Pineau, the hawkish French foreign minister. Meanwhile, Radio Moscow was translating into Arabic and broadcasting stories from American Movietone newsreels, which seemed to show US complicity with Britain and France. In one of these videos, which can still be watched on a reel-to-reel player at the US National Archive (which I also found transcribed in faded paper form in the State Archive of the Russian Federation alongside a scribbled directive to "translate into Arabic"), the famous American broadcaster Joe King declared that Nasser's nationalization of the canal had "upset the chancelleries of the free world," that it was a "seizure from private interests," and that it was Nasser's response to the West "for refusing to finance the Aswan Dam." Eisenhower was being sincere when he denounced Britain and France, but over the radio, it certainly didn't sound like it. Alongside the sound of cheering Egyptian crowds carrying Nasser atop their shoulders through the streets of Cairo, Radio Moscow translated Joe King's words, declaring the strategic waterway "a lifeline between the East and West."[28] In a later newsreel, King (now translated into Arabic and broadcast over Radio Moscow) described Nasser's return to Cairo from Alexandria, where he was met by a population that was "in a veritable nationalistic frenzy." From there, King reported that Dulles "seem[ed] to take the side of the West in the debate. . . . The door to a peaceful and fair solution [was] kept open, if only the government of Egypt [would] choose that way."[29] A week later, King declared that the Egyptian nationalization of the canal was an "aggressive action" that had led French, British, and American forces to "spring into action in the Mediterranean." Again, Eisenhower may have given speeches arguing for a peaceful solution, and in the back room Dulles may have been at loggerheads with his British and French counterparts in an effort to force their withdrawal from Egypt, but such realities would not have been clear to the average listener, trained to be skeptical of Western promises of peace and presented with American newsreels seeming to prove US collusion with Britain and France. Whether one listened to the BBC, Radio Moscow, or Voice of the Arabs, American collusion was an assumed fact. All three radio stations had different reasons for asserting that the United States had a vested interested in defending Western rights in the canal. Britain needed Eisenhower's legitimacy, the Soviet Union needed to bolster the image of the United States as an imperial power, and Ahmed Said needed a monolithic "West" against which Arab nationalists could rally.

Then Dulles attended the famous London Conference, to which Egypt, China, and all of the Arab nations whose territories lay in direct proximity to the canal were not invited. Each of the broadcasting services struggled to find the language to describe the London Conference. From the cloudy drizzle of the London morning, broadcasters transmitted events back to the Arab world. Again, Radio Moscow focused on the seeming collusion of Dulles with the British and French and his unwillingness to entrust the Suez Canal to Egypt. It remained focused on this story throughout the conference, especially after Dulles presented his separate plan that did not grant Egyptian sovereignty over the canal. Nasser, who was back in Cairo receiving hourly reports from the Soviet delegates, stood his ground, declaring again and again that he would not accept the supervision of the canal by an international organization. As the conference went on, Radio Moscow argued that if shipping routes needed to be internationalized in order to prevent any one country from holding the world hostage, then the rule would also have to apply to Gibraltar, Aden, Singapore, and Panama.[30] This put Dulles in an uncomfortable position. As Radio Moscow put it, "The United States is apprehensive that Panama may follow Egypt's example in wiping out all traces of imperialism in her territory.... This is the reason that Dulles is insisting Suez be put under foreign control, and this is the reason the United States did not invite Panama to the London Conference."[31] Immediately the VOA ceased talking about international governance of Suez, especially after Panamanians began to protest for sovereignty over their canal.[32] This was another message that made the US position in the crisis suspicious and confusing.

Meanwhile, the world of British broadcasting was in turmoil. John Rae, the Middle East representative at the BBC stationed in Cairo, wrote increasingly worried letters to Gordon Waterfield back in London as he and his staff made plans to move the Middle East office to Beirut and evacuated their families back to England. As Rae put it, if an English invasion did happen, "even the Lebanon won't be able to resist in joining the struggle in some way."[33] After attending one of Nasser's press conferences, Rae wrote frankly to Waterfield that he did not believe Nasser to be the "vile dictator depicted in the British Press." In fact, Rae had to admit that Nasser "made a good case for Egypt." And while Rae conceded to his friend back in Caversham that Nasser was a "pretty slippery customer," he could not for the life of him see how Britain could flout the UN Charter and impose any decision that the current London Conference might arrive at. Little did he know that his government had even darker plans.

In fact, it does not appear that any of the British stations knew of Eden and Mollet's secret invasion plan. Earlier in 1956, Eden's government had created the Information Coordination Executive (ICE), which was supposed to be responsible for managing psychological warfare in times of conflict. It brought together key personnel from the IRD, the Regional Information Office in Beirut, the BBC, the Colonial Office, the Ministry of Defense, the chief of staff, and the British embassy in Cairo. The original plan was that they would mobilize all the tools at their discretion (including black propaganda) to undermine Nasser in the event of war.[34] There was no way they could do their job, however, because they were kept in the dark about the invasion plan until the last minute—a sad consequence of Eden's growing secretiveness and illness.[35] ICE had expected that a long negotiation would follow Nasser's nationalization of the canal. Its personnel had also reiterated to Her Majesty's government the need for transparency in planning so that they could have enough notice to deal with reversals in policy. Otherwise, as one IRD officer put it, they would be "left too far out on a limb" to be of any use.[36] The agreed-upon themes in their propaganda offensive were the importance of honoring contracts (going after Nasser for abrogating his country's ninety-nine-year contract with the Suez Canal Company that had begun in 1869), the dangers of the canal's nationalization to other Arab states, the underlying communist conspiracy behind Nasser's actions, and how fair the British were being in their dealings with Egypt. This was a good plan for tackling the canal's nationalization, but it was not the kind of propaganda one adopts when preparing for an invasion, which normally includes messages about imminent physical danger, the brutality of the enemy, and the futility of resistance.

And so the BBC was caught largely unawares. On August 29, Rae wrote to Waterfield, "I would dearly like to know what is in the government's mind. . . . No doubt we shall keep our upper lips stiff in the approved fashion." Rae nonetheless refused to believe the rumors that the British and French might fabricate an excuse to "get" Nasser. He reminded his old friend that there was some merit in the Egyptian grievances, which had become submerged under a mounting tide of mutual mistrust, suspicions, and British oil interests. "But, alas, when in the last fifty years has there been any British attempt to meet a situation before it actually hit us over the head?" he scoffed. "I feel that it is highly probable that unless we do make some attempt to come to terms with Arab nationalism (instead of sneering at it and trying to jump on its head) we shall see a Communist Middle East within the next decade—and no amount of moribund Islam will save it."[37] Rae's comments were reflective of the ongoing suspicion among some British propaganda officers that Islam represented a weak bulwark against the appeals of international communism, which would find great appeal if the British government did not learn to come to terms with Arab nationalism.[38] After Rae and his wife Nonie evacuated to Beirut, Rae exchanged multiple letters with Bush house, the Central BBC Office, requesting that the compensation package for the cost of his move include the value of his mislaid socks (he was ultimately successful).[39] By August 24 it was clear that the London Conference would end with no resolution. Eden now had to decide whether to escalate the conflict or back away. As the BBC put it, the final goal, regardless of how it all shook out, was to "counter claims by Colonel Nasser that he had won."[40]

As Dulles worked desperately to obtain promises from the British and the French that they would not intervene militarily, over the air the rest of the world seemed to be doubling down on its willingness to fight. Voice of the Arabs replied to the failed conference and the latent threats coming from the West: "We await the next move, and we are prepared for anything."[41] "O Arabs! Redouble your solidarity and tighten your fists, for imperialism wants to rule your land forever!" Said proclaimed.[42] He embraced a full-blown language of Arab solidarity and military preparedness, including steady attacks on the United States. Voice of the Arabs ran stories claiming, "America has been plotting for two years to internationalize the canal," and "American workers are standing against Eisenhower in their support for the nationalization of the Canal Company." Mostly, Cairo lambasted the British and relished Nasser's steadfastness. "He is a stubborn militant soldier who would not abandon one atom of what he believes to be right."[43] Interviews aired daily on the preparedness of the Egyptian army, such that by September 7, General Abd al-Hakim Amir, the commander in chief, was giving daily briefings over the radio at 06:00 hours. "My confidence as regards . . . the safety of the situation is unbounded," he said.[44] Alongside this ran stories about the influx of Soviet pilots who were volunteering to help navigate ships through the canal. Indeed, when it came to talking about the damage done by imperialism and the imperative to defeat it, the link between the language of the Soviets and the Arab world was impossible to ignore. "We will continue to unmask, resist, and defeat imperialism and its agents," Ahmed Said intoned, sounding not unlike Soviet revolutionary discourse of the 1920s.

If a listener had tuned in solely to Voice of the Arabs, by September 10, Egypt would have seemed already victorious. Britain and France were puttering around in Europe, struggling to acquire an endorsement of their Suez plans from recalcitrant NATO allies, failing again to change Nasser's mind when they visited Cairo on September 9. Nasser appeared open to resuming normal shipping under the UN Charter, his position firm and honorable. It was true that English and French troops were massing in Cyprus and the Eastern Mediterranean, but again and again Egyptian military and political experts assured listeners that these were "no more than bombastic demonstrations which can never materialize." They pointed to the lack of support from Cypriots for such a venture, and said that such a rash choice would lead to war with the entire Arab community along with volunteers from around the world—all amid an economic downturn in Europe. "It will not happen," Said promised.[45] These reassurances seemed confirmed when, on September 12, Eisenhower declared that the United States would "not take part in any aggressive act," and that there would be no use of force by the United States, even if negotiations over Suez ceased.[46]

That evening, the BBC aired Eden's threat that "if Egypt continues to reject every endeavor to reach a peaceful settlement, a grave situation will ensue."[47] He proposed an Anglo-French association to administer the canal and ordered Western pilots and workers at the canal to leave their posts. The next day, Ahmed Said reassured his audience both at home and abroad that the Egyptian people remained resolute. "The Egyptian people want to take revenge on the British and are ready to sacrifice everything so that not a single British soldier can return to Egypt."[48] "If Eden thinks that Egypt will tremble and submit to him or to his proposed association, he is definitely mistaken. . . . He can continue his game, but it will only lead to his downfall." For people who could remember 1947, this sounded suspiciously like the reassurances from that summer that Europe would never dare to impose its will upon a majority Arab Palestinian population intent on determining its own fate.

Then, on September 23, Britain and France formally appealed to the UN Security Council. They attempted to find recourse and justification using the law, arguing that the Egyptians had violated an 1888 convention protecting the status quo of the canal. As it had in 1948, Radio Moscow reported that Britain and France were dredging up old agreements to justify their intervention and prove the illegality of the canal's nationalization. They actually read the text of the original 1888 convention over the air, which granted the free use of the canal "to all states at all times." "There is no connection," the Radio Moscow–sponsored Arabic speaker said slowly at dictation speed, "between Egypt's nationalization of the Suez Canal Company and the guarantee of free use of the Canal."[49] One hour later, Kol Israel responded, pointing out that the 1888 convention had been abrogated for years due to the Egyptian refusal of free passage through the canal to Israeli ships. And then, in what can only have been an attempt at a propaganda feint, they attacked Britain for its, "unbridled anti-Israeli propaganda."[50] Radio Moscow broadcasters then harkened to the now well-established language of peace. "It is plain that there are no grounds for the accusation against Egypt that its activities represent a threat to peace and violate the 1888 Convention. . . . Britain and France's appeal to the Security Council is a maneuver aimed at distracting public attention from their efforts to settle the Suez problem from a position of strength."[51] They were not wrong. They also repeatedly called into question the veracity of "certain British radio stations" (meaning Sharq al-Adna) that were disguising themselves as Arab. "Aware of this trickery," Radio Moscow declared on October 3, "Arab states are barring the way to imperialist propaganda carried out by British radio stations. The Lebanese Government is also closing down the British radio station in Beirut."[52] This was not true, but it helped to create a sense of pan-Arab solidarity that reached even to Britain's closest allies.

Again, as in 1947 Egypt argued that the UN had no right to arbitrate this decision. Like before, Arab radio, particularly Radio Cairo, declared that the current crisis was a test of the United Nations. "It either wins the respect of world public opinion," Nasser was quoted as saying, "or collapses as did the League of Nations."[53] "The question we now face," Ahmed Said asked his listeners, "is will the United Nations be a toy in the hands of imperialist countries which ignore the world conscience? . . . O Arabs! The word internationalization is only a new name for usurpation, domination, and joint colonization." This argument would be repeated again and again well into the twenty-first century. Radio Cairo aired on repeat a commentary from Anwar Sadat, who declared that the West was applying the "law of the jungle" in Egypt—an explicit inversion of the "law and order" arguments being made by Eden. "Nasser and Egypt will not pause like a beast of burden to be mounted by the Big Powers."[54]

As the early signs of autumn began to appear in New York, London, Paris, and Cairo, Dulles struggled to maintain a uniform US approach to the escalating crisis. It was not that Dulles and Eisenhower supported Nasser; they didn't. They were concerned about the optics of invasion and the damage to American consensus building and messaging in the Middle East.[55] Their worries were valid. The VOA was declaring US opposition to invasion every day, but the larger messaging was confusing and inconsistent. Dulles repeatedly claimed on the shortwave that the United States was opposed to British, French, and Israeli policies. At the same time, the domestic US media seemed to show continuing support for the invasion—support that provided ample fodder for stations like Radio Moscow and Voice of the Arabs. The United States had opposed allowing Arab representatives and Israel to attend the Security Council meeting, Radio Moscow reminded its listeners again and again.[56] American newspapers were printing full-page interviews with British diplomats while reflecting a profound ambiguity toward Nasser. On October 1, 1956, a *Newsweek* article came out in the United States stating that Kings Saud of Saudi Arabia and Faisal of Iraq were "patching [up] their dynastic feud to meet a greater common danger—Nasser and his pan-Arab dreams." The article also declared that "whatever the fate of the canal may be, the United States considers that Abd al-Nasir must go."[57] Radio Moscow immediately translated this article into Arabic and read it over the air, contrasting it with the language of seeming support for Egypt that was coming from the US State Department. "Who should we believe?" they asked. "The answer can be found in the policy of the United States." The Soviet broadcaster recounted the times earlier in the crisis when the United States had attempted to stop Nasser's nationalization of the canal, "resorting to economic and military threats, to diplomatic pressure and to direct intimidation. Everyone knows that the formulator of the plans for interference in Egypt's internal affairs is the U.S. State Department. All these facts prove that Dulles' statements are lies and hypocrisy."[58] Soviet stories in subsequent days claimed that American monopolists were pushing for a special consortium of oil companies that would grant concessions in Suez, similar to what was done in Iran in 1954.[59] Dulles may have been fighting for peace, but in the audiosphere, the verdict on US policy in Suez was far murkier.

. . .

On October 16, thirteen days before the invasion was to begin and six days before Britain, France, and Israel would meet to craft their invasion plan at Sévres, Voice of the Arabs seemed to predict the future. Summarizing an article that had just been printed in the newspaper *Al Akhbar* that morning, the broadcaster said the following: "British policy urges one country to attack another, then a third country to come to the aid of the country attacked. It advises the attacking country that the military forces which were sent to aid the attacked will not embark on aggression, but will merely maintain order, like a police force. Later it tells the country attacked that these forces are only to help defend it against foreign aggression."[60] The BBC Monitoring Service did not appear to pick up the broadcast, but the CIA did. There is no evidence that it made its way into higher diplomatic circles, although given that it was broadcast at 8:00 a.m. in Cairo, on a Tuesday, while everyone was heading to work or having their morning coffee, one can assume that thousands heard it. It was a description of what was to come.

In the context of the chaos that defined the audiosphere of 1956, the language of peace, the discourse of outrage and injury, and the promise of benevolent modernization were not easy to maintain for any of the broadcasting services. Ironically, even when a government embraced a policy of peace, as Dulles and Eisenhower did, making that believable had become difficult. This was the case not just because Radio Moscow and occasionally Radio Cairo accused them of collusion with the British, but also because they had, even by that point, built a rhetorical foundation that was only tenuously grounded in reality. Like their peers across the dial, the US stations' preoccupation with the Cold War, fear of Arab nationalism, and orientalist assumptions about their listeners had been the building blocks for a narrative that could barely hold up, even when they were being honest.

EIGHT

Cacophony

THE CRISIS OF SUEZ

THE ISRAELI INVASION began on October 29. For a regular listener, it would have been almost impossible to know what was going on with only the radio (and the press) as a source. Microfilmed transcripts from these days show that the BBC did its best to shy away from news about Suez, offering cursory reports as it had done in 1947.[1] It focused instead on the Soviet invasion of Hungary and ran stories on the morning's test match in Bombay, where Australia scored 386 for two wickets in reply to India's 251. At 9:00 p.m. GMT, they finally made the following mention of the invasion:

> Just over an hour ago, news came in that Israel forces have crossed the Egyptian border and attacked Egyptian positions. This operation followed Egyptian military interference with Israel sea and land communications. The five Algerian leaders arrested by the French have appeared in court. The Queen is attending a special film performance this evening in aid of [illegible] charities.[2]

And so began the war, between cricket scores and a special film screening for the queen. The first shots, according to the BBC, were fired by Egypt. At 11:00 p.m. GMT, the BBC aired this follow-up:

> A Foreign Office statement said the Government regarded the situation in the Middle East as serious, and were disturbed at the possibility of a breach of the peace there. British and United States diplomatic missions in Israel, Jordan, Egypt, and Syria have been instructed to warn subjects to leave these countries unless their work there is essential. In Moscow this evening, the Soviet Foreign Ministry told reporters that Russian troops in Budapest would be withdrawn as soon as the insurgents laid down their arms.

This short report did a lot of heavy lifting. It presented Eden's government as gravely concerned with Israeli aggression, thus completing the first step of the plan hatched at Sèvres. It gave the appearance of US and British cooperation as they evacuated their citizens from an event that they had not anticipated. Then it redirected attention to Hungary, painting the Soviet Union as the imperial aggressor giving ultimatums to freedom-loving Hungarians.

That morning, Voice of the Arabs declared that Egyptian officers were reporting to their units and that the Israeli plan for a major advance into Egyptian territory had failed.[3] Seconds later, further up the dial, Kol Israel announced in Arabic that the Israelis had crossed into the Egyptian frontier the previous night and were advancing toward the Suez Canal.[4] The BBC supported Kol Israel's claims, reporting an hour later that Israeli forces were indeed only eighteen miles from Suez. It then repeated every hour throughout the day the Israeli assertion that Egyptian commandos were indiscriminately murdering Israelis. The BBC was clearly following the directions of the Foreign Office. At noon, at the same time that Britain and France issued their "ultimatum" to Egypt and Israel (which Dulles described as "crude and brutal"), the BBC reported that the Egyptians had closed the Cairo airport thirty minutes before a large group of American families were due to evacuate out of the country to Amman. They did not report on the evacuation of British or French personnel. In fact, they put the Americans at the center of the story again and again, as though it was the Americans who had the most to worry about in terms of Egyptian reprisals. BBC reports throughout the day reiterated the statement that the Americans were in "consultation" with the British and French, quoting Eisenhower as saying the "United States has pledged itself to assist the victim of any aggression in the Middle East. We shall honor our pledge." The VOA also replayed this speech throughout the day.[5] When the BBC broadcast it, however, it sounded distinctly like the United States was arguing that it would send troops to stop the Israelis, so that when the British and French intervened, it would appear as though they were following the American lead. As we now know, this was not Eisenhower's intention. He was furious at his erstwhile allies, and his threat about intervening to protect victims was aimed as much at Eden, Mollet, and Pineau as it was at Ben-Gurion. That afternoon, Britain and France vetoed the US resolution in the UN Security Council calling on Israel to withdraw, making no mention of the veto over the air. It is not surprising that, behind the scenes, Dulles and Eisenhower were most concerned with the possibility of being lumped in with the French and British in the minds of Arab listeners—a thing that was definitely happening on the public stage. Such an eventuality, Dulles feared, would turn the newly independent countries "from us to the USSR."[6]

It was at this moment that the BBC's tortured position became apparent. Somehow it needed to navigate the strong demands of its government while still ostensibly remaining an independent organization. It dutifully aired Anthony Eden's speech at the House of Commons defending the "humanitarian" decision to occupy Port Said, Ismailia, and Suez—all done to "guarantee freedom of transit through the canal." Eden's speech was met with prolonged cheers. Then, against orders from Eden and the Foreign Office, the BBC aired the opposition's response to the speech. Yelling out amid heckling jeers, Hugh Gaitskill asked Eden by "what authority and what right he supposes that British and French forces are justified in armed intervention in this matter?" Gaitskill demanded that Eden take no steps before the UN had made a pronouncement, to which Eden replied that Israel and Egypt would be given twelve hours to respond to his ultimatum (it was Ivone Kirkpatrick, who had been in charge of British information activities in Palestine in 1947 and was Rex Keatings longtime pen pal, who gave those ultimatums to Egypt and Israel). This moment created serious tensions between the BBC and the British Foreign Office. Her Majesty's government wanted the BBC to convey a sense of British solidarity behind Eden, not schism. Interestingly, the BBC reported Gaitskill's rebuttal in the 6:00 p.m. news but pulled it at 10:00 p.m., chastened, at least momentarily, into compliance with Whitehall's wishes.

While the BBC might have found itself walking a tightrope, Sharq al-Adna had fallen off it. It was common knowledge in the broadcasting world and beyond that Sharq was just a covert British radio station pretending to be Arab. Back on April 5, the station had accidentally announced, "This is the Sharq al-Adna British Broadcasting Station, sorry, Sharq al-Adna Arabic Broadcasting Station."[7] Letters had poured into the Arabic newspapers, which Ahmed Said then read over the air.[8] For those who had been paying attention, Sharq had been British for a long time, but now it was obvious to everyone. Radio Moscow and Voice of the Arabs mentioned this fact hourly on the first day of the invasion, along with news that Sharq's entire Arab staff had resigned. Whatever conviction Sharq had once offered had now turned to calumny.

With Sharq dead in the water, the British Foreign Office and the IRD requisitioned it on October 30 and renamed it the Voice of Britain. "The British

Government has taken control of this radio station," the broadcaster declared at 3:02 p.m. GMT. "It will be known from now on as 'The Voice of Britain.'"[9] The earliest mention of the idea of the government taking over Sharq and renaming it appears to have come from Allan Lennox-Boyd, the Secretary of State for the Colonies, in a top-secret letter to Eden sent on May 30, 1956. The purpose of the letter was to discuss the incendiary Egyptian propaganda being directed at Yemen and Saudi Arabia that May. On the fourth page of his letter, Boyd wrote, "We should consider setting up a powerful station directed at undermining the Nasser regime in Egypt. Why not from the Near East Arab Broadcasting Service (Sharq al-Adna) itself? It would most certainly not be short of material!"[10] That September, Patrick Dean, an assistant undersecretary at the Foreign Office, wrote to John Rennie, the head of the IRD, that while Sharq could not put over the British point of view or openly criticize Nasser in a big way because it was pretending to be an Arab station (and the Arab staff were likely to desert if it did), "as soon as Nasser is gone, however, and a more friendly regime has been established in Egypt, the Arab staff in Sharq might be less averse to service."[11] Such was not the fate of the station, or of Nasser. Sharq instead became a casualty of the war.

After Sharq's rechristening as the Voice of Britain, it was put under the direction of the British governor of Cyprus, Brigadier Bernard Fergusson, who also had under his control a small printing press, a few Royal Air Force (RAF) pilots to drop leaflets sealed in canisters engineered to open up a thousand feet above the ground, some borrowed Kenyan "voice-aircraft" that would fly low conveying information, and a unit of trucks to drive around giving "instructions and exhortations."[12] Fergusson's task, assigned at the last minute, was to roll out a full British propaganda program in Egypt to support the Suez campaign, to be done in three phases. First, his program was to attack Egyptian morale; then work to minimize Egyptian interference; and then finally, after the Egyptians had been defeated, to rehabilitate and mend the morale of their malleable listeners.[13]

The BBC and Voice of Britain were opposed over the air by the Egyptians, Soviets, and Americans, who were also fighting to shape the narrative. That night, the VOA made it clear that the United States had not been consulted by the British and French and had no part in the threats coming from Whitehall.[14] At 8:00 p.m. EET (Cairo time), Radio Cairo and Radio Moscow announced that the Egyptian Air Force, using Russian jet fighters and bombers built in Czechoslovakia, had completely stopped the Israeli advance. They said that the Suez Canal was "in no way endangered by any military threat."[15] Ahmed Said claimed repeatedly that Egyptian forces were mopping up the Israelis, who were scattered across the Sinai, and had shot down seven Israeli aircraft.[16] None of this was true, but as would happen in 1967, it was seen as more important to maintain public morale than to convey the realities of the battlefield. This worked, at least temporarily. Either way, the average radio listener sitting in the el Fashawy coffee shop, enjoying the late hours of that temperate Cairo evening in October, would have had no clear sense of what was happening just one hundred miles north. That night, Nasser announced a general mobilization. "The [British and French] ultimatum constitutes an aggression against the rights of Egypt and her dignity," he said, "and it is a flagrant violation of the United Nations Charter."[17] Nasser had transformed the issue of the canal's ownership into an existential fight for national survival.

Listeners woke up the next morning, October 31, to hear the BBC reporting that Egypt had rejected the British and French ultimatum to withdraw from Port Said, Ismailia, and Suez. In the same broadcast, the BBC announced that the Israelis had accepted the British and French demand to withdraw to a distance of ten miles from the canal, just as planned, noting that the Israelis had made the concession under the assumption that Egypt would do the same.[18] It was all a ruse, as everyone would soon learn, and the evidence was already beginning to show. Half an hour later, the BBC reported that Britain and France had vetoed two separate US and Soviet resolutions at the UN Security Council calling for a ceasefire, while at the same time, RAF and French transport planes were taking off from Cyprus.[19] Meanwhile, Kol Israel reported that Israel had downed two Egyptian Vampire jets over Sinai, and that an Egyptian warship had bombarded Haifa Bay in the night, which the Israelis sank. Radio Paris declared that the "courage and resolution of the people of Israel were well known and it was recognized that Colonel Nasser's regime did not hesitate to use force and to violate human rights." Radio Moscow continued to bellow accusations of collusion and duplicity at the French, British, and Israelis—a message that Ahmed Said echoed at every turn.[20] "It is clear to every sober-minded person that there is a conspiracy against peace," Radio Moscow declared, "that the imperialist circles in Britain and France want to restore by force the old colonial regimes in the Middle East. This is colonialism, clear and naked."[21] All of it was couched in the language of peacekeeping—the Western powers were committed to the cessation of conflict, so committed, in fact, that they refused to sign a ceasefire agreement.

ВОЗВРАЩЕНИЕ ИЗ ЕГИПТА

Военная авантюра англо-французских интервентов в Египте за-
кончилась полным провалом. В результате этой авантюры престиж
и политические позиции Англии и Франции на Востоке и во всем
мире были еще более ослаблены, экономические затруднения
в этих странах усилились. *(Из газет)*

FIGURE 10. British lion and French rooster washed ashore after being rebuked by Egyptian sphynx. *Source:* "Vozvrashchenie iz Egipta" [Returning from Egypt], 1956, Kukryniksky.

Then, at 6:15 p.m. EET on October 31, the first bombs fell on Egyptian airfields. This news broke at different times depending on where listeners were on the radio dial. Radio Cairo reported it right away. Two hours later, at 8:00 p.m. EET, the BBC was reporting that the Israeli army had stopped, as instructed, at the "ultimatum line," ten miles east of the Canal, and Israeli soldiers had isolated the Gaza strip, which was known to house "Egypt's spy and sabotage school for commandos," in addition to about two hundred thousand Palestinian refugees. It was because of frequent raids by those refugees, the BBC declared, "in which grain was reaped and cattle stolen," that Israeli forces had "deliberately built up settlements along the border, in which land-workers carry rifles on their tractors and stand guard at night." At no point did the BBC report unequivocally that British and French bombs were falling on Egypt on October 31. Air raid sirens were going off, it said, but Cairo was calm, as though the sirens were an unnecessary precaution. The only excitement, the BBC reported, was at the British embassy, where "officials in short sleeves" were burning secret documents in incinerators put up in the embassy garden in anticipation of an illegal Egyptian raid that could unearth vital British national security secrets.[22] The creation of narrative through omission, coupled with the repeated claims that Israelis and British diplomats were largely acting in defense, put the British in the role of peacekeeper—a role for which the British diplomats and broadcasters expected their Arab listeners to be grateful.

The VOA broadcasters awoke the next morning exasperated to hear the Voice of the Arabs blaming the United States for being involved. As one USIA official put it, the situation was "impossible to get ahead of." In response to the accusations, the VOA, which had increased its Arabic transmissions by 120 percent to fourteen hours per day, aired Eisenhower's entire speech, translated into Arabic, in which he said that the use of force against Egypt was an "error."[23] The VOA promised that there would be no US involvement and expressed solidarity with the Egyptian plight.[24] Unfortunately, it also described Nasser's nationalization of the canal as a "needless aggravation" that had driven the Israelis, British, and French to "protect their vital interests." The VOA made sure to reaffirm its friendship with Britain, France, and Israel, who "have been subjected to grave and repeated provocations." The VOA may have been trying to placate both sides, but over the air, as listener surveys attested, this messaging engendered as much skepticism from Arab listeners as it did acceptance.[25]

The contradictions only continued in the days that followed. On November 1, the BBC famously went against Foreign Office commands. It again gave airtime to Hugh Gaitskill, who had been organizing against the invasion for weeks. It broadcast his full oppositional speech on the floor of the House of Commons deploring Eden's decision to use armed force against Egypt. That same day, however, on the hour every hour, it reported that Selwyn Lloyd, the foreign secretary, had denied any collusion between Britain and Israel over their invasion. It also aired the voice of Eden saying that he would not condemn Israel, "as the aggressor, in view of previous actions by Egypt, who has made clear her intentions to destroy Israel."[26] The standard history of the BBC in Suez tends to focus on its stalwart independence from the Foreign Office, despite immense pressure to collaborate. The story, like most, was much messier.

At exactly the same time, Radio Cairo announced that Egypt had broken off all relations with Britain and France and was considering withdrawing from the United Nations. Then, at 5:00 p.m. EET, Nasser came on the air. "The Egyptian people will fight a total war," he said "in defense of Egypt's freedom and independence." Harkening back explicitly to Winston Churchill's famous, "We will fight them on the beaches" speech, Nasser said, "We will fight them from village to village, we will fight them from place to place, and each Egyptian will be a soldier serving in the armed forces."[27] Whether Nasser or Said wrote this, we do not know, but it was a brilliant rhetorical turn. The speech was motivating in its own right, but for those who recognized it, it was a clear comparison of the Nazi invasion of Britain to the British invasion of Egypt.

Meanwhile, Voice of Britain and its new director, Fergusson, were also attempting to roll out their plan. Unfortunately for them, it did not survive the first day. Their most popular Egyptian staff refused to cooperate, and their Egyptian director refused to hire any of the Arabic speakers that the British sent. On the second day of the bombing, Fergusson realized that the Voice of Britain's Arab staff had not been airing the state-approved scripts and instead had been sending out one message, on a constant loop, that expressed the station's loyalty to the Egyptians and its disassociation from the British broadcasts that were intermittently interfering. Fergusson and his signal man put the entire staff under arrest and confined the Egyptian director of the station to his home.[28] In a gesture that resembled the standard Soviet media response to national crises, Voice of Britain created a playlist of Middle Eastern pop music and kept it on a loop.[29] Fergusson then set out to find new staff but could not locate any British-endorsed Egyptian Arabic speakers to take the microphone. Egyptians in the British political service were unwilling to go near it for fear that their voices would be recognized and their families would face reprisals. The Arabic speakers that Fergusson did eventually find were Algerian or Palestinian, and Egyptian listeners quickly concluded that they must be Jewish.[30]

Even Fergusson had to admit later that his psychological warfare endeavor was "devilishly bad" and "bedeviled by short-handedness, lack of experience, hasty mounting, and a cocoon of secrecy." He had bought planes from a Kenyan manufacturer to fly close to the earth, shouting messages from loudspeakers. After realizing what the uses would be of their low-flying aircraft, the Kenyan manufacturer sent the planes as promised, but stripped them of all their loudspeaker equipment. Fergusson's group devised a massive leaflet campaign with messages that read, "Remember, we have the might to attain our objective and we shall use all of it if necessary. Your choice is clear, either accept the Allied proposals or accept the consequences of Nasser's policy, which will bring heavy retribution, not only to the few who are guilty, but also to you, the many, who are innocent."[31] These messages undermined Eden's promises that the British government had no quarrel with the Egyptian people and was intent on intervening to protect them. It didn't really matter in the end what the pamphlets said. Fergusson soon realized that the printing press was broken, which held up the leaflet drop. Once they were printed and the Hastings RAF pilots got the planes in the air over Egypt, instead of exploding a thousand feet above the ground, the canisters full of leaflets did a free fall and opened at six feet over the ground, creating nice little mountains of paper. In future drops, they attempted to mitigate the problem by adding weight to the canisters in the form of sand, which led to years of jokes about how the British psychological warfare department spent the Suez invasion dropping sand on Egypt.

Such mistakes were representative of the entire British propaganda endeavor during the Suez Crisis. A fatal mixture of poor planning, hubris, and lack of coordination and communication from above, coupled with the general impossibility of the task, meant that the British services could only react desperately as each crisis came their way. Taken in the context of the larger audiosphere, it is clear that they were never able to control the narrative. Take for instance the British attempt to silence Voice of the Arabs. London had agreed early on that the first stick of dynamite would be dropped on the

Radio Cairo offices and broadcasting station, at which point Voice of Britain would take over its frequency. When the English and French air assault began, the RAF hit the offices of Radio Cairo in the city, having failed to realize that the transmitters were located miles away, on the edge of the desert.

Despite the BBC's and the Voice of Britain's best efforts to present a vision of unified British support for Eden's policies, evidence of popular British opposition to the invasion did make its way to the Middle East. Not only did Radio Moscow report regularly on the protests happening in Trafalgar Square, but the BBC was also now giving attention to the opposition. On the morning of November 2, it ran a full story on Aneurin Bevan, the Welsh Shadow Foreign Secretary, who had called Britain's conservatives "lynchers" in the House of Commons debate the night before. "Is Britain going to be bled in Egypt as France is bleeding herself to death in Algeria?!" he asked amid Labour cheers. "We are dishonoured!" he yelled. Key was the translation and conveyance of these speeches to listeners in the Middle East in Arabic, who, as surveys continued to attest, increasingly blamed the invasion on Whitehall's elite.[32] Most noticeable was the moment the next day when Radio Moscow reported, "Blood is being spilled on the earth God gave to man for happiness and prosperity. The peaceful life of the peoples is disturbed. . . . *The British imperialists are dishonored and will be bled in Egypt as France is being bled in Algeria.* We pray for retribution on the imperialists who have encroached on the freedom and independence of Egypt. May the holy words of the Quran—that Allah will subject to torments those who commit injustice—come true!"[33] The broadcast reflected the Soviet approach to propaganda since the 1940s: tolerance of religion as a part of its larger belief in the rights of all people to happiness and prosperity, the West's attack on peace, and the call to mobilize collectively against such aggression. Tucked in the speech were the exact words that Bevan had just used on the floor of Parliament, now cast as a call to arms. Days later, the Labour leader Gaitskill argued in a domestic BBC broadcast, "This was not a police action; we had taken the law into our own hands. How tragic it was that, at the very moment when the whole world should be united in denouncing the Russian aggression in Hungary, we—by our criminal folly—should have lost the moral leadership of which we were once so proud."[34] Radio Moscow quickly translated this into Arabic and broadcast it, omitting the bit about Hungary.[35]

That same morning, the Radio Cairo broadcaster's voice cut out in midsentence as British bombs fell on its desert transmitters, which had finally been located. A well-placed explosive dropped by the Canberra Bombers knocked the Voice of the Arabs radio transmitter out of commission. The historian Elie Podeh has argued that Radio Damascus picked up the frequency, while Kennett Love has claimed that the British Foreign Office quickly stole the frequency to broadcast Voice of Britain.[36] Either way, wherever it was on the dial, the Voice of Britain pulled no punches. "O Egyptian people," it declared, attempting to sound like Ahmed Said, "your broadcasting station has been destroyed. . . . Why has this befallen you? First because Abdel Nasser went mad and seized the Suez Canal which is of vital importance to the world."[37]

Voice of Britain had a moment of victory, but it was not to last. Later that day Nasser recorded a speech, which Voice of the Arabs managed to send out on a stored transmitter.[38] "The Egyptian people will not be silenced!" Ahmed Said bellowed, taking the mic after the ringing from Nasser's proclamations had ended. Two days later, Radio Cairo was back up full time at a weaker signal. The Egyptians developed a reputation for being indomitable. It seemed like no one could get them off the air.[39]

The crisis created an incredible opportunity for the Soviet propaganda project. Even the Americans had to acknowledge that the Western invasion and resulting scandal had offered a "golden opportunity to shake the foundations of Western influence in the Middle East—through skillful propaganda, without firing a shot."[40] The Soviets actually responded slowly to the outbreak of violence, not condemning the West until three days later, on the first of November.[41] But then the floodgates opened. "The voices of millions of people echo in every continent saying, 'Hands off Egypt!'" the Arabic-speaking Soviet announcer bellowed.[42]

Public attestations of solidarity from Soviet citizens for Egyptians were a steady feature. On November 4, Radio Moscow reported on a "spontaneous" gathering of five thousand Soviet workers, students, and housewives near the British embassy to "protest the criminal actions of the aggressors." This was followed by a protest at the French embassy that night. "Wrathful voices rang out, 'Shame on the Aggressors,' 'Down with the Imperialists!' and, 'Suez Belongs to Egypt!'"[43] Since the 1930s the Soviet people had become experts in orchestrating performances of public solidarity. These events had traditionally come in the form of grand spectacles attesting to the public's continued support for the Stalinist state. Beginning in the 1940s, the state apparatus exported these spectacles as a tool in the waging of the cultural Cold War. International solidarity with the cause of peace became a mass performance, played out in Soviet schools, offices, and factory floors, complete with petitions, public rallies, academic lectures, and marches, all of which were then photographed, documented, and exported to audiences around the world as evidence of the free Soviet people's sincere support for the working classes and colonized people who still suffered under the imperial yoke. On November 8, Radio Moscow reported that at the Egyptian embassy, demonstrators were handing embassy officials a score of letters and statements wishing the Egyptian people success in their "just struggle." Meanwhile, the Komsomol (the youth section of the Communist Party) gathered across the Soviet Union to air its condemnation of the "piratical attack on Egypt."[44] The next day, Radio Moscow broadcast ostensibly from a live gathering of thirty thousand students and faculty of Moscow University. The speaker, S. Sobolov, tied the notion of peace to the promised progress of the Soviet communist project. "Without peace our construction work will be retarded, the development of our science arrested, and our advance to the radiant future, to communism, hampered." The broadcast then switched to an interview with a factory worker, who said, "During the last war I lost my mother, brother, and my home. Being a mother of three children I know full well what war means. . . . Shame on the warmongers!" The image of the beleaguered mother and the Soviet experience of suffering in the Great Patriotic War legitimized the outrage of the Soviet people. Programming that same day included declarations of solidarity from the Trekhgornaya textile mill workers, Soviet medical workers at the Burdenko Institutue of Neurosurgery, and the Ministry of the Heavy Machine Industry.[45]

Such mass spectacles carried a myriad of meanings for the people participating in them. They were coerced public acts, performed out of obligation and long-standing habit. They were also sincere. Lots of Soviet citizens sympathized with the Egyptian cause. Also, such mobilizations of solidarity provided the only means by which Soviet populations could gather to critique imperialism and the trauma of overwhelming state power. They had no ability to safely protest the invasion of Hungary (although some did nonetheless), but they could implicitly stand in solidarity with the Hungarians by taking to the streets to defend the Egyptians. Regardless of the motivations that drove Soviet people into the streets that November, by all measures, their gatherings were powerful gestures that were appreciated by the Egyptian people. They seemed to show that the normal people of the Soviet Union cared in a real and tangible way about what happened in Suez. Radio Moscow was also the first to argue that the British and the French were using the UN as a veil for the invasion. They claimed that this was but the first step in "spreading colonial domination to all the liberated Asian and African countries."[46] In a reverse of the domino theory, it was "the imperialists" who were hatching a grand plan for global control.

These attestations of public support for Egypt might have seemed more genuine if it weren't for Hungary—a topic that Radio Moscow avoided as much as possible in its broadcasts to the Middle East. There is no mention of Hungary in Radio Moscow broadcasts on October 23. On that day, as Soviet tanks were rolling into Budapest, the broadcasters spent an hour talking about the ongoing Anglo-French-Egyptian negotiations and the relationship between oil and politics.[47] They focused on the dangers that the United States posed to Syrian and Egyptian sovereignty.[48] The US National Archive holds a report written by USIA officials on Soviet propaganda during the Suez Crisis. In it, they claim that Radio Moscow was arguing over the air that the West was fabricating false stories about events in Hungary in order to distract the world from the horrors the British, French, and Americans were perpetuating against the Egyptians.[49] This could be accurate, but the Soviet archives show no mention of Hungary at all in the October and November broadcasts. The Soviets instead spent October and November arguing that the United States was partially to blame for the Suez invasion.[50] "The United States has taken another step toward encouraging aggression against Egypt." The station declared on November 4 that "the shameful participation of America in these maneuvers once more shows the hypocrisy of the United States."[51] Hungary finally did appear in August 1957, when Radio Moscow reported on a visit made by two Egyptian newspapermen to Hungary. The Egyptian journalists could be heard declaring that "in Egypt no-one has any doubt that the aggression against Egypt last fall was organized by the same people who had their hands in the October events in Hungary."[52] Here, ten months after the Hungarian invasion, Radio Moscow was attempting to rewrite the story, holding Britain and the United States responsible for Suez *and* Hungary.

On November 16, broadcasters and journalists from Moscow, Washington, and London revealed the existence of the Anglo-French-Israeli conspiracy. In the end, the best-laid plans failed. International opinion turned against the British, French, and Israelis. Eden was left having to admit his calumny, while Nasser became the self-proclaimed leader of the Arab world. It was a critical moment that marked the ascendance of Arab nationalism and the collapse of Britain's hegemony in the Middle East.

Most diplomats and propaganda specialists, then and now, agree that the English broadcasting program during the Suez Crisis was an "incompetent" debacle.[53] Both the US and British efforts were disastrous. Both sides found themselves on the receiving end of Said's tirades with the juggernaut of Voice of the Arabs to back him.[54] The Suez Crisis destroyed the ability of the British to promote the Baghdad Pact as a counter to Egyptian power, ostensibly with Iraq at the forefront of the effort. Even the British Foreign Office had to admit that its half-hearted support of Iraq had been "dreadful."[55] It had promoted Iraq as the "champion" of Western modernization but had failed to provide the needed political support. It was, in the words of historian James Vaughan, a strategy "dangerously out of step with regional political realities" that contributed to the discrediting of Eden and Nuri Said and ultimately led to both of them being deposed from positions of power.[56] The officials working in the British Broadcasting and External Services offices came to the same conclusion. As John Rennie put it, "British broadcasting (particularly Shaq al-Adna) collapsed at the very moment when it was most needed."[57]

The role of the BBC in the crisis is still a point of debate. Some have argued that 1956 represented a critical moment in the history of English independent broadcasting, when the BBC stood resolutely against encroaching pressure from Eden's government to tow the official line.[58] Others have contended that the BBC cooperated in many crucial ways with Eden and that the British broadcasting program during the crisis was not nearly as independent as previously thought.[59] Throughout 1957, the BBC continued to defend British policy in the Middle East and denied charges that the Israelis had been co-conspirators. It reminded everyone that the ultimatum had been issued to Egypt and Israel, that the British had threatened to invade Israel if Jordan were attacked, and that British forces had evacuated the Suez Canal before they were supposed to. Britain had given Sudan independence, the BBC argued, and had supported Libyan independence and the wishes of Iraq and Jordan to end their treaties with Britain. The BBC argued repeatedly that Britain had remained a paragon of democracy during the crisis, citing as proof the fact that the British had debated the issue of Suez openly in Parliament. The BBC contrasted this with the censorship and dogma of Egypt, where no alternative opinions were allowed. It argued that the Egyptians had been consistently misinforming the Egyptian people about the numbers of casualties. Whether or not it made these arguments independently, the BBC certainly seemed to support the larger efforts by the British Foreign Office to recover what prestige it could and deflect blame. Even with this, many in the British Foreign Office were still furious that the BBC wasn't towing the line enough. It was difficult to be the global voice of a nation while also remaining independent from it.

British diplomats, journalists, and propagandists continued to search for the reasons for their failure. As in previous cases, the British and American broadcasters held Radio Moscow responsible for much of Nasser's victory. In the USIA's assessment of the Soviet broadcasting effort in the Middle East five weeks after the Israeli attack on Suez, it concluded that Radio Moscow had succeeded in increasing Arab solidarity and intransigence in negotiations, had intensified Arab hatred for Israel, had "reinforced and stimulated Arab distrust of the Western powers (including, the U.S.)," had incited individual violence and the sabotage of oil pipelines, was branding pro-Western Arab leaders like Iraq's Nuri Al-Said as "foreign stooges," had speculated on the "imminent dissolution of the Baghdad Pact," and had somehow managed to promote the message of Soviet solidarity without committing the USSR to any tangible material or military aid.[60] The power of Radio Moscow to have such a significant impact was unlikely. Ironically, an additional success that the USIA and the VOA failed to see in the Radio Moscow broadcasts was its ability to convey solidarity between the Soviet and Egyptian people. While Radio Moscow had provided live coverage of Soviet workers, peasants, and students rallying in support of Egypt during the crisis, at no point had the VOA talked about US citizens marching in the streets, signing petitions, or expressing their popular support for the people of Egypt. Never, too, did the USIA direct outrage explicitly and repeatedly at the British and the French. The most it could do was express its desire for a peaceful solution, which seemed to be in contrast to a general anti-Arab sentiment among the American public.

The Americans also provided a foil for Britain's failure in Suez. "It is [the Americans'] attitude," one British journalist noted, "which has helped to cause a movement for local independence in North Africa to degenerate into a murderous gangsterism. . . . It was they who refused to put any teeth into the Tripartite Declaration and thus make us an effective instrument for keeping peace between Israel and the Arabs."[61] The domestic British press and radio were particularly distressed at what they perceived to be the US treatment of Britain as an unequal and humiliated partner who overlooked the value of its allies in the Cold War. They felt that they had earned American loyalty due to their support of the United States in Korea. "We hoped that Americans would realize that without Britain and France even their strength might be unable to resist the spread of Communism throughout Europe, Asia, and Africa."[62] Or perhaps the United States was attempting, as Lord Vansittart put it in a letter to the *Daily Telegraph*, to "fall heir to the British Empire."[63] The Americans had to realize, he chided, "that there are two sides to this matter," the communist side or the British side.[64] Rumors spread that the Americans were using the oil shortage that resulted from the closing of the Suez Canal as a means of economic sanction and as an excuse to raise prices.

And as in times before, the British frequently settled on Orientalist explanations. Some even suspected that the promise of democracy itself had been a failed message from the beginning because it fell on the ears of a population that only understood the baser forms of social structuring. As the British Foreign Office Information Policy Department put it in an internal memo written in late September (while the plans for the invasion of Suez were being finalized), "Most Arabs although violently nationalist are not greatly interested in democracy as such."[65]

After Suez, the VOA "occupied the grey hinterland of being neither right nor wrong."[66] The United States had opposed British, French, and Israeli aggression but had failed to come to the aid of Nasser. This had the uncanny effect of souring its relationships with everyone in the crisis. As USIA officials noted internally, by the summer of 1956, after the failures of the London Conference and the Canal Users Association, a "certain disillusionment" toward America had settled in the minds of the British public. For British liberals, the United States had failed to broker a desperate peace. For British conservatives, they had failed to stand decisively beside their ally in order to force Nasser's capitulation. As the conservative *Daily Telegraph* wrote that September, "It is clear that only Britain and France are prepared to back a policy of international control of the Canal, if need be, with action."[67]

The VOA also saw this moment as an opportunity. It made multiple gestures to move into the space left by the disgraced British, particularly in Jordan and Iraq, and to become the new source of information and entertainment for listeners in the region. It isn't a coincidence that the United States decided to undertake a massive expansion of its Arabic Service in November 1956 with a new commitment to producing a better, more powerful message for audiences. The new director of the USIA, Arthur Larson, declared, "America and American ideals cannot be 'sold' abroad like cakes of soap, nor can the spirit of freedom be kept alive by pep talks. . . . What you have to do is keep truth itself alive."[68] What this meant in reality was that the VOA would harden against Nasser, with a commitment to combat Arab and Soviet radio in the Middle East. It meant that the United States would pick up the mantle of protecting the promise of democratic capitalism now that it had been dropped by the British. The VOA leadership eventually concluded that the Egyptian anti-imperialism tack was, in fact, a procommunist tack and had to be viewed in Cold War terms—a difficult pill to swallow given that the United States had helped to finance much of Radio Cairo's broadcasting infrastructure. The Voice of the Arab's criticism of the Eisenhower Doctrine as a device of US imperialism and Nasser's cooperation with Moscow had tipped the scales. On top of that, the British could not be trusted to handle the situation anymore. When Eisenhower declared that "any threat to Turkey, Persia, Pakistan, and Iraq" would be met with "the utmost gravity," it became clear that the United States would defend Western interests in the Middle East—a role that Great Britain had played up to that point.[69] At the end of January 1957, less than two months after the Suez Crisis, Larson flew to Karachi, New Delhi, Baghdad, Beirut, and Cairo. On his visits to local stations, he stressed the importance of broadcasts that would support the $200 million in foreign aid that Eisenhower hoped to send to the Middle East. They would now direct 9.5 hours of Arabic broadcasts to the area to combat the Voice of the Arabs, all while figuring out a more powerful way to reach audiences than the floating transmitter in Rhodes allowed. They would flood the USIA publications and libraries with images of dead Hungarians, killed at the hands of Soviet troops.[70] On top of this, VOA had to deal with the fact that only two of the fifty Americans involved in broadcasting in Egypt, Iraq, Jordan, Lebanon, Syria, and Sudan spoke fluent Arabic, and their language training program famously resembled a sixth-grade public school Spanish class.[71] As one USIA official admitted in the aftermath, "Adequate supervision is lacking."[72]

The Americans also had blame to spread. In mid-1957, USIA memos argued that Voice of the Arabs had contributed in a tangible way to the rise of sectarian strife in Lebanon over its adoption of the Eisenhower Doctrine and its tacit adherence to the Baghdad Pact. They blamed Voice of the Arabs for the rise of "pan-Arab fervor" among Kuwaitis, Muslim Filipinos, and nationalists in Bahrain. The USIA noted the cooperation of the Middle East News agency (which was supposed to be an independent news source but was largely funded by the Egyptian government) and TASS in spring of 1956.[73] The USIA's Office of Research and Intelligence was quick to note that the Voice of the Arab's objective of eliminating Western influence in the Middle East "happens also to be the primary Communist objective." One assessment in 1957 concluded that "the content of Moscow and Cairo propaganda shows a large degree of cooperation."[74] The USIA came to the conclusion that the "pro-Soviet attitude" of Egyptian propagandists created an increasing likelihood that they would "begin thinking in terms of Soviet propaganda themes rather than Egyptian directives."[75] This despite the fact that, by 1955, the Egyptian government had cracked down fairly successfully on communists in the country, arresting some and closely monitoring the Greek communists in Alexandria.[76]

If there was a victor in this story, it was the Voice of the Arabs and Ahmed Said. "O Arab Brothers," he began a broadcast in his characteristic cadence. "Do not say that the conspiracies of the colonialists have ended.... If the aggression of colonialism against Egypt has met with utter failure, it still thinks of plotting another aggression by which to secure victory."[77] The station became the mouthpiece for Arab unity and resistance against imperial aggression. More than anything, it was responsible for creating a viable vision of a pan-Arab movement led by the tenacious Abdul Nasser, which generated widespread popular consensus and set the stage for the creation of the UAR. And yet even Voice of the Arabs was unable to escape from the rhetorical modalities that had come to define it since 1953. It too was bound by the echo chamber that it had helped to create. While it was able to muster a powerful revolutionary, anti-imperialist message in 1956, its fate was ultimately not unlike those of its Western counterparts.

. . .

The consequences of the Suez Crisis were myriad and long lasting. It hastened the decolonization process, isolated Nuri al-Said, and set the stage for the Iraqi Revolution of 1958. It created a new alignment in the Middle East, pitting the US-supported royalist axis of Saudi Arabia, Iraq, and Jordan, plus Lebanon, against the Soviet-supported alliance of Egypt and Syria. It laid the groundwork for the 1967 Six-Day War by salting the earth between Egypt and Israel, saved the Soviet Union from facing what should have been a massive international outcry over the Hungarian invasion, emboldened Khrushchev in the use of brinksmanship and blackmail as a foreign policy, and was the catalyst for the Eisenhower Doctrine, which authorized the US use of military force to check "aggression" in the Middle East and provided financial aid and development to US allies in the region. It marked the height of Nasser's popularity, driving him to embrace the possibility of a united Arab nation, especially after the failed Anglo-American coups in Syria in 1957.[78] As Ahmed Said put it, the union of Syria and Egypt provided "the shield which protects Arabism against aggression."[79] It also drove Nasser, especially after the proclamation of the Eisenhower Doctrine, further into the arms of the Soviet Union. Most notably, it marked the death knell of the British Empire in the Middle East, turning what was to be a cause célèbre into an international disgrace.

The crisis also brought into stark relief the extent to which each of the great radio broadcasting services had become locked into long-standing linguistic regimes that circumscribed what they could say and how they could say it. By 1956 the audiosphere (particularly what was coming from Britain and the United States) had become a spectacle, separated from reality, constructed for the purposes of reinforcing state policy, nakedly exposed as a tool of power. In this chaotic world of post-truth (a reality that the West has only come to see clearly in the last two decades), the general promises of peace, development, and progress became increasingly suspect. This maelstrom contributed to the general disillusionment among Arab listeners—a disillusionment that at that point had been developing for decades. It was one thing to argue for one's love of peace and national determination during peacetime. It was another altogether to argue for it when one's nation was clearly responsible for disregarding those ideals. This was exactly what the British and French in Egypt, and the Soviets in Hungary, did. And while the United States in no way supported its allies' aggression, the combination of general mismanagement in its own information programs and the constant Soviet and Egyptian accusations of US collusion with the British, French, and Israelis left the United States consistently in the wrong camp in the eyes of many across the Middle East. This sense of distrust toward the current hegemonic structures of state power, both foreign and domestic, would only worsen in the years to come. Only Voice of the Arabs seemed to hold a claim to the truth for a sizeable percentage of the Arab world, not because it had spoken the truth, but because it had not been exposed and it carried a message of liberation and independence that many believed in deeply. But as with its counterparts on the dial, this claim was tenuous, and in the coming years it would face the same scrutiny and collapse.

NINE

Voices Carry

LANGUAGE AND THE CRISIS OF TRUTH

ON DECEMBER 26, 1956, the Egyptian embassies from Kabul to Tangier invited guests to visit at any time between 5:00 and 9:00 p.m. to see a twenty-minute film, *Aggression at Port Said*. The Egyptians played the film eight times that day, each time to a full house. There were no battle scenes in the film. Instead, the camera panned over leveled neighborhoods, cutting to an operating theater where a surgeon was removing shrapnel from a child's leg. The movie ended with sweeping views of the Egyptian flag flying grandly over the Suez Canal, guarded by resolute soldiers staring out over the vast expanse of water. In a final shot, the camera zoomed out to show a row of flags, each representing the nations of the Arab Middle East, with the Egyptian flag at the center, fluttering in the breeze. It was a reminder of the final price that was paid by the Egyptian people for the freedom and peace that the Arab world enjoyed. It was a promise of revolution and pan-Arab solidarity, inscribed upon the bodies of those who had paid the ultimate price for liberty.

Her Majesty's government was not pleased with the film. The British embassy in Kabul informed the British Foreign Office back in London that day that the movie "consisted entirely of post-battle shots: bodies, hospitals, ruins, ships 'sunk by the aggressors' etc."[1] The Foreign Office, which quickly requisitioned a copy of the film, noted in reply that the particularly gruesome sequence of the operating theater "might have been taken almost anywhere," commenting that the areas most badly destroyed in the film appeared to be "just slums." British diplomats who had attended the showings of the film conceded that audience members were horrified by what they saw. Viewers "clicked their tongues" and "hissed in the right places." This was to be expected, staff at the Kabul embassy remarked. The "Afghan mentality," as they put it, did not mind exaggeration.[2] And besides, it did not seem to matter to these audiences that the destroyed areas were slums. "The majority of Arabs—and for that matter the majority of Asiatics—live in hovels. The thing that counts with any audience, but particularly with any Asiatic audience, is not the commercial value of the destroyed buildings but the fact that they were human habitations."[3] Indeed. In an effort to reduce the damage done by the film, the undersecretary in charge of press and information banned it from domestic British television and commercial newsreels.

The USIA was also bothered by the film, not so much by the sensationalism of it as by its apparent communist origins. In the months that followed, the agency reported on "rumors spreading" that the film had been funded by Soviet-sponsored communist organizations from Syria to Algeria. In response, the American embassies in Syria and Iraq (two countries whose loyalties were most coveted by Washington, Moscow, and Cairo) pushed local magazines to publish photographs of benevolent British soldiers helping Egyptian civilians, with captions referring to the "ridiculous claims" made by Egyptian propaganda.[4]

The Soviet response to the film was glowing. Soviet and Chinese diplomats and officers attended the showings of the film in suits and full military uniform.[5] Over the air, Radio Moscow applauded the "strength and resiliency" of the Egyptian people who had rejected the Anglo-American assault on their sovereignty.[6] Broadcasts highlighted the heroic efforts of Soviet pilots who had worked with Egyptians to open the canal. They retold stories of local Soviet and Eastern European citizens who were now celebrating Egyptian liberation in the streets, followed by attestations of Egyptian gratitude for Soviet assistance. Such was the performance of Egyptian appreciation and friendship. As far as Radio Moscow was concerned, a grand victory had occurred for the forces standing against Anglo-American imperialism— a victory in which the Soviet Union had played no small part.

The stories behind the airing of *Aggression at Port Said* attest to the sentiments and difficulties that characterized the post-Suez period for all who were working over the air—difficulties that were caused in large part by their own lasting rhetorical practices and commitments. Chastened, British broadcasters resolved in the months to come to make amends with Nasser and to present a moderate alternative to Soviet totalitarianism and American "Coca-Colonization."[7] While they based their programming on the message of support for moderate, socialized reforms across the Middle

East, their opposition to anything that smacked of Nasserism and communism precluded them from addressing the rising anger of poor landless peasants across the Middle East.[8] Further up the dial, at the VOA, the disgrace of British radio seemed to create an opportunity. In the vacuum left by the British at Suez, American broadcasters resolved to differentiate the United States from the old colonial powers by offering an American-led alternative to European hegemony.[9] President Eisenhower advocated for steady intervention in the Middle East whenever the communist threat seemed to appear.[10] Consequently, the promise of US development and liberation for the Middle East quickly found itself having to tackle the contradictions caused by the American government's willingness to intervene in the internal affairs of Arab countries.

Similar difficulties besot the Khrushchev-era approach to the Middle East. For Radio Moscow, the Soviet Union's wholehearted support of Egypt in the crisis appeared to have paid off, establishing it as a great defender of Arab nationalist and socialist movements, standing against Anglo-American perfidy across the Middle East, and seeming to set a precedent for future Soviet support in the region. But the Khrushchev regime's promises of aid, peace, and anti-capitalist defense became increasingly difficult to deliver on as the decade wore on. Egypt's debt, Nasser's crackdown on communists and Ba'athist socialists, and his embrace of positive neutralism made many leaders in the Politburo ambivalent about the merits of Soviet support for Cairo.

Even Voice of the Arab's language of anti-colonialism and pan-Arab liberation carried with it a troubled paradox—a paradox that increasingly bore resemblances to the contradictions faced by the station's counterparts up and down the dial.[11] Nasser appeared resilient and victorious, poised to create a new pan-Arab state. Egyptian revolutionary propaganda promised a liberationist ideology that would unite Arab society. Over time, this revolutionary message created a trap from which Nasser and Voice of the Arabs could scarcely escape. If Nasser continued to embrace a revolutionary, Egyptian-led, liberationist ideology for the Arab world, he would forever be obliged to support the many nationalist republican movements that cropped up in opposition to the West. He would also be obliged to suppress alternative liberationist programs from within the Middle East that did not have him at the helm. If Nasser receded from the Egyptian-led revolutionary message and sought normalization with the West and his regional rivals, his and Egypt's identity as a revolutionary movement would be delegitimized. Such policies would shape the inter-Arab struggle, particularly between Egypt and Saudi Arabia, but also between Egypt and the Muslim Brotherhood.[12] All these contradictions had the potential to cast Egypt's secular, pan-Arab, liberationist narrative as yet another empty promise—a development that culminated in the collapse of 1967.

All of this happened against the backdrop of continuous political and economic upheaval across the region, alongside the escalating efforts of the Western powers to wage the Cold War by proxy. As a consequence, the contradictions in everyone's messaging became difficult to ignore. Western military interventions revealed the willingness of the United States to send troops to uphold its "peaceful" promises of capitalist development and democratic defense. The reciprocal demands made by Soviet gifts became easier to see as tensions arose over rising Egyptian debt and the Kremlin's need for clearer evidence of Arab fealty. Nasser's increasing authoritarianism, the breakup of the UAR, the disappointments of Arab socialism, his attacks on Hashemite leaders and the Muslim Brotherhood, and the devastating loss of the 1967 war all made the promise of secular liberation suspect.

One of the key reasons language failed to do the work that broadcasters needed it to was that in all of their narratives, their support for Arab peace and development hinged on the condition that the Arab world embrace a specific vision of Arab identity—what the historian Salim Yaqub has called "acceptable Arabism." [13] For the Americans, this required Nasser to take a side in the Cold War, to accept US aid and development, to find some reconciliation with Israel, and to ensure American access to oil. For the Soviet Union, "acceptable Arabism" did not necessarily require communist fealty, but it did expect performances of gratitude for Soviet aid and development, a certain replication of public messaging, a steady antagonism with the West, a positive trade relationship, and access to ports. For Whitehall, "acceptable Arabism" required the Arab accession to the return of Britain's steadying leadership, the rejection of Nasserism, and the repudiation of Soviet influence. Nasser increasingly defined "acceptable Arabism" as Nasserist Arabism, with his evolving dictatorship leading the charge against Western imperialism, internal enemies, and Zionism. He and his broadcasters argued that anyone who embraced the policies of the West or rejected the policies of Nasser's secular-bureaucratic-authoritarian regime was outside the pale of what it meant to be Arab. These narratives presented by the great powers about how listeners could perform their identities as "acceptable Arabs" were part of a genealogy that by this point had locked them into largely determined roles. They left no rhetorical or conceptual space for thinking about Arab identity outside of how they had defined it. This didn't stop that identity, or the language needed to describe it, from developing; it just stopped the broadcasters from being able to use it or deal with it. These mantras, stripped of their connections to Arab experience and emptied of believable promise, set the stage for the rise of political Islam. "With Nasser diminished," Said K. Aburish has noted, "the Islamic movements moved to assume the political leadership of the masses of [the] Arab Middle East."[14] In the decade between the Suez Crisis and the Six-Day War, an increasingly narrow vocabulary was available to the state-led broadcasters who sought, through language, to conceal the faults of power.

. . .

The British had the most pieces to put back together after Suez. Their first task was to figure out what to do with the Voice of Britain, formerly Sharq al-Adna. The station was not in a good place in 1957. It had seen all its Arab staff resign, had been outed as a tool of the British government, and had nowhere to house its transmitter (the "conditions in Cyprus were no longer hospitable" the British mission in Egypt informed Whitehall in 1957, meaning that they were being kicked out).[15] Her Majesty's treasury also had no interest in financing the cumbersome station. As Sir Alexander Johnston, the treasury's third secretary, put it, "we want to be completely quit of any financial burden in respect of a station which is putting out jazz music and advertisements for toothpaste."[16] The Voice of Britain had become a dead letter. In its place, the Foreign Office proposed the creation of a "composite" station that would air BBC broadcasts interspersed with advertisements, with the understanding that should another emergency arise, the UK government would take charge again.[17] This plan met with initial resistance, but the IRD and the BBC did eventually retool the station as a commercial endeavor, "directed to the uneducated masses in Arab countries with the object of attracting them away from Radio Cairo."[18] They created a current affairs program, "offering a new slant" on hot topics of the day alongside reports on trade and industry, with "thrilling plays of mystery and suspense," stories from Sinbad and Scheherazade, quiz shows, and travel programs.[19] The consequences of this were that the BBC grew significantly, taking on the lion's share of British broadcasting to the Middle East from this point on. Its reluctance to comply with Eden's mandates during the crisis may have caused internal consternation, but it meant that at least the BBC would be able to emerge from 1956 with a viable product that Arab populations were still willing to listen to.

In its efforts to counter Radio Cairo, to woo its listeners away from Voice of the Arabs, and to maintain some control over British messaging in the Middle East, the IRD also created a news-generating service that would address accusations lodged by Radio Cairo. It was called Transmission X. The workers at X received daily transcripts of Radio Cairo broadcasts from the BBC Monitoring Service. They crafted quick responses that were intended to be more in touch with current issues (with the help of the Regional Information Office [RIO] in Beirut), translated them into Arabic, and sent them out to other news venues across the Middle East. By 1962 the service was providing materials to the whole of Africa, the Middle East, Asia, and even South America and parts of Europe.[20]

As directed, the stories that came out of Transmission X avoided attacks on communist or socialist ideologies, instead focusing on the difficult living conditions of populations under the rule of communist governments.[21] As a consequence, stories that had once featured scholars attacking the ideological fallacies of communism were gone, replaced with more programs describing the working conditions on communal farms in the Soviet Union and the university students who were ordered to work there. They focused for the first time on Cuba, describing the rationing of food, the riots that were ostensibly happening on the streets of Havana, and the indoctrination that schoolchildren experienced. They made nods to the dangers of local communist parties in Africa and Latin America. As in decades past, these stories ostensibly functioned as object lessons meant to warn Middle Eastern listeners of similar dangers in their own countries. Only implicitly was ideology to blame for the suffering of populations living under communist rule.

The broadcasts coming from Transmission X were often so preoccupied with anti-Soviet programming that they failed to complete their larger objective of countering the Voice of the Arabs. Exposing the horrors of forced collectivization in the Soviet Union did not equate to an attack on Voice of the Arabs. In fact, Voice of the Arabs had little to say about Soviet collectivization, nor did it disagree with the British about the difficult conditions faced by populations in Eastern Europe and Cuba. What Voice of the Arabs *did* talk about in the 1950s and 1960s was the promise of the pan-Arab movement, Nasser's continuing campaign to promote Arab interests and modernization, his socialist reforms, the dangers of the more radical Ba'athists, and the constant threat of Western colonization, both military and economic. To these critiques, Transmission X could say nothing; it had sworn to maintain a tone of reconciliation with Nasser and silence on the rest. This was how narrow the British propaganda bandwidth had become, a fact that worried many in the IRD. In fact, there were some who argued that "rather than putting spokes in Nasser's wheels, we have actually helped spin them round."[22]

The US propaganda effort in the late 1950s and early 1960s also found itself unexpectedly hemmed in by what it could not say. The United States enjoyed a moment in the sun at the end of 1956 when it rebuked Britain, France, and Israel over the debacle in Suez. The USIA set out to construct a transmitter on Cyprus to improve the signal of the VOA.[23] Then, just as the possibility of developing a more subtle and genuine propaganda approach seemed to be on the horizon, the Eisenhower Doctrine was introduced in early 1957, promising American aid and military assistance against the "aggression" of "international communism" in the Middle East.[24] A coalition of anti-communist, pro-American Arab states would unite against an isolated Egypt and Syria, thereby ostensibly discrediting international communism and the idea of nonalignment in the Middle East.[25] The Eisenhower Doctrine became the justification for US military and political interventions in Jordan, Syria, and Lebanon over the next two years. It was behind the US reentry into the tripartite agreement with France and the United Kingdom, and it quietly allowed for America's restored relationship with Israel. By most accounts, it was a disastrous policy, resting on a "basic misreading of the Nasserist movement," that was rooted in a view of the Arab world as a pawn in the Cold War.[26] It also meant that the USIA and VOA would have to mobilize the language of peace and liberty to justify war and intervention. This mandate faced regular internal disagreements from VOA employees (just as the IRD did from British broadcasters) who wanted to report the "bad with the good" and chafed against the controlling tendencies of the "policy people" from the government who were stuck in a "sort of civil service aspic" in their efforts to make their language mold to a false reality.[27]

The US government also got involved in the "dirty business" of funding covert radio stations that did not have to follow the negotiated protocols of state radio. One such station was the Voice of Justice. Scholars continue to disagree over whether the station was British or CIA run.[28] The answer to this question may lie in a folder located in the British National Archives containing papers of the Information Policy Department at the

British Foreign Office. The folder holds the transcript of a Voice of Justice broadcast dated January 16, 1957. It was sent by the BBC Monitoring Service to the British Foreign Office a few days after the celebration of Egypt's Constitution Day. In the margins of the folder, a British Foreign Office worker whose name is unintelligible remarks that he or she had "heard of this station" and was thankful to the BBC for "obligingly obtaining the scripts from their U.S. contacts."[29] It seems clear that the station was under US control.

The transcripts of Voice of Justice broadcasts reveal the extent to which the American propaganda program was in a constant state of reaction and emulation with Voice of the Arabs in 1957 and beyond. The resemblances between Voice of Justice and Voice of the Arabs are unmistakable. The Voice of Justice broadcasts were delivered in florid, colloquial Arabic. They argued in powerful terms for the return of Abd al-Urabi, the grandson of Ahmad Urabi Pasha, to the Egyptian throne. The broadcast declared al-Urabi the "father of freedom and the constitution in Egypt" and Nasser a "blood shedder in an era of terrorism and blood, of steel and fire," who had cheated the people in his pursuit of personal power.[30] "Is it sufficient to have the constitution thrown into a drawer to consider Egypt a constitutional country?" the Voice of Justice broadcaster asked, emulating Said's trademark disdain. "Is it sufficient for Jamal Abd Al-Nasir to have the only copy of the constitution in his desk drawer to be considered a constitutional ruler, ruling Egypt in the name of the people?[31] Oh! Arab brothers, for this reason, we accuse the Egyptian president of swindling! Oh Jamal Abd Al-Nasir, enjoy your constitution day."[32] The strings of questions, the catchphrase calling on Arabs, the sarcasm—all of Said's most famous tactics were there in this American broadcast. Up and down the radio dial, there were now two state-run forms of expression to be heard: the standard state-sponsored promises of development, peace, and liberation coming from the BBC, the VOA, Radio Cairo, and Radio Moscow, and the high-voltage language of conflict, brinksmanship, and accusation coming from stations like Voice of the Arabs and Voice of Justice. One represented the rehearsed promises of state patronage given in return for acceptable Arab gratitude and fealty. The other sought simply to incite fear and anger. While many individual broadcasters remained committed to maintaining a degree of journalistic integrity, as far as their bosses were concerned, by 1962 they needed to "plug everything they have" and use any message that worked, regardless of its relationship to the truth.[33] Ironically, despite their seemingly different ideologies and goals, the broadcasters were all largely in agreement about how to make their point.

In the years that followed, the VOA and the USIA set out to promote a positive, friendly, sincere image of Americans as advocates for peace, technological development, and national liberation—a nation well on the way to fixing its race problems, filled with committed advocates for religious freedom around the world. Like the British, they too avoided explicit attacks on Nasser, recognizing the likelihood that such language would only inspire defensiveness in their listeners. As much as possible, they endeavored like the British to soften the view of capitalism as an exploitative economic structure, instead focusing on the ways that state-run social welfare programs in the United States were making the lives of workers and minorities better every day. They worked to counter the common misconceptions of Americans as "rich, materialistic, lacking in culture, jazz-happy, [and] full of gangsters" that had been promoted in Soviet and Egyptian propaganda as well as in numerous Hollywood films.[34]

In 1962 President John F. Kennedy attempted to reinvigorate the US propaganda program when he issued a memorandum on the USIA to its director, the famous radio broadcaster Edward R. Murrow. Kennedy warned that US national security could be lost due to the loss of effective international messaging, "piece by piece, country by country, without the firing of a single missile or the crossing of a single border." In addition to giving the USIA advisory rights on matters of foreign policy, Kennedy instructed it to "encourage constructive public support abroad for the goal of a peaceful world community of free and independent states, free to choose their own future and their own system so long as it does not threaten the freedom of others."[35] The USIA's job was to identify the United States as the qualified world leader of democracy and "unmask" anyone who tried to frustrate that objective. Indeed, as one US congressional study concluded (using the word *propaganda* in a positive light, seemingly for the first time), the USIA needed to "implant the notion that the future of the world belongs to democratic societies, to convince underdeveloped areas that that the U.S. wants to improve their technological ability, and to knock the myths that capitalism is exploitative and wants to dominate the world, and that communism is inevitable."[36] This sounded like a powerful new mandate, but in fact, it bore close resemblances to Truman's "Campaign of Truth" and Eisenhower's Plan 8, which had created the USIA. Much as in years before, the VOA provided political analysis, stories on American science and sporting achievements, conversations about religion, steady news reports, highlights of American cultural programs and international exchanges, and a constant stream of American music, which was by far its most popular draw.

Adding to the post-Suez audiosphere was Radio Moscow. Radio Moscow in the early 1960s narrowed its attention entirely on the Arab nationalist cause and the Western imperialist attempt to break up that unity.[37] Critical to Soviet propaganda was the message that the United States was taking over from the old European colonial powers in its pursuit of world domination. The Eisenhower Doctrine, Radio Moscow argued, was the American corollary to the Baghdad Pact. Similarly, it repeatedly made the claim that the United States was taking over for France in Algeria. Just as the British collapse had been caused by the bravery of the Egyptians in Suez, so too had the French collapse in Algeria and the resignation of Prime Minister Mollet been caused by mass protests over French imperialism by the Algerian people and the huge financial cost of that misadventure. Now it was France's "senior partner," which had helped the French to "eliminate Algerians with American weapons," that was stepping in to take over the new role of primary imperialist.[38] It was at this moment that the history lessons returned, except this time it was to paint the United States as a nation that did not know the history of the Middle East or the imperial West. Washington's leaders, Radio Moscow argued, were incapable of learning the lessons offered by the experiences of Britain, France, and Israel in Suez and Algeria. "They have not learned that to impose imperialism anywhere is a matter which history has doomed to failure."[39]

The opportunity to put those accusations into practice came quickly, in June 1957, when King Hussein of Jordan fired the communist leaders in his government. Radio Moscow accused the Americans of actively suppressing the nationalist movement in Jordan, arguing that Eisenhower had demanded the arrest of the communists inside the Jordanian government.[40] The broadcasters claimed that the American and British offer of financial aid to King Hussein was "blood money," given in return for his removal of his own people.[41] "Not a single country that receives US aid has become an industrial country or politically independent," Radio Moscow pointed out again and again.[42] It spoke of the Philippines and Turkey, countries still struggling with "backwardness," despite the seeming "generosity" of the United States. This would be the fate of nations that fell under the umbrella of the Eisenhower Doctrine, with aid only being offered on the condition that they suppress their own nationalism and concede to continued Israeli aggression. By the end of June, Radio Moscow was arguing that Washington was the producer of the "tragedy" unfolding in Jordan. "Washington is trying through her agents to isolate Jordan from the rest of the Arab countries and to turn this small country into a lackey."[43] Radio Moscow was admittedly not that far afield, given that Eisenhower and Dulles were in fact supportive of Hussein's crackdown on left-wing dissidents, even if it meant opposing representative government in Jordan.[44]

The perfidy of the United States only seemed to be reinforced when a second British and American coup attempt failed in Syria that same year. Syria in 1957 was the golden goose, the ally that everyone wanted, and "the fulcrum of geo-political hegemony in the Middle East."[45] It was also the target over which the United States and Britain found common cause.[46] In the plan to replace the current regime with a pro-Western government, the American and British scheme had hinged upon a great propaganda campaign, predicated on the belief that there was a sufficient domestic population in Syria that could be triggered into rising up.[47] The IRD and the USIA would make it appear as though the current Syrian regime was "the sponsor of plots, sabotage and violence directed against neighbouring governments" and would "goad" the Syrian and Egyptian radio station "into aggressive attacks upon neighbouring regimes."[48] This would, the IRD argued, make Syria's pro-Western neighbors feel morally obliged to intervene militarily, thereby justifying a takeover of the government. British short- and medium-wave transmitters would carry the messaging, while the CIA provided the "advisers" to Iraq, Lebanon, and Jordan.

The Soviets and Egyptians were not having any of it. While the British and American media blitz attempted to frame the Syrian coup attempt as a defense of democracy, Radio Moscow ran round-the-clock updates on the buildup of American-sponsored Turkish troops on the Syrian border.[49] "Today the system of colonialism is collapsing," the broadcasters reported, quoting an interview that Khrushchev had just given to the *New York Times*. "The ruling circles of the U.S.A. are . . . now playing the part of an international gendarme acting against the peoples who are struggling for freedom and independence."[50] "The Soviet people stand with the people of Syria," declared a Radio Moscow broadcaster in a story about aluminum factory workers in the Don Basin who had organized a "spontaneous march" in solidarity.[51] Just as in 1956, the Soviet popular performance of solidarity established a personal affinity between the people of the two regions.

Not surprisingly, the choicest words for the United States and Britain came from Voice of the Arabs. Every day in the summer and fall of 1957, Ahmed Said declared Cairo's allegiance to Syrian independence, recounting the Syrian government's abrupt removal of members of the US embassy involved in the attempt.[52] Finally, on October 13, Nasser sent soldiers to stand alongside the Syrians to stare across the border at the mobilized Turkish troops.

Needless to say, the Syrian coup, and its accompanying Anglo-American propaganda push, failed—another sign of the vast chasm that lay between the Arab world and the British/US understanding of the Arab world. In his history/memoir of the USIA, Alvin Snyder argues that the VOA's messaging was never going to work if the United States "didn't clean up its act at home." He cites the "tempest-tossed" Vietnam War and the street violence of the 1960s as evidence that US domestic chaos "undermined America's ability to project itself as a role model."[53] But audiences in the Middle East did not need to look to Vietnam and Detroit for such examples. The situation in Syria was reflective of the West's continued belief in the power of propaganda, despite the failures that it had just experienced in Suez. It indicated the ongoing conviction on the part of the Eisenhower administration that the United States could continue to overthrow unfriendly regimes in the postcolonial world as it had done in Iran and Guatemala. It showed an Anglo-American belief in the manipulability of the Arab world. It exposed the West's conviction that communism and Arab nationalism were two sides of the same problematic coin. The British historian George Kirk wrote in 1960 that the Egyptians had "hurr[ied] to succour Syria with an unneeded umbrella," implying that the Syrians had not needed such protection from Egypt and would have likely benefited from an Anglo-American-led regime change.[54] This perspective had been cultivated by British diplomats and media for years at that point, and it had largely become Eisenhower's perspective. It nonetheless bore little resemblance to the popular views of most Syrians, who may have felt ambiguous about the current regime but had no interest in replacing it with an Anglo-American puppet. It also reinforced the clear position that Nasser had achieved by the end of the decade as the voice of pan-Arab identity and neutralism.

The following January, Nasser promised a "new dawn in Arab history," the creation of the UAR.[55] While scholarship on the UAR tells a complex story of shifting internal alliances, over the radio, the combining of the nations of Egypt and Syria was a pure victory. In the words of Ahmed Said, it represented a manifestation of the "will of the Arab people as a result of long struggle." It appeared to be the culmination of Arab destiny, a confirmation of Nasser's mandate to lead, a strong repudiation of the West, and evidence of the Arab ability to overcome "imperialist plots." Underlying all of these messages was the UAR's promise of revolution. As Said put it, "It has become the duty of the UAR to support free Arabs everywhere, whether in their struggle against imperialism or against the underlings of imperialism [at home] who are more dangerous than imperialism."[56] More than ever, the success of the pan-Arab revolution now hinged on the person of Nasser. Stories abounded on Voice of the Arabs of Jordanians and Iraqis celebrating in the streets, shouting Nasser's name and demanding to be added to the UAR. Not an hour passed without the radio describing the crowds that gathered to celebrate the leader and his vision.

Nasser was taking a gamble in making such promises, which became apparent in the ever more Manichean language coming from Voice of the Arabs. If he could unite the Arab world behind his banner, that would deal a strong blow to his imperial, Hashemite, and Ba'athist enemies. He would become the next Napoleon, bringing the revolution on a tank instead of a horse. These were the grand aspirations that had shaped Voice of the Arabs messaging since 1953 and completely dominated it now. If his unification plan failed, however, he would be the one to carry the bulk of the blame. From this point forward, there was only space over the air for claims of victory and warnings of invasion and infiltration.

By 1958 the UAR's promise of liberation had come to include a panoply of revolutionary movements. Ahmed Said accused the British of "intrigues, bloodshed, and use of force" for the last century and a half upon "the sons of Muscat" in Oman.[57] "Defend your right! Dignity for the Arabs!" Said called out that February. Borrowing a page from Radio Moscow, Voice of the Arabs aired reports on gatherings of Egyptian engineers, housewives, and factory workers who declared their support for the "sacred liberation war waged by the Arab people in Algeria against French imperialism and in Oman against the British."[58] On March 7, only two months after the creation of the UAR, Said declared Yemen's inclusion in the UAR to be imminent, "the dream of the free generation and the desire of Arabs and Arab rulers everywhere . . . neither dominated by any pact nor its ruler humiliated by the dollar."[59] This was what the promise of liberation looked like, free of Western coercion, liberated from local forces that allied with the West, based on the promise of Nasser's forceful leadership and protection.

Then the British and Americans suffered a third blow in their efforts to influence the political ecosphere of the Middle East, this time in Iraq. On July 14, 1958, Iraq's Free Officer's Movement overthrew its pro-Western leaders, Nuri al-Said, King Faisal, and 'Abd al-Ilah. Thus began the Iraqi Revolution that ended the Hashemite dynasty and Iraq's alliance with the Baghdad Pact. In the wake of the unexpected coup, the British and Americans renamed the Baghdad Pact the Central Treaty Organization (CENTO) and moved the organization's headquarters to Ankara. That same year, the United States became an associate member. Not surprisingly, the USIA and the IRD blamed the overthrow on the Soviets and Radio Cairo.[60] Radio Moscow, meanwhile, expressed solidarity with the revolution, framing it as a workers' seizure of power from an outdated regime. It interspersed promises of support with constant caveats that the revolution had been spontaneous and not of Soviet design. Radio Cairo continued to lay claim to the pan-Arab cause, seeking to fold Arab nationalist sentiments and the Iraqi Revolution into the UAR's larger embrace.

A number of scholars have argued that the Iraqi Revolution, not the Suez Crisis, marked Britain's withdrawal from the region and the "orderly transfer of power" to the United States as the gendarme of anti-communist neocolonialism in the Middle East.[61] The shifting voices that filled the audiosphere in the late 1950s reflected this reality. The BBC continued to broadcast to large audiences, but it was the USIA that doubled down on the argument that events in Syria and Iraq represented a real threat to democracy and liberty in the Middle East. The VOA grew rapidly, both in its Arabic-speaking staff and its broadcasting hours. The VOA had always been the little brother to Britain's gargantuan propaganda program in the Middle East; now it was dictating messaging and policy. As the VOA stepped into this new position, its broadcasters believed they were able to offer a new, fresh approach that would win back the hearts and minds of Arab listeners who had grown cold toward the West because of outdated British colonial programming. In reality, very little of the USIA's new programming was new. It was mired in the same assumptions and contradictions that had defined the Western approach for decades.

The first demonstration of the VOA's muscle occurred in the summer of 1958, when the United States sent troops to prop up its ally, Camille Chamoun, whose precarious hold on power in Lebanon (now surrounded by enemy republics) seemed to be fading by the day. The USIA framed American military intervention in Lebanon as the protection of a legitimate leader and

FIGURE 11. Resolute Arab man holding back attacking flags of Britain and the United States with his rifle. *Source:* "Ostanovit' Agressora" [Stop the aggressors], 1958, Nikolai Tereshchenko. © 2024 Artists Rights Society (ARS), New York/UPRAVIS, Moscow.

ally from violent rebellion, couched in the now well-developed language of communist threat and economic aid. Over the air, the VOA framed the intervention as a new approach to supporting democracy in the Middle East. "The United States is committed to developing the confidence of the Arab people in the economic future of their own countries of the Middle East as a whole," the broadcasters declared.[62] If this sentence seems familiar, it is because it is an almost verbatim quote from George Marshall's famous Marshall Plan speech, given at Harvard University in 1947, with "Middle East" now substituted for "Europe."[63] Just as had been the case in 1947, the flow of American goods and soldiers into the Middle East represented American largess and defense of freedom against tyranny. For the VOA, the sending of marines to Beirut was an act of peace intended to preserve liberty. Like the British in decades past, the USIA found itself having to argue that Lebanon's dictatorship was best suited to defend the cause of liberty.

The VOA also justified the decision to send the US military into Lebanon with the argument that if the United States did not honor the obligations of the Eisenhower Doctrine, the Soviet Union would "push harder than ever, and border countries will submit to them."[64] The State Department was aware that Nasser and the Soviet Union had not spearheaded the

Iraqi coup. We know that the Soviet Union and Nasser were deeply concerned with the violence happening in the Fertile Crescent. We also know that Nasser had no interest in communism. And yet publicly this was the argument that spread out from the VOA. Reiterating Allen Dulles's promises to American members of Congress when cultivating approval for the intervention, the VOA argued that the Soviet Union was "undoubtedly behind" Nasser and the republican unrest happening in Lebanon and Iraq. Here was the domino theory articulated in (and to) the Middle East five years before it became a staple of articulated American foreign policy in Vietnam.

Critically, none of the Soviet, American, or British state departments and broadcasting programs seemed interested in (or perhaps capable of) acknowledging the places where their counterparts were telling the truth or where they shared the same interests. Dulles and Eisenhower were convinced of the Soviet project to spread global communism and of Nasser's collusion with the East. The Soviets were convinced of the American imperialist project. None of these convictions were as clear as the superpowers believed them to be. For his part, Nasser seemed most capable of seeing these realities but was still unwilling to acknowledge them in public. These assumptions dictated each program's master narratives, which had come about from decades of cultivated language and belief. Internal perceptions rooted in racism, imperialism, or ideology provided the track on which each side traveled. Every track also impacted the direction of the others. While Nasser may have been uninterested in communism, Radio Cairo nonetheless sided frequently with the Soviet Union and borrowed communist critiques of capitalist imperialism and encirclement. This in turn impacted how the Americans and British perceived the Egyptian stance on global communism. While Eisenhower may have been reticent about extending American military power in the Middle East, the VOA spent hundreds of hours justifying it, alongside the Eisenhower Doctrine and the Baghdad Pact. And while Khrushchev may have had no designs to spread global communism in the region, Radio Moscow's steady vitriol against the United States and Britain did little to assuage Western fears of aggressive communism. It didn't matter if these narratives weren't real if everyone believed them to be so.

As surveys revealed, Arabic-speaking listeners were even more unwilling to listen to the Americans than to the British. At least the British workers at the broadcasting services took the time to learn Arabic and had lived in the Middle East.[65] Worries over the loss of legitimacy faced by the VOA were such that in 1961 Wisconsin senator Alexander Wiley declared to his

AID GIVEN - AND AID REFUSED

Aid and technical assistance are very much in the news today.

In the Communist world, the Soviet Union has admitted - for the first time - that its aid has strings attached. This emerged in Moscow's threat to Iraq, that Russian economic assistance might be cut off because of Baghdad's campaign against the Kurdish rebels.

Commenting on the Moscow announcement, the Syrian paper Al-Ba'th said: "This unjust campaign is a strange violation of a principle which the USSR has for long adopted and to which it has repeated its adherence; namely, non-interference in the internal affairs of other States."

In another Communist capital, Peking, the Government has described the damage done to the Chinese economy as a result of Moscow's halt on aid and technical assistance.

In the free world, an American newspaper, the Chicago Daily News, recently paid tribute to British aid to developing countries. Its columnist, Norman Ross, said the British aid record was one to be proud of.

August 6, 1963

مساعدات تعطى ٠٠٠ ومساعدات ترفض

تحتل انها• المساعدات الفنية وغيرها مكانا بارزا في صحف هذه الايام ، وقد اعترف الاتحاد السوفياتي لاول مرة في تاريخه بان المساعدات التي يقدمها هي رهن بشروط معينة • وجاء ذلك في التهديد الذي وجهته موسكو الى العراق بانها ستضطر الى قطع المساعدات الاقتصادية السوفياتية بسبب الحملة التي تشنها بغداد ضد الثوار الاكراد •

وعلقت صحيفة " البعث " السورية على اذاعة موسكو بقولها : " ان عذه الحملة الظالمة هي في الواقع انتهاك للمبدأ الذى طالما تبجحت روسيا باعتناقه وكررت تمسكها به ، الا وهو مبدأ عدم التدخل في الشرؤن الداخلية للبلدان الاخرى •"

وفي بكين اسهبت الحكومة الصينية الشيوعية في رصف الاضرار التي لحقت بالاقتصاد الصيني من جراء قطع موسكو المساعدات الفنية وغيرها عن الصين الشيوعية•

اما في العالم الحر فقد اشادت اخيرا صحيفة الدايلي نيوز التي تصدر في شيكاغو بالمساعدات التي تقدمها بريطانيا الى البلدان الناشئة ، وقال محرر عامودها نورمان روس — ان سجل المساعدات البريطانية يدعو الى الفخر والاعتزاز ، ولا سيما ان مساعمات بريطانيا وحدها في هذا المضمار فاقت مساهمات الاتحاد السوفياتي وجميع دول الكتلة الصينية السوفياتية مجتمعة• واضاف المحرر بقوله :

" وقدمت بريطانيا منذ عام ١٩٥٦ ما يقرب من مليارى دولار الى البلدان الناشئة كان اكثر من النصف بمثابة منح مباشرة لا مجال لتسديدها ، وجاءت في المرتبة الثالثة بعد الولايات المتحدة وفرنسا في ما قدمته من مساعدات ٠ اما ما قدمته بالنسبة لمجموع انتاجها فهو جواز لنسبة ما قدمناه نحن •

" وكان نصيب الهند ما يقرب من ثلاثين بالمائة من هذا المبلغ بينما نالت بلدان افريقيا الناشئة ما يزيد على نصفه ، ولقد انفقت بريطانيا ما يزيد على خمسائة مليون دولار في بلدان مشروع كولومبو في جنوب آسيا الشرقي لوحدها منذ عام ١٩٥١٠•

وهناك /٠٠٠•

FIGURE 12. Transcript of British broadcast questioning underlying designs behind Soviet aid to the Middle East. *Source:* 1962 IRD Broadcast, "Middle East: Pamphlets and Articles Issued in December 1962," TNA, FO 1110/1689 Foreign Office: Information Research Department, 1962.

colleagues on the floor of Congress that "the cold figures on international shortwave broadcasting show the Voice of America lagging behind Radio Moscow. Radio Peiping, and Radio Cairo."[66] It did not help that the Soviet Union was now reporting daily on the violence being visited on civil rights activists and children entering desegregated schools across America.

Then another war broke out that backed all the broadcasting programs into an even tighter corner. On September 26, 1962, a group of Yemeni army officers orchestrated a coup that led to the overthrow and attempted murder of Yemen's new imam, the prince Muhammad al-Badr, who had been on the throne for only eight days following his father's death. The new leaders declared Yemen a republic, standing against the royalists loyal to al-Badr, who had the support of other army officers, merchants, the Zaydi tribes from the north, and the British and Americans. Radio Cairo and Radio Moscow quickly came to the aid of the new revolutionary regime, broadcasting throughout that fall their fealty to the republican cause.

By the time the Yemeni war began, both Nasser and Khrushchev had something to prove there. Syrian officers had recently pulled the country out of the UAR, dashing the great pan-Arab plan and damaging Nasser's reputation in the process. Egypt was facing worsening scarcities of domestic goods, a rising trade deficit, high debt payments, soaring defense costs, and a shortage of foreign currency. Nasser saw the joint effort with the Soviets in Yemen as a way to regain lost legitimacy and leadership. It was also an opportunity to support the anti-royalist, anti-imperialist cause.[67] It was a similar story for Khrushchev, who had announced in 1961 that the Soviet Union was morally obliged to aid "Third World" liberation movements that were struggling against colonial domination, even if they were not socialists.[68] As many Khrushchev scholars have noted, his decision to help the Egyptians in their support of Yemen came from the same complex personal and political impulses that drove him to assist Fidel Castro in Cuba and Patrice Lumumba in Congo.[69] By helping revolutionaries abroad, he hoped to reinforce his own image as a man of action and conviction. Yemen was going to be a propaganda victory—a chance to show Khrushchev's and Nasser's power and constancy as the leaders of a pan-Arab, secular, republican movement that was resurging across the Middle East.

But it was not to be. Despite the Radio Moscow stories on the Soviet Union's dispatching of planes and pilots to the Middle East, and despite the daily broadcasts from Voice of the Arabs attesting to the heroic freedom fighters who were keeping the British- and American-backed royalists at bay, on the ground the war was long, inconclusive, and costly. It famously became a quagmire that threatened Egyptian social and economic solvency, set the stage for the Six-Day War, and marked the decline of Egypt and the promise of secular Arab nationalism.

In the years that followed Voice of the Arabs placed blame for the continued fighting in Yemen squarely on the shoulders of the West. As Ahmed Said put it, "The undeniable objective of this pact is to dominate the Middle East and ensure that it remains within the sphere of western influence." He blamed King Hussein of Jordan for providing trained men and weapons, artillery, and mortars.[70] He saved his deepest ire for the British, who held fast to their one remaining foothold in Aden, which was the second largest port in the world and the headquarters of the British Middle East command. As propagandists have known for centuries, the easiest way to justify the strengthening of authoritarian power is to conjure the threat of outside invasion. Such threats fund militaries, stave off calls for reform, conceal weaknesses in leadership, allow for shows of individual heroism, transform public performances of allegiance into a prerequisite for citizenship and patriotism, and justify the suppression of domestic protest. Like its Soviet, British, and American counterparts, this became the project of Voice of the Arabs.

In London, Ahmed Said became Whitehall's foil for explaining away anti-British and anti-Western sentiment in the Middle East. The British were the first of the Western allies to argue that the Egyptian-Yemeni alliance represented a radical threat to Saudi Arabia, their holdings in Aden, general peninsular stability, freedom, peace, democracy, and so forth. True to form, high-ranking British politicians and ministers of defense argued that "anti-Egyptian propaganda in the Yemen" was needed immediately.[71] Because Ahmed Said was the greatest thorn in the side of British broadcasting, he was its most convenient scapegoat.

Ahmed Said's role as foe and foil for the British government and its broadcasters was most clearly exhibited in the summer of 1965, when he visited Britain as a part of a five-person UAR delegation (now without Syria). He and his colleagues were in London for discussions on the proxy war in Yemen and the continued British colonization of Aden and the Aden Protectorate (South Arabia). Said's presence in the delegation was both a testament to the power that he wielded in the world of Middle Eastern public opinion and an explicit signal to the British that the UAR perceived itself to be operating from a position of strength. Said would take notes and report back on what he saw, over the air. This, everyone knew.

Said's presence in the delegation made national news in the United Kingdom and sparked heated debate on the floor of the House of Commons. On the day of the delegation's arrival, Colin Jackson and George Thomson, both Labour members of Parliament (MPs), argued that, given the arrival of the UAR delegation, now was a good time to send a British group to Cairo. Nigel Fisher, a Conservative MP who had recently worked as a minister for Commonwealth Relations, clambered his way to the podium and declared it completely unsuitable to be hosting the delegation or to entertain the prospect of sending a British group to the UAR, "in view of continued terrorist activities inspired from Cairo which have resulted in the killing of British Service personnel and Arab civilians." He then asked indignantly, "Can the Honorable Gentleman (referring to Thomson) tell me why the director of Cairo Radio, which has been responsible for the most anti-British propaganda for years, is now the honored guest of Her Majesty's Government in London?" Sir Barret Janner (Labour) then jumped in to ask Thomson if he was planning on discussing the propaganda problem with Nasser and Ahmed Said. "Will you express to this individual [meaning Said] . . . that we highly deprecate the kind of propaganda emanating day by day from Radio Cairo?" Reginald Maudling, the foreign affairs spokesman for the Tories, then declared it "incredible" that Said should be standing on British soil "as an honored guest."[72] At this point, Sir Godfrey Nicholson, the Conservative MP from Farnham, asked Thomson pointedly whether he understood the gravity of having Said in the country. "There comes a point at which turning the other cheek is interpreted as weakness," he quipped, to much applause.[73] Said had become for the world the voice of anti-colonialism on the radio— a symbol of British decline, an example of Arab independence for some, and a reflection of Orientalist stereotypes about Arab emotionality and duplicity for others.

Said then had his chance to respond. Later that very day, Said, who was comfortably ensconced at a posh London hotel, told the *Daily Mirror* that he preferred "not to be thought of as anti-British, but pro-Arab." Then, in a gesture that threw the British Foreign Office into a maelstrom, he invited MP Nicholson to Cairo to broadcast his views on air, on the Voice of the Arabs.[74] Predictably, the Foreign Office declined the offer. In internal documents, the staff agreed that they could not be certain that Cairo Radio would not play tricks with whatever an MP said on the air. "And even if they allowed any effective British statements to be made, Said would make his own style of reply and the exchange might develop into a positively harmful public debate."[75] When Said returned to Cairo that July, the Foreign Office listened closely to his broadcasts, expressing despair that Said's tone was "as bad as ever."[76] It appeared to everyone that the Egyptians were controlling the public sphere. True to form, when Arab anti-British sentiment continued in the Middle East that July over British interference in the Emirate of Sharjah (now the United Arab Emirates) over the deposition of Saqr bin Sultan Al Qasimi, the British Foreign Office first blamed Ahmed Said.[77]

For their part, the Egyptians continued to make good use of the British menace. For the last decade, the British had proved a handy enemy for rallying populations behind Nasser's banner as the defender of the Arab world against aggressive Western imperialism. The decision to send Said with the delegation in the summer of 1965 was part of the larger strategy to provide nonstop evidence of the English threat. When the talks did not go well, Said was there to recount the story of their failure in full narrative glory upon his return: "While we met in London to find a suitable solution for the question of the British presence in the occupied South; while British propaganda [made it] look as if she was ready to reach an understanding and arrive at a point which could be a basis for a solution to the problem; while liberal-minded people inside Britain herself were calling for an end to the imperialist obstinacy and outdated mentality which still dictates British policy; Britain took in secrecy and behind everybody all the necessary steps and measures which led to its end."[78] He said of the Organization for the Liberation of the Occupied South, which was fighting to push the British out of South Arabia: "With gun and bullet we shall terrorize the intruders and the enemies of the people. The price of freedom is high and its path is long and difficult. . . . There is no force however powerful that can turn the people of the south from their will and aspirations. . . .The British government should know that the time of misrepresentations has gone for good."[79] He spoke of the "graveyard" that South Arabia had become for British soldiers. "The wolves are falling in the jungle," he said, again mobilizing the image of the predatory animal brought to its knees. "And the remainder will meet the same fate if they do not leave."[80] While we know that many of the crises that unfolded in the south in those years revolved around internecine problems, over the radio it was the British who could be held to blame for the UAR's failures and the British who appeared to have lost when the UAR was successful.

Indeed, for Voice of the Arabs, the West became the primary culprit for explaining the UAR's difficulties in creating the pan-Arab state—a state that

Nasser had long envisioned but had proven unable to create. The narrative that the West stood in the way of achieving Arab unity had been around for a long time. This was a useful story, and it was in many ways true. The crusade against the West had been a critical part of defining Egypt's revolutionary identity and had provided a common enemy that would unite the Arab world. It also helped to smooth over the bitter struggles for power that often characterized the inter-Arab political and social world. After the Syrian secession from the UAR in 1961, Nasser found his dream of a pan-Arab republic fading. While the causes of the Syrian secession were rooted in a myriad of Syrian resentments toward Nasser's centralizing, pro-Egyptian mission, this was not a story that Voice of the Arabs could recount. Instead, Nasser's propaganda program blamed the loss of Syria on Britain, the United States, Israel, Turkey, Iran, Iraq, and Saudi Arabia. All appeared to share the blame for the floundering of the pan-Arab cause, made worse now by the crisis in Yemen.

By 1962, Ahmed Said and the Voice of the Arabs found themselves in a position where there were lots of things they could not say. Tensions in Yemen continued to escalate, with republican attacks on British-controlled South Arabia being followed by British, and then UAR and Soviet, retaliation. Each time, Ahmed Said claimed an Arab victory over the failing imperialists, each time arguing that pan-Arab unity was right around the corner. In the end, the Yemeni conflict drove the Saudis and the British into a rapprochement and pushed Egypt into deeper debt with the Soviet Union—all as it struggled to engage in a radical socialization drive at home. Popular discontent in Egypt grew, and the patina surrounding Nasser began to rust. Not only was Egypt unable defeat the British in the south or the Americans and Saudis in the north, but by 1962 it also could not manufacture sufficient support among the many tribes that dominated Yemeni society. Egypt had become a modern, secular state whose legitimacy rested on its ability to argue for a revolutionary ideal based on a shared vision of a nationalist, pan-Arab future. Ironically, when the Egyptians found themselves repeatedly unable to sell their project to their erstwhile allies in Yemen, they turned to none other than the British for advice on what to do. Salah al-Din al-Hadidi, the Egyptian commander of military intelligence, admitted in his memoir years later that after they realized that digging wells and treating the sick were not going to work in swaying the Yemeni population to the republican side, they turned to the British for ideas. It was Lawrence of Arabia's work in establishing cooperation with local sheikhs in the First World War, and his purchasing of loyalty with silver and gold when possible, that served as the inspiration for the Egyptian creation of the Administration of Tribal Affairs in 1962.[81]

None of this could appear on the radio. In the summer of 1963, Ahmed Said traveled to San'a and, over the Yemeni airwaves, declared that the Egyptians would not leave Yemen as long as it did not have an army "capable of undermining the monarchist regime in Saudi Arabia."[82] Even anti-Israeli rhetoric became useful in the fight for Yemeni hearts and minds. As numerous scholars have noted, the plight of Palestine and its refugees had become (and still is) a useful tool for Arab leaders that could be deployed in the fight to defend their domestic and international policies. As the war in Yemen became increasingly unpopular at home and abroad, Nasser, Ahmed Said, and Nasser's great advocate in print, Muhammed Haykal, turned to the argument that fighting for republicans in Yemen was tantamount to fighting for the Palestinian cause against Israeli aggression. This idea carried such lasting power that Said wrote of it fifty years later, arguing that Egypt got embroiled in Yemen in part because of the "sweeping wave of pressure to liberate Palestine."[83]

Absent, too, were stories over Egyptian radio about the single-party system created by the 1956 Egyptian Constitution as well as Nasser's ongoing assault on the Muslim Brotherhood and the Ba'athist movement. In the sources that we have, only Israeli radio speaks of the Muslim Brotherhood after 1956, noting when Nasser purged its members from his government, including Sad Jabr at-Tamimin, who worked for Voice of the Arabs as a jamming specialist, and Amin Ismail, who was an assistant director for the EBS.[84] Scant mentions appeared in September 1965 of the vast conspiracy by the Muslim Brotherhood to commit assassinations and overthrow the state—a conspiracy foiled by Egypt's Secret Service. Stories of victorious pan-Arab popular solidarity supporting Nasserist anti-imperialism, socialism, and secularism did not sit comfortably alongside conversations about internal Egyptian and Syrian groups who were interested in nonsecular (in the case of the Muslim Brotherhood) or non-Nasserist socialist (in the case of the Ba'athists) socio-political-economic systems. Over the Voice of the Arabs, there was only one unified voice that spoke for the Arab people. This was so at all the state-run radio programs, where brooking internal dissent was a clear admission of weakness.

To the casual listener, it would also have sounded like Voice of the Arabs and Radio Moscow were speaking as allies over the air; upon closer listening, however, the cracks had already started to show. This became particularly apparent after Nasser gave his famous speech in May 1962, in which he explained the differences between Arab socialism and Soviet communism; reiterated his belief in private property, landownership, and religion; declared a crackdown on local communist and socialist movements (particularly Ba'athists); and asserted that he could bring about a happy democracy without the help of Marxism-Leninism—all while also arguing for the Arab world's continued need for Soviet assistance and protection.[85]

Historians have traditionally argued that the deterioration of Soviet and Egyptian relations began sometime between 1967 and Nasser's death in 1970.[86] More recently, Jesse Ferris has contended that the deterioration started much earlier, with the fall of Khrushchev in October 1964. There is evidence that not only is Ferris's assessment correct, but at least in the world of radio and propaganda, the Egyptians were mobilizing anti-Soviet rhetoric at least as early as January 1963, during the early months of the joint military campaign in Yemen. While Voice of the Arabs remained positive about the Egyptian relationship with the Soviet Union, Egyptian covert radio began to argue that the Soviet Union's intentions in the Middle East were similar to those of the West. The transcripts of Egyptian covert radio are sadly only available through the CIA-monitored Foreign Broadcast Information Service. It is perhaps not surprising that the CIA paid attention, when, on January 10, Cairo's alternative station, the Voice of the Arab Nation, warned that the Soviet Union was "trying to implement its policy in the Arab east . . . endeavoring to benefit from western pressure . . . by granting [the Arab people] aid to withstand this pressure, not because of its desire to liberate the Arab people from western imperialism but because of an ambition to expand its influence in the Arab world."[87] The Voice of the Arab Nation connected this skepticism about Soviet interests in Yemen and Egypt to the general idea that *all* of the West, the Soviet Union included, presented a threat to Arab unity. The broadcast claimed that "some" Arab governments had declared themselves to be aligned with neither the West nor the East, but with "positive neutrality, nonalignment, true Arab nationalism, and democratic rule" (referring to Egypt). It then went on to list the countries that had pursued such independence: Jordan and Iraq, which had fallen under British influence; Saudi Arabia, which was under the thumb of the Americans; and Syria, which had been "turned into a battlefield for influence" between the French, English, Americans, and communists. But the Soviets were also a threat, the broadcaster concluded. "The Arab people can no longer be deceived by imported slogans. . . . Everyone—Western imperialism, Eastern imperialism, the bases of the two types of imperialism, and their stooges and lackeys—know that the Arab giant has set forth."[88] Ironically, Russia's historic ability to claim both Western and Eastern identity was now being used against it. Its professed ability to bring Eastern culture to the heathen West and Western modernity to the backward East was increasingly exposed as a ruse for an imperial project. By 1963 it was clear that the long-standing Egyptian undercurrent of ambiguity toward the Soviet Union had become more visible.

· · ·

The audiosphere became a hardened place in the period between the Suez Crisis and the 1967 Six-Day War. One gets the sense, after reading thousands of transcripts from this decade, that while there were many broadcasters and journalists who endeavored sincerely to report the truth to their listening public, they were overshadowed by state-run forces interested in promoting a message whose content was determined at every point by their interest in retaining power. It is no coincidence that memoirs written by journalists from these years speak repeatedly of their frustration with heavy-handed, bureaucratic civil servants who increasingly stepped in to control what got said over the air and in print.

What got said over the air was a product of older forces that had been at play in shaping the audiosphere since the 1940s—the promises of liberty, self-determination, and peace; the assurances of economic development; the threat of invasion and ideological infiltration—none of it was new. Not only this, but the rhetorical tools used to promote those messages were largely the same across the radio dial—the steady outrage; the commitment to truth amidst a sea of lies; the attestations of deep concern for the needs of listening populations; the claims to expertise, wealth, generosity, and good leadership; the harkening to religious themes; the creation of group identities based on shared antagonisms; the calls for righteous mobilization; even the phrasing of sentences and the use of particular metaphors—all could be found on every station. This was a reality of the audiosphere, despite the fact that the broadcasting programs were in opposition to each other and were seeking differing allegiances from their audiences.

These messages were filled with conditions for what it meant to be "Arab"—conditions that local populations increasingly rejected as manipulative and hypocritical. As Johan Franzén has shown, most Arab listeners wanted nothing to do with the US and British "turgid and indigestible," mass produced anti-communist material that had no connection to the experiences of local populations on the ground.[89] While socialist movements cropped up across the Middle East in the following years, most of them were not interested in Moscow, much less Britain. Meanwhile, Sayyid Qutb, the influential Egyptian advocate for the creation of an Islamist state (who was executed by Nasser's regime in 1966), called on Arabs to upend the hegemonic social, political, and discursive order created by the West, by its allies in the Middle East, and by Nasser's secular authoritarianism. At the foundation of his thinking was the idea that there was no authentic center of representative power in the Middle East. He summoned Arabs across the region to "refute the false and baseless with a statement of truth proclaimed by Islam."[90] When the constant assurances coming from the state that it would improve society went unfulfilled again and again, Islamic movements stepped in to take over leadership of the Arab Middle East.[91] By 1967, what it meant to be Arab was no longer being defined by the great powers, whose hold on the narrative had become delegitimized by years of "false and baseless" promises. The hopeful pursuit of modernization and liberation that had characterized the postwar era came to an end, as did some of the power of the people and states who had made those promises.

TEN

Poisonous Propaganda or Productive Progress to Peace

1967 AND THE COLLAPSE OF THE AUDIOSPHERE

ON APRIL 6, 1967, a major aerial battle broke out over the Golan Heights between Israel and Syria, with Israeli pilots downing six Syrian MiGs, followed by a flyby over Damascus. Nasser, who had been receiving false intelligence from the Soviets showing that the Israelis were planning an attack on Syria, called the Arab world to attention. On May 14, Nasser ordered Egyptian soldiers to march into the previously demilitarized Sinai. He closed the Straits of Tiran to Israeli vessels. Troops mobilized in Syria and Jordan.

War was coming. "We are fully ready and prepared to face racialist Zionism and those who stand behind it," Nasser declared over the radio. "If Israel, backed by imperialism and reaction, believes that the time has come to undermine the great Arab cause and the whole Arab revolutionary movement, it will be met with deadly blows and an explosion which will destroy and eliminate it from the area forever."[1] Israel also mobilized, and on June 5 it launched a series of preemptive air strikes against Egyptian airfields and other facilities, along with a ground offensive in the Gaza Strip and Sinai. Egypt was caught unawares, with most of its air force taken out and its soldiers forced to retreat entirely out of Sinai within six days. Jordan and Iraq proved reluctant allies, refusing to commit major forces to the collapsing effort. Saudi Arabia's King Faisal also withheld sending promised support. Voice of the Arabs and Radio Damascus, meanwhile, promoted two messages: that Arab victory was still assured and that any setbacks were caused by direct American and British military assistance to the Israelis.

In the end, what was supposed to have been a resolute show of pan-Arab defense and liberation ended in resounding defeat. Over twenty thousand Arab troops died in the war, and hundreds of thousands of Palestinians and Syrians were forced to flee from the West Bank and the Golan Heights.[2] In the wake of the debacle, Nasser famously tendered his resignation. Egyptians poured out into the streets, demanding that he remain, calling for continued war against Israel, Britain, and the United States. Nasser returned, but he and his propagandists could not maintain the ruse for long. The historian Paul Fussell famously wrote that every war is ironic because every war is worse than expected.[3] Nowhere was this truer than in Egypt in 1967. For years, Nasser's regime had argued that the Egyptian army was fully modernized and expertly trained. Special parades, songs, poems, banners, and rituals reinforced the promise of victory. The "drone" of victory was everywhere, in company names, car brands, store fronts, and public health initiatives. This was to have been the moment of liberation and reunion for Palestinians, the settling of scores with Israel, and the manifestation of unified Arab power for the entire Middle East.

Instead, it ended in death, destruction, and more diaspora. In a matter of hours, revolutionary Egypt collapsed, "a laughing-stock" whose touted promises of strength were little more than words.[4] People who were alive in Egypt, Syria, Iraq, and Jordan during those fateful months remember the sense of disbelief that reverberated through the populace as they realized that Nasser's assurances had been more delusion than descriptions of reality. As the novelist Naguib Mahfouz wrote, "Never before or after in my life had I ever experienced such a shattering of consciousness and shock as I felt at that moment."[5] Scholars, essayists, and poets have since argued that 1967 represented a "rude awakening from the sweet dream" of Nasser's pan-Arab ascendancy. For writers like Tawfiq al-Hakim, Nizar Qabbani, and Ahmed Baha' al-Din, the psychological trauma of the defeat hinged on the fact that state rhetoric had framed the impending battle as an assured, historic victory of Arab empowerment and renewal—only to find their nation left humiliated and in tatters. It was not just a military defeat; it was a delegitimation of Arab modernization and of the pan-Arab nationalist ideology that undergirded the Nasser regime.[6] It was, for the secular Arab world, the end of victory culture.[7]

At the center of the war's brutal irony buzzed the audiosphere. Voice of the Arabs famously stayed on the air throughout most of the war, telling listeners across the Arab world that victory was imminent. On the second morning, although it was already clear that the Israelis had gained the upper hand, Egyptian state radio continued to report positively on the Egyptian and Syrian armies' progress. Most listeners believed what they heard. Winston Burdette, who was a reporter for CBS in Cairo that June, wrote later that there was no panic in the streets that day. On the contrary, "there was jubilation." Cheers and chanting followed the radio's reports that twenty-three Israeli planes had been shot down, followed quickly by a correction that, in fact, seventy planes had been downed already.[8] Voice of the Arabs gave false information regarding troop movements and casualty numbers. It was not until later that people realized the falsity of what they had heard and learned about the casualties. Here was the source of the great irony. All those expectations—of a pan-Arab superpower, of a revolutionary defeat of Israel, and of a grand developmental transformation through nationalized five-year plans that would bring prosperity to even the lowliest citizens—all turned out to be false. It was arguably the failure of these expectations and this rhetoric that tolled the last bell for Nasser's pan-Arab dream. It was on the air that those expectations had been created, and it was on the air that those promises collapsed.

Like the histories of the Nakhba and Suez, the amount of writing on the Six-Day War and its consequences is voluminous. Social scientists have meticulously traced the infrastructural weaknesses in Nasser's Egypt, chronicling its bloated civil and industrial workforce; its indebted economy; its collapsing domestic social contract; its exploding population; its conflicts with other pan-Arab movements, especially the Ba'athists; its crumbling relationship with the United States, Britain, and the Soviet Union; its increasing authoritarianism; its lost legitimacy following Syria's retreat from the UAR; and its crippling war in Yemen.[9] Anthropologists have also paid attention to the emotional damage that Arab populations experienced as a consequence of the defeat.[10] To this day, historians and laypeople speak of the trauma inflicted by Ahmed Said and the "Big Lie" of Arab victory that he promoted on the radio in those fateful days.

Missing from the historical record is an examination of what actually was said over the radio. The story, it turns out, is much more complicated than popular memory would have us believe. Contrary to popular opinion, Ahmed Said and Voice of the Arabs were not single-handedly responsible for the falsities that coursed over the air that summer, nor were they saying anything new. *All* Egyptian and Syrian radio in those days touted the assured victory of the Arab armies and targeted the United States as the real threat behind Israel. They used the now entrenched language of pan-Arab solidarity, labeling their Arab enemies as "reactionaries." They leaned on poetic meter and metaphor to conjure a vision of a powerful Arab alliance that would ultimately be victorious. These were the very same tools that had worked successfully during the Suez Crisis. Just as critically, such arguments were not exclusive to Said or to the Egyptians and the Syrians. Radio Moscow, the VOA, and even the BBC constructed particular visions of the conflict to suit their needs, based on decades of discursive use and reuse, that were also only tangentially connected to what was really happening on the ground. The Soviet Union blamed the United States, feigning support for an Arab world it had no intention of going to war to defend. The VOA claimed innocence, ignoring the role that American arms sales had played in escalating the crisis. The BBC watched with smug dismay, quietly reminding its listeners of what happens when the calming hand of empire is pulled away, ignoring the role of Britain in creating the crisis in the first place. The falsities that defined that fateful summer had become a defining feature of the entire audiospace, and lying was a feature from which the varying state broadcasters could scarcely escape.

While the state rhetoric of 1967 was not new, that year did nonetheless mark a pivotal, culminating moment. The betrayal of the audiosphere and the disillusionment that it precipitated helped to usher in a new era when certain Arab populations resolved to take their liberation and their language into their own hands, when fewer and fewer people were willing to buy the stories they were being fed, and when the United States assumed the role of colonial antagonist that it arguably still plays to this day.[11] Laila Khaled, the famous militant who participated in two airplane hijackings in 1969 and 1970 with the Popular Front for the Liberation of Palestine, said as much when she argued for the building of new, more authentic, "symbolic meanings" for language and action. The promises of state-run modernization and representation from the West were moribund. Far from providing the promised development that would liberate an independent Arab world, the Americans, she argued, had instead used their vast resources to supply the arms and money to Israel that had kept Palestinians in exile for over two decades.[12] The same applied to Nasser, whose pan-Arab nationalism had become, in Khaled's words, "a spent force in historical terms . . . repressive, managerial."[13] These were the "historical circumstances of the 1960s," when disillusioned populations across the globe rose up against the ideas and leaders that had failed to deliver on postwar promises of "freedom and prosperity."[14] Because so much of what they had been told was false, all of it became worthy of rejection, including the promises of liberal democracy and modernization. The radio played a critical role in mapping and enabling this collapse.

...

If one were only listening to Egyptian and Syrian radio in the late spring of 1967, it would have appeared as though Egypt was on the brink of war with the United States. On May 11, 1967, Egyptian and Syrian radio broadcasts were filled with news that the Israelis were amassing soldiers on the Syrian border, backed by US logistical support.[15] As Muhammad Haykal, the chief editor of the newspaper *Al-Ahram*, put it when he took to the microphone the next day, "Like a monstrous spider, the United States has been slowly building a web in which it plans to entangle Egypt and Syria."[16] American sins were myriad. The United States promised friendship, all while arming Israel and funding Saudi Arabia in the Yemeni war. "Like a sword of Damocles," the United States held Egypt hostage through its need for American wheat. It also sowed discord at home, financing the Muslim Brotherhood, which, Haykal warned, "acts like a hidden mine under the surface of political life in Egypt—funded graciously by the CIA." Even more troublesome, Haykal declared, was the fact that the country had been lulled into complacency by the appeal of easy American wheat and the requests of President Lyndon Johnson to avoid violence. This was the moment when Egypt had to choose between accepting the politically charged and humiliating gifts of the West or taking the harder path by refusing those gifts and the obligations they engendered. Egypt would choose the hard path, Haykal claimed: "Egypt will tackle the cobwebs of the huge monstrous spider that seeks to paralyze its movements."[17]

By 1967 the tone of Egyptian and Syrian radio had settled into familiar tropes. Listeners would have recognized Ahmed Said's anaphoric prose when he declared, "We challenge you, Israel. No, in fact we do not address the challenge to you, Israel, because you are unworthy of our challenge. But we challenge you, America. We challenge you, gangsters of the Bay of Pigs. We challenge you with death which is claiming your soldiers in Vietnam. We challenge you to come near, with Israel, to our gulf of Aqaba."[18] Also familiar would have been his catchphrase: "Oh Arabs, The United States is Israel. Oh Arabs, have you heard the latest news of the United States or rather of Israel, the news of Israel or rather of the United States?"[19] Recognizable, too, would have been his matter-of-fact conveyance of complex ideas: "It has been proved that collusion has been carried out between Washington and Tel Aviv."[20] Said now equated the United States with Israel, transferring to it from Britain the title of imperial aggressor. "Today, the

United States is standing with the remnants of Western colonialism in an attempt to conquer the people and their will, and to rid them of their rights and sovereignty." Radio Damascus similarly told its listeners that the CIA was to blame for the "sinful creation of confusion among the ranks of the citizens."[21] All of this language was well established in the lexicon of Voice of the Arabs by 1967.

Running alongside accusations of American and British complicity, the standard message from Cairo in the months before the war was that the Egyptian armies were fully capable of waging a successful conflict. In the decades since the 1967 war, Ahmed Said has borne much of the blame for promising an Egyptian victory amid defeat in those fateful days. In truth, Voice of the Arabs was one of many channels that claimed Egyptian readiness on the battlefield. Radio Cairo, which was the larger radio channel that oversaw all state-led radio in Egypt, had been interviewing the Egyptian commanders of the Eastern front and of land forces since mid-May. General Abd al-Mushin Murtaji, the commander of the Sinai front, reported on May 18 that Egyptian forces were "prepared for this battle," with "adequate forces to counter Israel effectively." He reported that Israel's possession of modern weapons "does not mean it has gained supremacy over us nor does it pose any sudden danger," and that the morale of the military was "very high."[22] The next day, Field Marshal Abd al-Hakim took the microphone. "I say very frankly that nobody inside or outside the Arab east should doubt that the UAR will strike any attempt at aggression with all its might. It is time for the policy of braggadocio and conceit pursued by the Israeli enemy to be decisively ended."[23] As Radio Cairo put it, "Reactionary defeatism and collusion with imperialism and the U.S. arms deals with Israel are not enough to provide security and protection for the enemy. The main UAR forces can deal crushing blows to the enemy. Meanwhile, the Egyptian Army operating in Yemen can carry out its heroic role there. . . . Remnants of imperialism's crumbling system are now in retreat."[24] Meanwhile, the Syrian foreign minister, Ibrahim Makhus, argued over Voice of the Arabs:

> All of Egypt's revolutionary potential has been put into the battle. . . . Zionism, reaction, and colonialism have overlooked the fact that revolutionary forces always hold the reins of initiative. . . . This initiative is not confined merely to military mobilization, which has been completed in both countries to such an extent that both armies have become one, but also to the initiating of all revolutionary movements by the toiling masses everywhere in the Arab homeland. . . . We challenge the Israeli gangs and the U.S. Sixth

Fleet to make the first move. Then the Arab homeland would be a grave for colonialism and for Israel.[25]

As many listeners would later realize, the braggadocio of revolutionary victory was very much alive at home. One would never have predicted that massive protests by students and workers would be erupting against Nasser's regime in a matter of months, followed by the UAR's outlawing of demonstrations and the training of riot police.

When looking for proof of Egypt's inevitable victory, the radio stations turned again and again to the precedent set in Suez eleven years earlier. Just as Nasser had been triumphant against the British, French, and Israelis, so too would he be against the Israelis and Americans. By 1967 the state had rewritten the history of Suez to be a story of Egyptian military victory over the Israelis. The story of Suez was now used as an example of unified Arab action, with the military defeats and internecine struggles of those years smoothed over to present a stirring example of what was possible when the entire Muslim-Arab world came together to fight. Such was the claim of the exiled Saudi king, Saud bin Abdulaziz, from his pyrrhic perch before a Radio Cairo microphone: "Just as Saudi Arabia stood with our sister, Egypt, during the treacherous aggression in Suez, so too will we today."[26] Saud, who had been replaced as king of Saudi Arabia by his brother Faisal in 1964 and was now in exile in Cairo, still claimed to speak for his country, offering useful proof to Egyptian listeners that Nasser had united all of the Arab world. The victorious legacy of Suez was so critical that Nasser chose to make it the topic of one of his major speeches, which he delivered to the UAR Air Force Advanced Command and which was broadcast on Radio Cairo on May 23, the day he closed the Gulf of Aqaba to Israel. "On the night of 29 October 1956, the Israeli aggression against us began." Nasser proceeded to deliver a history lesson on the Suez Crisis to his air force commanders.

> In 1956, we did not have the opportunity to fight Israel directly. Despite our withdrawal, Israel was unable to occupy any of our positions except after we left them. Israel created a big uproar, boasted, and said a great deal about the Sinai campaign and the Sinai battle. Every one of you know all the rubbish that was said. They probably believed it themselves.[27]

The question of what people believe when they speak was now, as ever, in question. It was here that Nasser inscribed the might of the Egyptian army and air force upon the past: "Ben Gurion refused to undertake anything unless he was given a guarantee that [France and Britain] would protect him from the Egyptian bombers and Air Force. This is why France sent fighter planes to Ben Gurion and why Britain pledged to bomb Egyptian airfields.... This goes to show how much they feared Egyptian forces.... Gurion could not attack Egypt out of fear of the Egyptian Air Force and bombers." And that was then, in 1956, when Egypt had had only a few Ilyushin bombers. Now, he argued, they had many. Israel now was not backed by Britain and France. "It has the United States, which supports it and supplies it with arms, but the world cannot again accept the plotting which took place in 1956." For Nasser, the current conflict offered a chance to set the military record straight, to "make the world see matters in their true perspective." As in 1956, the language of the dog entered Nasser's vocabulary to describe his rivals. Again, Israel's victory or loss was dependent upon outside help. Nasser spoke of the shared deceits coming out of Israel in 1956 and 1967: first the pretense of invasion and now the "false message that Egypt [was] bogged down in Yemen. Of course they say that we are bogged down in Yemen. We are in Yemen. But they seem to believe the lies they have been saying all these years." Nasser contrasted this with the "accurate information" he had recently received, just as he had in 1956, regarding Israel's military movements. The speech offered a convincing historical precedent, positing victory in the current crisis as an inevitability based on all the variables that it shared with the previous crisis.

The Egyptian and Syrian language of blame took on a decidedly Soviet tone, a trend that had been developing for years and was reflective of the leftist turn in Syrian politics in the previous years. As Radio Damascus put it, "The revolution has successfully placed all the popular sectors under arms to crush any conspiratorial attempt by the bourgeois feudalist elements within the country, and any attempt from abroad by imperialist, reactionary, and Zionist allies."[28] This was undoubtedly a reflection of the ideological convictions of Syria's leadership, but by 1967, expressions of anti-imperialist outrage were also indivisible from Soviet revolutionary rhetoric. Broadcasts like this could easily have been a domestic Soviet radio broadcast from 1937, with its identification of internal, bourgeois, feudalist conspirators and international, reactionary, and often Zionist enemies of the state. Much like in the high Stalinist period, Radio Damascus called for popular mobilization to annihilate spies and agents. This had been the rhetorical platform of the Stalinist show trials of the prewar period. Now this language was applied to

Syria, Egypt, and those who threatened their increasingly authoritarian understanding of what defined Arab cohesion.

Scholars continue to debate the role that the Soviet Union played in inciting the 1967 war, but there can be no doubt that over the air at least, Radio Moscow held the United States responsible for Israel's mobilization, what Washington and London would later call the "Big Lie." "Apparently the democratic regime set up in Syria is not to the liking of the United States," Radio Moscow declared in mid-May.[29] And again the next day: "This is nothing less than another conspiracy of the American imperialists and the Israeli rulers, who are toeing the U.S. line against the Arab people. . . . The United States is prodding Israel to new provocations against Syria."[30] Most pronounced in Radio Moscow's broadcasts was the tendency to instrumentalize Israel as a tool of US manipulation: "Once again, the imperialists use Israel as their instrument. . . . Israel is a small country with a population of only 2 million. The Tel Aviv Government's budget shows a big deficit year after year, and yet Israel is constantly developing, particularly in Africa." And the next day, "It is now evident that the growing tension in the region was the aim of American imperialism and figured in plans laid down by the CIA."[31] In fact, Radio Moscow did everything in its power to deemphasize the role of Israel in the conflict, seeing it merely as a US pawn. "The Israeli military orchestra did not begin to play until the U.S. maestros raised their baton."[32]

As Nasser had done, Radio Moscow argued that the United States had always been in a position of exploitation and collusion in the Middle East, revising the history of 1956 to make the Americans culpable for the British and French invasion of Suez. "Washington's connection with the organizers of the [1956] coup is evident," the Moscow broadcaster declared. Arab listeners tuning in to the radio in late May 1967 were not just hearing the message of American and British historical perfidy from Ahmed Said and Nasser; they could find corroboration of the narrative of Western involvement across multiple frequencies.

On top of this, Radio Moscow returned daily to the ongoing civil rights movement inside the United States. The USIA sent frantic letters back to Washington with news that Radio Moscow was airing memorandums written by Malcolm X pleading for Nasser's support against white American violence and declaring the Civil Rights Bill a "trick."[33] All of these broadcasts served a myriad of long familiar functions for the Soviet leadership. They established the United States as the true antagonist in the story, now replacing Britain as the imperial culprit. In a fashion similar to Said's, seldom did Radio Moscow speak simply of the "United States" or "America." The threat was "American imperialism," as in, "Who is pushing the Israeli ruling circles into new, dangerous adventures? The matter concerns simply one more plot of American imperialism."[34] Laying responsibility for the crisis at the feet of the United States also stripped from the Israelis any responsibility for their own success. Down the road, this argument provided an explanation for Egypt and Syria's defeat, arguing that they were not defeated by the Israelis but by the much bigger and more powerful Americans. Claims of American CIA involvement in Israel and Syria also fell in line with Radio Moscow's larger crusade against US foreign policy globally. If the United States was willing to intervene in Greece and Vietnam, it argued, then why not also in Israel and Syria?[35]

On the flip side of the coin, Radio Moscow continued to argue that the Soviet Union represented the only real ally of the Arab cause. As in decades past, Moscow cited Soviet generosity as the cause for Arab successes: "All the victories won by the Arab peoples in the struggle against imperialism and reaction, and all the important transformations in the Arab world, are inviolably linked with the victory of the Great October Socialist Revolution and with the extensive aid provided by the USSR in the past and present."[36] Many Arabs believed that the Soviet Union would come to their aid in the event of war because it sounded like they were promising just that. In a long list of slogans and songs heard by the CIA over Radio Damascus and Radio Cairo in the week preceding the war, the airwaves repeatedly assured listeners that the Soviet Union had promised to face all threats to Arab independence with "the resolute resistance of the Soviet Union and all peace-loving states."[37] This was seconded in print. The Cairo newspaper *Al-Jumhuriyah* printed this headline on May 24: "Soviet Union Supports Arabs and Warns Israel and Its Instigators."[38] *Al-Ahram*, one of the most widely circulated newspapers in Egypt, known for its in-depth coverage of domestic and international news, wrote: "The Soviet Government officially expresses its resolute support for the Arab countries' stand against aggression. . . . The Soviet Union warns that it will resist any aggression."[39] This was an almost exact match to the front-page stories about Soviet martial support during the Suez Crisis eleven years earlier. Meanwhile, the Syrian newspaper *Al-Ba'ath* had as its headline: "Soviet Warning to Imperialist Powers Which Support Israel."[40] The same text appeared in the Iraqi and Lebanese press. To be clear, the Arab radio stations did not fabricate these assurances of support.

A day earlier, Radio Moscow had promised that "should anyone try to unleash aggression in the Near East, he would meet not only with the united strength of Arab countries but also with strong opposition from the Soviet Union and all peace-loving states."[41] On May 24 TASS listed proudly in Arabic and English the Arab presses that were printing the Soviet promises of support.[42]

The British and Americans desperately denied the accusations of collusion coming from Cairo and Moscow, but they, too, were not free from dissimulation. The British effort seemed to be motivated primarily by a desire not to replicate 1956, at least not over the air. Britain would present itself as an innocent observer in the latest crisis. The BBC echoed this by taking Britain largely out of the story in its broadcasts. Throughout its coverage of Nasser's order that UN forces withdraw from the Syrian border and the subsequent debates that happened on the floor of the UN, the BBC only quoted American representatives, never British ones (although we know from the records that Hugh Foot, Lord Caradon, the UK representative to the UN, spoke about the UN's obligation to manage the crisis). The BBC reported instead that the United States was taking the lead in efforts to "keep the peace."[43] This was a shocking change from 1956, when the cause of peace had offered a manufactured justification for war. Tellingly, even the presence of British ships in the Mediterranean (an issue that Nasser protested vehemently in these days) did not make it onto the BBC airwaves in 1967.

There would be no direct threats levied by Britain this time. Instead, the BBC (and the government that it represented) plied its trade in commentary and criticism of others. On May 25, the day after the UN Security Council failed to issue any resolution on the rising tensions, the BBC reported that Moscow would "do well to keep in mind her responsibility as a great power."[44] One hour later, Radio Moscow replied, calling out the BBC by name for "trying to fabricate an anti-Soviet smokescreen to mask their own policy, which endangers peace.... London radio's assurances that the alleged source of tension in the Middle East is the Soviet aid to the progressive Arab states are simply absurd."[45] In the days that followed, the BBC continued to position Britain as a well-meaning state, interested in fair play but most decidedly not in charge. It reported on the evacuations of British and American women and children from Cairo, a message that for centuries has conjured heartrending images of innocents driven in haste and confusion from their homes.[46] Interestingly, this particular broadcast aired immediately before a story on the general strike happening in Aden, which had been called that day by pro-Nasserist nationalists to protest the alleged molestation of Arab schoolgirls by British troops in Yemen. These contested images of children under siege provided a prism for understanding the troubled British situation in the entire region. Either it was a testament to the BBC's commitment to tell the truth unvarnished, or it was an unfortunate accident that the two stories fell one after the other. Either way, for the listener these stories were bound together by the thread of the suffering child, one the British child evacuating to avoid Arab violence and the other the Arab child being victimized by British sexual predation. There is no mistaking the discomfiture that came in the next broadcast with news of Sir Francis Chichester's expected arrival in Portsmouth after his solo circumnavigation of the globe by ship. It was a momentous feat, but as Ahmed Said put it later that day, "It just doesn't matter when there are thousands of lives at stake." Even more telling are the sections of BBC broadcasts that were crossed out and never read over the air—sections that reported on clashes in late May between "Israeli patrols and the Arab guerilla force known as the Palestinian Liberation Army," and news that ten thousand people were rallying in Peking in support for Egypt and Syria.[47]

In critical ways, the BBC contributed to the arguments being made in Cairo and Moscow about the dangerous possibility of American invasion. On the evening of May 24, the same night that Radio Cairo, Voice of the Arabs, and Radio Moscow were laying blame for the heightening of tensions on Washington's doorstep, the BBC told its listeners, "Egypt has been told by the Americans that they regard the denial of free passage through the Gulf as an act of aggression and would act against it, both inside and outside the United Nations. According to informed sources, the use of force was not excluded."[48] And again, later that night, the BBC reported that while the White House spokesman was "answering questions obscurely," the US position was that "if all else fails, force cannot be ruled out."[49] It did not help that the BBC was also reporting on American casualties in Vietnam, which reached an all-time high in May 1967. What emerged was an image of the Johnson administration preparing for one war in order to distract attention from another.

And what of the USIA? Whether or not a desire for war or peace drove American foreign policy during those heady days remains up for debate. There is no question that State Department officials and the VOA believed themselves to be seeking peace. They had spoken repeatedly over the years about the need to avoid "getting in a lather every time some neutralist leader makes a violent speech," pointing to the mistake that Dulles had made in 1956 by pulling funding from the Aswan Dam after Nasser signed his arms deal with the Czechoslovakians.[50] VOA broadcasters did not want to isolate Egypt within the Arab world, since, as Lucius Battle (the US ambassador to the UAR) put it, "This was tried in the days of the 'Eisenhower doctrine,'" and it failed.[51] Peace with Nasser was critical, or at least the semblance of it was.

Thus when, on May 17, President Johnson called Israeli prime minister Levi Eshkol, US officials claimed that Johnson's main purpose was to "urge restraint" and "to persuade the Israelis not to take matters into their own hands."[52] And on March 23, when Nasser threatened to close the Gulf of Aqaba to Israeli ships, US State Department officials argued that they were intervening solely to "stay Israel's hand" and "protect the rule of international law."[53] Johnson apparently sent "another restraining message" to the Israelis after Egypt and Jordan signed their defensive pact on May 30 (the full text of which was read over the air on Radio Cairo on May 30).[54] Ironically, in the same folder in the LBJ Presidential Archive that holds these attestations of peace and restraint are documents listing the one hundred M-113 A1 armored personnel carriers, Skyhawk A-4H aircraft, Hawk missile systems, and Patton tank spare parts that the United States was expediting shipment of to Israel in the coming days.[55] Also in this same folder are memos from Walt Rostow to Johnson warning him of the risk in supporting Israel for US oil interests in the Arab world: "Our greatest single liability— and one of the USSR's greatest assets—is the sincere Arab belief that the 'Zionists exercise a veto on US policy.'"[56] Rostow was perhaps not wrong, although the sale of arms didn't help the US claim of peaceful mediation.

Over the air, the VOA replayed Johnson's May 23 declaration that the United States had "always opposed—as we oppose in other parts of the world at this very moment—the efforts of other nations to resolve their problems with their neighbors by the aggression route."[57] It also read out Dean Rusk's June 5 declaration that the United States would "devote all its energies to bring about an end to the fighting and a new beginning of programs to assure peace and development."[58] More than ever, peace had become a word used by any and all to justify policy.

The VOA nonetheless faced steady rebuttal over the air. When the Johnson administration protested Nasser's closing of the Straits of Aqaba to Israeli ships, Voice of the Arabs was the first to point out Johnson's seeming hypocrisy. "How strange for a country like the United States, which kills the

Vietnamese people, overthrows legitimate governments, mobilizes its intelligence to interfere in the internal affairs of other countries, concocts plots against the people of Latin America, backs the racist South African government against U.N. resolutions, stands against Lumumba's legitimate government in Congo—how strange it is for it to come out and speak to us about the importance of international law. . . . This is not peace."[59] Similarly, Radio Moscow was quick to point out the hypocrisy of the US appeals to peace and to position itself as the authentic defender of the peaceful ideal. "Regions that are thousands of kilometers distant from one another have been linked by Washington's single strategy," the Soviet broadcaster Gelihy Shakhov said over the air in late May. "I refer to the U.S. global offensive against the peoples of all continents against the cause of independence and peace."[60] It would not have been unreasonable as a listener to choose to believe the Egyptian, Syrian, and Soviet story.

For Nasser, as for the VOA and Radio Moscow, peace would come at the end of war, or alternatively, there would be war for the cause of peace. While Radio Jerusalem continued to call for the "consolidation of peace in our region," Nasser called the idea of peace itself into question.[61] "There is talk about peace now," he said over the radio at the end of May. "What is peace? If there is a true desire for peace, we say that we also work for peace. But does peace mean that we should ignore the rights of the Palestinian people because of the lapse of time? Does peace mean that we should concede our rights?"[62] Ahmed Said echoed him: "The Arab world ridicules American gangsterism and imperialism's concept of peace."[63] What peace really meant in the spring of 1967 was not clear, but that too was a familiar phenomenon.

Religious rhetoric and iconography also ran like an undercurrent through the radio broadcasts of 1967, setting the stage for the religious banner under which Anwar Sadat would consolidate power and wage the 1973 war. Scholars have convincingly noted that the use of religious language and imagery in state parlance was a phenomenon of the 1970s, ushered in as a part of Sadat's larger effort to eradicate Arab nationalism and Nasserism from the political sphere through an alliance with Islamic nationalists. There is no record of Voice of the Arabs telling Egyptians that "God and his angels" were fighting on the side of the Egyptians or of stories of the Prophet walking among the soldiers, as there would be in 1973.[64] But the religious call to arms was there in 1967. Again and again, generals, politicians, and broadcasters made the argument that the Arab armies would overcome Israel through the force of their religious drive to liberate Palestinians from bondage. "This is the day we have been waiting for in the holy war to retrieve the usurped land for its owners," General Murtaji told Voice of the Arabs that May.[65] It is not easy to find the discrete moment when a zeitgeist begins. It seems clear, however, that Ahmed Said, Nasser, and his generals made regular use of religious arguments over the radio to unify and embolden soldiers and civilians on the eve of the 1967 war. Interestingly, the use of religious rhetoric to describe the coming conflict was not limited to the Arab broadcasters. The BBC, echoing the words of Prime Minister Harold Wilson, warned its listeners that the crisis had "all the dangers of a Holy War."[66]

Stories also abounded about the high morale of Egyptian soldiers petitioning to go to war, all in contrast to Israeli soldiers, who were better armed but were only there because the Israeli government forced them to be. This was not the first or last time in history that the argument would be made by generals that victory could be achieved by the élan of a motivated infantry against superior weaponry. Joseph Joffre had made the same claim when calculating French odds against the German machine gun in 1914. Both generals would find themselves sorely mistaken. Murtaji's use of religious, liberationist rhetoric had a long precedent, as this book has shown. At issue was the deep irony that such rhetoric exposed when set against the realities of the war's experience. Ironically, Murtaji, the general who promised a holy war driven by high morale, famously withdrew his staff on the first day of fighting, leaving his troops to retreat without command and failing to notify the general staff in Cairo or his commanders in the field.

In the days that followed, as tensions escalated, Radio Cairo and Radio Damascus continued to argue that their soldiers were ready for war; that the Israelis and Americans represented an amoral, existential, but nonetheless beatable threat; and that the Soviet Union was committed to coming to their aid. Stories of American, Soviet, and British fleets in the Mediterranean were mixed with declarations from rabbis in New York calling on all Jews to rally for Israel. When, on May 30, King Hussein of Jordan signed a five-year defensive pact with Nasser, the language of pan-Arab unity returned in force.[67] Every hour that day, Voice of the Arabs replayed Nasser's declaration that "everything is forgotten in the face of Israel," meaning that Egypt and Jordan had buried the hatchet for the sake of this larger cause. The BBC then repeated this line that afternoon.[68] Even after it became clear that Syria would not join the pact with Jordan (finding the alliance "distasteful" and arguing that Jordan and Saudi Arabia were not to be trusted since they were "stooges of American imperialism"), the unity of the Arab world seemed like a daunting new reality.[69] To outside observers, these declarations of unity were "electrifying," as the BBC put it, patching up bitter rivalries and showing the pro-Western Hussein's capacity for making peace with his opponents. One story that was crossed out on the BBC's agenda included a report on widespread Arab rejoicing in London accompanied by portraits of King Hussein and Prime Minister Nasser displayed together.[70]

As had been the case in 1956, it was nigh impossible to sort fact from fiction after the fighting broke out. Following are excerpts from some of the transcripts of broadcasts aired in the first days of the war, taken from multiple archives and merged into one master transcript. They show as best as possible conversations that raged over the airwaves in those fateful days in 1967. This material is included to allow us to sit in these moments, to perhaps feel for a second what it might have been like to change the channel on our radios in Cairo in the summer of 1967, to read these sources with a critical eye, born from having developed an understanding of their linguistic, political, and cultural histories, and to show how these various sources can be woven together to reveal something new. Here are the half-truths, loaded language, repetition, and common enemy intimacies that had developed in the two preceding decades. They offer a glimpse into the audiosphere, revealing the long-used tropes of the different broadcasting stations and the profound difficulties that any listener would have had in discerning fact from fiction. For consistency, all times have been standardized to Cairo Mean Time:

June 5
0900: Kol Israel—The battle started at 4 AM after Egyptian mortar batteries laid a barrage of fire on four Israeli Kibbutzim along the Gaza border.[71]

0920: Radio Amman—The Arab nation has united. . . . Rest assured and be joyful about the imminent return and liberation.[72]

0940: Radio Cairo—Israel began its aggression at 0900 hours today with air raids over UAR airports in Cairo and the Canal Zone.[73]

0945: Kol Israel—The Israeli army has shot down 10 Egyptian planes and a large number of planes at the Egyptian airport.

1041: Voice of the Arabs (in Hebrew)—People of Israel, we shot down 44 Israeli air planes in our first reaction to your soldiers' aggression. Our forces are now attacking you everywhere, in every oasis, in every village. We shall broadcast in Hebrew starting from 1145 on the 388.1 meter medium wave.[74]

1053: Voice of the Arabs—The Israeli enemy started a full-scale land and air attack on the United Arab Republic. The United Arab Republic, standing today to repel the aggression and crush it, declares that it will be carrying out a sacred duty, that the Israeli enemy and those who support it now must bear the consequences which are bound to befall the aggressors.[75]

1253: Radio Amman—The Jordanian, Iraqi, and Syrian air forces are carrying out joint air operations and bombing targets inside our occupied territory. All kinds of supplies and fuel are available. There is no need to worry in this respect. Everyone should go to work calmly.[76]

[VOA Cairo and VOA Beirut are taken offline by the Egyptian and Iraqi governments.[77] VOA broadcasting continues from Rhodes.]

1600: Radio Moscow—Everyone is, of course, aware that Israel would not have committed such extreme action had it not been for the backing it enjoys from the imperialists. . . . It is clear that the entire Arab world is now offering collective support to the UAR which is now repelling the attacks of the Israeli forces.[78]

1600: Voice of America—The United States has called on everyone to support the United Nations Security Council's efforts to bring about an immediate cease-fire in the Middle East. [This broadcast again at 17:30.[79] Meanwhile, the VOA begins around-the-clock English-language broadcasts and increases its Arabic transmissions from six to eleven hours a day.[80]]

1900: BBC—In London, the Foreign Secretary, Mr. Brown, said Britain's immediate aim was to bring about an early ceasefire. . . . He told the House of Commons that Britain was not concerned to take sides, and her forces in the area had been told to avoid any involvement.[81]

1930: Radio Moscow—American senators such as Javits and the leaders of the British Conservatives are openly pushing Israel onto the path of military adventures. It is reported that Washington and London are probing the possibility of creating an anti-Arab bloc of Western maritime powers under the pretext of ensuring freedom of navigation in the Gulf of Aqaba, that is, in territorial waters of the UAR.[82]

2100: BBC—There have been mob attacks on British Embassies. . . . The United States has proclaimed its neutrality in the conflict in thought, word, and deed.[83]

2200: BBC—Britain and the United States have both announced that they are not taking sides in the conflict. [The BBC broadcast this again at 23:00, 23:40, and 24:00, and on June 6 at 03:00, 05:00, 06:00, 07:00, and 08:00.]

2230: Voice of the Arabs—Plotters do not admit anything easily. Lies are the slogans and cover of plots.[84]

June 6

0115: Kol Israel—Today [meaning June 5], we dealt a strong blow to the Egyptian, Jordanian, and Syrain air forces and attained air supremacy in the entire region. . . . In today's battle we destroyed about 400 enemy planes. . . . [W]e lost 19 pilots. Their families have been informed.[85]

0637: Radio Cairo—The Supreme Command of the armed forces in the UAR announces that it has now become certain that, in a comprehensive manner, the United States and Britain are taking part in the Israeli military aggression as far as the air operations are concerned. . . . The American and British planes have created an air umbrella over Israel.[86] [This message was repeated again at 07:03.]

0800: VOA—It has never been US policy to support Israel against the Arab states. Like the Soviet Union, Britain, France, and a majority of the members of the United Nations, the US favored the establishment of Israel as a state in 1948. But the US certainly did not support the Israeli use of force against Egypt in 1956. The basic US policy has always been to work for the peace and stability of the area.[87]

0800: Kol Israel—Egyptian soldiers in Sinai: The Israeli forces are advancing on all roads. It is useless for you to fight. Your fighting will mean your final death and destruction. Leave this place immediately and return to Egypt, for only that will help you, and it is your only hope to stay alive.[88]

0830: Radio Baghdad—America has deceived the world. America and Britain lied to [word indistinct] and to all states when they declared that they would adopt a neutral position toward the current armed struggle between the Arabs and the Zionists. But we knew full well that America was lying. We knew that Britain was lying, too. . . . With the firm determination of heroic men and the help of God we shall destroy America, Britain, and all their fleets.[89]

0900: BBC—A British government spokesman has denied an Egyptian claim that British aircraft have been helping Israel. . . . The American Secretary of State, Mr. Rusk, said last night that the United States was neutral in the sense that she had no forces involved in the war. . . . The Egyptian charge—broadcast over Cairo Radio—said both British and American aircraft-carriers had been helping the Israelis; that their planes had provided air cover for Israeli forces and that they had played an actual part in operations against Jordan. Later, Amman Radio said that Jordan had been bombed by aircraft from three foreign aircraft-carriers in the Mediterranean. And Damascus Radio said a captured Israeli pilot had allegedly revealed that seventeen British jets with their pilots had arrived at an Israeli military air base ten days ago and that they had bombed targets in Syria and Egypt yesterday. These allegations are categorically false.[90]

0925: Radio Damascus—[Interview with the captured Israeli pilot, 1st Lieutenant Abraham Zilakh, on the air.] 17 British Vulcan planes came from Cyprus to the Ikron airbase in Israel ten days ago with a mission to attack Arab targets. . . . Yes, British planes attacked targets in Egypt and Syria from their base in Cyprus and returned to their base.[91]

1001: Radio Cairo—[Nasser asserts,] I have indisputable proof of Anglo-American air intervention on the Jordanian and Egyptian fronts.[92]

1430: Radio Moscow—Now in these grave days when the Arab countries are being subjected to a fresh aggression, the Soviet Union stands on their side with all firmness.[93]

1440: Voice of America—In the past few years, seventy-five per cent of all arms flowing into the Middle East have come from the Soviet Union.[94] In the meantime, the US has provided economic aid to Arab states. Our economic aid to the UAR—over $1.1 billion—was greater than our aid to Israel.[95]

1400: BBC—In London, the Foreign Office and the Ministry of Defense have repeated strong denials that there is any British intervention in the war.

1600: Radio Moscow—The Arab command said today that it had real proof of interference by United States and British aircraft on the Israeli side.[96]

1605: Voice of America—[Secretary of State Dean Rusk speaking in a statement outside the West Lobby of the Whitehouse:] We categorically deny charges made on Voice of the Arabs that US carrier-based planes have taken part in attacks on Egypt.[97]

1700: BBC—Britain and the United States have again categorically denied Arab accusations that they have intervened in the war in support of Israel. . . . This is a malicious fabrications and there is not a grain of truth in it. British statements say measures to interrupt the normal flow of oil supplies or to close the Suez Canal are therefore totally unjustified.[98]

2002: Voice of the Arabs (Ahmed Said)—The United States is the enemy. The United States, Arabs, is the enemy of the peoples, the killer of life, and the shedder of blood. Its aircraft protect the Zionists from Arab bombing. . . . Our battle today, the battle being fought by the Arab armies with every sacrifice and every offering, is against the United States, firstly, secondly, and thirdly. Lastly it is against the Zionist bands, very much lastly. . . . Here, United States, here in the Arab homeland, we buried Britain's greatness. Here, United States, we shall bury the imperialist base, Israel. Here we shall bury the American international gangsterism. Here Arabs, dig graves everywhere; dig them for every US person; dig them, Arabs; dig it, Arabs; dig it, Arabs.[99]

1900: Radio Algiers—America is not only supplying Israel with soldiers, aircraft, and tanks under the protection of the Sixth Fleet. It is also supplying it with napalm.[100]

June 7

1000: Radio Moscow—Sudan, Iraq, Yemen, Syria, and Lebanon have broken off diplomatic relations with the United States and Britain.[101]

1200: BBC—The BBC Arabic Service is from today broadcasting an extra 7½ hours a day, providing continuous coverage from 0345 to 2100. . . .

The story of British involvement in the current conflict is a malicious and mischievous invention deliberately spread by the Egyptian government. The Ministry of Defense says allegations that British Canberra bombers have taken part in bombing Egyptian positions in Sinai are complete lies.[102]

1230: BBC—The Egyptian newspaper, *Al Ahram*, reports that the US has supplied arms to Israel through its Wheelus Air Base and Israeli personnel are being trained at Wheelus.[103] [This broadcast solicits frantic letters from BBC London to the station in Cairo demanding that news be corroborated before it is reported. As the station put it, "BBC Broadcasts overseas containing unsupported Arab propaganda is having the very quick repercussion of encouraging mobs in Arab capitals to beat up British and American embassies, consulates, libraries, etc."[104]]

1500: Radio Moscow—US aircraft have been sighted over Ishmailia.[105]

1900: Radio Damascus—US infantrymen have taken part in the battle for Jerusalem.

1930: Radio Peking—US imperialists, acting in partnership with British imperialism, have sent its air force to participate in Israel's war of aggression against the Arab states.[106]

2000: Kol Israel—Today the main Egyptian Army in Sinai has been defeated.

2052: Voice of the Arabs [Shaykh of al-Azhar, Hasan Mamun, speaking:] Our gallant soldiers, the hour of victory has struck, victory of the enemy of God—Israel. . . . God will torture them at your hands and will shame them. God will shame the Jews and will grant you victory over them.[107]

June 8

[By this time, Egyptian forces have been largely routed from Sinai and are in retreat.]

0300: BBC—[At this moment, Jordan backs off from supporting the lie of US and British complicity.] A report from Amman says that Jordan denies any knowledge of British or American military aircraft operating over her territory.[108]

0545: Radio Damascus—Our armed forces have scored decisive victories—enemy positions overrun, their tanks and fortifications blown up, and 10 Zionist planes shot down.[109]

1010: Voice of the Arabs—Brave storm troops, the news of your operations yesterday are good tidings along the road to victory: the shelling of Galilee settlements, the destruction of a number of enemy vehicles and armored cars, the blowing up of the bridge between Lydda and Jerusalem. . . . Brave storm troops, on to more victories![110]

1600: BBC—Radio Cairo said among other things that fifty American planes took off today from Wheelus airbase in Libya to attack Arab forces. The Libyan radio has since repeatedly broadcast an American Embassy denial that any planes had left the base to help Israel.[111]

1732: Radio Amman—[Jordan now justifies its withdrawal, laying blame at
Egypt's feet for failure to provide air cover.] Our armed forces willingly
offered sacrifices of honor and glory. They were undaunted by the larger
enemy force and its air supremacy. . . . Our forces did not fear death
when they faced the enemy without air cover. . . . As a result, and as
the almighty had destined, our heroes fell on the battlefield . . . When
the Security Council ordered a cease-fire yesterday, . . . we decided to
comply. . . . What was left of our forces was compelled to retreat with a
broken heart. . . . Although the setback we have suffered is worse than
expected, it is best that we submit to the will of God.[112]

1800: Voice of the Arabs—At 7:30 this morning three American planes
with US Air Force markings were seen flying over the Suez Canal from
north to south. Our forces along the Canal spotted them. Today, this
very day, the US Department of Defense admitted the presence of a US
ship only 15 miles north of Sinai. Today, this very day, the US can clearly
be seen to be taking part in the battle.[113]

1815: Radio Damascus—The US Sixth Fleet is continuing its suspicious role
of helping the Zionist gangs in their present ordeal during which they
received crushing blows in today's battles.[114]

1820: Radio Libya—Our soil was never used and will never be used against
the Arabs. Radio broadcasts alleging this use have contributed to tensions
between friends.[115]

1900: BBC—One of Egypt's allies, Libya, has been broadcasting American
denials of Egyptian accusations that American aircraft from a base in
Libya have been helping Israel. The Libyan Radio has repeatedly quoted
the American Embassy, denying that American aircraft at Wheelus
airbase in Libya took off today to attack Arab forces.[116]

1930: Voice of the Arabs (Ahmed Said)—The deep grave we have dug
extending from Kuwait to Maghreb, we have prepared for the burial of
aggression. . . . Today, this very day, the United States is clearly seen to
be taking part in the battle. . . . Today, when the Arab forces have begun
in Sinai to rain violent blows on the forces of Israel, a fact admitted by
London radio, today, O Arabs, when the Syrian Arab forces are achieving triumph after triumph in the occupied territory, today, O Arabs,
the United States has no alternative but to come out into the open,
intervening for the protection of Israel. . . . We shall fight. O Arabs, we
have plenty in our bag, we have arms which we have saved to be used in
the battle against the United States and Britain. We have what could
guarantee the destruction of every house in Israel at the very same time as
we are repulsing the aggression by the Chicago and Texas gangs. We have
the battlefield with 100 million people. We have the oil. . . . We have the
Suez Canal. . . . O Arabs, we have plenty in the bag![117]

2300: BBC—The Israeli authorities have released a recording of what they
say is a monitored telephone call between President Nasser and King

Hussein on Tuesday morning. During the conversation the two leaders discussed whether to say British and American planes had intervened in support of Israel. We should note that Jordan has already denied any knowledge of British or American military aircraft operating over her territory. [BBC rebroadcast this news at 23:40 and on June 9 at 01:00, 02:00, 03:00, 05:00, 06:00, 07:00, 08:00, 09:00, 10:00, 11:00, 12:00, and 01:30 a.m. in Hebrew.[118]]

June 9

0900: Radio Damascus—One of the two Israeli pilots taken prisoner yesterday by Iraq stated that he and other Israeli pilots traveled by helicopter to a US aircraft carrier from which they flew directly to the front. Facts are being revealed daily on the Anglo-American-Zionist collusion in the imperialist aggression. Washington drew up the plan assigning each a role in the aggression.[119]

1700: Radio Moscow—[A broadcast with the title, "The Soviet People Support the People of Egypt" is scratched out in the program record and replaced with a story entitled, "Shame upon the Israeli Aggressors." The transcript is completely redacted.[120]]

1843: Radio Cairo—[Nasser speaking:] We cannot hide from ourselves that we have faced a grave setback in the last few days. . . . Evidence is clear of the existence of imperialist collusion with the enemy . . . without any exaggeration, the enemy was operating with an air force *three times stronger than his normal force.* . . . There were many honorable and marvelous efforts. . . . I have taken a decision. . . . I have decided to give up completely and to return to the ranks of the masses and do my duty with them like every other citizen.[121]

2000: VOA—In this crisis, as before, the US has opposed acts of hostility and acts likely to lead to war. The US did everything in its power to find a peaceful solution to the crisis before the fighting broke out. It used its influence with all involved in an effort to prevent the outbreak of fighting. In the first hours of the war, the Israelis destroyed most of the Egyptian, Syrian, and Jordanian Air Forces. Arab leaders, particularly in Cairo, were unwilling or unable to admit this great loss. So the story of US intervention was invented as an excuse.[122]

The confusion over the air did not stop on June 9. In fact, Damascus continued to report on June 11 that Arab radar had tracked enemy places piloted by Americans coming from Anglo-American aircraft carriers.[123] On June 12, Voice of the Arabs was still arguing that captured Israeli pilots had been carrying maps and aerial photographs of Egyptian positions, "which could only have been taken by the famous U.S. U-2 planes."[124] As late as June 24, Voice of the Arabs was still claiming that the present peace talks merely represented "big power bargaining," to support the US-UK "imperialist plot" against the Arabs.

The audosphere's implosion continued to have an impact long after the war was over. British diplomats spoke of the increased tension in Aden that had happened as a result of "Cairo's lie about British intervention in the Arab-Israeli war," noting the many letters arriving in the BBC's postbox accusing Britain of siding with Israel.[125] George Thompson, the British Minister of State for Foreign Affairs, proclaimed on the floor of the House of Commons that his government would use "every resource available to pin down the lies put out by Cairo about alleged British and American involvement in the Arab-Israeli war."[126] The BBC office in London sent folders of letters back and forth to Cairo on the topic of "how to counter the Big Lie," discussing how the service might exploit the silence of Radio Moscow, show the impracticality of a British air intervention, and how the Israeli army managed to orchestrate such devastating attacks, and giving lots of attention to Nasser's general chicanery.[127] King Hussein of Jordan, desperate to mend broken ties with his Western allies, could be heard every hour on the hour on the BBC claiming that there was no evidence of American or British intervention.[128] Meanwhile, Lyndon Johnson's government demanded a public retraction from Radio Cairo before the resumption of diplomatic relations could occur. As one US State Department document outlined on June 14, the "New Nailing of the Big Lie" had "poisoned the well of trust. There can be no decent relations with those who make such destructive charges. . . . Two roads lie ahead: poisonous propaganda or productive progress to peace. The U.S. will stick to the path of Peace, but can handle a propaganda war if one is forced."[129] Nasser initially denied any responsibility for the lie and blamed King Hussein of Jordan for its genesis. This explanation Ahmed Said repeated over the radio during the following year.

Historians have debated for years the reasons for Nasser choosing to expel the UN from Sinai and nationalize the Straits of Tiran. Most agree that he did not want a war any more than the Israelis, Syrians, or Soviets did. Perhaps he believed that he could nationalize the straits without inciting Israel to fight. Perhaps he believed he could keep skirmishes localized and stop the crisis from escalating. What becomes very clear from reading these transcripts is that Nasser was attempting to recreate Suez. As he had done a decade earlier, he would use the threat of invasion to rally the Arab world behind him and give him a victory after years of struggle and uncertainty. In order for the story to work, he had to have Britain, and now the United States, running the show from their imperialist stoop. Such meddling would enrage the world, just as it had done before. This is why the lie was so critical. It became even more necessary after the Israeli victory on the first day. As many noted at the time, Nasser needed something to explain the defeat, and it was unthinkable that Israel could wreak such damage on its own. Nasser, Said, and Haykal created an image of a victorious Arab world that didn't just improve reality but offered a complete substitute for it.

American and British diplomats and broadcasters began referring to the false reporting coming from Cairo, Damascus, and Amman as the "Big Lie" as early as June 7. By then this phrase, the "Big Lie," had been around for awhile. The idea that cultures need a grand lie to maintain social harmony goes back to Plato. Big lies appeared during the English Civil War, in the Protocols of the Elders of Zion, in Walter Duranty's claims of a well-fed Ukrainian populace in the 1930s, in Adolf Hitler's construction of the Jewish menace, and in Charles de Gaulle's claims that the French had all been partisans in World War II. When Said proclaimed a victory for Arab forces on June 9, he was participating in a long tradition of bolstering one's political legitimacy based on a foundation of nonfacts. The philosopher Hannah Arendt argued in 1961 that lies had always been considered necessary in politics, but there was something new to the phenomenon of rewriting recent history in front of the very people who had been there to witness it. This phenomenon—this tension in real time between constructed reality and lived experience—had been in the Arab world for decades by that point. And it was not just one constructed image, one lie, that hovered in the audiosphere; it was many, coming from lots of directions, supporting a myriad of political and economic goals. All those lies, whether they were the "Big Lie" or the many that came before it, whether they came from Nasser or Moscow or Washington or Whitehall, had become, by 1967, unremarkable for their banality. If you have enough Big Lies, eventually they aren't big anymore. As soon as the Big Lie becomes commonplace, nothing in the rhetorical world becomes believable. The public has to either untether itself from its demand for the truth or reject all of the images and rhetoric that it has been fed and start over, seeking truth in a new language.

This is what happened in 1967. The audiosphere had collapsed, and with it, Nasser's claim to revolutionary legitimacy, the ostensible power of the unified Arab world, and the trust of millions who had believed that Palestinian liberation was just around the corner. Arendt argued that public lies always contain an element of violence, since organized lying carries inside it a call to destroy what it has decided to deny. This was indeed the case. The dominant historical narrative presents the Six-Day War as *the* watershed moment that opened the door for new religious leaders to consolidate their power in Egypt and elsewhere in the Middle East. Scholars have argued that pan-Arabism died with the 1967 defeat, that it was Nasser's Waterloo.[130] In the immediate aftermath of the defeat, Nasser's biggest critics were from nationalist and socialist circles who saw him as a moribund relic of bourgeois thinking. But there was also a growing Islamist national response to the crisis, which saw Nasser's failed secular promise of development and prosperity as yet another remnant of imperial meddling that was incongruous with the more authentic approach to government and civil society prescribed by the Quran. The moment of that collapse may have come in 1967, but it had been a long time coming.

Conclusion

IN 2017, a year before his death, Ahmed Said began publishing chapters of his memoir online.[1] In it, he claimed that he was merely following orders in 1967 when he proclaimed an Arab victory. He also argued, more to the point, that "the war of the radio stations imposed this call." He was right. By 1967 there was little else that he could say. Decades of practice had led all the broadcasters to a place where their language was profoundly limited. Would Said have been able, after years of proclaiming the indomitable strength of the Egyptian army, to admit on day one that they had fallen? Or was the linguistic regime in which he existed only capable of handling one story, one master narrative?

The state-run broadcasting services examined in this book all set out with similar goals: to build fear, loyalty, consensus, mobilization, and compliance. Their ideological differences may have been pronounced, but their methods and aspirations were the same. All of them believed that if they just told the simple truth as they saw it, their missives would upend the "slander and misinformation" being reported about them up and down the dial.[2] What they believed the truth to be shifted over time, but they all were sure of their command of it. The simpler the world and its problems became, the more easily that message could be packaged into sound bites and then mobilized.

They also all sought to cultivate Arab desires for independence and citizenship into collective support for state power. Over decades, the various broadcasting services had built a vast scaffolding of meaning and significance that sought to define the self, the group, and the Other. Danger and threat were the cornerstone of those identities, as were the promises of security, progress, and order, offered to those who adequately performed their gratitude. These identities were intended to shape how people understood events and to discipline their relationships with the outside world. They conflated the preservation of the self with the state. By 1960 even Nasser's Egypt was using the language of freedom and liberty to construct a police state. Indeed, after the Six-Day War, the rhetoric of Egyptian state radio sounded more and more like the voices of the West, a phenomenon that senior employees in the Egyptian government reported on regularly.[3] They laid claim to the truth and marked what was false. They shaped and filtered every plan, every approach. At their core, their similarities lay in the fact that they were all assuming a language of power, of reified enemies and allies.

One of the intentions of this book has been to grapple with the dialogized nature of this world. None of the broadcasting services existed in a vacuum. When they devised their programs and wrote their transcripts, broadcasters were always in conversation with the other programs that were coursing across the airwaves. Sometimes they did this explicitly, such as when the BBC responded directly to Said's claims of British collusion with Israel in 1967. At other times the call and response was more implicit, such as when Radio Moscow highlighted the help given by Soviet pilots on the Suez Canal in 1956, only to see similar stories emerge on the BBC and the VOA. Historian Melani McAlister has chronicled how decades of repeated representations of the Middle East in American domestic media created an echo chamber for understandings of Middle Eastern identities, which then set the stage for the expansionist nationalism that drove US policy over the last seventy years. *Frequencies of Deceit* has attempted to show the "discursive power of conjuncture," not in American domestic rhetoric as McAlister has done, but in the messaging of the propagandists who sought to influence the hearts and minds of their Middle Eastern audiences.[4] This conjuncture did not just happen inside the confines of each national broadcasting service; it also happened between the services, creating a constantly self-reinforcing, autopoietic system of language, identity, and representation.

This regression to a shared scaffolding of meaning and signification that characterized the Middle Eastern audiosphere in the 1950s and 1960s came from numerous interwoven forces. Cold War terminology helped to create a "totalizing concept of modernization."[5] The rhetoric of Cold War modernization was indeed central to creating the crisis of faith that the Arab world faced in the 1960s. That language came from many directions, including the Soviet Union, and it was shaped irreducibly by the audiosphere itself. It was this space that provided the reiterative environment for that broadcasting language to develop. It is to this shared scaffolding that this book has directed its attention, offering a history, or a "genealogical reading," of that shared space and the contested discourses, identities, and meanings that inhabited it.[6]

There were issues with this scaffolding, however. This decades-long progression toward discursive hegemony, which happened at the expense of alternative voices and identities in the audiospace of state-run propaganda, was of course part of a much larger global phenomenon that arguably continues to this day. The constrained, autocatalytic, pedagogical language of the developed modern colonial state performs a critical role in building entire sociogenic worlds.[7] It can turn coercion into "freedom," consent and collaboration into "civilization," civil rights activism into a crisis of law and order, and dissent into treason.[8] More critically, this constructed, conceptual world *understands* coercion *as freedom*, consent *as civilization,* and dissent *as abnormal and irrational.* That world seems to be filled with humans who take these understandings as ontogenic truths instead of seeing them as the sociogenic, constructed myths that they are.[9] This was the world that defined much of the audiospace by 1967, complete with the limitations and exclusions that this world inscribed, and it is arguably the world we inhabit today.

The implications of this tenuous relationship between representation and experience were disastrous in the long run. In the process of cultivating domestic consensus and international prestige, the propagandists and their governments created a world that by the 1960s was losing its ability to act beyond those representations. It was hemmed in by a tired and circumscribed language, with each country playing its prescribed role—a role that each worked hard to preserve. As this language fed on itself, it became increasingly impossible to avoid any step but escalation, limiting the range of possible responses. This was a process that had started decades earlier and continued well past the moment in 1967 when Ahmed Said found himself having only one possible response to a declaration of war.

Numerous scholars have noted that the Egyptian defeat in 1967 "shook the faith of millions in [Nasser], the champion of Arab revolution."[10] This was compounded by the decades-long argument that colonialism represented a "broken promise" that had guaranteed modernization, democracy, and liberation but had never delivered.[11] Over time, when Arab populations began to imagine for themselves identities beyond the circumscribed parameters of the state's discursive confines, they challenged the hegemonic connections between sign and reference that the state broadcasters had established for decades. New sounds coming from nonstate sources became more important, offering the voices of "Islamic counterpublics" that more accurately reflected people's experiences and aspirations.[12] The international broadcasting programs played a key role in engendering that loss of faith in the state-led secular solution to modern social development. Since 1953, Voice of the Arabs had captured its audiences through anti-imperialist, revolutionary language. This language rested on an argument that envisaged the Western powers and their allies as morally bankrupt enemies whose designs centered on the creation of puppet regimes intent on reactionary exploitation. This was a battle between good and evil, easily understood. The Soviets, the British, and the Americans did the same. At some level, so much of what limited and defined the rhetoric of propaganda in the Middle East was based on the idea that there were fixed cultural differences that defined the Arab people and those who were speaking to them.

Those structures of meaning not only closely resembled each other in the end, but also collectively embraced shared practices that necessarily silenced other possible articulations of the self, the group, and even the state.[13] There was little room in the language of mainstream propaganda for the experiences and aspirations of populations who saw Islam as an avenue for political economy and development, for instance. Nor was there much space for conceptualizing and articulating nonalignment as an ideology that could exist outside of Nasserist or Western frameworks. This failure of language has to be considered when seeking the causes for the rising popularity of alternative grassroots solutions to state formation in the Middle East in this period. Such voices offered alternative ways of understanding and articulating the nature of liberty and legitimacy. They represented a turn away from the West and Nasser's secular dictatorship toward traditional, religious, and subaltern socioeconomic structures that offered a different way of making sense of the world and a means for expressing frustration with the rhetorical regime that had become so confining. When changes at the rhetorical level became inconsistent with lived experiences, those structures began to crack. This happened in part because the circumscribed language could not sustain the imaginations or the realities of the Arab experience.

NOTES

INTRODUCTION

Epigraph: "U.S. Admits Ship in Water Off Sinai Coast," FBIS, Cairo Domestic Service in Arabic, June 8, 1967, 17:30 GMT.

1. "Radios on Hire," *Palestinian Post,* June 4, 1947, 2.

2. David Wood and Robert Bernasconi, eds., *Derrida and Difference* (Evanston, IL: Northwestern University Press, 1988).

3. Letter from Edwin Samuel to Cyril Conner, October 1, 1946, Countries: Palestine: Palestine Broadcasting Service, BBCWAC, E1/1140; Jacob Stoyanovsky, *The Mandate for Palestine: A Contribution to the Theory and Practice of International Mandates* (Westport, CT: Hyperion Press, orig. 1928, 1979); and H. J. Simson, *British Rule, and Rebellion* (1937; Salisbury, NC: Documentary Publications, 1977).

4. Vladimir Aleksandrovich Gurko-Kriazin, *Natsional'no-osvoboditel'noe dvizhenie na Blizhnem Vostoke. Siriia i Palestina, Kilikiia, Mesopotamiia i Egipet* (Moskva: Mospoligraf, 1923); and L. B. Gurevich', *Siriia, Palestina, Mesopotamiia: (Mandatnye strany)* (Leningrad: Nauka i shkola, 1925).

5. Musa al-ʿAlami, *'Ibrat Filastin (The Lesson of Palestine)* (Beirut: n.p., 1949); and Qustantin Zurayq, *Maʿna al-Nakbah* [The meaning of the disaster] (Bayrut: Dar al-ʿIlm li-al-Malayin, 1948).

6. "Common enemy intimacy" is the practice of people coming together through their shared dislike for a common person or group. Brooke S. Dunbar, "Connection and Disconnection in Online Spaces: An Analysis of Semantic, Latent, and Cultural Themes across Reddit" (PhD diss., Regent University, n.d.), 104.

7. Ngugi wa Thiong'o, *Decolonising the Mind: The Politics of Language in African Literature* (Oxford: James Currey/Heinemann, 1986), 7; and Richard Wright, Amritjit Singh, and Gunnar Myrdal, *The Color Curtain: A Report on the Bandung Conference* (Jackson: University Press of Mississippi, 1995), 200.

8. Malcolm H. Kerr, *The Arab Cold War: Gamal Abd Al Nasir and His Rivals, 1958 to 1970,* 3rd ed. (New York: Oxford University Press, 2020).

9. M. M. Bakhtin, *The Dialogic Imagination: Four Essays*, ed. Michael Holquist, trans. Caryl Emerson, rev. ed. (Austin: University of Texas Press, 1982), 75; Donna Haraway, *Simians, Cyborgs, and Women: The Reinvention of Nature* (New York: Routledge, 2015), 190–91; and Alexei Yurchak, *Everything Was Forever, Until It Was No More: The Last Soviet Generation* (Princeton, NJ: Princeton University Press, 2005), 18.

10. Claude Lefort, *The Political Forms of Modern Society: Bureaucracy, Democracy, Totalitarianism*, ed. David Thompson (Cambridge, MA: MIT Press, 1986), 211–12.

11. Excellent organizational histories of the British and American propaganda programs in the Middle East include Andrew Defty, *Britain, America and Anti-Communist Propaganda 1945–53: The Information Research Department* (Routledge, 2004); Paul Lashmar and James Oliver, *Britain's Secret Propaganda War* (Stroud, Gloucestershire: Sutton Publishing, 1999); Peter Partner, *Arab Voices: The BBC Arabic Service, 1938–1988* (London: British Broadcasting Corp., 1988); Gary D. Rawnsley, "Overt and Covert: The Voice of Britain and Black Radio Broadcasting in the Suez Crisis, 1956," *Intelligence and National Security* 11, no. 3 (July 1, 1996): 497–522; Simon Collier, "Countering Communist and Nasserite Propaganda: The Foreign Office Information Research Department in the Middle East and Africa, 1954–1963" (PhD diss., University of Hertfordshire, 2013); Douglas A. Boyd, "Sharq Al-Adna/The Voice of Britain: The UK's 'Secret' Arabic Radio Station and Suez War Propaganda Disaster," *Gazette* (Leiden, Netherlands) 65, no. 6 (December 1, 2003): 443–55; and Johan Franzén, "Losing Hearts and Minds in Iraq: Britain, Cold War Propaganda and the Challenge of Communism, 1945–58," *Historical Research* 83, no. 222 (2010): 747–62.

12. James Vaughan, *The Failure of American and British Propaganda in the Middle East, 1945–1957: Unconquerable Minds* (Houndmills, Basingstoke: Palgrave Macmillan, 2005); James Vaughan, "Propaganda by Proxy? Britain, America, and Arab Radio Broadcasting, 1953–1957," *Historical Journal of Film, Radio and Television* 22, no. 2 (June 1, 2002): 157–72; James R. Vaughan, "The BBC's External Services and the Middle East before the Suez Crisis," *Historical Journal of Film, Radio & Television* 28, no. 4 (October 2008): 499–514; James Vaughan, "'Cloak without Dagger': How the Information Research Department Fought Britain's Cold War in the Middle East, 1948–56," *Cold War History* 4, no. 3 (April 1, 2004): 56–84; Tony Shaw, *Eden, Suez, and the Mass Media : Propaganda and Persuasion during the Suez Crisis* (London: I. B. Tauris, 1996); Tony Shaw, "The Information Research Department of the British Foreign Office and the Korean War, 1950–53," *Journal of Contemporary History* 34, no. 2 (April 1, 1999): 263–81; Susan L. Carruthers, *Winning Hearts and Minds: British Governments, the Media and Colonial Counter-Insurgency 1944–1960* (London: UNKNO, 1995); Andrea L. Stanton, *This Is Jerusalem Calling: State Radio in Mandate Palestine* (Austin: University of Texas Press, 2013); Andrea L. Stanton, "Situating Radio in the Soundscape of Mandate Palestine," *Jerusalem Quarterly*, no. 86 (Summer 2021): 97–116; Andrea L. Stanton, "Who Heard What When: Learning from Radio Broadcasting Hours and

Programs in Jerusalem," *International Journal of Middle East Studies* 48, no. 1 (February 2016): 141–45; Melani McAlister, *Epic Encounters: Culture, Media, and U.S. Interests in the Middle East since 1945* (Berkeley: University of California Press, 2005); Gary D. Rawnsley, *Radio Diplomacy and Propaganda: The BBC and VOA in International Politics, 1956–64*, Studies in Diplomacy (New York: St. Martin's Press, 1996); and Gary D. Rawnsley, ed., *Cold-War Propaganda in the 1950* (Houndmills, Basingstoke: Palgrave Macmillan, 1999).

13. McAlister, *Epic Encounters*, 3.

14. Kerr, *Arab Cold War*; Elie Kedourie, *The Chatham House Version: And Other Middle Eastern Studies* (Chicago: Ivan R. Dee, 2004); and Jesse Ferris, *Nasser's Gamble: How Intervention in Yemen Caused the Six-Day War and the Decline of Egyptian Power* (Princeton, NJ: Princeton University Press, 2012).

15. Two histories of Soviet international propaganda are still considered the benchmarks and have been useful in the research for this book. See Frederick Charles Barghoorn, *Soviet Foreign Propaganda* (Princeton, NJ: Princeton University Press, 1964); and Martin Ebon, *The Soviet Propaganda Machine* (New York: McGraw-Hill, 1987). The history of Radio Cairo and Voice of the Arabs has been the subject of some excellent recent studies. See Anas Alahmed, "Voice of the Arabs Radio: Its Effects and Political Power during the Nasser Era (1953–1967)," SSRN Scholarly Paper (Rochester, NY, March 12, 2011); Douglas A. Boyd, "Development of Egypt's Radio: 'Voice of the Arabs' under Nasser," *Journalism Quarterly* 52, no. 4 (Winter 1975): 645; Douglas A. Boyd, "Egyptian Radio: Tool of Political and National Development," Journalism Monographs no. 48 (Association for Education in Journalism, February 1, 1977); and Nawal Musleh-Motut, "The Development of Pan-Arab Broadcasting Under Authoritarian Regimes: A Comparison of Sawt Al-Arab ('Voice of the Arabs') and Al Jazeera News Channel" (master's thesis, Simon Fraser University, 2006).

16. While Radio Damascus, Radio Beirut, and Voice of Israel make appearances here, I could not give them the attention that they arguably deserve.

17. I was able to complete my work at the Russian State Archive (GARF) before the current war in Ukraine began.

18. Antonio Gramsci and Teun van Dijk have explored this idea in depth. See Antonio Gramsci, *Selections from the Prison Notebooks*, ed. Quintin Hoare and Geoffrey Nowell Smith (1971; London: International Publishers, 1989), 195; and Teun van Dijk, "El Análisis Crítico Del Discurso," *Anthropos*, no. 186 (October 1999): 27.

19. Alahmed, "Voice of the Arabs Radio," 21; Michael Frishkopf, ed., *Music and Media in the Arab World* (Cairo: American University in Cairo Press, 2010), 13; William A. Rugh, *Arab Mass Media: Newspapers, Radio, and Television in Arab Politics* (Westport, CT: Praeger, 2004), ch. 9; and Elie Podeh and Onn Winckler, eds., *Rethinking Nasserism: Revolution and Historical Memory in Modern Egypt* (Gainesville: University Press of Florida, 2004), 26.

20. Podeh and Winckler, *Rethinking Nasserism*, 26.

21. Bakhtin, *Dialogic Imagination*.

22. Bakhtin, 424.

23. This phenomenon is observed by Lisa Wedeen in her analysis of Syria under the Asad regime. Her work echoes the observations made by James Scott, Peter Sloterdijk, and Slavoj Žižek. Lisa Wedeen, "Acting 'As If': Symbolic Politics and Social Control in Syria," *Comparative Studies in Society and History* 40, no. 3 (1998): 503–23; James C. Scott, *Domination and the Arts of Resistance: Hidden Transcripts*, rev. ed. (New Haven, CT: Yale University Press, 1992); Peter Sloterdijk and Andreas Huyssen, *Critique of Cynical Reason* (Minneapolis: University of Minnesota Press, 1988); and Slavoj Žižek, *For They Know Not What They Do: Enjoyment as a Political Factor* (London: Verso, 2002).

24. Pierre Bourdieu, John B. Thompson, and Gino Raymond, *Language and Symbolic Power* (Cambridge, MA: Harvard University Press, 1991), 111.

25. Avi Shlaim, *Collusion across the Jordan: King Abdullah, the Zionist Movement and the Partition of Palestine* (Oxford: Clarendon Press, 1989); and Benny Morris, *The Birth of the Palestinian Refugee Problem, 1947–49* (Cambridge: Cambridge University Press, 1989).

1. THE RISE OF A "RADIOYAZIK"

1. Naomi Shepherd, *Ploughing Sand: British Rule in Palestine, 1917–1948* (New Brunswick, NJ: Rutgers University Press, 2000); Rory Miller, *Britain, Palestine and Empire: The Mandate Years* (London: Routledge, 2016); Vaughan, "Propaganda by Proxy?," 157–72; Asa Briggs, *History of Broadcasting in the United Kingdom*, vol. 2, *The Golden Age of Wireless* (Oxford: Oxford University Press, 1995); Kate Utting, "The Strategic Information Campaign: Lessons from the British Experience in Palestine 1945–1948," *Contemporary Security Policy* 28, no. 1 (April 1, 2007): 42–62; Carruthers, *Winning Hearts and Minds*; Stanton, *This Is Jerusalem Calling*; Andrea L. Stanton, "Part of Imperial Communications," *Media History* 19, no. 4 (November 1, 2013): 423; Stanton, "Who Heard What When," 141–45; and Stanton, "Situating Radio in the Soundscape," 97–116.

2. Shepherd, *Ploughing Sand*.

3. Vaughan, *Failure of American and British Propaganda*, 9; and Miller, *Britain, Palestine and Empire*.

4. Utting, "Strategic Information Campaign," 56. Utting argues that, in fact, the British propagandists were given an impossible task and that propaganda is never sufficient in stopping counterinsurgency.

5. Barghoorn, *Soviet Foreign Propaganda*; Clive Rose, *The Soviet Propaganda Network: A Directory of Organisations Serving Soviet Foreign Policy* (London: Pinter Publishers, 1988); Zygmunt Nagorski, "Soviet International Propaganda: Its Role, Effectiveness, and Future," *Annals of the American Academy of Political and Social Science* 398 (1971): 130–39; Anne Boyer, *Soviet Foreign Propaganda: An Annotated Bibliography* ([Washington, DC]: United States Information Agency, Agency Library, 1971); Marian Kirsch Leighton, *Soviet Propaganda as a Foreign Policy Tool*

(New York: Freedom House, 1990); Ebon, *Soviet Propaganda Machine*; and Kristin Roth-Ey, *Moscow Prime Time: How the Soviet Union Built the Media Empire That Lost the Cultural Cold War* (Ithaca, NY: Cornell University Press, 2011).

6. W. F. Flicke, *War Secrets in the Ether* (Laguna Hills, CA: Aegean Park Press, 1977), 2:288.

7. Roth-Ey, *Moscow Prime Time*, 16.

8. Masha Kirasirova, *The Eastern International: Arabs, Central Asians, and Jews in the Soviet Union's Anticolonial Empire* (New York: Oxford University Press, 2024), 3.

9. "Palestine Police," 1946, MECA, GB165-0361, Keating Box 2, 2/6/5, 2.

10. Rex Keating, *The Trumpets of Tutankhamun: Adventures of a Radio Pioneer in the Middle East* (Basingstoke: Fisher Miller, 1999), 74.

11. Keating, 74; and Keating Diary, MECA, GB165-0361, Keating Box 1, 1947 Journal, February 5, 1947.

12. Rex Keating, "Between Ourselves," March 14, 1947, MECA, GB165-0361, Keating Box 2, 2/6/3, 1.

13. Contribution by H. Wiedermann to the 21st Anniversary Programme of the German Service, October 1959; Weekly Note, March 31–April 6, 1942, cited in A. Briggs, *The War of Words* (Oxford: Oxford University Press, 1970), 381, 390.

14. Al Jawzi Al Maqdisi, Nasri (2010), "Tarikh al-Itha'a al-Filastiniyya Huna al-Quds," cited in Anthony McNicholas, "Sharq al-Adna: Covert British Radio and the Development of Arab Broadcasting," *Middle East Journal of Culture and Communication* 13, no. 3 (November 27, 2020): 15.

15. Vaughan, *Failure of American and British Propaganda*, 35.

16. Stanton, *This Is Jerusalem Calling*, 23.

17. Stanton, 4.

18. Neither man was new to the propaganda game. Conner, the father of the famed novelist Penelope Gilliat, had worked in the BBC Newcastle office before going through a bad divorce and moving into international broadcasting. Kirkpatrick had been an aide to Prime Minister Neville Chamberlain during the Munich Conference in 1938 and had worked as the director of the Ministry of Information in the Second World War. He went on to become Permanent Under-Secretary in the Foreign Office and was partially responsible for British policy during the 1956 Suez Crisis.

19. Letter from Edwin Samuel to Cyril Conner, October 1, 1946, folder: "Countries: Palestine: Palestine Broadcasting Service," BBCWAC, Reading, UK, E1/1140.

20. The seventeen-acre space was lined in redoubts every ten feet, with two layers of barbed wire, armed guards, and sniper towers. The city's residents humorously named it "Bevingrad" after the British foreign minister, Ernest Bevin. The area had been built up and owned by Russia in the 1860s and had passed into Ottoman and British control since then (explaining the "grad" suffix). Yishuv residents of Jerusalem also sometimes sardonically called the complex the "British concentration camp" and its residents "displaced people." The British Mandate had become fodder for bad jokes about the Holocaust.

21. *Falastin*, October 4, 1946, 3, MDCA.

22. *Palestine Post*, October 4, 1946, 2, AUCA.

23. Letter from Cyril Conner to the BBC main office, April 6, 1946. "Middle East Broadcasting," BBCWAC, E1/666.8; and Bernard Fergusson, *The Trumpet in the Hall, 1930–1958* (London: Collins, 1970), 201–2.

24. Defty, *Britain, America and Anti-Communist Propaganda*, 62.

25. "Propaganda in Middle East: Publicity Directive," TNA, FO 953/61 Foreign Office: Information Policy Department and Regional Information Departments, 1947.

26. Defty, *Britain, America and Anti-Communist Propaganda*, 43, 103.

27. "Propaganda in Middle East: Publicity Directive," TNA, FO 953/61 Foreign Office: Information Policy Department and Regional Information Departments, 1947.

28. "Russia May Leave Iran to Save Face," FBIS, in Arabic to Palestine, March 24, 1946, 7:00 a.m. EST-C.

29. "Aljaliya fi radiu alQuds waltahayyuz alwadih lilyahud" [The community on Radio Al-Quds and the clear bias towards the Jews], *Falastin*, October 15, 1947, 2.

30. Edwin Samuel, *A Lifetime in Jerusalem: The Memoirs of the Second Viscount Samuel* (New York: Routledge, 1970), 207.

31. The Samuels were one of the most prominent Yishuv families in Britain, with Sir Herbert Samuel going on to serve as the head of the Liberal Party in the 1930s. Ironically, Sir Herbert Samuel had been the one to invite Muhammad Amin Al-Huseyni to be the mufti of Jerusalem in 1921, not knowing at the time that the mufti would eventually become the leader of the Palestinian nationalist movement and a collaborator with the Nazis. Philip Mattar, "The Mufti of Jerusalem and the Politics of Palestine," *Middle East Journal* 42, no. 2 (1988): 229.

32. Letter from Mr. Rex Keating of Jerusalem to Mr. Conner, September 10, 1947, folder: "Countries: Palestine: Palestine Broadcasting Service," BBCWAC, E1/1140.

33. Douglas A. Boyd, *Broadcasting in the Arab World : A Survey of the Electronic Media in the Middle East* (Ames: Iowa State University Press, 1993).

34. "Wireless Programmes," *Palestine Post*, April 28, 1947, 2, NLI.

35. "Madha fi radiu alQuds mudir alidha'at yatahadath 'an alidha'at alyahudia" [The director of the Palestine Broadcasting Service talks about the Jewish broadcasts], *Falastin*, August 16, 1945, 1.

36. "Bin Ghwryun yatahadath masa'an 'ams min radiu al-Quds," *Falastin*, January 12, 1947, 1.

37. "Wireless Programmes," 6.

38. "(Kakaw) almistar Brown ba'd (halib) almistar alqasi jawza' kafaa biallah mahazil ya radiu al-Quds," *Falastin*, May 1, 1947, 2.

39. "Tasarufat wasa'at 'ala mata ya radiu alQuds?," *Falastin*, February 23, 1947, 4.

40. Rex Keating, "Between Ourselves: P.B.S. Introduces 'Second Programme,'" *Radio Week*, date unknown, folder: "Countries: Palestine: Palestine Broadcasting Service," BBCWAC, E1/1140, 1.

41. Brochure, P.B.S. Second Programme, "Cultural Broadcasts in English Covering January, February and March 1948," MECA, GB165-0361, Keating Box 2, folder 2/5/7.

42. Rex Keating, 'Between Ourselves,' March 14, 1947, MECA, GB165-0361, Keating Box 2, folder 2/6/3, 1.

43. Memoranda, TNA, CAB 66/64, War Cabinet, W.P. (45)201–W.P. (45) 250, vol. 64, April 4, 1945, 58–62.

44. Peter Partner, *Arab Voices: The BBC Arabic Service, 1938–1988* (London: British Broadcasting Corp., 1988), 68.

45. The wireless programs for daily radio broadcasts in Palestine can be found at the National Library of Israel. These examples are taken from April 27, April 28, May 6, May 11, July 18, July 1, July 20, and December 4, 1947.

46. Partner, *Arab Voices*, 65.

47. Microfilm, BBC broadcast transcript, January 1, 1947, 10:15 a.m., BBCWAC

48. Ibid.

49. Ibid.

50. Report to the Joint Directors-General by E. G. D. Living, "BBC and the Middle East," 1942, folder "Middle East: 1942–1949," BBCWAC, E2 400.

51. This claim has been made by a number of historians, most pointedly Vaughan, *Failure of American and British Propaganda*.

52. Report to the Joint Directors-General by E. G. D. Living, "BBC and the Middle East," 1942, folder: "Middle East: 1942–1949," BBCWAC, E2 400.

53. Ibid.

54. "Arabs Prefer British to UNO Control," FBIS, London, in Arabic to the Middle East, November 13, 1946, 10:00 a.m. EST.

55. "Palestine and German Problems Debated," FBIS, London, in Arabic to the Middle East, February 25, 1947, 2:15 a.m. EST, 112.

56. Mark Tessler, *A History of the Israeli-Palestinian Conflict*, 2nd ed. (Bloomington: Indiana University Press, 2009), 185.

57. "Palestine and German Problems Debated," FBIS, London, in Arabic to the Middle East, February 25, 1947, 2:15 a.m. EST, 112.

58. V. I. Lenin, *Polnoye sobraniie sochinenii: Pyat'desyat pervyi tom* (Moscow: Izdatel'stvo "Prospekt," 2013), 130.

59. Aleksandr Arkad'yevich Sherel', *Audiokul'tura XX veka: Istoriia, esteticheskiie zakonomernosti, osobennosti vliianiia na auditoriiu* (Moscow: Progress-Traditsiya, 2004), 19.

60. Jeffrey Brooks, *Thank You, Comrade Stalin! Soviet Public Culture from Revolution to Cold War* (Princeton, NJ: Princeton University Press, 2000); and Stephen Lovell, *Russia in the Microphone Age: A History of Soviet Radio, 1919–1970*, Oxford Studies in Modern European History (Oxford: Oxford University Press, 2015), 3.

61. Ebon, *Soviet Propaganda Machine*, 286.

62. Boyd, *Broadcasting in the Arab World*, 296. Radio Peace and Progress's transmitting hours were short, however, and it never attracted the kind of listenership that Arab audience surveys acknowledged.

63. Roth-Ey, *Moscow Prime Time.*

64. Roth-Ey, 16.

65. The BBC aired such stories occasionally, but by and large, it was more interested in highlighting the cultural and scientific "gifts" that the West had brought to the world. This assessment is taken from a reading of daily BBC radio show titles, listed each morning in the Palestinian newspapers between 1945 and 1947. The daily show titles can be found in the pages of the *Palestine Post* and *Falastin,* which have been digitized and are available at the National Library of Israel.

66. "Programmy peredach za 1 ianvaria—31 iiunia, 1947," Komitet po radioveshchaniiu i televideniiu pri SSSR, Otdel veshchanie na Arabskie strany, GARF f. P6903, op. 25, d. 27, l. 64–95.

67. And it did seem to work, at least on paper. Kazakhstan underwent an astonishing transformation from 1940 onward, with huge growth in electrification, industrial development, education, and urbanization. No mention was ever made of the forced collectivization and environmental devastation of the 1930s. Great leaps forward are more exciting when the costs are left in the footnotes.

68. "Gosudarstvennye assignovaniia na prosveshchenoe v SSSR i kapitalisticheskikh stranakh," and "Programmy peredach za 1 ianvaria—31 iiunia, 1947," Komitet po radioveshchaniiu i televideniiu pri SSSR, Otdel veshchanie na Arabskie strany, GARF f. P6903, op. 25, d. 27, l. 39, 74.

69. Ibid., l. 64–95.

70. Brooks, *Thank You, Comrade Stalin!.*

71. Brooks.

72. "Pravda" Replies to Major Beamish, *Palestine Post*, August 18, 1947, 1, NLI.

73. "Programmy peredach za 1 ianvaria—31 iiunia, 1947," Komitet po radioveshchaniiu i televideniiu pri SSSR, Otdel veshchanie na Arabskie strany, GARF f. P6903, op. 25, d. 27, l. 64–95. This is also cited in Rósa Magnúsdóttir, *Enemy Number One: The United States of America in Soviet Ideology and Propaganda, 1945–1959* (New York: Oxford University Press, 2018), 4–5.

74. "New Year Round the World," *Palestine Post*, January 1, 1947, 3, NLI.

75. "Programmy peredach za 1 ianvaria—31 iiunia, 1947," Komitet po radioveshchaniiu i televideniiu pri SSSR, Otdel veshchanie na Arabskie strany, GARF, f. P6903, op. 25, d. 27, l. 15.

76. "Imperialism Inflames Palestine Enmities," FBIS, Moscow, in Arabic to the Near and Middle East, May 23, 1947, 12 noon EST—L, BB7.

77. "Programmy peredach za 1 ianvaria—31 iiunia, 1947," Komitet po radioveshchaniiu i televideniiu pri SSSR, Otdel veshchanie na Arabskie strany, GARF, f. P6903, op. 25, d. 27, l. 153.

78. Contribution by H. Wiedermann to the 21st Anniversary Programme of the German Service, October 1959, Weekly Note, March 31–April 6, 1942, cited in Briggs, *War of Words*, 381, 390.

79. Amazingly, this broadcast series is cited in the Russian Federation Archives and in the British National Archives. The British Foreign Office was listening with great interest. "Material on Russian Orthodox Celebrations for BBC," TNA, FO

1110/84, Foreign Office: Information Research Department, 1948; and "The Falsification of History" (Фалсификаторы истории)—"Programmy peredach za 1 ianvaria—31 iiunia, 1948," Komitet po radioveshchaniiu i televideniiu pri SSSR, Otdel veshchanie na Arabskie strany, GARF f. P6903, op. 25, d. 27, l. 41–52.

80. Barghoorn, *Soviet Foreign Propaganda.*

81. Donald Raleigh, "Languages of Power: How the Saratov Bolsheviks Imagined Their Enemies," *Slavic Review* 57, no. 2 (1998): 322.

82. GARF, f. 6903, op. 25., d. 27. l. 45.

83. Sherel', *Audiokul'tura XX veka*, 23.

84. Peter Danchin, "Muslims in a Secular State: Islamic Law and Constitutions Islam in America," *University of Maryland Law Journal of Race, Religion, Gender and Class* 11, no. 1 (January 1, 2011): 4.

85. "Programmy peredach za 1 ianvaria—31 iiunia, 1947," Komitet po radioveshchaniiu i televideniiu pri SSSR, Otdel veshchanie na Arabskie strany, GARF f. P6903, op. 25, d. 86, l. 14.

86. "Radiu Musku yatahim alFatikan bialfashia" [Radio Moscow accuses the Vatican of fascism], *Falastin*, April 2, 1946, 1.

87. "Material on Russian Orthodox Celebrations for BBC," TNA, FO 1110/84, Foreign Office: Information Research Department, 1947; "Falsifikatory istorii," and "Programmy peredach za 1 ianvaria—31 iiunia, 1947," Komitet po radioveshchaniiu i televideniiu pri SSSR, Otdel veshchanie na Arabskie strany, GARF f. P6903, op. 25, d. 27, l. 41–52; and Victoria Smolkin, *A Sacred Space Is Never Empty: A History of Soviet Atheism*, illus. ed. (Woodstock, Oxfordshire: Princeton University Press, 2018).

88. "Programmy peredach za 1 ianvaria—31 iiunia, 1947," Komitet po radioveshchaniiu i televideniiu pri SSSR, Otdel veshchanie na Arabskie strany, GARF f. P6903, op. 25, d. 27, l. 157.

89. "Programmy peredach za 1 ianvaria—31 iiunia, 1947," Komitet po radioveshchaniiu i televideniiu pri SSSR, Otdel veshchanie na Arabskie strany, GARF, f. P6903, op. 25, d. 27, l. 80–81. See also "Programmy peredach za 1 ianvaria—31 iiunia, 1948," Komitet po radioveshchaniiu i televideniiu pri SSSR, Otdel veshchanie na Arabskie strany, GARF f. P6903, op. 25, d. 2, l. 2.

90. "Programmy peredach za 1 ianvaria—31 iiunia, 1947," Komitet po radioveshchaniiu i televideniiu pri SSSR, Otdel veshchanie na Arabskie strany, GARF, f. P6903, op. 25, d. 27, l. 80–81.

91. "British Talk to Quit Palestine Doubted," FBIS, Moscow, in Persian to the Near and Middle East, October 14, 1947, 12:30 p.m. EST—L.

92. "Imperialism Inflames Palestine Enmities," FBIS, Moscow, in Arabic to the Near and Middle East, May 23, 1947, 12 noon EST—L, BB7.

93. "Programmy peredach za 1 ianvaria—31 iiunia, 1947," Komitet po radioveshchaniiu i televideniiu pri SSSR, Otdel veshchanie na Arabskie strany, GARF, f. P6903, op. 25, d. 27, l. 82.

94. Ibid.

95. Ervand Abrahamian, "Ali Shariati: Ideologue of the Iranian Revolution," *Merip Reports* 12 (February 1982): 45.

96. Michael Ignatieff, "The Nightmare From Which We Are Trying to Awake," in *The Warrior's Honor: Ethnic War and the Modern Conscience* (London: Chatto and Windus, 1998), 166–90.

2. THE RESONANCE MACHINE IS BORN

1. HC Debates, February 18, 1947, vol. 433, cc988.

2. There is a vast literature on the UN Special Committee on Palestine, their tour of Palestine, their recommendations, and the UN General Assembly's vote, which led to the creation of the state of Israel. Much of it is highly partisan and political, following the trajectory of traditional Israeli historiography, but giving way in recent years to a revisionist school. For a general review of this literature, see Nicholas E. Roberts, "Re-Remembering the Mandate: Historiographical Debates and Revisionist History in the Study of British Palestine," *History Compass* 9, no. 3 (2011): 215–30.

3. William E. Connolly, "The Evangelical-Capitalist Resonance Machine," *Political Theory* 33, no. 6 (2005): 870.

4. Boyd, *Broadcasting in the Arab World*, 85.

5. "What Do You Know about Egyptian Broadcasting?," in *Arab Broadcasts*, trans. F. Yousef, 63–77 (July 1971), cited in Boyd, *Broadcasting in the Arab World*, 18.

6. Louise M. Bourgault, *Mass Media in Sub-Saharan Africa* (Bloomington: Indiana University Press, 1995). After the British departed, the PBS became Kol Isreal, the Voice of Israel. Derek Jonathan Penslar, "Transmitting Jewish Culture: Radio in Israel," *Jewish Social Studies* 10, no. 1 (2003): 1–29; and Douglas A. Boyd, "Hebrew-Language Clandestine Radio Broadcasting During the British Palestin Mandate," *Journal of Radio Studies* 6, no. 1 (1999): 101–15.

7. "Jewish News Agency Distorts Facts," FBIS, Beirut, in Arabic to the Near East, March 4, 1947, 6:00 a.m. EST.

8. "Britain and U.S. to Split Palestine," FBIS, Cairo, in Arabic to the Middle East, May 26, 1947, 7:30 a.m. EST.

9. "First International Organization," FBIS, Jerusalem, in Arabic to the Near East, July 21, 1947, 2:00 p.m. EST.

10. "Belief in UN in Balance," FBIS, Sharq al-Adna in Arabic to the Near East, April 28, 1947, 10:00 a.m. EST.

11. Clifton Daniels, "Irgun Bars Truce Unless British Let Refugees Enter," *New York Times*, February 18, 1947, 1.

12. "Palestine Press Reaction," FBIS, Paris, in Arabic to the Middle East, April 29, 1947, 11:45 a.m. EST.

13. "Palestine UNO Inquiry Would Help Jews," FBIS, Radio Tunis in Arabic to North Africa and the Near East, April. 4, 1947, 2:25 p.m. EST.

14. Keating's Diaries, MECA, GB165-0361, Keating Box 1, 1947 Journal, January 10 and 29, 1947.

15. "Palestine UNO Inquiry Would Help Jews," FBIS, Radio Tunis in Arabic to North Africa and the Near East, April 4, 1947, 2:25 p.m. EST.

16. "Arabs Should Not Pin Hopes on UN," FBIS, Radio Cairo in Arabic to North Africa and the Near East, August 27, 1947, 1:30 p.m. EST.

17. "No Clash with Jews," FBIS, Jerusalem, in Arabic to the Near East, July 25, 1947, 11:00 a.m. EST.

18. "4,000 Monthly Yishuv Immigration," FBIS, Damascus, in Arabic to the Middle East, April 10, 1947, 12 noon EST.

19. Shepherd, *Ploughing Sand*, 222.

20. "Arab Reaction to UN Session Reported," FBIS, Sharq al-Adna, Jaffa, in Arabic to the Near East, May 17, 1947, 11:00 a.m. EST.

21. "Treaty Modifications Sought," FBIS, Sharq al-Adna, Jaffa, in Arabic to the Near East, April. 15, 1947, 10:00 a.m. EST.

22. "Arab Reaction to UN Session Reported," FBIS, Sharq al-Adna, Jaffa, in Arabic to the Near East, May 17, 1947, 11:00 a.m. EST.

23. Z. Elpeleg and Shmuel Himelstein, *The Grand Mufti: Haj Amin al-Hussaini, Founder of the Palestinian National Movement* (Frank Cass, 1993), 83–84. This is disturbingly glossed over in David Dalin, *Icon of Evil: Hitler's Mufti and the Rise of Radical Islam* (New York: Routledge, 2017), 83.

24. "Egypt Criticized by Palestine Arabs," FBIS, Radio Beirut in Arabic to North Africa and the Near East, April. 5, 1947, 12 noon EST.

25. "Complete British Evacuation Demanded," FBIS, Radio Cairo in Arabic to North Africa and the Near East, May 18, 1947, 1:30 p.m. EST.

26. "Palestine's Importance," FBIS, Beirut, in Arabic to the Near East, March 4, 1947, 12:00 noon EST.

27. "Palestine's Importance," FBIS, Beirut, in Arabic to the Near East, March 4, 1947, 12:00 noon EST.

28. Michael Doran, *Pan-Arabism before Nasser: Egyptian Power Politics and the Palestine Question* (New York: Oxford University Press, 2002), 5.

29. United Nations, "Itinerary of the Special Committee in Palestine," in Official Records of the Second Session of the General Assembly, Supplement no. 11, *United Nations Special Committee on Palestine, Report to the General Assembly*, vol. 2 (Lake Success, NY: UN, 1947), 4–5.

30. "U.N. Palestine Inquiry Opens," *La Crosse Tribune*, June 16, 1947, 1.

31. "Irgun Secret Radio Seized," *Ottawa Journal*, June 19, 1947, 6.

32. "Imperialism Inflames Palestine Enmities," FBIS, Radio Moscow in Arabic to the Near East, May 23, 1947, 12 noon EST.

33. "Crisis Result of Bevin's Foreign Policy," FBIS, Radio Moscow in Arabic to the Near East, June 4, 1947, 10:30 a.m. EST.

34. "Workers' Unity Solution for Palestine," FBIS, Radio Moscow in Arabic to the Near East, June 5, 1947, 12 noon EST.

35. Elad Ben-Dror, "The Arab Struggle against Partition: The International Arena of Summer 1947," *Middle Eastern Studies* 43, no. 2 (2007): 269.

36. "Arab Attitude to Commission Undecided," FBIS, Radio Damascus in Arabic to the Near East, June 8, 1947, 7:45 a.m. EST.

37. "Practical Solution Impossible," FBIS, Radio Moscow in Arabic to the Near East, June 6, 1947, 1:00 p.m. EST.

38. "Palestine Arabs Boycott Polish Goods," FBIS, Radio Moscow in Arabic to the Near East, June 10, 1947, 5:30 a.m. EST.

39. "Palestine Group Revokes UNSCOP Support," FBIS, Radio Cairo in Arabic to the Near East, June 16, 1947, 2:13 p.m. EST.

40. "Palestine in Arabic: 23 May 1945–20 October 1947," BBCWAC, box RIII, 5104480B.

41. Ibid. See a description of the broadcast from the Exodus in the *Palestine Post*, July 18, 1947, 1.

42. "Palestine in Arabic: 23 May 1945–20 October 1947," BBCWAC, box RIII, 5104480B.

43. "Palestine in Arabic: 23 May 1945–20 October 1947," BBCWAC, box RIII, 5104480B. This folder holds, among other things, clippings of international press stories in English on the exodus incident. See also the *Palestine Post*, July 21, 1947, 1.

44. "Severance of Relations," FBIS, Radio Beirut in Arabic to the Near East, July 25, 1947, 12:00 noon EST.

45. One other archive would be worth examining, the Maspero Archive in Cairo. Currently, scholars are being granted very limited access, even when they have all the required credentials and permissions.

46. Alan Swarc, "Illegal Immigration to Palestine 1945–1948: The French Connection" (PhD diss., University College London, 2006), 76.

47. "Arabs Sacrificed for U.S. Elections," FBIS, Damascus, in Arabic to Syria and the Near East, October 28, 1947, 2:00 p.m. EST.

48. "Russia Protects Palestine Veto Right," FBIS, Damascus, in Arabic to Syria and the Near East, November 10, 1947, 2:00 p.m. EST.

49. "UNSCOP Proposals Rejected," FBIS, Cairo, in Arabic to North Africa and the Near East, September 16, 1947, 12 noon EST. In this citation, the CIA actually listed the broadcasts on this topic that were coming from many sources, including PBS, Radio Damascus, and Radio Cairo.

50. "Iraqi Democrats Reject UNSCOP Decision," FBIS, Sharq al-Adna, Jaffa, in Arabic to the Near East, September 14, 1947, 11:00 a.m. EST.

51. "Disagreements Denied," FBIS, Sharq al-Adna, Jaffa, in Arabic to the Near East, September. 19, 1947, 11:00 a.m. EST.

52. Preamble, United Nations Charter, 1945, www.un.org/en/sections/un-charter/preamble/index.html.

53. "Cancelation of Oil Grants Threatened," FBIS, Egyptian Home Service, Cairo, September 30, 1947, 7:30 a.m. EST.

54. "Arabs Will 'Give America a Lesson,'" FBIS, Jerusalem, in Arabic to Palestine, October 17, 1947, 1:00 p.m. EST.

55. "U.S. Thwarts Soviet on Intervention," FBIS, Beirut, in Arabic to the Middle East, October 9, 1947, 1:00 p.m. EST.

56. Yacoub Haider Abdulrahman, "United Nations' Role in the Palestinian-Israeli Conflict, 1947–1950" (PhD diss., Golden Gate University, 1990), 47.

57. "Arabs Sacrificed for U.S. Elections," FBIS, Damascus, in Arabic to Syria and the Near East, October 28, 1947, 2:00 p.m. EST. Amazingly, after the UN vote in November, in which the Soviet Union and the United States both voted for partition, Radio Damascus would declare that the Soviets had "defeated" the United States during the vote. See "USSR Defeats on U.S. Palestine Pact," FBIS, Damascus, in Arabic to Syria and the Near East, November 11, 1947, 2:00 p.m. EST.

58. "Irgun Prefers Russian Plan to U.S.," FBIS, Damascus, in Arabic to Syria and the Near East, November 6, 1947, 7:30 a.m. EST.

59. Douglas Little, *American Orientalism: The United States and the Middle East since 1945* (Chapel Hill: University of North Carolina Press, 2009), 11.

60. Heonik Kwon, *The Other Cold War*, Columbia Studies in International and Global History (New York: Columbia University Press, 2010).

61. Letter from Wadsworth to Byrnes, July 10, 1946, NARA, RG84, Cairo Embassy 1936–55, box 151, no. 1266. Also cited in Vaughan, *Failure of American and British Propaganda*, 133; and Bruce J. Evensen, "Truman, Palestine and the Cold War," *Middle Eastern Studies* 28, no. 1 (1992): 121.

62. Vaughan, *Failure of American and British Propaganda*, 129–30.

63. Vaughan, 130–31.

64. Abdulrahman, "United Nations' Role the Palestinian-Israeli Conflict," 93.

65. "Arab World Passes through Critical Stage," FBIS, Sharq al-Adna in Arabic to the Middle East, September 1, 1947, 12:30 p.m. EST.

66. Ibid.

67. "Iraqi Indignation," FBIS, Sharq al-Adna, Jaffa, in Arabic to the Near East, October 14, 1947, 11:00 a.m. EST.

68. "Soviet Partition Support Irks Arabs," FBIS, Sharq al-Adna, Jaffa, in Arabic to the Near East, October 14, 1947, 1:30 p.m. EST.

69. "USSR Zone Abets Jewish Emigration," FBIS, London, in Arabic to Syria and the Near East, September 25, 1947, 9:30 p.m. EST.

70. "Arabs Hear Soviet View of Palestine," FBIS, Moscow, in Arabic to the Near and Middle East, November 14, 1947, 12 noon EST.

71. "British Talk to Quit Palestine Doubted," FBIS, Moscow, in Persian to the Near and Middle East, October 14, 1947, 12:30 p.m. EST.

72. "Programmy peredach za 1 ianvaria—31 iiunia, 1948," Komitet po radioveshchaniiu i televideniiu pri SSSR, Otdel veshchanie na Arabskie strany, GARF f. P6903, op. 25, d. 25, l.1.

73. National Weather Service, New York, NY, History Page, November 12, 1947, www.weather.gov/okx/history.

74. "Britain as Target," FBIS, Beirut, in Arabic to the Near East, November 12, 1947, 12 noon EST.

75. "Brochure of the P.B.S. Second Programme, "Cultural Broadcasts in English Covering August, September, October, 1947," MECA, GB165-0361, Keating Box 2, folder 2/5/7.

76. Keating Diary, MECA, GB165-0361, Keating Box 1, 1947 Journal, November 28, 1947.

77. Microfilm, BBC broadcast rranscript, November 29, 1947, 11:00 p.m., BBCWAC

78. Microfilm, BBC broadcast transcripts, November 30, 1947. 6:00 a.m., BBCWAC

79. Ibid, 7:00 a.m.

80. Ibid, 8:00 a.m.

81. Ibid.

82. Microfilm, BBC broadcast transcript, December 1, 1947, 11:00 a.m., BBCWAC.

83. Microfilm, BBC broadcast transcript, November 30, 1947, 6:20 a.m., BBCWAC.

84. Microfilm, BBC broadcast transcript, November 30, 1947, 8:20 a.m., BBCWAC.

85. Keating's Diary, MECA, GB165-0361, Keating Box 1, November 29, 1947.

86. Keating's Diary, MECA, GB165-0361, Keating Box 1, 1947 Journal, December 4, 1947.

87. Keating Diary, MECA, GB165-0361, Keating Box 1, 1947 Journal, November 30, 1947.

88. Keating Diary, MECA, GB165-0361, Keating Box 1, 1947 Journal, December 1, 1947.

89. Keating Diary, MECA, GB165-0361, Keating Box 1, 1947 Journal, December 22, 1947. This story was corroborated through a conversation that I had with Keating's second wife, Elizabeth Keating.

90. Letter from Rex Keating to Cyril Conner, December 23, 1947, folder: "Countries: Palestine: Palestine Broadcasting Service," BBCWAC, E1/1140.

91. "The Secret People," 1948, MECA, GB165-0361, Keating Box 2, 2/6/6, 1.

92. Letter from Edwin Samuel to Azmi Nashashibi, April 16, 1948, MECA, GB165-0361, Keating Box 2, 2/7/6.

93. Keating's Diary, MECA, GB165-0361, Keating Box 1, 1947–1948 Journals, December 5, 1947–April 28, 1948.

94. Penslar, "Transmitting Jewish Culture," 5.

95. "Arab Reaction Balks Palestine Peace," FBIS, Moscow, in Arabic to the Near East, January 20, 1948, 12 noon EST.

96. Ibid.

97. David Cesarani, *Major Farran's Hat: Murder, Scandal and Britain's War Against Jewish Terrorism, 1945–1948* (London: William Heinemann, 2009), viii.

98. Microfilm, BBC broadcast transcript, November 30, 1947, 8:00 a.m., BBCWAC.

99. "British Agents behind Arab Revolt," FBIS, Moscow, in Arabic to the Near East, January 11, 1948, 12:02 p.m. EST.

100. "Jews Repudiate Deir Yassin Atrocity," FBIS, Hagana Radio, Clandestine, in Arabic to the Near East, April 12, 1948, 1:00 p.m. EST.

3. "IMAGINE, O ARABS!"

1. Hugh Wilford, "The Information Research Department: Britain's Secret Cold War Weapon Revealed," *Review of International Studies* 24, no. 3 (1998): 353.

2. Musleh-Motut, "Development of Pan-Arab Broadcasting.".

3. Elie Podeh, "The Drift Towards Neutrality: Egyptian Foreign Policy during the Early Nasserist Era, 1952–55," *Middle Eastern Studies*, December 6, 2006, 161.

4. Alahmed, "Voice of the Arabs Radio; Boyd, "Development of Egypt's Radio," 645; Musleh-Motut, *Development of Pan-Arab Broadcasting.*

5. Voice of the Arabs, "Cairo Radio and Broadcasting Services," Commentary by Ahmed Rashad Ali, May 6, 1956, TNA, FO 371/119221, Foreign Office: Political Departments: General Correspondence from 1906–1966.

6. BBCM IV, 668, May 1–7, 1956, reel 336, 25.

7. "Programmy peredach za 1 maia—31 avgusta, 1956," Komitet po radioveshchaniiu i televideniiu pri SSSR, Otdel veshchanie na Arabskie strany, GARF f. P6903, op. 25, d. 271, l. 88.

8. BBC Engineering Information Department, "Egypt: Estimated External Output," March 13, 1956, BBCWAC, E8/153/1, World Index of External Broadcast, Near & Middle East.

9. "Albathu fi alsutur," MASPERO, The Egyptian Radio and Television Federation, Cairo, 1.

10. Keith Kyle, *Suez: Britain's End of Empire in the Middle East*, reprint ed. (London: I. B. Tauris, 2011), 34.

11. "Radio Organisations[sic] Basic Data—Asia & Middle East A-H," BBCWAC, E3/996/1.

12. Ibid.

13. BBC Engineering Information Department, "Egypt: Estimated External Output," March 13, 1956, BBCWAC, E8/153/1, World Index of External Broadcast, Near & Middle East.

14. Ibid.

15. Osgood Carruthers, "'Voice of the Arabs' Stirs Mideast: Broadcasts Are Now Most Potent Propaganda Aimed at West and the U.S.," *New York Times*, January 15, 1956, E5.

16. "Egypt's External Propaganda," August 1, 1957, NARA, RG 306, US Information Agency, Office of Research and Analysis, entry A1 1033, Research Reports, 1956–1959, container 3, 11.

17. "Egyptian Broadcasting Service Transmissions," July 27, 1956, "Arrangements for Extended BBC Monitoring Coverage," TNA, FO 1110/945 Foreign Office: Information Research Department, 1956.

18. "Egypt's External Propaganda," August 1, 1957, NARA, RG 306, US Information Agency, Office of Research and Analysis, entry A1 1033, Research Reports, 1956–1959, container 3, 7.

19. A. I. Dawisha, "The Role of Propaganda in Egypt's Arab Policy, 1955–1967," *International Relations* 5, no. 2 (1975): 897.

20. Alahmed, "Voice of the Arabs Radio," 4; and Vaughan, "Propaganda by Proxy?," 157.

21. Cypher, "Egyptian Saudi Yemeni Pact," British Foreign Office translation, April 26, 1956, "Anti-British Propaganda in the Middle East," TNA, FO 371/119303—Foreign Office: Political Departments: General Correspondence from 1906–1966, Africa: Egypt, 1956.

22. Gillian Kennedy, *From Independence to Revolution: Egypt's Islamists and the Contest for Power* (New York: Hurst, 2017), 41.

23. Cairo to Secretary of State, January 19, 1955, NARA, RG 59, 682.87/1-1955, cited also in Podeh, "Drift towards Neutrality," 168. See also Elie Podeh, *The Quest for Hegemony in the Arab World: The Struggle over the Baghdad Pact* (New York: Brill, 2022); Reem Abou-El-Fadl, "Neutralism Made Positive: Egyptian Anti-Colonialism on the Road to Bandung," *British Journal of Middle Eastern Studies* 42, no. 2 (2014): 219–40; and Georgiana G. Stevens, "Arab Neutralism and Bandung," *Middle East Journal* 11, no. 2 (1957): 139–52.

24. Podeh, "Drift towards Neutrality," 167; and Muhammad Hasanayn Haykal, *Milaffat Al-Suways: Harb Al-Thalathin Sanatan* (Cairo: Markaz al-Ahram lil-Tarjamah wa-al-Nashr, 1986), 318.

25. Carruthers, "'Voice of the Arabs' Stirs Mideast," E5.

26. Radio Cairo, "West Seen Embittered by Arab Freedom," FBIS, Cairo, in Arabic, July 24, 1954, 18:20 GMT.

27. Karl Popper, "The Conspiracy Theory of Society," in *Conspiracy Theories: The Philosophical Debate*, ed. David Coady (London: Routledge, 2019), 14.

28. Gregory Currie, "Why Irony Is Pretence," in *The Architecture of the Imagination: New Essays on Pretence, Possibility, and Fiction*, ed. Shaun Nichols (Oxford: Oxford University Press, 2006), 111–33.

29. British Foreign Office to Cairo, May 10, 1956, "Cairo Radio and Broadcasting Services," TNA, FO 371/119221, Foreign Office: Political Departments: General Correspondence from 1906–1966.

30. Ahmed Said, Voice of the Arabs, May 1, 1956, SWB, IV, 672, reel 336, 13.

31. Voice of the Arabs, "Cairo Radio and Broadcasting Services," Commentary by Ahmad Said, May 8, 1956, TNA, FO 371/119221, Foreign Office: Political Departments: General Correspondence from 1906–1966, 4.

32. British Foreign Office to Cairo, May 10, 1956, "Cairo Radio and Broadcasting Services," TNA, FO 371/119221, Foreign Office: Political Departments: General Correspondence from 1906–1966.

33. "Ahmed Said. Huna Sawt al-Arab," *Albawwabat Niuz*, May 5, 2018.

34. BBCM IV, 668, May 1–7, 1956, reel 336, 25.

35. BBCM IV, 683, June 22, 1956, reel 336, 22.

36. Voice of the Arabs, "Cairo Radio and Broadcasting Services," Commentary by Ahmed Shawkat, May 7, 1956, TNA, FO 371/119221, Foreign Office: Political Departments: General Correspondence from 1906–1966.

37. Ibid.

38. Ibid.

39. "Audience Research O/S, General Overseas Service, Middle East/South Asia Panels, 1952–1960," BBCWAC, E3/51.

40. "Programma radioperedach redaktsii veshchaniia dlia arabskiikh stran na sredy," Komitet po radioveshchaniiu i televideniiu pri SSSR, 20 iiulia, 1954, GARF, f. P6903, op. 25, d. 271, l. 63–110.

41. Daniel J. Gilman, *Cairo Pop: Youth Music in Contemporary Egypt* (Minneapolis: University of Minnesota Press, 2014), 20.

42. Ahmed Said, "Huna Sawt al-Arab."

43. "Wafat Mudhie Alnuksat Fi Dhikraha," *al'amsar*, June 5, 2018.

44. Anne Dillon, *The Construction of Martyrdom in the English Catholic Community, 1535–1603* (London: Routledge, 2016); David Cook, *Martyrdom in Islam* (Cambridge: Cambridge University Press, 2007); Bill Rolston, "When Everywhere Is Karbala: Murals, Martyrdom and Propaganda in Iran," *Memory Studies* 13, no. 1 (February 1, 2020): 3–23; and Andreas Marklund, "The Manly Sacrifice: Martial Manliness and Patriotic Martyrdom in Nordic Propaganda during the Great Northern War," *Gender & History* 25, no. 1 (April 2013): 150–69.

45. Tony Shaw, "Martyrs, Miracles, and Martians: Religion and Cold War Cinematic Propaganda in the 1950s," *Journal of Cold War Studies* 4, no. 2 (2002): 3–5.

46. BBCM IV, 662, April 4–6, 1956, reel 336, 29.

47. Margaret Peacock, *Innocent Weapons: The Soviet and American Politics of Childhood in the Cold War*, New Cold War History (Chapel Hill: University of North Carolina Press, 2014).

48. "Programma radioperedach redaktsii veshchaniia dlia arabskiikh stran na sredy," Komitet po radioveshchaniiu i televideniiu pri SSSR, 20 iiulia, 1954, GARF, f.P6903, op. 25, d. 271, l. 63–110.

49. BBCM IV, 663, April 18–21, 1956, reel 336, 17.

50. BBCM IV, 668, May 1–7, 1956, reel 336, 24.

51. Robert Conquest, *The Great Terror: A Reassessment* (New York: Oxford University Press, 1990).

52. Bethan Johnson, "The Role of Animals in National Socialist Propaganda," *Fair Observer* (blog), January 5, 2022.

53. Vasilii Semenovich Grossman, *Vse techet . . .* (Frankfurt am Main: Posev, 1974), 74.

54. Bahrain to Foreign Office, March 12, 1956, "Egyptian Propaganda in Middle East," TNA, PREM 11/1450—Prime Minister's Office: Correspondence and Papers, 1954–1964, 1.

55. British Foreign Office to Cairo, April 25, 1956, "Cairo Radio and Broadcasting Services," TNA, FO 371/119221, Foreign Office: Political Departments: General Correspondence from 1906–1966.

56. Voice of the Arabs, "Cairo Radio and Broadcasting Services," Commentary by Ahmad Said, May 6, 1956, TNA, FO 371/119221, Foreign Office: Political Departments: General Correspondence from 1906–1966.

57. Christian Lange, "Eternal Sunshine of the Spotless Mind: Light and Luminous Being in Islamic Theology," *Critical Research on Religion* 9, no. 2 (August 1, 2021): 143.

58. Christian Lange, *Paradise and Hell in Islamic Traditions*, reprint ed. (New York: Cambridge University Press, 2015), 120.

59. Abu Nu'aym al-Isfahani, *Sifat Al-Janna*, ed. Ali Rida b. 'Abdallah b. 'Ali Rida (Beirut: Dar al-Ma'mun li-l-Turath, 1995), 5; and Suyuti, *Al-Budur al-Safira Fi 'ulum al-Akhira*, ed. Abu 'Abdallah M. al-Shafi'i (Beirut: Dar al-Kutub, 1996), 620.

60. Lange, "Eternal Sunshine of the Spotless Mind," 152.

61. Hadi Gharabaghi, "Documentary Diplomacy and Audiovisual Modernization: A Cold War Genealogy of Arab Cinema during the 1950s through American Declassified Archives," in *Cinema of the Arab World: Contemporary Directions in Theory and Practice*, ed. Terri Ginsberg and Chris Lippard, Global Cinema (Cham: Springer International Publishing, 2020), 5.

62. BBCM IV, 663, April 18–21, 1956, reel 336, 17.

63. Foreign Office to Cairo, March 13, 1956, "Egyptian Propaganda in Middle East," TNA, PREM 11/1450—Prime Minister's Office: Correspondence and Papers, 1954–1964, 1–2.

64. Henri Lefebvre et al., *State, Space, World: Selected Essays* (Minneapolis: University of Minnesota Press, 2009), 175.

65. BBCM IV, 684, June 24, 1956, reel 336, 24.

66. British Foreign Office to Cairo, April 30, 1956, "Cairo Radio and Broadcasting Services," TNA, FO 371/119221, Foreign Office: Political Departments: General Correspondence from 1906–1966.

67. Information Department, Baghdad, to IRD, January 12, 1954, TNA, FO 1110/700/PR 1093/1/G, cited in Vaughan, "'Cloak without Dagger,'" 63.

68. BBCM IV, 662–692, April 10–July 24, 1956, reel 336, 26.

69. BBCM IV, 662–692, April 10–July 24, 1956, reel 336, 27.

70. BBCM IV, 664, April 10–17, 1956, reel 336, 3.

71. BBCM IV, 663, April 18–21, 1956, reel 336, 24 .

72. "Situation Report on Egypt and Egyptian Relations," September 1, 1955, NARA, RG 306, US Information Agency, Office of Research and Intelligence, entry A1 1022, Intelligence Bulletins, Memorandums and Summaries: 1954–1956, container 6, 3.

73. BBCM IV, 662, April 4–6, 1956, reel 336, 31

74. BBCM IV, 662, April 4–6, 1956, reel 336, 31.

75. J. L. Austin, *How to Do Things with Words*, ed. J. O. Urmson (Eastford, CT: Martino Fine Books, 2018).

76. For more on post-structural critiques of language and its formation of meaning, see Jacob Torfing, *New Theories of Discourse: Laclau, Mouffe and Zizek* (Toronto: Wiley-Blackwell, 1999); and Jacques Derrida, *Writing and Difference*, trans. Alan Bass (Chicago: University of Chicago Press, 2017).

77. Ernesto Laclau and Chantal Mouffe, *Hegemony and Socialist Strategy: Towards a Radical Democratic Politics*, 2nd ed. (London: Verso, 2014), 111.

4. THE POWER OF PEACE

1. John Maynard Keynes, *The Economic Consequences of the Peace* (CreateSpace Independent Publishing Platform, 2012).

2. Brooks, *Thank You, Comrade Stalin!*.

3. Scholars have done important work on the history of the Middle East peace process. They have traced the role of inter-Arab and inter-Israeli politics in shaping the ongoing conflict between Israel and the Arab world. They have sought to understand how issues of perception, belief, and identity have made the peace process so difficult over many decades. Some have held the West, particularly the United States, accountable for the failure to reach peace, tracing how American foreign policy has repeatedly destabilized the region and led to the normalization of Israeli hegemony. Others have argued that the ability to control the language of peace and to establish oneself as the defender of it was a vital step in the fight for soft power in the emerging global Cold War. Madiha Rashid al Madfai, *Jordan, the United States and the Middle East Peace Process, 1974–1991* (Cambridge: Cambridge University Press, 1993); Alasdair Drysdale and Raymond A. Hinnebusch, *Syria and the Middle East Peace Process* (New York: Council on Foreign Relations, 1991); Hassan A. Barari, *Israeli Politics and the Middle East Peace Process, 1988–2002* (London: Routledge, 2004); Greg McLaughlin and Stephen Baker, *The Propaganda of Peace: The Role of Media and Culture in the Northern Ireland Peace Process* (Bristol: Intellect Books, 2010), 11; Eran Halperin et al., "Promoting the Middle East Peace Process by Changing Beliefs About Group Malleability," *Science* 333, no. 6050 (September 23, 2011): 1767; N. Haslam, L. Rothschild, and D. Ernst, "Essentialist Beliefs about Social Categories," *The British Journal of Social Psychology* 39, pt. 1 (March 2000): 113; I. William Zartman, ed., *Peacemaking in International Conflict: Methods and Techniques*, rev. ed. (Washington, DC: United States Institute of Peace, 2007), 61; Avi Shlaim, *War and Peace in the Middle East: A Critique of American Policy* (New York: Whittle Books, 1994); Edward W. Said, *Peace and Its Discontents: Essays on Palestine in the Middle East Peace Process* (New York: Knopf Doubleday, 2012), xxv; Petra Goedde, *The Politics of Peace: A Global Cold War History*, illus. ed. (New York: Oxford University Press, 2019); Walter L. Hixson, *Parting the Curtain: Propaganda, Culture, and the Cold War, 1945–1961*, (New York: Palgrave Macmillan, 1998); Kenneth Alan Osgood, *Total Cold War: Eisenhower's Secret Propaganda Battle at Home and Abroad* (Lawrence: University of Kansas,

2006); and Ira Chernus, "The Word 'Peace' as a Weapon of (Cold) War," *Peace Review* 10, no. 4 (December 1998): 605.

4. Said, *Peace and Its Discontents*, xiii.

5. Raymond G. Cowherd, "The Soviet Peace Offensive," *Current History* 19, no. 109 (1950): 129.

6. Jeffrey Brooks, "When the Cold War Did Not End: The Soviet Peace Offensive of 1953 and the American Response," Wilson Center Occasional Papers, no. 278 (2000): 4.

7. Komitet po radioveshchaniiu i televideniiu pri SSSR, "Programma radioperedach redaktsii veshchaniia dlia arabsckikh stran na sredy, 20 iiuliia, 1954," GARF f. P6903, op. 25, d. 271, l. 63–110.

8. Frederick Charles Barghoorn, *Soviet Cultural Offensive* (Princeton, NJ: Princeton University Press, 2015), 221.

9. Komitet po radioveshchaniiu i televideniiu pri SSSR, "Programma radioperedach redaktsii veshchaniia dlia arabsckikh stran na sredy, 20 iuliia, 1954," GARF f. P6903, op. 25, d. 271, l. 87.

10. "Programmy peredach za 1 ianvaria—1 iiunia, 1950," Komitet po radioveshchaniiu i televideniiu pri SSSR, GARF, f. P6903, op. 25, d. 86, l. 12; and "Programmy peredach za 1 maia—31 avgusta," Komitet po radioveshchaniiu i televideniiu pri SSSR, GARF f. P6903, op. 25, d. 271, l. 88.

11. Radio Moscow, "Egypt Offers to Enroll Autherine Lucy," FBIS, Radio Moscow in Arabic, March 15, 1956, 15:30 GMT. And of course, because this source comes from the Central Intelligence Agency, it means that the Americans knew that the Soviets and Egyptians were talking about Lucy.

12. Radio Moscow, "Sudan Gained Freedom Despite Britain," FBIS, Moscow, in Arabic, January 1, 1956, 15:30 GMT.

13. Information Research Department, "Current Developments in Communist Tactics in the Middle East," Middle East Regional Meetings, TNA, FO 1110/508 Foreign Office: Information Research Department, 1952.

14. Radio Moscow, "Egypt Right Morally to Nationalize Suez," FBIS, Moscow, in Arabic, July 31, 1956, 18:30 GMT.

15. Articles in the Arab press identify Sharq al-Adna as being British funded in early 1955. See "Thalath 'iidhaeat min alqahira," *Akher Sa'ah,* January 13, 1955.

16. Information Research Department, "Current Developments in Communist Tactics in the Middle East," Middle East Regional Meetings, TNA, FO 1110/508 Foreign Office: Information Research Department, 1952.

17. "Soviet Activities and Propaganda in Egypt," December 17, 1955, HU OSA, 300-1-2-65402.

18. Joel Beinin, "Labor, Capital, and the State in Nasserist Egypt, 1952–1961," *International Journal of Middle East Studies* 21, no. 1 (1989): 71.

19. Komitet po radioveshchaniiu i televideniiu pri SSSR, "Literaturnye peredachi Arabckogo otdela, 1952–1953–1954, Teksty peredach," GARF f. 6903, op. 24, d. 24, l. 1–6.

20. Eckart Woertz, "The Food Weapon: Geopolitics in the Middle East," in *Oil for Food: The Global Food Crisis and the Middle East*, ed. Eckart Woertz (Oxford: Oxford University Press, 2013), 106.

21. Barry Riley, "The Marshall Plan Era," in *The Political History of American Food Aid: An Uneasy Benevolence*, ed. Barry Riley (New York: Oxford University Press, 2017), 137.

22. Komitet po radioveshchaniiu i televideniiu pri SSSR, "Internatsional'nye peredachi, 1952–1953–1954, teksty peredach," GARF, f. 6903, op. 24, d. 25 l. 17.

23. Radio Moscow, "USSR Near East Stand Backs Peace Aims," FBIS, Moscow, in Arabic, February 15, 1956, 18:30 GMT.

24. Radio Moscow, "USSR Would Help Egypt Build Aswan Dam," FBIS, Moscow, in Arabic, August 1, 1956, 15:30 GMT.

25. Komitet po radioveshchaniiu i televideniiua pri SSSR, "Teksty peredach 'a zashchity mira,' 1951–1952," GARF, f. 6903, op. 24, d. 24, l. 2.

26. Macrotrends, "Uzbekistan Population Growth Rate 1950–2022," www.macrotrends.net; and A. R. Omran and F. Roudi, "The Middle East Population Puzzle," *Population Bulletin* 48, no. 1 (July 1993): 1.

27. Gil Feiler, "Housing Policy in Egypt," *Middle Eastern Studies* 28, no. 2 (April 1, 1992): 295.

28. "Schast'e uzbekskoi materi," Komitet po radioveshchaniiu i televideniiu pri SSSR, Programma radioperedach redaktsii dlia arabskiix stran, 2 iiulia 1956, GARF f. P6903, op 25, d. 271, l. 63–110.

29. Ibid.

30. Mervat F. Hatem, "Economic and Political Liberation in Egypt and the Demise of State Feminism," *International Journal of Middle East Studies* 24, no. 2 (1992): 231.

31. "Russia Fails to Show Real Peace Desire," May 28, 1953, 4, "The US News Review," Records of the US Information Agency, Publications about the United States, 1953–1999, *USA News Review* (English/Arabic) 1951–1961, NARA, RG 306, entry 1053, box 502, folder 1953, 2 of 3.

32. "Worldwide Communist Propaganda Activities in 1954," January 15, 1955, NARA, RG 306, Office of Research and Intelligence, entry A1 1022, Intelligence Bulletins, Memorandums and Summaries: 1954–1956, container 4, II-3, IV-4.

33. "Akhbar alwilayat almutahida," May 28, 1953, 14, "The U.S. News Review," Records of the US Information Agency, Publications about the United States, 1953–1999, *USA News Review* (English/Arabic) 1951–1961, NARA, RG 306, entry 1053, box 502, folder 1953, 2 of 3.

34. "The Strategy of Soviet Propaganda," in *Proceedings of the Academy of Political Sciences* (New York: Columbia University, 1951), 214.

35. "USIA Broadcast Titles," NARA, RG 306, entry A1 23, box 2.

36. "Translation of 'Imperialist Propaganda of the United States—A Threat to the Peace and Security of Nations,'" June 2, 1955, NARA, RG 306, Office of Research and Intelligence, entry A1 1022, Intelligence Bulletins, Memorandums and Summaries, 1954–1956, container 2, 3.

37. Ibid., 1; and "Worldwide Communist Propaganda Activities in 1954," January 15, 1955, NARA, RG 306, Office of Research and Intelligence, entry A1 1022, Intelligence Bulletins, Memorandums and Summaries, 1954–1956, container 4, III-1.

38. "USIA Broadcast Titles," NARA, RG 306, entry A1 23, box 2.

39. William Faulkner, "Faith or Fear," *Atlantic*, August 1, 1953.

40. ""Yatimu tatheer biree'," akhbar alwilayat almutahida, June 11, 1953, 6, Records of the US Information Agency, Publications about the United States, 1953–1999, *USA News Review* (English/Arabic) 1951–1961, NARA, RG 306, entry 1053, box 502, folder 1953, 2 of 3.

41. PRO, FO 1110/591/PRG53/1, Information Division, Beirut to Information Office, Tel Aviv, June 10, 1953. James Vaughan notes correctly that this mirrored the USIA's approach. See USNA, RG 306, 250/67/26/06, USIA Feature Packets, Non-Recurring Subjects 1953–58, box 1, kit no. 14, "Words and Deeds," undated, cited in Vaughan, "'Cloak without Dagger,'" 69.

42. "Middle East; Communist Peace Campaign," TNA, FO 1110/384 Foreign Office: Information Research Department, 1951.

43. "Middle East Regional Meetings," December 31, 1952, TNA, FO 1110/508/PR67/1.

44. Radio Moscow, "Nasir Hails New Egyptian Constitution," FBIS, Moscow, in Arabic, January 18, 1955, 17:30 GMT.

45. "Programmy peredach za 1 maia—31 avgusta," Komitet po radioveshchaniiu i televideniiu pri SSSR, Otdel veshchanie na Arabskie strany, GARF f. P6903, op. 25, d. 271, l. 99.

46. A. A. Fursenko, ed., *Prezidium TsK KPSS: 1954–1964: V Trekh Tomakh*, vol. 1 (Moscow: ROSSPEN, 2015), 152.

5. THE ECHO CHAMBER

1. This argument has been made by a number of historians. See Nicholas J. Cull, *The Cold War and the United States Information Agency: American Propaganda and Public Diplomacy, 1945–1989*, illus. ed. (Cambridge: Cambridge University Press, 2009); and Osgood, *Total Cold War*.

2. Frances Stonor Saunders, *The Cultural Cold War: The CIA and the World of Arts and Letters* (New York: New Press, 2000), 2.

3. Osgood, *Total Cold War*.

4. Elie Podeh, "The Perils of Ambiguity: The United States and the Baghdad Pact," in *The Middle East and the United States*, ed. David Lesch (Boulder, CO: Westview Press, 2007), 87.

5. Rawnsley, *Radio Diplomacy and Propaganda*, 8.

6. Victoria de Grazia, *Irresistible Empire: America's Advance through Twentieth-Century Europe* (Cambridge, MA: Belknap Press, 2006). See also Hixson, *Parting the Curtain*.

7. Bakhtin, *Dialogic Imagination*, 259.

8. Brett Gary, *The Nervous Liberals: Propaganda Anxieties from World War I to the Cold War*, Columbia Studies in Contemporary American History (New York: Columbia University Press, 1999).

9. As Justin Hart notes, this process of paying attention to the US image abroad started in the mid-1930s. Justin Hart, *Empire of Ideas: The Origins of Public Diplomacy and the Transformation of U.S. Foreign Policy* (Oxford; New York: Oxford University Press, 2013).

10. Department of State, "Semi-Annual Report of the Secretary of State to Congress on the International Information and Educational Exchange Program," FRUS, January 1–June 30, 1948, 23.

11. Chester Bowles, "The Crisis That Faces Us Will Not Wait: The Crisis Will Not Wait," *New York Times*, November 27, 1955, sec. Magazine, 245.

12. Richard J. Aldrich, *The Hidden Hand* (Woodstock, NY: Overlook Books, 2003), 149. Cited also in Richard Aldrich, "Putting Culture into the Cold War: The Cultural Relations Department (CRD) and British Covert Information Warfare," *Intelligence and National Security* 18, no. 2 (June 1, 2003): 110.

13. Report accompanying H.R. 3342, cited in Robert William Pirsein, *The Voice of America: A History of the International Broadcasting Activities of the United States Government, 1940–1962*, Dissertations in Broadcasting (New York: Arno Press, 1979), 138. See also Frank A. Ninkovich, *The Diplomacy of Ideas: U.S. Foreign Policy and Cultural Relations, 1938–1950* (Cambridge: Cambridge University Press, 1981); and Emily T. Metzgar, "Public Diplomacy, Smith-Mundt and the American Public," *Communication Law and Policy* 17, no. 1 (December 1, 2012): 67–101.

14. "U.S. Adds Arabic Program: Voice of America Broadcasts a Greeting by Truman," *New York Times*, January 2, 1950, 6.

15. Hart, *Empire of Ideas*, 4.

16. "Voice of America Fact Sheet," March 1, 1953, NARA, RG 59, entry 1053, box 503, Voice of American Historical Files, 1.

17. Letter from Alan Warfield, FBIS, to R. Marriott at the BBC Monitoring Service, October 7, 1952, "Anti-Communist Propaganda," BBCWAC, E2/325/2.

18. Osgood, *Total Cold War*.

19. Hart, *Empire of Ideas*, 9, 108.

20. Hart, 200.

21. USIA, "Third Review of Operations", July–December 1954, NARA RG306, Review of Operations Reports:8/1953-12/1971, box 2, 19. Like Radio Moscow, VOA recorded its shows in Washington and then sent them to the Middle East through transmitters.

22. "An Appraisal of the Contribution of Research Officers," May 6, 1956, NARA RG 306, Records of the United States Information Agency, Office of Research and Intelligence, Headquarters Subject Files, 1955–1970, entry 1048, box 2, 3.

23. "I'dha'āt sawt amrika yukhatit lisaʿatayn min albaramij alʿarabiya," March 26, 1953, 2, "The U.S. News Review," Records of the US Information

Agency, Publications about the United States, 1953–1999, *USA News Review* (English/Arabic) 1951–1961, NARA, RG 306, entry 1053, box 502, folder 1953, 1 of 3.

24. "Sayatimu alihtifal bi'id al'ummal fi alwilayat almutahida," akhbar al-wilayat almutahida, August 28, 1952, 3, "The U.S. News Review," August 19, 1953, Records of the US Information Agency, Publications about the United States, 1953–1999, *USA News Review* (English/Arabic) 1951–1961, NARA, RG 306, entry 1053, box 502, folder 1952, 2 of 2.

25. Karl Marx, *Capital: A Critique of Political Economy*, vol. 1 (CreateSpace Independent Publishing Platform, 2010), ch. 10.

26. "Al-ra'smaliya aljadida," akhbar alwilayat almutahida, September 24, 1953, 8, Records of the US Information Agency, Publications about the United States, 1953–1999, *USA News Review* (English/Arabic) 1951–1961, NARA, RG 306, entry 1053, box 502, folder 1953, 2 of 3.

27. Timothy Johnston, *Being Soviet: Identity, Rumour, and Everyday Life under Stalin, 1939–53* (Oxford; New York: Oxford University Press, 2011), 169–81; Peter Kenez, *A History of the Soviet Union from the Beginning to the End*, 2nd ed. (New York: Cambridge University Press, 2006), 182–83; and Dina Fainberg, *Cold War Correspondents: Soviet and American Reporters on the Ideological Frontlines* (Baltimore, MD: Johns Hopkins University Press, 2021), 169–73.

28. "Jababara: alshuyu'iyun khatar 'ala aljami'," akhbar alwilayat almutahida, August 17, 1953, 7, Records of the US Information Agency, Publications about the United States, 1953–1999, *USA News Review* (English/Arabic) 1951–1961, NARA, RG 306, entry 1053, box 502, folder 1953, 2 of 3.

29. "Vystuplenie dzhamalia musa, delegate arabskogo rabochego kongressa," Komitet po radioveshchaniiu i televideniiu pri SSSR, Teksty peredach redaktsii veshania na arabskie strany/Sovetskaia tematika za 1 ianvaria—14 avgusta, 1951, GARF, f. 6903, op. 24, d. 23, l. 6–7; and "Al'islam yahtadir fi alitihad alsufiti," akh-bar alwilayat almutahida, November 13, 1952, 13, NARA, RG 306, entry 1053, box 502, folder 1952, 2 of 2.

30. "alfajawat bayn alṭariqa alshuyu'iya alsufitiya waalṭariqa al'islāmiya," akh-bar alwilayat almutahida, August 27, 1953, 4, NARA, RG 306, entry 1053, box 502, folder 1953, 2 of 3.

31. "Al-shuyu'iya hiya 'aduw almu'taqadat al'islamiya," akhbar alwilayat almuta-hida, July 9, 1953, 3, NARA, RG 306, entry 1053, box 502, folder 1953, 2 of 3.

32. "Al'islam yahtadir fi alitihad alsufiti," akhbar alwilayat almutahida, Novem-ber 13, 1952, 13, "The U.S. News Review," August 19, 1953, NARA, RG 306, entry 1053, box 502, folder 1952, 2 of 2.

33. "Almuslimun fi rusia," 'akhbar alwilayat almutahida, February 12, 1953, 3, NARA, RG 306, entry 1053, box 502, folder 1953, 1 of 3.

34. Ibid.

35. This line was read out over the floor of the US Congress by Alexander Wiley, a Wisconsin Republican senator, 107 Cong. Rec. 850, A317 (January 17, 1961) (state-ment of Sen. Wiley).

36. Elie Abel, "Eisenhower, Eden Caution Asia and Africa on Red Aid," *New York Times*, February 2, 1956, 1. For more on the different motives that drove US and British support for the Baghdad Pact, see Nigel John Ashton, "The Hijacking of a Pact: The Formation of the Baghdad Pact and Anglo-American Tensions in the Middle East, 1955–1958," *Review of International Studies* 19, no. 2 (April 1993): 123–37.

37. "Poland Was to Send Coal to Egypt", November 21, 1956, HU OSA 300-1-2-76668; Records of Radio Free Europe/Radio Liberty Research Institute: General Records: Information Items; and Open Society Archives at Central European University, Budapest.

38. Radio Listening, "Statistical Tables for USIS Library Study in Alexandria, UAR," NARA, RG 306, Records of the US Information Agency, Office of Research, Country Project Files, 1951–1964, entry 1015, 1953, box 26, 3–6.

39. Ralph White, "The Philosophy of the BBC," November 30, 1953, NARA, RG 306, entry P 160, Special Reports: 1953–1997, container 2.

40. Mary Dudziak, *Cold War Civil Rights: Race and the Image of American Democracy* (Princeton, NJ: Princeton University Press, 2000), 6; Penny Von Eschen, *Race Against Empire* (Ithaca, NY: Cornell University Press, 1997); and Thomas Borstelmann, *The Cold War and the Color Line: American Race Relations in the Global Arena* (Cambridge, MA: Harvard University Press, 2001).

41. Quoted in Frank A. Ninkovich, *U.S. Information Policy and Cultural Diplomacy* (New York: Foreign Policy Association, 1996), 24.

42. Penny M. Von Eschen, *Satchmo Blows up the World: Jazz Ambassadors Play the Cold War* (Cambridge, MA: Harvard University Press, 2004), 5.

43. "Glavnaia redaktziia propagandy na zarubezhnye strany," 13 fevralia 1964 r., GARF, f. 6903, op 25, d. 15, l. 68.

44. "Teksty peredach redaktsii veshaniia na arabskie strany/Sovetskaia tematika za 1 ianvaria—14 avgusta, 1951," Komitet po radioveshchaniiu i televideniiu pri SSSR, GARF f. 6903, op. 24, d. 23.

45. "'Alf mabruk lishah 'iran," akhbar alwilayat almutahida, September 3, 1953, 4, *USA News Review* (English/Arabic) 1951–1961, NARA, RG 306, entry 1053, box 502, folder 1953, 2 of 3.

46. "News of Iran," Moving Images Relating to US Domestic and International Activities, NARA RG 306, ARC ID 48548.

47. Bryant Buckingham, US consul, Isfahan, "IRI Debriefing Report," USIA, March 31, 1955, NARA, RG 306, entry P 160, Special Reports: 1953–1997, container 8, ARC 5664216.

48. USIA Office of Research and Analysis, "Ten Years of Soviet Radio Propaganda to Iran, 1949–1959," August 14, 1959, P-40-59, NARA RG 306, entry A1 1033, Research Reports; 1956–1959, container 7, ARC 1074148, 1.

49. USIA, "IRI Reaction Report, Communist Propaganda Treatment of the Iran Spy Trials in Selected Countries," December 21, 1954, NARA, RG 306, entry P 160, Special Reports: 1953–1997, container 5; and "Literaturnye peredaii Arabskogo otdela 1952–1953–1954, Teksty peredach,"Komitet po radioveshchaniiu i televideniiu pri SSSR," GARF f. 6903, op. 24, d. 24, l. 17.

50. Bryant Buckingham, US consul, Isfahan, "IRI Debriefing Report," USIA, March 31, 1955, NARA, RG 306, entry P 160, Special Reports: 1953–1997, container 8, ARC 5664216.

51. USIA, "IRI Reaction Report, Communist Propaganda Treatment of the Iran Spy Trials in Selected Countries," December 21, 1954, NARA, RG 306, entry P160, Special Reports: 1953–1997, container 5.

52. Ibid.

53. Bryant Buckingham, US consul, Isfahan, "IRI Debriefing Report," USIA, March 31, 1955, NARA, RG 306, entry P 160, Special Reports: 1953–1997, container 8, ARC 5664216.

54. Vaughan, "Propaganda by Proxy?,"168.

55. "Soviet Activities and Propaganda in Egypt," November 1955. HU OSA 300-1-2-65402; Records of Radio Free Europe/Radio Liberty Research Institute: General Records: Information Items; and Open Society Archives at Central European University, Budapest.

56. "Small Arms for Egypt Shipped from Bratislava as 'Gravel,'" December 31, 1955, HU OSA 300-1-2-65850; Records of Radio Free Europe/Radio Liberty Research Institute: General Records: Information Items; and Open Society Archives at Central European University, Budapest.

57. *Foreign Relations of the United States*, FRUS, 1955–7, XV, 388.

58. "Soviet Activities and Propaganda in Egypt," December 17, 1955, HU OSA 300-1-2-65402; Records of Radio Free Europe/Radio Liberty Research Institute: General Records: Information Items; and Open Society Archives at Central European University, Budapest.

59. March 8 through October 22, 1956. See general collection, HU OSA 300-1-2; Records of Radio Free Europe/Radio Liberty Research Institute: General Records: Information Items; and Open Society Archives, Budapest.

60. "Current Indications of Communist Trade Offensive in the Arab States," November 29, 1955, NARA, RG 306, US Information Agency, Office of Research and Intelligence, entry A1 1022, Intelligence Bulletins, Memorandums and Summaries: 1954–1956, container 1, ARC 1073965, 3.

61. Vaughan, "Propaganda by Proxy?," 160.

62. Letter to C. D. Jackson, DDE, C. D. Jackson: Papers 1931–1967, box 29 (Arab Affairs), cited in Vaughan, "Propaganda by Proxy?," 160.

6. BRITAIN'S STRUGGLE FOR AIR

1. Vaughan, *Failure of American and British Propaganda*; Collier, "Countering Communist and Nasserite Propaganda"; Briggs, *History of Broadcasting in the United Kingdom*,; Rawnsley, *Radio Diplomacy and Propaganda*; McNicholas, "Sharq Al-Adna"; and Boyd, "Sharq Al-Adna."

2. "Middle East Regional Meetings," December 31, 1952, TNA, FO 1110/508/PR67/1.

3. Vaughan, "BBC's External Services," 50. See also Wilford, "Information Research Department"; Shaw, "Information Research Department"; Vaughan, "'Cloak without Dagger'"; Defty, *Britain, America and Anti-Communist Propaganda*; and Collier, "Countering Communist and Nasserite Propaganda."

4. C.E.O. Investigation, April 14, 1954, "Foreign Office Arabic Service," BBCWAC, E2 784/1.

5. Partner, *Arab Voices*, 92.

6. "Arabic Expansion Service," 1957, BBCWAC, E2 626/2.

7. Letter from John Whitehead, BBC Middle East Representative, to the BBC A.H.P.O., December 21, 1950, BBCWAC, E12/236/5, Publicity O.S., Middle East Representative, file 4.

8. BBCWAC, E2 784/1.

9. BBC Eastern Service Listener Research Unit, "Quarterly Listener Research Report," April 15, 1955, BBCWAC, E3/189/1, Arabic Service, Listener Correspondence Reports, 1955–1963. The BBC did its listener surveys by selecting at random from Syrian and Egyptian telephone directories.

10. Letter from Ralph Stevenson to Sir Thomas Rapp, BMEO, February 22, 1951, "British Technicians in the Arab World," "Propaganda: Middle East Publicity for British Middle East Office in Middle East Countries," TNA, FO 957/132, Foreign Office, British Middle East Office Cairo, and Department of Technical Cooperation, Middle East Development Division, 1951, 2.

11. Letter from Anthony Haigh, Senior Information Officer in the Middle East, British Embassy, Cairo, to E. J. Howes, First Secretary, British Legation, Beirut, January 7, 1949, TNA, FO 1110/225. Haigh sent the same letter to legations in Damascus and Baghdad.

12. Harold Beeley, "The Changing Role of British International Propaganda," *Annals of the American Academy of Political and Social Science* 398, no. 1 (November 1, 1971): 126.

13. "Intel for Foreign Office and Whitehall distribution on Anti-Communism," February 10, 1956, TNA, FO/111/907/PR1034/2. Also cited in Collier, "Countering Communist and Nasserite Propaganda," 66.

14. W. Scott Lucas and C J. Morris, "A Very British Crusade: The Information Research Department and the Origins of the Cold War," in *British Intelligence, Strategy and the Cold War*, ed. Richard J. Aldrich (London: Routledge, 1992), 86; Wesley K. Wark, "Coming in from the Cold: British Propaganda and Red Army Defectors, 1945–1952," *International History Review* 9, no. 1 (1987): 50; Lyn Smith, "Covert British Propaganda: The Information Research Department, 1947–77," *Millennium: Journal of International Studies* 9, no. 1 (1980): 68; Wilford, "Information Research Department," 354; Defty, *Britain, America and Anti-Communist Propaganda*; Collier, "Countering Communist and Nasserite Propaganda"; and John Jenks, *British Propaganda and News Media in the Cold War* (Edinburgh: Edinburgh University Press, 2006).

15. Letter from Anthony Haigh to Ralph Murray at the Information Research Department, Foreign Office, February 5, 1949, TNA, FO 1110/225.

16. Office of Information Research, Foreign Office, Draft of Anti-Communist Radio Programme, February 1949, TNA, FO 1110/225.

17. Ibid.

18. Ibid.

19. Vaughan, *Failure of American and British Propaganda*, 114–19.

20. "Publicity O.S. Middle East Representative, file 5B, 1953–1953," BBCWAC, E12/236/7.

21. Denise M. Lynn, *Where Is Juliet Stuart Poyntz? Gender, Spycraft, and Anti-Stalinism in the Early Cold War* (Amherst: University of Massachusetts Press, 2021), x.

22. Office of Information Research, Foreign Office, Draft of Anti-Communist Radio Programme, February 1949, TNA, FO 1110/225.

23. "Middle East, Use of Material in Middle East and Cyprus," April 1, 1949, TNA, FO 1110/226 Foreign Office: Information Research Department.

24. "USIA Broadcast Titles," NARA, RG 306, entry A1 23, box 2.

25. Phillip Deery, "Confronting the Cominform: George Orwell and the Cold War Offensive of the Information Research Department, 1948–50," *Labour History* 73, no. 1 (November 1, 1997): 220.

26. "Middle East, Use of Material in Middle East and Cyprus," March 7, 1949, TNA, FO 1110/226, Foreign Office: Information Research Department.

27. Deery, "Confronting the Cominform," 220.

28. "Material in Arabic for Colonial Office, Middle East," August 1956, TNA, FO 1110/942/PR10704/54. See also Nicholas John Cull, David Holbrook Culbert, and David Welch, *Propaganda and Mass Persuasion: A Historical Encyclopedia, 1500 to the Present* (Santa Barbara: ABC-CLIO, 2003); and Garth Jowett and Victoria O'Donnell, *Propaganda and Persuasion*, 2nd ed. (Newbury Park, CA: Sage Publications, 1992).

29. "Material in Arabic for Colonial Office, Middle East," August 1956, TNA, FO 1110/942/PR10704/54.

30. CAE Shuckburgh (IRD) to Sir Roger Stevens, August 24, 1954, TNA, FO 1110/676/PR1034/4/G. Also cited in Collier, "Countering Communist and Nasserite Propaganda," 45.

31. "Publicity O.S. Middle East Representative, file 5B, 1952–1953," BBCWAC, E12/236/7.

32. Ibid.

33. Ibid.

34. TNA, FO 1110/591/PRG53/1, Information Division, Beirut to Information Office, Tel Aviv, June 10, 1953.

35. Ibid. James Vaughan notes correctly that this mirrored the USIA's approach. See USNA, RG 306, 250/67/26/06, USIA Feature Packets, Non-Recurring Subjects 1953–58, box 1, kit no. 14, "Words and Deeds," undated, cited in Vaughan, "'Cloak without Dagger,'" 69.

36. "Middle East; Communist Peace Campaign," TNA, FO 1110/384 Foreign Office: Information Research Department, 1951.

37. BBCM IV, 671, May 11, 1956, reel 336, 13. These are examples taken from this day, but similar reports were done every day.

38. BBCM IV, 662, April 4–6, 1956, reel 336, 26.

39. "Chapman Andrews to Bowker," September 23, 1953, PRO, FO 1110/PRG104/75/G.

40. Near East Arab Broadcasting Station, April 26, 1951, "Propaganda: Middle East Publicity for British Middle East Office in Middle East Countries," TNA, FO 957/132, Foreign Office, British Middle East Office Cairo, and Department of Technical Cooperation, Middle East Development Division, 1951, 2.

41. "Publicity O.S. Middle East Representative, file 5B, 1952–1953," BBCWAC, E12/236/7.

42. "Publicity O.S. Middle East Representative, file 5B, 1952–1953," BBCWAC, E12/236/7.

43. "British Technicians in the Arab World," folder Propaganda: Middle East Publicity for British Middle East Office in Middle East Countries, TNA, FO 957/132, Foreign Office, British Middle East Office Cairo, and Department of Technical Cooperation, Middle East Development Division, 1951, 7.

44. "Publicity O.S. Middle East Representative, file 5B, 1953–1953," BBCWAC, E12/236/7.

45. "Chapman Andrews to Bowker," September 23, 1953, PRO, FO 1110/PRG104/75/G.

46. RW Fay (British Embassy, Triploi) to LC Glass (British Middle East Office), November 5, 1954, TNA, FO 1110/660/PR1013/5. Also cited in Collier, "Countering Communist and Nasserite Propaganda," 45.

47. BBC Eastern Service Listener Research Unit, Arabic Service, Listener Correspondence Reports, 1955–1963, "Quarterly Listener Research Report," August 20, 1955, BBCWAC, E3/189/1, 22.

48. John Rae, Report, "Broadcasting in the Middle East," Egypt: Middle East Representative, BBCWAC E1/1850/1.

49. Overseas Audience Research, "Reactions to the Arabic Service," Arabic Service, Listener Correspondence Reports, 1955–1963, BBCWAC E3/189/1, 3.

50. "British Technicians in the Arab World," "Propaganda: Middle East Publicity for British Middle East Office in Middle East Countries," TNA, FO 957/132, Foreign Office, British Middle East Office Cairo, and Department of Technical Cooperation, Middle East Development Division, 1951, 8.

51. Letter from John Whitehead, BBC Middle East Representative to the BBC, to the A.H.P.O., December 6, 1950, BBC Written Archives Centre, E12/236/5, Publicity O.S., Middle East Representative, file 4, 1950.

52. Vaughan, "Propaganda by Proxy?," June 2002, 157–71.

53. BBCM, September 17, 1956, "Arrangements for Extended BBC Monitoring Coverage," TNA, FO 1110/945 Foreign Office: Information Research Department, 1956.

54. Miles Copeland, *The Game of Nations: The Amorality of Power Politics* (New York: Simon & Schuster, 1970), 247, cited in Boyd, "Development of Egypt's Radio," 646.

55. "Arrangements for Extended BBC Monitoring Coverage," TNA, FO 1110/945 Foreign Office: Information Research Department, 1956.

56. Carruthers, "'Voice of the Arabs,'" E5.

57. TNA, PRO, FO 371/52310/E769/96, Shaw to Hull, August 18, 1945, enclosed memorandum by J. B. Glubb, "The New Relationship, July 1, 1945. Also cited in James R. Vaughan, "'A Certain Idea of Britain': British Cultural Diplomacy in the Middle East, 1945–57," *Contemporary British History* 19, no. 2 (June 1, 2005): 154.

58. Osgood Carruthers, "Cairo Broadcasts Irk London, Paris: Inflammatory Talks to Africa Incite Natives to Revolt Against 'Imperialists,'" *New York Times*, March 1, 1956, 2.

59. Rawnsley, "Overt and Covert," 502.

60. Ahmed Said, Voice of the Arabs, April 4–6, 1956, BBCM, IV, 662, reel 336, 1.

61. Transcribed by the Information Research Department at the British Foreign Office, "Anti-British Propaganda in the Middle East," TNA, FO 371/119303, Foreign Office: Political Departments: General Correspondence from 1906–1966. Africa: Egypt, 1956, 3–4.

62. "Now It Is War of Words," *Daily Mail,* March 15, 1956, 5.

63. "Propaganda in Middle East," TNA, FO 953/1631, Foreign Office: Information Policy Department and Regional Information Departments, 1956.

64. Glubb letter to Douglas Boyd, April 17, 1973, cited in Boyd, "Development of Egypt's Radio," 648.

65. Rawnsley, *Radio Diplomacy and Propaganda*, 207.

66. Rawnsley, "Overt and Covert," 503.

67. BBC Written Archives, "Political Question and Answer," June 1956, 92, 20, and November 1956, 137, 30. Also cited in Rawnsley, *Radio Diplomacy and Propaganda*, 32.

68. Information Research Department, "The Task of Covert Propaganda in the Middle East," February 7, 1942, TNA, FO 1110/508/PR67/35.

69. Information Research Department, "The Task of Covert Propaganda in the Middle East," February 7, 1942, TNA, FO 1110/508/PR67/35.

70. The absence of conversation about the problem of Israel for Arab populations has also been noted by Simon Collier in his excellent dissertation. Collier, "Countering Communist and Nasserite Propaganda," 57.

71. "Broadcasting in Arabic," December 1953, TNA, FO 953/1563/PB1041/1, cited in Vaughan, "Propaganda by Proxy?," 160.

72. "Chapman Andrews to Bowker," September 23, 1953, TNA, FO 1110/PRG104/75/G, cited in Vaughan, "Propaganda by Proxy?," 160.

73. Vaughan, *Failure of American and British Propaganda.*

74. "Anti-Communist Propaganda in Egypt," TNA, FO 1110/316/PR43/8/G, February 18, 1950.

75. Publicity O.S., Middle East Representative, file 4, 1950, BBCWAC, E12/236/5.

76. Michael Kemper and Artemy M. Kalinovsky, eds., *Reassessing Orientalism: Interlocking Orientologies during the Cold War* (London: Routledge, 2015), 5; and

Joep Leerssen, *National Thought in Europe: A Cultural History* (Amsterdam: Amsterdam University Press, 2010), 11–26.

77. BBCM IV, 662, April 4–6, 1956, reel 336, 26.

78. "Programmy peredach za 1 ianv—30 apr, 1956," Komitet po radioveshchaniiu i televideniiu pri SSSR, Otdel veshchanie na Arabskie strany, GARF, f. P6903, op. 25, d. 270.

79. "British Experts," FBIS, Sharq Al-Adna in Arabic, April 9, 1956, 15:30 GMT.

80. Michael B. Oren, "A Winter of Discontent: Britain's Crisis in Jordan, December 1955–March 1956," *International Journal of Middle East Studies* 22, no. 2 (1990): 178.

81. "Clarification of USSR Statement Urged," FBIS, Jerusalem, in Hebrew, Israeli Home Service, April 18, 1956, 11:30 GMT.

7. THE ELEVENTH HOUR

1. Douglas Little, "A Puppet in Search of a Puppeteer? The United States, King Hussein, and Jordan, 1953–1970," *International History Review* 17, no. 3 (1995): 512–44.

2. John Darwin, *Britain and Decolonisation: The Retreat from Empire in the Post-War World* (Houndmills, Basingstoke: Palgrave, 1988), 210.

3. Eden letter, July 27, 1956, FRUS, vol. 16, 357.

4. David Tal, "Israel's Road to the 1956 War," *International Journal of Middle East Studies* 28, no. 1 (1996): 59–81.

5. The USIA was aware of why relations with Nasser had cooled. It identified these points of contention in a situation report in 1955: "Situation Report on Egypt and Egyptian Relations," September 1, 1955, RG 306, US Information Agency, Office of Research and Intelligence, entry A1 1022, Intelligence Bulletins, Memorandums and Summaries, 1954–1956, container 6, 1.

6. "How the Suez Canal Is Operated," August 29, 1956, NARA, RG 306, US Information Agency, Office of Research and Intelligence, entry A1 1022, Intelligence Bulletins, Memorandums and Summaries, 1954–1956, container 1, ARC 1073965, 2.

7. James Eayrs, ed., *The Commonwealth and Suez a Documentary Survey* (London: Oxford University Press, 1964).

8. UNRWA Report to the UN General Assembly November 1–December 14, 1956; and Derek Varble, *The Suez Crisis 1956* (Oxford: Osprey Publishing, 2003), 46.

9. Varble, *Suez Crisis 1956*, 87; and Eayrs, *Commonwealth and Suez*, 173.

10. Noam Chomsky, *The Fateful Triangle: The United States, Israel, and the Palestinians* (Boston: Noontide Press, 1983), 187–91.

11. Shaw, *Eden, Suez, and the Mass Media*; Rawnsley, "Overt and Covert"; and Gary David Rawnsley, "Cold War Radio in Crisis: The BBC Overseas Services, the Suez Crisis and the 1956 Hungarian … ," *Historical Journal of Film, Radio & Television* 16, no. 2 (June 1996): 197. See also Huw Bennett, "'Words Are Cheaper than Bullets': Britain's Psychological Warfare in the Middle East, 1945–60," *Intelligence*

and National Security 34, no. 7 (November 10, 2019): 925–44; Stephen Blackwell, "Britain, the United States and the Syrian Crisis, 1957," *Diplomacy & Statecraft* 11, no. 3 (November 1, 2000): 139–58; Boyd, "Sharq Al-Adna"; Lindsay Frederick Braun, "Suez Reconsidered: Anthony Eden's Orientalism and the Suez Crisis," *Historian* 65, no. 3 (2003): 535–61; Briggs, *History of Broadcasting in the United Kingdom*, vol. 5, 1995; Shih-Yu Chou, "Constructing National Interests: Narrating the Suez Crisis," *International Critical Thought* 8, no. 3 (July 3, 2018): 453–67; Haykal, *Milaffat Al-Suways*; Kyle, *Suez*; Guy Laron, *Origins of the Suez Crisis: Postwar Development Diplomacy and the Struggle over Third World Industrialization, 1945–1956* (Washington, DC: Woodrow Wilson Center Press; Baltimore, MD: Johns Hopkins University Press, 2013); Lashmar and Oliver, *Britain's Secret Propaganda War*; J. M. Lee, "British Cultural Diplomacy and the Cold War: 1946–61," *Diplomacy & Statecraft* 9, no. 1 (March 1, 1998): 112–34; Kennett Love, *Suez: The Twice-Fought War; A History* (New York: McGraw-Hill, 1969); W. Scott Lucas, *Divided We Stand: Britain, The US and the Suez Crisis*, new ed. (London: Sceptre, 1996); McNicholas, "Sharq Al-Adna"; Podeh, *Quest for Hegemony in the Arab World*; O. M. Smolansky, "Moscow and the Suez Crisis, 1956: A Reappraisal," *Political Science Quarterly* 80, no. 4 (1965): 581–605; Alex von Tunzelmann, *Blood and Sand: Suez, Hungary, and Eisenhower's Campaign for Peace* (New York: Harper, 2016); Vaughan, "BBC's External Services"; Geoffrey Warner, "The United States and the Suez Crisis," *International Affairs (Royal Institute of International Affairs 1944–)* 67, no. 2 (1991): 303–17; and Gordon Waterfield, "Suez and the Role of Broadcasting," *Listener* 76, no. 1970 (December 29, 1966): 947–49.

12. Radio Cairo, "Text of Nasser's Speech in Alexandria," FBIS, Cairo, in Arabic, July 26, 1741, 18:30 GMT, A1–A20.

13. Kol Israel, "Nasser Makes Israel Chief Target," FBIS, Jerusalem, in English, July 29, 1956, 21:15 GMT.

14. Kol Israel, "Israeli Rights Test of Nasser Sincerity," FBIS, Jerusalem, in English, August 5, 1956, 21:15 GMT.

15. Rae to Waterfield, "Egypt: Middle East Representative," July 27, 1956, BBCWAC, E1/1850/1.

16. Microfilm, July 26, 1956, 20:00 GMT, BBCWAC.

17. "Khartoum University," FBIS, Limmasol al-Adna [*sic*] in Arabic, July 25, 1956, 18:00 GMT.

18. Radio Moscow, "West Reacts Violently to Suez Move, FBIS, Moscow, in Arabic, July 28, 1956, 16:00 GMT.

19. Ibid.

20. Bismark famously altered the Kaiser's Ems telegram in 1870 before publishing it in order to incite French and German anger and jump-start the Franco-Prussian War.

21. Radio Moscow, "Nasser Nationalizes Suez," FBIS, Moscow, in Arabic, July 27, 1956, 15:40 GMT.

22. Radio Cairo, "Text of Nasser's Speech in Alexandria," FBIS, Cairo, in Arabic, July 26, 1956, 18:30 GMT, A14–A15. It is a lingering sign of Western orientalism that Nasser's famous speeches have not been published in English translation.

23. Radio Moscow, "Suez Situation Strengthens Arab Unity," FBIS, Moscow, in Arabic, August 7, 1950, 04:45 GMT.

24. "Programma radioperedach redaktsii veshchaniia dlia arabckikh stran na sredy, 2 iiulia, 1956 g, Egpetskii narod—khoziain i sebia doma," Komitet po radio-veshchaniiu i televideniiu pri SSSR, GARF f. P6903, op. 25, d. 271, l. 63–110; and Radio Moscow, "Gunboat Diplomacy Must Not Be Repeated," FBIS, Moscow, in Arabic, August 4, 1956, 15:40 GMT.

25. Ahmed Said, Voice of the Arabs, April 10–July 24, 1956, BBCM, IV, 662–92, reel 336, 1.

26. Radio Cairo, "Arab Unity Lauded," FBIS, Cairo, in Arabic, August 2, 1956, 18:30 GMT.

27. "Situation Report on Egypt and Egyptian Relations," September 1, 1955, NARA, RG 306, US Information Agency, Office of Research and Intelligence, entry A1 1022, Intelligence Bulletins, Memorandums and Summaries, 1954–1956, container 6, 7.

28. The newsreel is cited in the Russian archives at Komitet po radioveshchaniiu i televideniiu pri SSSR, "Programma padioperedach redaktsii veshchaniia dlia arab-skikh stran na sredy, 5 avgusta 1956 g," GARF f. P6903, op. 25, d. 271, l. 63–110. I found the original text of the newsreel at Movietone News, "Nasser's Seizure of Suez Creates Tension in the West," August, 1956, NARA, RG263, Records of the Central Intelligence Agency, 1894–2002, Moving Images Relating to Intelligence and International Relations, 1947–1984, Egypt and Gamal Abdel Nasser, 1956, ARC 644640.

29. "Return of Secretary of State John Foster Dulles, Speech from Whitehouse on the Suez Canal," September 22, 1956, NARA, RG 306, Production Library Audio Recordings, 1999–2005, ARC 120092.

30. Voice of the Arabs, "Dulles Plan 'Contradictions' Noted," FBIS, Moscow, in Arabic, August 22, 1956, 06:00 GMT.

31. Radio Moscow, "Panama Doubts Guide Dulles Policy," FBIS, Moscow, in Arabic, September 15, 1956, 18:30 GMT.

32. Federico Vélez, "From the Suez to the Panama Canal and Beyond: Gamal Abdel Nasser's Influence in Latin America," *Varia Historia* 31 (April 2015): 163.

33. Rae to Waterfield, "Egypt: Middle East Representative," August 13, 1956, BBCWAC, E1/1850/1. In the end, this was not to be the case. Camille Chamoun's pro-British orientation and fear of Nasser's potential takeover of Lebanon guaranteed, in the words of the historian William Harris, "that he would tilt towards the West when cornered." Lebanon kept its ties with Britain and France throughout the crisis, but Rae's concerns about the overwhelming looming loss of British legitimacy in the Arab world were well founded. See William Harris, *Lebanon: A History* (Oxford: Oxford University Press, 2012), 209.

34. Lucas, *Divided We Stand*, 132.

35. Stephen Dorril, *MI6: Inside the Covert World of Her Majesty's Secret Intelligence Service* (New York: Free Press, 2000), 641.

36. "Top Secret: Propaganda and Political Warfare in the Middle East," K. E. Oakeshott (IRD) to Hugh Carleton-Greene, October 1956, BBCWAC, R34/1580/1.

37. Rae to Waterfield, "Egypt: Middle East Representative," August 29, 1956, BBCWAC, E1/1850/1.

38. Walter Z. Laqueur, *Communism and Nationalism in the Middle East* (London: Routledge & Kegan Paul, 1956). See also Vaughan, "'Cloak without Dagger,'" 63.

39. Patrick Ramsey, obituary of John Rae, "Distinguished Head of the Monitoring Service," *Prospero: The Newspaper for BBC Pensioners*, no. 3 (April 2012): 10.

40. "Record of Meeting of Advisory Committee," August 24, 1956, Middle East: Advisory Committee on Political Warfare," TNA, FO 1110/880, Foreign Office: Information Research Department, 2.

41. Voice of the Arabs, "Failure of Suez Conference was Inevitable," FBIS, Cairo, in Arabic, August 24, 1956, 06:00 GMT.

42. Voice of the Arabs, "Canal Issue Excuse for Western Domination," FBIS, Cairo, in Arabic, August 22, 1956, 19:56 GMT.

43. Radio Cairo, "Press Discusses Suez Issue, Spy Case," FBIS, Cairo, in Arabic, August 31, 1956, 06:00 GMT.

44. Radio Cairo, "Commander Says Army is Fully Prepared," FBIS, Cairo, in Arabic, September 3, 1956, 06:06 GMT.

45. Radio Cairo, "Anglo-French Plot Against Peace Decried," FBIS, Cairo, in Arabic, September 12, 1956, 18:30 GMT.

46. Radio Cairo, "Western Leaders' Statements Draw Comment," FBIS, Cairo, in Arabic, September 12, 1956, 06:00 GMT.

47. Microfilm, Eden Statement, September 12, 1956, 20:00 GMT, BBCWAC.

48. Radio Cairo, "People Are Ready for Any Sacrifice," FBIS, Cairo, in Arabic, September 13, 1956, 16:30 GMT.

49. Radio Moscow, "1888 Convention Upholds Egypt's Actions," FBIS, Moscow, in Arabic, October 8, 1956, 18:30 GMT.

50. Kol israel, Israeli Home Service, "Comments on Armistice Commission," FBIS, Jerusalem, in Hebrew, October 8, 1956, 19:30 GMT.

51. Radio Moscow, "Western Charges Against Egypt Unfounded," FBIS, Moscow, in Arabic, September 29, 1956, 20:30 GMT.

52. Radio Moscow, "Arab States Move to Ban BBC Stations," FBIS, Moscow, in Arabic, October 3, 1956, 05:45 GMT.

53. Radio Cairo, "Nasir Says Suez Question will Test U.N.," FBIS, Cairo, in Arabic, October 7, 1956, 1500.

54. Radio Cairo, "Press Suspicious of UN Discussions," FBIS, Cairo, in Arabic, September 26, 0600, 18:30 GMT.

55. Dulles telegram, October 5, 1956, FRUS, vol. 16, 648–50.

56. Behind the scenes, the State Department had been stating clearly since March that because of Nasser's failure to reach a settlement with Israel, his opposition to the Baghdad Pact, his purchasing of arms from Czechoslovakia, his willingness to accept Soviet aid, and his anti-Western propaganda machine, it was "unlikely" to be "able to work with Nasser in the foreseeable future." Wilkins memo, March 14, 1956, FRUS, vol. 15, 352–53. As far as we know, there were no

Soviet attempts going on to orchestrate extralegal regime changes in Egypt or Syria. Britain and the United States could not make the same claim. For more on the US coup attempts in Syria, start with Hugh Wilford, *America's Great Game: The CIA's Secret Arabists and the Shaping of the Modern Middle East* (New York: Basic Books, 2013).

57. "A Suez Compromise? Don't Count on It," *Newsweek*, October 1, 1956, 40.

58. Radio Moscow, "Lies and Hypocrisy," FBIS, Moscow, in Arabic, October 5, 1956, 18:30 GMT.

59. Radio Moscow, "U.S. Monopolists Plan Suez Consortium," FBIS, Moscow, in Arabic, October 6, 1956, 02:45 GMT.

60. Radio Cairo, "Comments on British Policies," FBIS, Cairo, in Arabic, October 16, 1956, 06:00 GMT.

8. CACOPHANY

1. Recent histories of this period have argued that the BBC fell under significant government control during the early days of the Suez Crisis. The broadcast transcripts from these days substantiate that claim. Shaw, *Eden, Suez, and the Mass Media*; Vaughan, *Failure of American and British Propaganda*; and Simon Potter, *Broadcasting Empire: The BBC and the British World, 1922–1970* (Oxford: Oxford University Press, 2012), 197.

2. These transcripts are available at the BBC Written Archives Center (BBC-WAC) in Caversham, UK, on microfilm, sorted by date. For all citations to BBC reports in this chapter, refer to these transcripts unless otherwise stated.

3. Letter from A. J. Williams at the British Embassy Cairo to L. C. W. Figg at the Information Research Department, Foreign Office, London, September 12, 1956, "Egypt: Distribution of Material," TNA, FO 1110/893, Foreign Office: Information Research Department, 1956.

4. Kol Israel, "War Erupts," FBIS, Jerusalem, in Arabic, October 29, 1956, 06:00 GMT.

5. NARA, RG 306, entry P 160, Special Reports; 1953–1997, container 11, ARC 5664213, 7.

6. Dulles memo, October 30, 1956, FRUS, vol. 16, 863.

7. Sharq al-Adna, May 11, 1956, BBCM IV, 336, 2.

8. Summary of World Broadcasts, BBC, Middle East, part 4, 671, May 11, 1956, reel 336, 2.

9. "Britain Takes over Sharq al-Adna Radio," FBIS, Limassol, Sharq al-Adna Radio in Arabic to the Near East, October 30, 1956, 15:02 GMT.

10. Lennox-Boyd to Anthony Eden, May 30, 1956, "Egyptian Propaganda in Middle East," TNA, PREM 11/1450, Prime Minister's Office: Correspondence and Papers, 1954–1964, 4.

11. Dean to Smith, September 26, 1956, "Middle East, Broadcasting to the Region," TNA, FO 1110/947, Foreign Office: Information Research Department, 1956, 1.

12. Fergusson, *Trumpet in the Hall*, 261. The Information Policy Department's Sidney Hebblethwaite took over directorship of the Voice of Britain on December 3, 1956. Rawnsley, "Overt and Covert," 506.

13. TNA, AIR20/9570, "Suez: Psychological Warfare," E3, Annex, cited in Rawnsley, "Overt and Covert," 507.

14. Voice of America, November. 30, 1956, BBCM, IV, 662–92, reel 336, 45.

15. Radio Moscow, November. 30, 1956, BBCM, IV, 662–92, reel 336, 47.

16. Radio Cairo, "General Mobilization Announced," FBIS, Cairo, in Arabic, October 30, 1956, 18:00 GMT.

17. Lahav Pnina, "The Suez Crisis of 1956 and Its Aftermath: A Comparative Study of Constitutions, Use of Force, Diplomacy and International Relations," *Boston University Law Review* 95 (2015): 1299.

18. Microfilm, BBC broadcast transcript, October 31, 1956, 06:00 GMT, BBCWAC.

19. Microfilm, BBC broadcast transcript, October 31, 1956, 06:30 GMT, BBCWAC.

20. Varying stations, all transcribed in FBIS, October 31, 1956.

21. Information Research Department, "Communist Propaganda and Developments in the Middle East," October 15–November 15, 1956, TNA, FO 1110/948, Foreign Office: Information Research Department," 1956, 5.

22. Microfilm, BBC broadcast transcript, October 31, 1956, 06:30 GMT, BBCWAC.

23. BBC Eastern Service Listener Research Unit, "Quarterly Listener Research Report," August 20, 1955, BBC Written Archives Centre, E3/189/1, Arabic Service, Listener Correspondence Reports, 1955–1963; and Edwin Dale, "U.S. to Limit Acts to Its Step in U.N.: Defers Further Moves Now on Middle East Crisis U.S.," *New York Times*, November 1, 1956, 1.

24. Pirsein argues that the VOA was very pro-Arab during the crisis. This may have been true, but the messaging was not so clear. Pirsein, *Voice of America*, 362.

25. NARA, RG 306, entry P 160, Special Reports; 1953–1997, container 11, ARC 5664213, 7.

26. Microfilm, BBC broadcast transcript, November 1, 1956, BBCWAC.

27. "Nasser Declares Total War," FBIS, November 1, 1956, 15:00 GMT.

28. Fergusson, *Trumpet in the Hall*, 269.

29. The Soviets famously looped *Swan Lake* when Leonid Brezhnev died and when the Chernobyl disaster happened.

30. Fergusson, *Trumpet in the Hall*, 263.

31. Microfilm, BBC broadcast transcript, November 4, 1956, 05:40 GMT, BBCWAC.

32. BBC Eastern Service Listener Research Unit, "Quarterly Listener Research Report," August 20, 1955, BBC Written Archives Centre, E3/189/1, Arabic Service, Listener Correspondence Reports, 1955–1963.

33. Information Research Department, "Communist Propaganda and Developments in the Middle East," October 15–November 15, 1956, TNA, FO

1110/948, Foreign Office: Information Research Department," 1956, 5. Emphasis added.

34. "Mr. Gaitskill's Attack on the Government's Policy," *Guardian,* November 5, 1956.

35. "Programmy peredach za 1 sentabria—31 dekabria, 1956," Komitet po radio-veshchaniii i televideniiu pri SSSR, Otdel veshchanie na Arabskie strany, GARF, f. P6903, op. 25, d. 272 l. 45–72.

36. Elie Podeh, "The Struggle over Arab Hegemony after the Suez Crisis," *Middle Eastern Studies* 29, no. 1 (January 1, 1993): 96.

37. Love, *Suez,* 529.

38. Rawnsley, "Overt and Covert," 59.

39. Love, *Suez,* 529.

40. Brian McCauley, "Hungary and Suez, 1956: The Limits of Soviet and American Power," *Journal of Contemporary History* 16, no. 4 (1981): 785.

41. McCauley.

42. Radio Moscow, "World Condemns Continued Egypt Attack," FBIS, Moscow, in Arabic, November 5, 1956, 9:30 GMT.

43. Radio Moscow, "USSR People, Churches Protest Attach," FBIS, Moscow, in Arabic, November 6, 1956, 00:01 GMT.

44. Information Research Department, "Communist Propaganda and Developments in the Middle East," October 15–November 15, 1956, TNA, FO 1110/948, Foreign Office: Information Research Department," 1956, 8.

45. Radio Moscow, "Moscow Meetings," FBIS, Moscow, in Arabic, November 9, 1956, 13:05 GMT.

46. Radio Moscow, "British, French use UN for as Veil," FBIS, Moscow, in Arabic, November 9, 1956, 15:30 GMT.

47. "Programmy peredach za 1 sentabria—31 dekabria, 1956," Komitet po radio-veshchaniii i televideniiu pri SSSR, Otdel veshchanie na Arabskie strany, GARF, f. P6903, op. 25, d. 272, l. 45–72.

48. "S-22-56, Soviet Propaganda to the Near East in the Current Crisis," NARA, RG 306, entry P 160, Special Reports; 1953–1997, container 11, ARC 5664213, 7.

49. Ibid.

50. "Telegrafnozh Agentsvo Sovetskogo Soioza, Upravlenie inostrannoi informatsii," 1956, GARF, f. 4459, op. 27, d. 17814, l. 135.

51. Radio Moscow, "US Encourages Middle East Aggression," FBIS, Moscow, in Arabic, November 13, 1956, 12:30 GMT.

52. "Visit of Two Egyptian Journalists in Hungary," August 4, 1957, HU OSA 398-0-1-1471; Records of the UN Special Committee on the Problem of Hungary: UN Documents; and Open Society Archives at Central European University, Budapest.

53. Rawnsley, "Overt and Covert," 500.

54. Vaughan, "Propaganda by Proxy?," 170.

55. TNA, FO 953/1741/P1041/71, Baghdad Embassy to IPD, July 17, 1957, cited in Vaughan, "Propaganda by Proxy?,"169.

56. Vaughan, 170.

57. John Rennie, "Broadcasting to the Middle East from Cyprus," November 27, 1956, "Middle East, Information and Cultural Work," TNA, FO 1110/949, Foreign Office: Information Research Department, 1956.

58. Vaughan, "BBC's External Services," 499.

59. Shaw, *Eden, Suez, and the Mass Media: Propaganda and Persuasion during the Suez Crisis.*

60. "S-22-56, Soviet Propaganda to the Near East in the Current Crisis," NARA, RG 306, entry P 160, Special Reports; 1953–1997, container 11, ARC 5664213, 1–5.

61. USIA, Office of Research and Intelligence, Report, "The Nature and Extent of British Press Criticism of the United States in Light of the Suez Crisis," January 24, 1957, 6, NARA, RG306, Research Reports 1956–1959, 1957, P-4, ARC 6819321.

62. Ibid., 7.

63. Ibid.

64. Ibid.

65. "Propaganda in Middle East," TNA, FO 953/1633, Foreign Office: Information Policy Department and Regional Information Departments, 1956.

66. Rawnsley, *Radio Diplomacy and Propaganda*, 59.

67. USIA, Office of Research and Intelligence, Report, "The Nature and Extent of British Press Criticism of the United States in Light of the Suez Crisis," January 24, 1957, 3, NARA, RG306, Research Reports 1956–1959, 1957, P-4, ARC 6819321.

68. "The Voice in Arabic," *New York Times*, December 28, 1956, 18.

69. TNA FO953/1634/P1041/89, December 8, 1956, cited in Rawnsley, *Radio Diplomacy and Propaganda*, 63.

70. "Progress of Iran," 1957, NARA, RG 306, US Information Agency, entry P 46, Master File Copies of Field Publications, 1951–1979, container 1.5, ARC 1126039, 3.

71. James Reston, "Mideast Propaganda Drive Mapped by Administration: U.S. Increases Propaganda," *New York Times*, January 23, 1957, 1.

72. Oren Stephens, "USIA Meets the Test: A Study of Fast Output During the Hungarian and Suez Crisis," June 1957, 140, cited in Pirsein, *Voice of America*, 362.

73. "Egypt's External Propaganda," August 1, 1957, NARA, RG 306, US Information Agency, Office of Research and Analysis, entry A1 1033, Research Reports, 1956–1959, container 3, 16.

74. Ibid., 23.

75. Ibid., 1–10.

76. "Situation Report on Egypt and Egyptian Relations," September 1, 1955, NARA, RG 306, US Information Agency, Office of Research and Intelligence, entry A1 1022, Intelligence Bulletins, Memorandums and Summaries: 1954–1956, container 6, 5.

77. Ahmed Said, *Voice of the Arabs*, December 9, 1956, BBCM IV, 120, December 11, 1956. Also cited also in Collier, "Countering Communist and Nasserite Propaganda," 96.

78. David W. Lesch, *Syria and the United States: Eisenhower's Cold War in the Middle East* (Boulder, CO: Westview Press, 1992).

79. BBCM, no. 458, January 24, 1958, 1.

9. VOICES CARRY

1. Letter from Kabul Chancery to the British Foreign Office Information Policy Department, December 29, 1956, "Propaganda in Middle East," TNA, FO 953/1738, Foreign Office: Information Policy Department and Regional Information Departments, 1957, 1. Later documents in this folder show that the film was shown in Cairo and Algiers. There was an attempt to show the film at a packed cinema in Tunis on January 25, 1957. The event began with anti-colonial poems, which "aroused the audience." Then a long delay ensued when the organizers realized that they had a 35mm projector for a 16mm film. They made a hasty attempt to borrow a 16mm projector from other cinemas, finally even going to the USIA for one (it was closed). They then had to apologize to the packed crowd and dismiss everyone.

2. Ibid.

3. Ibid., 2.

4. "Publicity on Port Said: Use of Films and Propaganda," January 31, 1957, NARA, RG 306, US Information Agency, Office of Research and Analysis, entry A1 1033, Research Reports, 1956–1959, container 3, 1.

5. Letter from Kabul Chancery to the British Foreign Office Information Policy Department, December 29, 1956, "Propaganda in Middle East," TNA, FO 953/1738, Foreign Office: Information Policy Department and Regional Information Departments, 1957, 4.

6. "Programmy peredach za 1 sentabria—31 dekabria, 1956," Komitet po radioveshchaniiu i televideniiu pri SSSR, Otdel veshchanie na Arabskie strany, GARF, f. P6903, op. 25, d. 272 l. 278.

7. Reinhold Wagnleitner, *Coca-Colonization and the Cold War: The Cultural Mission of the United States in Austria after the Second World War* (Chapel Hill: University of North Carolina Press, 1994).

8. Franzén, "Losing Hearts and Minds in Iraq," 1.

9. McAlister, *Epic Encounters*, 40.

10. Nigel John Ashton, *Eisenhower, Macmillan and the Problem of Nasser: Anglo-American Relations and Arab Nationalism, 1955–59* (New York: Palgrave Macmillan, 1996).

11. Ferris, *Nasser's Gamble*, 6.

12. As Jesse Ferris has argued, it was this inter-Arab struggle, not the Arab-Israeli conflict, that provided the "central axis around which Middle Eastern politics revolved" during the Cold War in the 1950s and early 1960s. Ferris, 2.

13. Salim Yaqub, *Containing Arab Nationalism: The Eisenhower Doctrine and the Middle East* (Chapel Hill: University of North Carolina Press, 2005), 20.

14. Said K. Aburish, *A Brutal Friendship: The West and The Arab Elite* (New York: St. Martin's Griffin, 1998), 58.

15. Letter from Egypt and Jordan Mission to Information Research Department, "Propaganda in Middle East," TNA, FO 953/1739, Foreign Office: Information Policy Department and Regional Information Departments, 1957.

16. Letter from UK Treasury to P. F. Grey at the Foreign Office, "Broadcasting from Cyprus," January 9, 1957, TNA, FO 1110/971/PR139/48.

17. "Voice of Britain: Decision to Phase Out," Foreign Office: Information Research Department, January 8, 1957, TNA, FO 1110/971.

18. Working Party on Broadcasting in the Middle East, Minutes of First Meeting on 22 February 22, 1957, "Establishment of Broadcasting Service in Middle East to Counter Influence of Radio Cairo," TNA, DO 35/9645, Dominions Office and Commonwealth Relations Office: Original Correspondence, 1957–58.

19. "Extension of Arabic Broadcasts from London," July 10, 1956, "Arabic Service Expansion," BBCWAC, E2 626/1.

20. "Distribution of Transmission 'X,'" July 1962, TNA, FO 1110/1583/PR1125/19.

21. IRD/BMEO Minutes, February 17, 1955, TNA, FO 111-/832/PR10104/21/G; and Collier, "Countering Communist and Nasserite Propaganda," 143.

22. "Britain's Public Relations in the Middle East," paper by D. A. Scott-Reid (publicity manager for the Iraq Petroleum Company Ltd.), December 20, 1956, TNA, FO 953/1740/P1041/39.

23. Stephens to Toner, April 16, 1958, Dwight D. Eisenhower Presidential Library, White House Office, Staff Research Group Records 1956–61, box 21, folder: United States Information Agency 1-350, cited in Vaughan, "'Cloak without Dagger,'" 77.

24. Eisenhower speech, January 5, 1957, Scripps Library, box: OL100020204, ID: dde_1957_0105, 5969.

25. For more on the history of the Eisenhower Doctrine, see Yaqub, *Containing Arab Nationalism.*

26. Yaqub, *Containing Arab Nationalism,* 1–20.

27. John W. Henderson, *The United States Information Agency* (New York: Praeger, 1969), 164; and Alvin A. Snyder, *Warriors of Disinformation: American Propaganda, Soviet Lies, and the Winning of the Cold War; An Insider's Account* (New York: Arcade Publishing, 1995), 16.

28. Gary Rawnsley points to fact that the CIA was using "Voice of Justice" in 1958. Rawnsley, "Overt and Covert." Vaughan points out that the CIA may not have been the "original operators." Vaughan, *Failure of American and British Propaganda,* 209.

29. "Voice of Justice" transcript, January 16, 1957, "Sharq el Adera Broadcasting Station: 'Voice of the Arabs' Broadcasting Station in Egypt," TNA, FO 953/1786, Foreign Office: Information Policy Department and Regional Information Departments: Registered Files, 1957.

30. Ibid.

31. It is interesting to note the fus-ha (الفصحى) transliteration of Nasser's name here, instead of the Egyptian (المصري) transliteration.

32. "Voice of Justice" transcript, January 16, 1957, "Sharq el Adera Broadcasting Station: 'Voice of the Arabs' Broadcasting Station in Egypt," TNA, FO 953/1786, Foreign Office: Information Policy Department and Regional Information Departments: Registered Files, 1957.

33. Snyder, *Warriors of Disinformation*, 41.

34. *Variety*, April 20, 1955.

35. Henderson, *United States Information Agency*, 66.

36. Legislative Reference Service, Library of Congress, *The U.S. Ideological Effort: Government Agencies and Programs*, study prepared for the House Subcommittee on International Organizations and Movements of the Committee on Foreign Affairs, January 3, 1964.

37. Interestingly, in the Radio Moscow transcripts that we have, which come from the Soviet archives, the BBC Monitoring Service, and the FBIS, there is no mention of communism in all the discussions of the Jordanian crisis. In fact, much as the British did, the word *communism* stopped being a term that Radio Moscow used in its Arabic broadcasts altogether.

38. Radio Moscow, "U.S. Seeks France's Place in Algeria," FBIS, Moscow in Arabic, June 19, 1957, 18:30 GMT.

39. Ibid.

40. Radio Moscow, "U.S. Ambassador Demands Jordan Arrests," FBIS, Moscow in Arabic, June 11, 1957, 12:30 GMT.

41. Radio Moscow, "U.S.-U.K. Talks Plot Arab Break-up," FBIS, Moscow in Arabic, June 18, 1957, 15:30 GMT.

42. Radio Moscow, "U.S. Aid Only Keeps Countries Backward," FBIS, Moscow in Arabic, June 27, 1957, 04:45 GMT.

43. "Programmy peredach za 1 sentabria—31 dekabria, 1957," Komitet po radio-veshchaniiu i televideniiu pri SSSR, Otdel veshchanie na Arabskie strany, GARF, f. P6903, op. 25, d. 289 l. 142.

44. Yaqub, *Containing Arab Nationalism*, 137.

45. Philip Anderson, "'Summer Madness': The Crisis in Syria, August–October 1957," *British Journal of Middle Eastern Studies* 22, nos. 1/2 (1995): 21.

46. Blackwell, "Britain, the United States and the Syrian Crisis," 140.

47. "Final Report of the Joint U.S.–U.K. Working Group on Syria," September 18, 1957, Duncan Sandys papers (DSND) 6/35, Churchill College Archives, Cambridge; and Matthew Jones, "The 'Preferred Plan': The Anglo-American Working Group Report on Covert Action in Syria, 1957," *Intelligence and National Security* 19, no. 3 (September 1, 2004): 406.

48. "IV. Psychological Program," September 18, 1957, Duncan Sandys papers (DSND) 6/35, Churchill College Archives, Cambridge. See also David Lesch, "The 1957 American-Syrian Crisis: Globalist Policy in a Regional Reality," in *The Middle East and the United States: A Historical and Political Reassessment*, ed. David Lesch, 4th ed. (Boulder, CO: Westview Press, 2007), 106.

49. Radio Moscow, "U.S. Aims to make Syria another Jordan," FBIS, Moscow in Arabic, June 29, 1957, 17:30 GMT.

50. "Programmy peredach za 1 sentabria—31 dekabria, 1957," Komitet po radio-veshchaniiu i televideniiu pri SSSR, Otdel veshchanie na Arabskie strany, GARF, f. P6903, op. 25, d. 289 l. 154; and "Text of Khrushchev Interview on Wide Range of Issues Between East and West," *New York Times*, October 10, 1957, quoted in NARA, USIA, RG 306, entry P 160, Special Reports (s): 1953–1997, box 12, S-39-57, October 25, 1957, 1–2.

51. "Programmy peredach za 1 sentabria—31 dekabria, 1957," Komitet po radio-veshchaniiu i televideniiu pri SSSR, Otdel veshchanie na Arabskie strany, GARF, f. P6903, op. 25, d. 289 l. 154.

52. Blackwell, "Britain, the United States and the Syrian Crisis," 145.

53. Snyder, *Warriors of Disinformation*, 19. See also Jeremi Suri, *Power and Protest: Global Revolution and the Rise of Detente* (Cambridge, MA: Harvard University Press, 2003).

54. George Kirk, "The Syrian Crisis of 1957—Fact and Fiction," *International Affairs (Royal Institute of International Affairs 1944–)* 36, no. 1 (1960): 61.

55. R. Takeyh, *The Origins of the Eisenhower Doctrine: The US, Britain and Nasser's Egypt, 1953–57* (Houndmills, Basingstoke: Palgrave Macmillan, 2000), 151.

56. Voice of the Arabs, "Jordanians, Iraqis Protest False Union," FBIS, March 1, 1958, 18:45 GMT.

57. Voice of the Arabs, "Muscat Must Throw Off British Control," FBIS, February 25, 1958, 10:50 GMT.

58. Voice of the Arabs, "Combine Egypt, Syria Unions," FBIS, March 3, 1958, 20:00 GMT.

59. Voice of the Arabs, "Ahmad Said Hails Yemeni Union with UAR," FBIS, March 4, 1820, 10:50 GMT.

60. Boyd, *Broadcasting in the Arab World*, 325–29.

61. Ritchie Ovendale, *Britain, the United States, and the Transfer of Power in the Middle East, 1945–1962* (London: Leicester University Press, 1996); Ashton, *Eisenhower, Macmillan and Nasser*; Blackwell, "Britain, the United States and the Syrian Crisis"; and Takeyh, *Origins of the Eisenhower Doctrine*.

62. This line is taken from a Soviet transcription of a VOA broadcast, which was then requoted in a Radio Moscow broadcast. "Programmy peredach za 1 senta-bria–31 dekabria, 1958," Komitet po radioveshchaniiu i televideniiu pri SSSR, Otdel veshchanie na Arabskie strany, GARF, f. P6903, op. 25, d. 352.

63. Marshall's original line was, "The remedy lies in breaking the vicious cycle and restoring the confidence of the European people in the economic future of their own countries and of Europe as a whole." George Marshall, "The Marshall Plan Speech," Harvard University, June 5, 1947, www.marshallfoundation.org/the-marshall-plan/speech/.

64. "Egypt's External Propaganda," August 1, 1957, NARA, RG 306, USIA, Office of Research and Analysis, entry A1 1033, Research Reports, 1956–1959, container 3, 27;

and Memorandum of conversation, Eisenhower, J. F. Dulles, et al., July 14, 1958, FRUS, 1958–1960, 11, item 160. Also cited in Yaqub, *Containing Arab Nationalism*, 224.

65. "Establishment of Broadcasting Service in Middle East to Counter Influence of Radio Cairo," TNA, DO 35/9645, Dominions Office and Commonwealth Relations Office: Original Correspondence, 1957–58.

66. Alexander Wiley, "Voice of America, How Loud Is It?," , 107 Cong. Rec. A6696 (August 25, 1961).

67. Ferris, *Nasser's Gamble*.

68. A. A. Fursenko and Timothy J. Naftali, *Khrushchev's Cold War: The Inside Story of an American Adversary* (New York: Norton, 2006), 80–82, 292–95; Odd Arne Westad, *The Global Cold War: Third World Interventions and the Making of Our Times* (New York: Cambridge University Press, 2005), 67–70; and William Taubman, *Khrushchev: The Man and His Era*, reprint ed. (New York: W. W. Norton, 2004), 348, 354, 487.

69. Fursenko and Naftali, *Khrushchev's Cold War*, 292–322; Melvyn P. Leffler, *For the Soul of Mankind: The United States, the Soviet Union, and the Cold War* (New York: Hill and Wang, 2008), 161–74; and Walter LaFeber, *America, Russia, and the Cold War, 1945–2006*, 10th ed. (Boston: McGraw-Hill, 2008), 204.

70. "Haykal Assails CENTO Influence in Area," FBIC, Cairo Domestic Service in Arabic, March 8, 1963, 15:30 GMT.

71. Thornycroft to Douglas-Home, April 22, 1964, TNA, DEFE 13/569. Also cited in Robert McNamara, *Britain, Nasser and the Balance of Power in the Middle East, 1952–1977: From the Egyptian Revolution to the Six Day War* (London: Routledge, 2019), 193.

72. The transcript of this interaction can be found at "Oral Answers on the House of Commons, Middle East (Ministerial Visits)," June 21, 1965, 1188–92, in "Radio Cairo Reports on Propaganda Broadcasts," June 1965, Foreign Office: Political Departments: General Correspondence from 1906–1966, TNA, FO 371/183949/VG1432/1.

73. Thomson did visit Cairo on September 24, 1965, one day before the British government suspended the South Arabian constitution and violence exploded in the streets. Nasser refused to see Thomson. Everyone agreed that the trip was a failure. See "UAR Radio Propaganda since Mr. Thomson's visit to Cairo," Foreign Office, October 15, 1965, TNA, FO 371/183949/VG1432/7.

74. "Cairo 'Hate' Man's Visit Angers MPs," *Daily Mirror*, June 22, 1965, 6.

75. Letter to R. A. Fyjis-Walker, Cairo, from R. T. Higgins, Foreign Office, June 28, 1965, TNA, FO 371/183949/VG1432/1.

76. Foreign Office, "Survey of Cairo Radio after Said's return to Cairo," August 16, 1965, TNA, FO 371/183949/VG1432/4.

77. Foreign Office letters, July 26, 1965, TNA, FO 371/183949/VG1432/3.

78. Voice of the Arabs in Arabic, August 14, 1965, 17:20 GMT, TNA, FO 371/183949/VG1432/4.

79. Ibid.

80. Ibid.

81. Salah al-Din al-Hadidi, *Shahid 'ala Harb al-Yaman* (Cairo: Maktabat Madbuli, 1984), 72.

82. "Yemeni Strength Recedes UAR Evacuation," FBIS, Jerusalem Domestic Service in Hebrew, June 15, 1963, 17:00 GMT.

83. Ahmed Said, *Harb al'idha'at alsirriyah . . .'abwab janibihim 1967* (Cairo: Maspiro, 2017). Some chapters of this work were published in *Majallat al'idha'at waaltilifiyun* (Radio and TV Magazine), February 1, 2017.

84. "Nasir Begins Muslim Brotherhood Purge," FBIS, Israel, in Arabic to Israel and the Near East, May 20, 1957, 11:15 GMT.

85. Jay Walz, "Nasser Defines Arab Socialism," *New York Times*, May 27, 1962.

86. Isabella Ginor and Gideon Remez, *Foxbats over Dimona: The Soviets' Nuclear Gamble in the Six-Day War* (New Haven, CT: Yale University Press, 2007).

87. "Clandestine Voice Attacks West, East," FBIS, Voice of the Arab Nation in Arabic, January 10, 1963, 10:00 GMT.

88. Ibid.

89. Letter from British Embassy, Baghdad, Information Division to British Embassy, Beirut, Information Division, January 12, 1954, TNA, PRO, FO 1110/700/PR1093/IG/S.810/2/54. Also cited in Franzén, "Losing Hearts and Minds in Iraq," 757.

90. Sayyid Quṭb, *This Religion of Islam*, Ishaat-e-Islam Trust (Delhi: Markazi Maktaba Islami, 1974), 9, cited in John Calvert, *Sayyid Qutb and the Origins of Radical Islamism* (New York: Oxford University Press, 2018), 2.

91. Dr. Nathan J. Citino, *Envisioning the Arab Future: Modernization in US-Arab Relations, 1945–1967* (Cambridge: Cambridge University Press, 2017), 252.

10. POISONOUS PROPAGANDA OR PRODUCTIVE PROGRESS TO PEACE

1. "Cairo Comments on National Mobilization," FBIS, Cairo Domestic Service in Arabic, May 16, 1967, 11:30 GMT.

2. Robert Bowker, *Palestinian Refugees: Mythology, Identity, and the Search for Peace* (Boulder, CO: Lynne Rienner, 2003), 81; and David McDowall, *Palestine and Israel: The Uprising and Beyond* (Berkeley: University of California Press, 1991), 84.

3. Paul Fussell, *The Great War and Modern Memory*, new ed. (Oxford: Oxford University Press, 2013), 7.

4. Tawfiq al-Hakim, *The Return of Consciousness* (London: Palgrave Macmillan, 1974), 53.

5. R. Al-Naqqash, *Nagib Mahfuz: Safahat min Mudakiratihi wa 'adwa' jadidah 'ala 'adabihi wa hayatihi* (Cairo: Ahram, 1998), 272.

6. Fawaz A. Gerges, *Making the Arab World: Nasser, Qutb, and the Clash That Shaped the Middle East* (Princeton, NJ: Princeton University Press, 2019), 300.

7. This observation is made about the United States in the 1960s as well. See Tom Engelhardt, *The End of Victory Culture: Cold War America and the Disillusioning of a Generation* (New York: Basic Books, 1995).

8. Winston Burdette, interview by Mike Shuster, *The Mideast: A Century of Conflict*, pt. 4, *The 1967 Six Day War*, NPR, October 3, 2002. See also Michael B. Oren, *Six Days of War: June 1967 and the Making of the Modern Middle East* (New York: Presidio Press, 2003).

9. Kennedy, *From Independence to Revolution*, 60; J. Waterbury, *The Egypt of Nasser and Sadat: The Political Economy of Two Regimes* (Princeton, NJ: Princeton University Press, 1992); Beinin, "Labor, Capital, and the State"; Constantine Zurayk, *Ma'na alNakba Mujaddadan* (Beirut: Dar al'ilm lilmalayyin, 1967); Moshe Gat, "Britain and Israel before and after the Six Day War, June 1967: From Support to Hostility," *Contemporary British History* 18, no. 1 (March 1, 2004): 54–77; Moshe Gat, "Nasser and the Six Day War, 5 June 1967: A Premeditated Strategy or An Inexorable Drift to War?," *Israel Affairs* 11, no. 4 (December 1, 2005): 608–35; Yossi Goldstein, "The Six Day War: The War That No One Wanted," *Israel Affairs* 24, no. 5 (September 3, 2018): 767–84; and Yaacov Ro'i and Boris Morozov, *The Soviet Union and the June 1967 Six Day War* (Washington, DC: Woodrow Wilson Center Press; Stanford, CA: Stanford University Press, 2008).

10. Ibrahim M. Abu-Rabi', *Contemporary Arab Thought: Studies in Post-1967 Arab Intellectual History* (London: Pluto Press, 2004); Elizabeth Suzanne Kassab, *Contemporary Arab Thought: Cultural Critique in Comparative Perspective* (New York: Columbia University Press, 2009); Walter Armbrust, *Mass Culture and Modernism in Egypt*, illus. ed. (Cambridge: Cambridge University Press, 1996); Tamara Maatouk, "On the Heels of 1967: Chahine, Cinema, and Emotional Response(s) to the Defeat," *International Journal of Middle East Studies* 55, no. 1 (February 2023): 25–42; Sune Haugbolle, "The New Arab Left and 1967," *British Journal of Middle Eastern Studies* 44, no. 4 (October 2, 2017): 497–512; Fouad Ajami, *The Arab Predicament: Arab Political Thought and Practice since 1967*, 2nd ed. (Cambridge: Cambridge University Press, 1992); Mériam N. Belli, *An Incurable Past: Nasser's Egypt Then and Now*, reprint ed. (Gainesville: University Press of Florida, 2017).

11. Citino, *Envisioning the Arab Future*, 266.

12. Citino, 269.

13. Leila Khaled, *My People Shall Live: The Autobiography of a Revolutionary* (London: Hodder and Stoughton, 1973), 90, 136.

14. Citino, *Envisioning the Arab Future*, 272.

15. The White House knew that Moscow and Syria were feeding this false information to Nasser but chose not to tell him that the reports of Israeli concentrations were unfounded. The archives suggest that Walt Rostow and his staff held off on speaking with Nasser about it because they feared the Israelis might, in fact, decide to execute a surprise attack. LBJ, National Security File, National Security Council Histories, Middle East Crisis, May 12–June 19, 1967, box 17, vol. 1, tabs 1–10, [1 of 2], 2.

16. "Haykal on 'Violence' Stage of U.S. Relations," FBIS, Cairo Domestic Service in Arabic, May 12, 1967, 14:45 GMT.

17. Jesse Ferris also notes the "bellicosity" with which the Egyptian media assailed the United States. Ferris, *Nasser's Gamble*, 265.

18. "We Challenge You, America," FBIS, Cairo Voice of the Arabs in Arabic, May 23, 1967, 11:34 GMT.

19. "Ahmad Said Commentary," Voice of the Arabs, in Arabic, FBIS, May 27, 1967, 11:30 GMT.

20. "Atlantic Alliance Colludes with Israel," Voice of the Arabs in Arabic, FBIS, May 25, 1967, 11:22 GMT.

21. "Syrian Military Governor Issues Statement," FBIS, Damascus Domestic Service in Arabic, May 7, 1967, 22:00 GMT.

22. "UAR General Speaks on Israeli Confrontation," FBIS, Cairo Domestic Service in Arabic, May 18, 1967, 23:00 GMT.

23. FBIS, Cairo Domestic Service in Arabic, May 19, 1967, 04:00 GMT.

24. "Amir Statement," FBIS, Cairo Domestic Service in Arabic, May 19, 1967, 04:00 GMT.

25. "Syrian Foreign Minister's Remarks," FBIS, Cairo Voice of the Arabs to the Arab World, May 18, 1967, 17:15 GMT.

26. "Saud Urges United Arab Action Against Israel," FBIS, Cairo, Voice of the Arabs to the Arab World, May 21, 1967, 17:09 GMT.

27. "Abd al-Nasir: Gulf of Aqaba Closed to Israel," FBIS, Cairo, May 21, 1967, 17:09 GMT.

28. "Syrian Military Governor Issues Statement," FBIS, Damascus Domestic Service in Arabic, May 7, 1967, 22:00 GMT.

29. "Yefimov Commentary," FBIS, Moscow, in Arabic, May 19, 1967, 18:00 GMT.

30. "Activities of Imperialists," FBIS, Moscow, in Arabic, May 22, 1967, 20:00 GMT.

31. "Imperialist Aims," FBIS, Moscow, in Arabic to the Arab World, May 23, 1967, 19:00 GMT.

32. "Primakov in Pravda," FBIS, Moscow, in Arabic to the Arab World, May 28, 1967, 17:30 GMT.

33. Memorandum from USIA Cairo, May 18, 1967, LBJ, 3 UAR, box 159, 1 of 2, 2.

34. "Imperialist Aims," FBIS, Moscow, in Arabic to the Arab World, May 23, 1967, 19:00 GMT.

35. "Algerian Conference Discusses Arab Socialism," FBIS, Moscow Peace and Progress, in English to Africa, May 23, 1967, 14:30 GMT.

36. Ibid.

37. "Damascus and Egypt Radio Broadcasts Crisis Slogans," FBIS, Radio Damascus and Radio Cairo, May 23, 1967, 04:00–21:30 GMT.

38. *Al-Jumhuriyah*, May 24, 2023.

39. *Al-Ahram*, May 24, 2023.

40. *Al-Ba'ath*, May 24, 2023.

41. "USSR to Support Arab States If Attacked," FBIS, Moscow, TASS International Service in Arabic, May 23, 1967, 20:47 GMT.

42. "Praise for Soviet Statement," FBIS, Moscow, TASS International Service in Arabic and English, May 24, 1967, 16:23 GMT.

43. Microfilm, BBC broadcast transcript, May 24, 1967, 10:00 GMT, BBCWAC.

44. Microfilm, BBC broadcast transcript, "Middle East—Brown," May 25, 17:00 GMT, BBCWAC.

45. A scouring of the BBC transcripts does not reveal the broadcast that Radio Moscow is referring to. See the Radio Moscow broadcast "Praise for Soviet Statement," FBIS, Moscow, TASS International Service in Arabic and English, May 25, 1967, 18:00 GMT.

46. Microfilm, BBC broadcast transcript, "Middle East—Embassy," May 26, 1967, 13:00 GMT, BBCWAC.

47. Microfilm, BBC broadcast transcript, May 25, 1967, 08:00 GMT, BBCWAC.

48. Microfilm, BBC broadcast transcript, "Middle East—American Warning," May 25, 1967, 22:00 GMT, BBCWAC.

49. Microfilm, BBC broadcast transcript, "Middle East—Warning," May 24, 1967, 23:00 GMT, BBCWAC.

50. R. W. Komer, Memorandum for the President, December 31, 1964, LBJ, National Security File, Country File, Middle East—UAR, box 159, 1 of 2, 2.

51. Memo from Battle to Secretary of State, December 3, 1964, LBJ, National Security File, Country File, Middle East—UAR, box 159, 1 of 2.

52. LBJ, National Security File, National Security Council Histories, Middle East Crisis, May 12–June 19, 1967, box 17, vol. 1, tabs 1–10, [1 of 2], 2.

53. Ibid., 3.

54. Ibid., 5; and "Husayn, Abd al Nasir Sign Defense Agreement," FBIS, Cairo Domestic Service, May 30, 1967, 13:35 GMT.

55. "Israeli Aid," LBJ, National Security File, National Security Council Histories, Middle East Crisis, May 12–June 19, 1967, box 17, vol. 1, tabs 1–10, [1 of 2].

56. Memorandum for the President, May 8, 1967, LBJ, National Security File, National Security Council Histories, Middle East Crisis, May 12–June 19, 1967, box 17, vol. 1, tabs 1–10, [1 of 2].

57. "Remarks of the President on the Near East Situation," May 23, 1967, 6:10 EST, LBJ, National Security File, National Security Council Histories, Middle East Crisis, May 12–June 19, 1967, box 17.

58. LBJ, National Security File, National Security Council Histories, Middle East Crisis, May 12–June 19, 1967, box 17, vol. 1, tabs 1–10, [1 of 2], 6.

59. "Sovereignty over Aqaba Gulf 'Indisputable,'" FBIS, Cairo Domestic Service in Arabic, May 23, 1967, 11:30 GMT.

60. "Washington Instigates Aggression Worldwide," FBIS, Moscow, TASS International Service in Arabic, May 23, 1967, 16:30 GMT.

61. "UAR Action Constitutes Aggression," FBIS, Jerusalem, Israel Domestic Service in Hebrew, in Arabic, May 23, 1967, 18:45 GMT.

62. "Abd al-Nasir: Gulf of Aqaba Closed to Israel," FBIS, Cairo Domestic Service in Arabic, May 21, 1967, 17:09 GMT.

63. "Further Comment," FBIS, Cairo, Voice of the Arabs in Arabic to the Arab World, May 23, 1967, 18:00 GMT.

64. M. H. Heikal, *Altariq 'ila Ramadan* (Beirut: Dal al-Nahar, 1975), cited in Gerges, *Making the Arab World*, 326.

65. "UAR General Speaks on Israeli Confrontation," FBIS, Cairo Domestic Service in Arabic, May 18, 1967, 23:00 GMT.

66. Microfilm, BBC broadcast transcript, May 31, 1967, 22:00 GMT, BBCWAC.

67. Behind the scenes, Hussein was writing to President Johnson asking him to publicly disassociate the United States from the Israelis, to profess neutrality, and to promise it would not interfere. LBJ, National Security File, National Security Council Histories, Middle East Crisis, May 12–June 19, 1967, box 17, vol. 3, tabs 81–95, tab 91.

68. "Nasir Speech," FBIS, Cairo Domestic Service in Arabic, May 30, 1967, 13:40 GMT; and microfilm, BBC broadcast transcript, "Jordan," May 30, 1967, 22:00 GMT, BBCWAC.

69. "Amman Accused of Obstructing Liberation War," FBIS, Damascus Domestic Service in Arabic, June 1, 1967, 11:15 GMT.

70. Microfilm, BBC broadcast transcript, May 31, 1967, 20:00 GMT, BBCWAC.

71. "Chronology," LBJ, National Security File, National Security Council Histories, Middle East Crisis, May 12–June 19, 1967, box 18, vol. 3, tabs 81–95.

72. "Aggression Noted in Slogan," FBIS, Amman Domestic Service in Arabic, June 5, 1967, 07:20 GMT.

73. "Chronology," LBJ, National Security File, National Security Council Histories, Middle East Crisis, May 12–June 19, 1967, box 18, vol. 3, tabs 81–95.

74. "Newscast for Israelis Reports 'Aggression,'" FBIS, Cairo Voice of the Arabs in Hebrew, June 5, 1967, 08:41 GMT.

75. "Communique Reports Israeli 'Full Aggression,'" FBIS, Cairo Voice of the Arabs in Arabic to the Arab World, June 5, 1967, 08:53 GMT.

76. "Joint Command Proclamation," FBIS, Amman Domestic Service in Arabic, June 5, 1967, 10:53 GMT.

77. "Middle East Crisis Coverage—Near East & South Asia Division," LBJ Library, Papers of Leaonard H. Marx, box 31, 1.

78. "U.S. Instigation," FBIS, Moscow, in Arabic to the Arab World, June 5, 1967, 14:00 GMT.

79. "British and American Neutrality in the Middle East War: Coverage in External Services News Bulletins," BBCWAC, E2/787/1, Foreign Office Middle East Crisis, 1967, 1.

80. "THE BIG LIE: Case History of Charges of U.S. Involvement in Middle East Crisis," NARA, USIA, RG 306, entry P 160, Special Reports: 1953–1997, container 23, ARC 5664216, S-6-67, 19.

81. "British and American Neutrality in the Middle East War: Coverage in External Services News Bulletins," BBCWAC, E2/787/1, Foreign Office Middle East Crisis, 1967, 1.

82. Komitet po radioveshchaniyu i televideniyu pri SSSR, "Kommentarii, besedy i stat'i na Mezhdunarodnyye temy," 1967, GARF, f. R6903, op. 25, d. 1644, l. 201.

83. "British and American Neutrality in the Middle East War: Coverage in External Services News Bulletins," BBCWAC, E2/787/1, Foreign Office Middle East Crisis, 1967, 1.

84. "THE BIG LIE: Case History of Charges of U.S. Involvement in Middle East Crisis," NARA, USIA, RG 306, entry P 160, Special Reports: 1953-1997, container 23, ARC 5664216, S-6-67, 1.

85. "Army, Air Force Leaders Detail Enemy Losses," FBIS, Jerusalem, Israeli Domestic Service in Hebrew, June 5, 1967, 23:15 GMT.

86. "Aircraft Carriers Participate," FBIS, Cairo Domestic Service in Arabic, June 6, 1967, 04:37 GMT.

87. USIA Office of Policy and Research, "Broadcasting Points," August 9, 1967, LBJ, National Security File Agency File, box 75.

88. "Warning to Egyptian Troops," FBIS, Jerusalem, Israel in Arabic to the Arab World, June 6, 1967, 06:00 GMT.

89. "Imperialist Aircover for Israel Is Aggression," FBIS, Baghdad Domestic Service in Arabic, June 6, 1967, 06:30 GMT.

90. "British and American Neutrality in the Middle East War: Coverage in External Services News Bulletins," BBCWAC, E2/787/1, Foreign Office Middle East Crisis, 1967, 2.

91. "Government Implicates U.S., U.K., in Raids—Interview with Downed Pilot," FBIS, Damascus Domestic Service in Arabic, June 6, 1967, 14:00 GMT.

92. "THE BIG LIE: Case History of Charges of U.S. Involvement in Middle East Crisis," NARA, USIA, RG 306, entry P 160, Special Reports: 1953–1997, container 23, ARC 5664216, S-6-67, 11.

93. "Comment for Arab Listeners," FBIS, Moscow, in Arabic to the Arab World, June 6, 1967, 12:30 GMT.

94. USIA Office of Policy and Research, "Broadcasting Points," August 9, 1967, LBJ, National Security File Agency File, box 75.

95. USIA Office of Policy and Research, "Broadcasting Points," August 9, 1967, LBJ, National Security File Agency File, box 75.

96. "THE BIG LIE: Case History of Charges of U.S. Involvement in Middle East Crisis," NARA, USIA, RG 306, entry P 160, Special Reports: 1953–1997, container 23, ARC 5664216, S-6-67, 8.

97. "Statement of Secretary Dean Rusk," June 6, 1967, LBJ, National Security File, National Security Council Histories, Middle East Crisis, May 12–June 19, 1967, box 18, vol. 4, tabs 111–27.

98. "British and American Neutrality in the Middle East War: Coverage in External Services News Bulletins," BBCWAC, E2/787/1, Foreign Office Middle East Crisis, 1967, 3.

99. "Our Battle Is with the U.S.," FBIS, Cairo Domestic Service in Arabic (Commentary by Ahmed Said), June 6, 1967, 18:02 GMT.

100. "THE BIG LIE: Case History of Charges of U.S. Involvement in Middle East Crisis," NARA, USIA, RG 306, entry P 160, Special Reports: 1953–1997, container 23, ARC 5664216, S-6-67, 4.

101. "More Diplomatic Breaks," FBIS, Moscow TASS, June 7, 1967, 08:35 GMT.

102. "Announcement to Press Agencies," June 7, 1967, "Middle East Crisis," BBCWAC, E2/824/1; and "British and American Neutrality in the Middle East War: Coverage in External Services News Bulletins," BBCWAC, E2/787/1, Foreign Office Middle East Crisis, 1967, 5.

103. "THE BIG LIE: Case History of Charges of U.S. Involvement in Middle East Crisis," NARA, USIA, RG 306, entry P 160, Special Reports: 1953–1997, container 23, ARC 5664216, S-6-67, 11.

104. External Services Branch, Foreign, Middle East Crisis, "Audience Research Radio Organizations Basic Data Asia and the Middle East, A-H," June 7, 1967, BBC Archive, E3/996/1, 5

105. "Memo from CIA to White House Situation Room," June 7, 1967, LBJ, National Security File, National Security Council Histories, Middle East Crisis, May 12–June 19, 1967, box 18, vol. 5, tabs 170–73. In later memos, the CIA notes that there is no threat of Soviet intervention in the war. They also note Israel's disappointment at the lack of US support.

106. "THE BIG LIE: Case History of Charges of U.S. Involvement in Middle East Crisis," NARA, USIA, RG 306, entry P 160, Special Reports: 1953–1997, container 23, ARC 5664216, S-6-67, 8.

107. "Beseech Forces to Kill Enemy," FBIS, Cairo Domestic Service in Arabic, June 7, 1967, 16:52 GMT.

108. "British and American Neutrality in the Middle East War: Coverage in External Services News Bulletins," BBCWAC, E2/787/1, Foreign Office Middle East Crisis, 1967, 8.

109. Comment," FBIS, Damascus Domestic Service in Arabic, June 8, 1967, 03:45 GMT.

110. "Beseech Forces to Kill Enemy," FBIS, Cairo Domestic Service in Arabic, June 7, 1967, 16:52 GMT.

111. "British and American Neutrality in the Middle East War: Coverage in External Services News Bulletins," BBCWAC, E2/787/1, Foreign Office Middle East Crisis, 1967, 9.

112. "King Husayn Says Setback Worse than Expected," FBIS, Amman Domestic Service in Arabic, June 8, 1967, 15:32 GMT.

113. "THE BIG LIE: Case History of Charges of U.S. Involvement in Middle East Crisis," NARA, USIA, RG 306, entry P 160, Special Reports: 1953–1997, container 23, ARC 5664216, S-6-67, 3.

114. Ibid., 6.

115. Ibid., 15.

116. "British and American Neutrality in the Middle East War: Coverage in External Services News Bulletins," BBCWAC, E2/787/1, Foreign Office Middle East Crisis, 1967, 9.

117. "U.S. Admits Ship in Water Off Sinai Coast," FBIS, Cairo Domestic Service in Arabic, June 8, 1967, 17:30 GMT.

118. "British and American Neutrality in the Middle East War: Coverage in External Services News Bulletins," BBCWAC, E2/787/1, Foreign Office Middle East Crisis, 1967, 10.

119. "THE BIG LIE: Case History of Charges of U.S. Involvement in Middle East Crisis," NARA, USIA, RG 306, entry P 160, Special Reports: 1953–1997, container 23, ARC 5664216, S-6-67, 3.

120. Komitet po radioveshchaniiu i televideniiu pri SSSR, "Teksty peredach redaktsii veshaniia na arabskie strany/Sovetskaia tematika, 10 Iunia, 1967," GARF, f. 6903, op. 25, d. 1579, l. n/a.

121. "Abd an-Nasir Speech Announcing his Resignation," FBIS, Cairo Domestic Service in Arabic, June 7, 1967, 16:43 GMT. The *Sunday Times* article was written by Anthony Cowdy and entitled, "Britain Nails the Big Lie." A copy of it is in this same folder in the BBWAC.

122. USIA Office of Policy and Research, "Broadcasting Points," August 9, 1967, LBJ, National Security File Agency File, box 75.

123. "THE BIG LIE: Case History of Charges of U.S. Involvement in Middle East Crisis," NARA, USIA, RG 306, entry P 160, Special Reports: 1953–1997, container 23, ARC 5664216, S-6-67, 4.

124. Ibid., 5.

125. "Arabic Service, Listener Correspondence Reports," BBCWAC, E3/189/2.

126. "British and American Neutrality in the Middle East War: Coverage in External Services News Bulletins," July 6, 1967, Foreign Office: Middle East Crisis, BBCWAC, E2/787/1, 11.

127. Memo by Sir Denis Greenhill, Deputy Under-Secretary of State, Foreign Office, June 19, 1967, Foreign Office: Middle East Crisis, BBCWAC, E2/787/1, 1.

128. "British and American Neutrality in the Middle East War: Coverage in External Services News Bulletins," July 6, 1967, Foreign Office: Middle East Crisis, BBCWAC, E2/787/1, 12.

129. "Another Possible Outline," June 14, 1967, LBJ, National Security File, National Security Council Histories, Middle East Crisis, May 12–June 19, 1967, box 18, vol. 5, tabs 170–73.

130. Fouad Ajami, "The End of Pan-Arabism," *Foreign Affairs*, December 1, 1978, 355–73; N. Y. Hitti, "Al'amal al'arabi ba'ada alhazimah," in *Ḥarb Yunyu 1967 Ba'da alhazimah*, ed. L. Al-Kholi (Cairo: Ahram, 1997), 196–207.

CONCLUSION

1. Said, *Harb al'iidhaeat Alsiriyati*.

2. Leonard Marx, LBJ Archive, Administrative History, USIA, vol. 1, box 1, 5-111.

3. Boyd, *Broadcasting in the Arab World*, 331–32.

4. McAlister, *Epic Encounters*, 269.

5. Citino, *Envisioning the Arab Future*, 275.

6. Michel Foucault, *The Foucault Reader*, ed. Paul Rabinow (New York: Pantheon, 1984). See his essay "Nietzsche, Genealogy, History."

7. Katherine McKittrick, ed., *Sylvia Wynter: On Being Human as Praxis* (Durham, NC: Duke University Press, 2015); Frantz Fanon, *Black Skin White Masks: The Experiences of a Black Man in a White World* (New York: Grove Press, 1967); Gramsci, *Selections from the Prison Notebooks*; and Aimé Césaire, *Discourse on Colonialism*, trans. Joan Pinkham (New York: Monthly Review Press, 2001).

8. Gramsci, *Selections from the Prison Notebooks*, 242.

9. Fanon, *Black Skin White Masks*.

10. Ferris, *Nasser's Gamble*, 295.

11. Dipesh Chakrabarty, "Legacies of Bandung: Decolonization and the Politics of Culture," in *Making a World after Empire: The Bandung Moment and Its Political Afterlives*, ed. Christopher Lee (Athens: Ohio University Press, 2010), 46.

12. Charles Hirschkind, *The Ethical Soundscape: Cassette Sermons and Islamic Counterpublics* (New York: Columbia University Press, 2009).

13. Roxanne Lynn Doty, "Aporia: A Critical Exploration of the Agent-Structure Problematique in International Relations Theory," *European Journal of International Relations* 3, no. 3 (September 1, 1997): 378.

BIBLIOGRAPHY

Abdulrahman, Yacoub Haider. "United Nations' Role in the Palestinian-Israeli Conflict, 1947–1950." PhD diss., Golden Gate University, 1990.Abou-El-Fadl, Reem. "Neutralism Made Positive: Egyptian Anti-Colonialism on the Road to Bandung." *British Journal of Middle Eastern Studies* 42, no. 2 (2014): 219–40.

Abrahamian, Ervand. "Ali Shariati: Ideologue of the Iranian Revolution." *Merip Reports* 102 (February 1982): 24–28.

Abu Nu'aym al-Isfahani. *Sifat Al-Janna*. 3 vols. Edited by 'Ali Rida b. 'Abdallah b. 'Ali Rida. Beirut: Dar al-Ma'mun li-l-Turath, 1995.

Abu-Rabi', Ibrahim M. *Contemporary Arab Thought: Studies in Post-1967 Arab Intellectual History*. London: Pluto Press, 2004.

Aburish, Said K. *A Brutal Friendship: The West and the Arab Elite*. New York: St. Martin's Griffin, 1998.

Ajami, Fouad. *The Arab Predicament: Arab Political Thought and Practice since 1967*. 2nd ed. Cambridge: Cambridge University Press, 1992.

———. "The End of Pan-Arabism." *Foreign Affairs*, December 1, 1978.

Alahmed, Anas. "Voice of the Arabs Radio: Its Effects and Political Power during the Nasser Era (1953–1967)." SSRN Scholarly Paper. Rochester, NY, March 12, 2011.

'Alami, Musa al-. *'Ibrat Filastin (The Lesson of Palestine)*. Beirut: n.p., 1949.

Aldrich, Richard J., ed. *British Intelligence, Strategy and the Cold War, 1945–51*. London: Routledge, 1992.

———. *The Hidden Hand*. Woodstock, NY: Overlook Books, 2003.

———. "Putting Culture into the Cold War: The Cultural Relations Department (CRD) and British Covert Information Warfare." *Intelligence and National Security* 18, no. 2 (June 1, 2003): 109–33.

Al-Naqqash, R. *Naguib Nahfouz: Safahat Min Mudhakkiratihi Wa Adwa' Jadida 'ala Adabiha Wa Hayatihi* [Naguib Mahfouz: New pages of his memoirs and new highlights on his literature and life]. Cairo: Ahram, 1998.

Anderson, Philip. "'Summer Madness': The Crisis in Syria, August–October 1957." *British Journal of Middle Eastern Studies* 22, nos. 1/2 (1995): 21–42.

Armbrust, Walter. *Mass Culture and Modernism in Egypt*. Cambridge: Cambridge University Press, 1996.

Ashton, Nigel John. *Eisenhower, Macmillan and the Problem of Nasser: Anglo-American Relations and Arab Nationalism, 1955–59*. New York: Palgrave Macmillan, 1996.

———. "The Hijacking of a Pact: The Formation of the Baghdad Pact and Anglo-American Tensions in the Middle East, 1955–1958." *Review of International Studies* 19, no. 2 (April 1993): 123–37.

Austin, J. L. *How to Do Things with Words*. Edited by J. O. Urmson. Eastford, CT: Martino Fine Books, 2018.

Bakhtin, M. M. *The Dialogic Imagination: Four Essays*. Edited by Michael Holquist. Translated by Caryl Emerson. Austin: University of Texas Press, 1981.

Barari, Hassan A. *Israeli Politics and the Middle East Peace Process, 1988–2002*. London: Routledge, 2004.

Barghoorn, Frederick Charles. *Soviet Cultural Offensive*. Princeton, NJ: Princeton University Press, 2015.

———. *Soviet Foreign Propaganda*. Princeton, NJ: Princeton University Press, 1964.

Baumann, Mario. "'Propaganda Fights' and 'Disinformation Campaigns': The Discourse on Information Warfare in Russia-West Relations." *Contemporary Politics* 26, no. 3 (May 26, 2020): 288–307.

Beeley, Harold. "The Changing Role of British International Propaganda." *Annals of the American Academy of Political and Social Science* 398, no. 1 (November 1, 1971): 124–29.

Beinin, Joel. "Labor, Capital, and the State in Nasserist Egypt, 1952–1961." *International Journal of Middle East Studies* 21, no. 1 (1989): 71–90.

Belli, Mériam N. *An Incurable Past: Nasser's Egypt Then and Now*. Gainesville: University Press of Florida, 2017.

Ben-Dror, Elad. "The Arab Struggle against Partition: The International Arena of Summer 1947." *Middle Eastern Studies* 43, no. 2 (2007): 259–93.

Bennett, Huw. "'Words Are Cheaper than Bullets': Britain's Psychological Warfare in the Middle East, 1945–60." *Intelligence and National Security* 34, no. 7 (November 10, 2019): 925–44.

Blackwell, Stephen. "Britain, the United States and the Syrian Crisis, 1957." *Diplomacy & Statecraft* 11, no. 3 (November 1, 2000): 139–58.

Bogart, Leo, and Agnes Bogart. *Cool Words, Cold War: A New Look at USIA's Premises for Propaganda*. Washington, DC: American University Press, 1995.

Borstelmann, Thomas. *The Cold War and the Color Line: American Race Relations in the Global Arena*. Cambridge, MA: Harvard University Press, 2001.

Bourdieu, Pierre, John B. (John Brookshire) Thompson, and Gino Raymond. *Language and Symbolic Power*. Cambridge, MA: Harvard University Press, 1991.

Bourgault, Louise M. *Mass Media in Sub-Saharan Africa*. Bloomington: Indiana University Press, 1995.

Bowker, Robert. *Palestinian Refugees: Mythology, Identity, and the Search for Peace*. Boulder, CO: Lynne Rienner, 2003.Boyd, Douglas A. *Broadcasting in the Arab*

World: A Survey of the Electronic Media in the Middle East. Ames: Iowa State
University Press, 1993.

———. "Development of Egypt's Radio: 'Voice of the Arabs' under Nasser." *Journalism Quarterly* 52, no. 4 (Winter 1975): 645.

———. "Egyptian Radio: Tool of Political and National Development." Journalism
Monographs No. 48. Association for Education in Journalism, February 1, 1977.

———. "Hebrew-Language Clandestine Radio Broadcasting during the British Palestine Mandate." *Journal of Radio Studies* 6, no. 1 (1999): 101–15.

———. "Sharq Al-Adna/The Voice of Britain: The UK's 'Secret' Arabic Radio Station and Suez War Propaganda Disaster." *Gazette* (Leiden, Netherlands) 65, no. 6
(December 1, 2003): 443–55.

Boyer, Anne. *Soviet Foreign Propaganda: An Annotated Bibliography*. [Washington,
DC]: US Information Agency, Agency Library, 1971.

Braun, Lindsay Frederick. "Suez Reconsidered: Anthony Eden's Orientalism and the
Suez Crisis." *Historian* 65, no. 3 (2003): 535–61.

Briggs, Asa. *The History of Broadcasting in the United Kingdom*. Vol. 2, *The Golden
Age of Wireless*. Oxford: Oxford University Press, 1995.

———. *The History of Broadcasting in the United Kingdom*. Vol. 5, *Competition*.
Oxford: Oxford University Press, 1995.

———. *The War of Words*. Oxford: Oxford University Press, 1970.

Brooks, Jeffrey. *Thank You, Comrade Stalin! Soviet Public Culture from Revolution to
Cold War*. Princeton, NJ: Princeton University Press, 2000.

———. "When the Cold War Did Not End: The Soviet Peace Offensive of 1953 and
the American Response." Occasional Papers, Wilson Center, no. 278. 2000.

Burkhalter, Thomas. *Local Music Scenes and Globalization: Transnational Platforms
in Beirut*. New York: Routledge, 2015.

Calvert, John. *Sayyid Qutb and the Origins of Radical Islamism*. New York: Oxford
University Press, 2018.

Carruthers, Susan L. *Winning Hearts and Minds: British Governments, the Media
and Colonial Counter-Insurgency, 1944–1960*. London: UNKNO, 1995.

Castillo, Greg. *Cold War on the Home Front: The Soft Power of Midcentury Design*.
Minneapolis: University of Minnesota Press, 2010.

Césaire, Aimé. *Discourse on Colonialism*. Translated by Joan Pinkham. New York:
Monthly Review Press, 2001.

Cesarani, David. *Major Farran's Hat: Murder, Scandal and Britain's War against Jewish Terrorism, 1945–1948*. London: William Heinemann, 2009.

Chakrabarty, Dipesh. "The Legacies of Bandung: Decolonization and the Politics of
Culture." In *Making a World after Empire: The Bandung Moment and Its Political Afterlives*, edited by Christopher Lee, 45–68. Athens: Ohio University Press,
2010.

Chernus, Ira. "The Word 'Peace' as a Weapon of (Cold) War." *Peace Review* 10, no. 4
(December 1998): 605.

Chomsky, Noam. *The Fateful Triangle: The United States, Israel, and the Palestinians*.
Boston: Noontide Press, 1983.

Chou, Shih-Yu. "Constructing National Interests: Narrating the Suez Crisis." *International Critical Thought* 8, no. 3 (July 3, 2018): 453–67.

Citino, Dr. Nathan J. *Envisioning the Arab Future: Modernization in US-Arab Relations, 1945–1967*. Cambridge: Cambridge University Press, 2017.

Cohen, Lizabeth. *A Consumers' Republic: The Politics of Mass Consumption in Postwar America*. New York: Vintage, 2008.

Collier, Simon. "Countering Communist and Nasserite Propaganda: The Foreign Office Information Research Department in the Middle East and Africa, 1954–1963." PhD diss., University of Hertfordshire, 2013.

Connolly, William E. "The Evangelical-Capitalist Resonance Machine." *Political Theory* 33, no. 6 (2005): 869–86.

Conquest, Robert. *The Great Terror: A Reassessment*. New York: Oxford University Press, 1990.

Cook, David. *Martyrdom in Islam*. Cambridge: Cambridge University Press, 2007.

Copeland, Miles. *The Game of Nations: The Amorality of Power Politics*. New York: Simon & Schuster, 1970.

Cowherd, Raymond G. "The Soviet Peace Offensive." *Current History* 19, no. 109 (1950): 129–34.

Cull, Nicholas J. *The Cold War and the United States Information Agency: American Propaganda and Public Diplomacy, 1945–1989*. Cambridge: Cambridge University Press, 2009.

Cull, Nicholas John, David Holbrook Culbert, and David Welch. *Propaganda and Mass Persuasion: A Historical Encyclopedia, 1500 to the Present*. Santa Barbara: ABC-CLIO, 2003.

Currie, Gregory. "Why Irony Is Pretence." In *The Architecture of the Imagination: New Essays on Pretence, Possibility, and Fiction*, edited by Shaun Nichols, 111–33. Oxford: Oxford University Press, 2006.

Dalin, David. *Icon of Evil: Hitler's Mufti and the Rise of Radical Islam*. New York: Routledge, 2017.

Danchin, Peter. "Muslims in a Secular State: Islamic Law and Constitutions Islam in America." *University of Maryland Law Journal of Race, Religion, Gender and Class* 11, no. 1 (January 1, 2011): 59.

Darwin, John. *Britain and Decolonisation: The Retreat from Empire in the Post-War World*. Houndmills, Basingstoke: Palgrave, 1988.

Dawisha, A. I. "The Role of Propaganda in Egypt's Arab Policy, 1955–1967." *International Relations* 5, no. 2 (1975): 897–907.

Deery, Phillip. "Confronting the Cominform: George Orwell and the Cold War Offensive of the Information Research Department, 1948–50." *Labour History* 73, no. 1 (November 1, 1997): 219–26.

Defty, Andrew. *Britain, America and Anti-Communist Propaganda, 1945–53: The Information Research Department*. London: Routledge, 2004.

Derrida, Jacques. *Writing and Difference*. Translated by Alan Bass. Chicago: University of Chicago Press, 2017.

Dijk, Teun van. "El Análisis Crítico del Discurso." *Anthropos*, no. 186 (October 1999): 23–36.

Dillon, Anne. *The Construction of Martyrdom in the English Catholic Community, 1535–1603*. London: Routledge, 2016.

Doran, Michael. *Pan-Arabism before Nasser: Egyptian Power Politics and the Palestine Question*. New York: Oxford University Press, 2002.

Dorril, Stephen. *MI6: Inside the Covert World of Her Majesty's Secret Intelligence Service*. New York: Free Press, 2000.

Doty, Roxanne Lynn. "Aporia: A Critical Exploration of the Agent-Structure Problematique in International Relations Theory." *European Journal of International Relations* 3, no. 3 (September 1, 1997): 365–92.

Drysdale, Alasdair, and Raymond A. Hinnebusch. *Syria and the Middle East Peace Process*. New York: Council on Foreign Relations, 1991.

Dudziak, Mary. *Cold War Civil Rights: Race and the Image of American Democracy*. Princeton, NJ: Princeton University Press, 2000.

Dunbar, Brooke S. "Connection and Disconnection in Online Spaces: An Analysis of Semantic, Latent, and Cultural Themes across Reddit." PhD diss., Regent University, n. d.

Eayrs, James ed. *The Commonwealth and Suez a Documentary Survey*. London: Oxford University Press, 1964.

Ebon, Martin. *The Soviet Propaganda Machine*. New York: McGraw-Hill, 1987.

Elpeleg, Z., and Shmuel Himelstein. *The Grand Mufti: Haj Amin al-Hussaini, Founder of the Palestinian National Movement*. Portland, OR: Frank Cass, 1993.

Engelhardt, Tom. *The End of Victory Culture: Cold War America and the Disillusioning of a Generation*. New York: Basic Books, 1995.

Evensen, Bruce J. "Truman, Palestine and the Cold War." *Middle Eastern Studies* 28, no. 1 (1992): 120–56.

Fahmy, Ziad. *Street Sounds: Listening to Everyday Life in Modern Egypt*. Stanford, CA: Stanford University Press, 2020.

Fainberg, Dina. *Cold War Correspondents: Soviet and American Reporters on the Ideological Frontlines*. Baltimore, MD: Johns Hopkins University Press, 2021.

Fanon, Frantz. *Black Skin White Masks: The Experiences of a Black Man in a White World*. New York: Grove Press, 1967.

Faulkner, William. "Faith or Fear." *Atlantic*, August 1, 1953.

Feiler, Gil. "Housing Policy in Egypt." *Middle Eastern Studies* 28, no. 2 (April 1, 1992): 295–312.

Fergusson, Bernard. *The Trumpet in the Hall, 1930–1958*. London: Collins, 1970.

Ferris, Jesse. *Nasser's Gamble: How Intervention in Yemen Caused the Six-Day War and the Decline of Egyptian Power*. Princeton, NJ: Princeton University Press, 2012.

Flicke, W. F. *War Secrets in the Ether*. Vol. 2. Laguna Hills, CA: Aegean Park Press, 1977.

Foucault, Michel. *The Foucault Reader*. Edited by Paul Rabinow. New York: Pantheon, 1984.

Franzén, Johan. "Losing Hearts and Minds in Iraq: Britain, Cold War Propaganda and the Challenge of Communism, 1945–58." *Historical Research* 83, no. 222 (2010): 747–62.

Frishkopf, Michael, ed. *Music and Media in the Arab World*. Cairo: American University in Cairo Press, 2010.

Fursenko, A. A., ed. *Prezidium TsK KPSS: 1954–1964: V Trekh Tomakh*. Vol. 1. Moscow: ROSSPEN, 2015.

Fursenko, A. A., and Timothy J. Naftali. *Khrushchev's Cold War: The Inside Story of an American Adversary*. New York: Norton, 2006.

Fussell, Paul. *The Great War and Modern Memory*. Oxford: Oxford University Press, 2013.

Gary, Brett. *The Nervous Liberals: Propaganda Anxieties from World War I to the Cold War*. Columbia Studies in Contemporary American History. New York: Columbia University Press, 1999.

Gat, Moshe. "Britain and Israel before and after the Six Day War, June 1967: From Support to Hostility." *Contemporary British History* 18, no. 1 (March 1, 2004): 54–77.

———. "Nasser and the Six Day War, 5 June 1967: A Premeditated Strategy or an Inexorable Drift to War?" *Israel Affairs* 11, no. 4 (December 1, 2005): 608–35.

Gerges, Fawaz A. *Making the Arab World: Nasser, Qutb, and the Clash That Shaped the Middle East*. Princeton, NJ: Princeton University Press, 2019.

Gharabaghi, Hadi. "Documentary Diplomacy and Audiovisual Modernization: A Cold War Genealogy of Arab Cinema during the 1950s through American Declassified Archives." In *Cinema of the Arab World: Contemporary Directions in Theory and Practice*, edited by Terri Ginsberg and Chris Lippard, 3–43. Global Cinema. Cham: Springer International Publishing, 2020.

Gilman, Daniel J. *Cairo Pop: Youth Music in Contemporary Egypt*. Minneapolis: University of Minnesota Press, 2014.

Ginor, Isabella, and Gideon Remez. *Foxbats over Dimona: The Soviets' Nuclear Gamble in the Six-Day War*. New Haven, CT: Yale University Press, 2007.

Goedde, Petra. *The Politics of Peace: A Global Cold War History*. New York: Oxford University Press, 2019.

Goldstein, Yossi. "The Six Day War: The War That No One Wanted." *Israel Affairs* 24, no. 5 (September 3, 2018): 767–84.

Gramsci, Antonio. *Selections from the Prison Notebooks*. Edited by Quintin Hoare and Geoffrey Nowell Smith. 1971. Reprint, London: International Publishers, 1989.

Grazia, Victoria de. *Irresistible Empire: America's Advance through Twentieth-Century Europe*. Cambridge, MA: Belknap Press, 2006.

Grossman, Vasiliĭ Semenovich. *Vse techet. . . .* Frankfurt am Main: Posev, 1974.

Gurevich', L. B. *Siriia, Palestina, Mesopotamiia: (Mandatnye strany)*. Leningrad: Nauka i skola, 1925.

Gurko-Kriazin, Vladimir Aleksandrovich. *Natsional'no-osvoboditel'noe dvizhenie na Blizhnem Vostoke: Siriia i Palestina, Kilikiia, Mesopotamiia i Egipet*. Moscow: Mospoligraf, 1923.

Hadidi, Salah al-Din al-. *Shahid 'ala Harb al-Yaman*. Cairo: Maktabat Madbuli, 1984.

Hahn, Peter L. *Crisis and Crossfire the United States and the Middle East since 1945*. Washington, DC: Potomac Books, Inc., 2005.

Hakim, Tawfiq, al-. *The Return of Consciousness*. London: Palgrave Macmillan, 1974.

Halperin, Eran, Alexandra G. Russell, Kali H. Trzesniewski, James J. Gross, and Carol S. Dweck. "Promoting the Middle East Peace Process by Changing Beliefs about Group Malleability." *Science* 333, no. 6050 (September 23, 2011): 1767–69.

Hamilton, Shane. *Supermarket USA: Food and Power in the Cold War Farms Race*. New Haven, CT: Yale University Press, 2018.

Haraway, Donna. *Simians, Cyborgs, and Women: The Reinvention of Nature*. New York: Routledge, 2015.

Harris, William. *Lebanon: A History*. Oxford: Oxford University Press, 2012.

Hart, Justin. *Empire of Ideas: The Origins of Public Diplomacy and the Transformation of U.S. Foreign Policy*. Oxford: Oxford University Press, 2013.

Haslam, N., L. Rothschild, and D. Ernst. "Essentialist Beliefs about Social Categories." *British Journal of Social Psychology* 39, pt. 1 (March 2000): 113–27.

Hatem, Mervat F. "Economic and Political Liberation in Egypt and the Demise of State Feminism." *International Journal of Middle East Studies* 24, no. 2 (1992): 231–51.

Haugbolle, Sune. "The New Arab Left and 1967." *British Journal of Middle Eastern Studies* 44, no. 4 (October 2, 2017): 497–512.

Haykal, Muhammad Hasanayn. *Milaffat Al-Suways: Harb Al-Thalathin Sanatan*. Cairo: Markaz al-Ahram lil-Tarjamah wa-al-Nashr, 1986.

Heikal, Mohamed. *Al-Tariq Ella Ramadan* [The road to Ramadan]. Beirut: Dal al-Nahar, 1975.

Henderson, John W. *The United States Information Agency*. New York: Praeger, 1969.

Hirschkind, Charles. *The Ethical Soundscape: Cassette Sermons and Islamic Counterpublics*. New York: Columbia University Press, 2009.

Hitti, N. Y. "Al-'Amal al-'Arabi Ba'ada al-Hazimab" [The Arab action after the defeat]. In *Harb Yunyu 1967 Ba'ada al-Hazimab* [The June 1967 war after 30 years], edited by L. Al-Kholi, 196–207. Cairo: Ahram, 1997.

Hixson, Walter L. *Parting the Curtain: Propaganda, Culture, and the Cold War, 1945–1961*. New York: Palgrave Macmillan, 1998.

Ignatieff, Michael. "The Nightmare from Which We Are Trying to Awake." In *The Warrior's Honor: Ethnic War and the Modern Conscience*, 166–90. London: Chatto and Windus, 1998.

Jenks, John. *British Propaganda and News Media in the Cold War*. Edinburgh: Edinburgh University Press, 2006.

Johnson, Bethan. "The Role of Animals in National Socialist Propaganda." *Fair Observer* (blog). January 5, 2022. www.fairobserver.com/world-news/the-role-of-animals-in-national-socialist-propaganda-87653/.

Johnston, Timothy. *Being Soviet: Identity, Rumour, and Everyday Life under Stalin, 1939–53*. Oxford: Oxford University Press, 2011.

Jones, Matthew. "The 'Preferred Plan': The Anglo-American Working Group Report on Covert Action in Syria, 1957." *Intelligence and National Security* 19, no. 3 (September 1, 2004): 401–15.

Jowett, Garth, and Victoria O'Donnell. *Propaganda and Persuasion*. 2nd ed. Newbury Park, CA: Sage Publications, 1992.

Kassab, Elizabeth Suzanne. *Contemporary Arab Thought: Cultural Critique in Comparative Perspective*. New York: Columbia University Press, 2009.

Keating, Rex. *The Trumpets of Tutankhamun: Adventures of a Radio Pioneer in the Middle East*. London: Fisher Miller, 1999.

Kedourie, Elie. *The Chatham House Version: And Other Middle Eastern Studies*. Chicago: Ivan R. Dee, 2004.

Kemper, Michael, and Artemy M. Kalinovsky, eds. *Reassessing Orientalism: Interlocking Orientologies during the Cold War*. London: Routledge, 2015.

Kenez, Peter. *A History of the Soviet Union from the Beginning to the End*. 2nd ed. New York: Cambridge University Press, 2006.

Kennedy, Gillian. *From Independence to Revolution: Egypt's Islamists and the Contest for Power*. New York: Hurst, 2017.

Kerr, Malcolm H. *The Arab Cold War: Gamal Abd Al Nasir and His Rivals, 1958 to 1970*. 3rd ed. New York: Oxford University Press, 2020.

Keynes, John Maynard. *The Economic Consequences of the Peace*. Seattle: CreateSpace Independent Publishing Platform, 2012.

Khaled, Leila. *My People Shall Live: The Autobiography of a Revolutionary*. London: Hodder and Stoughton, 1973.

Kirasirova, Masha. *The Eastern International: Arabs, Central Asians, and Jews in the Soviet Union's Anticolonial Empire*. New York: Oxford University Press, 2024.

Kirk, George. "The Syrian Crisis of 1957—Fact and Fiction." *International Affairs (Royal Institute of International Affairs 1944–)* 36, no. 1 (1960): 58–61.

Kwon, Heonik. *The Other Cold War*. Columbia Studies in International and Global History. New York: Columbia University Press, 2010.

Kyle, Keith. *Suez: Britain's End of Empire in the Middle East*. London: I. B. Tauris, 2011.

Laclau, Ernesto, and Chantal Mouffe. *Hegemony and Socialist Strategy: Towards a Radical Democratic Politics*. 2nd ed. London: Verso, 2014.

LaFeber, Walter. *America, Russia, and the Cold War, 1945–2006*. 10th ed. Boston: McGraw-Hill, 2008.

Lange, Christian. "Eternal Sunshine of the Spotless Mind: Light and Luminous Being in Islamic Theology." *Critical Research on Religion* 9, no. 2 (August 1, 2021): 142–56.

———. *Paradise and Hell in Islamic Traditions*. New York: Cambridge University Press, 2015.

Laqueur, Walter Z. *Communism and Nationalism in the Middle East*. 3rd ed. London: Routledge & Kegan Paul, 1956.

Laron, Guy. *Origins of the Suez Crisis: Postwar Development Diplomacy and the Struggle over Third World Industrialization, 1945–1956*. Washington, DC:

Woodrow Wilson Center Press; Baltimore, MD: Johns Hopkins University Press, 2013.

Larson, Deborah Welch. *Anatomy of Mistrust: U.S.-Soviet Relations during the Cold War*. Cornell Studies in Security Affairs. Ithaca, NY: Cornell University Press, 1997.

Lashmar, Paul, and James Oliver. *Britain's Secret Propaganda War*. Stroud, Gloucestershire: Sutton Publishing, 1999.

Lee, Christopher, ed. *Making a World after Empire: The Bandung Moment and Its Political Afterlives*. Athens: Ohio University Press, 2010.

Lee, J. M. "British Cultural Diplomacy and the Cold War: 1946–61." *Diplomacy & Statecraft* 9, no. 1 (March 1, 1998): 112–34.

Leerssen, Joep. *National Thought in Europe: A Cultural History*. Amsterdam: Amsterdam University Press, 2010.

Lefebvre, Henri, Stuart Elden, Neil Brenner, and Gerald Moore. *State, Space, World: Selected Essays*. Minneapolis: University of Minnesota Press, 2009.

Leffler, Melvyn P. *For the Soul of Mankind: The United States, the Soviet Union, and the Cold War*. New York: Hill and Wang, 2008.

Lefort, Claude. *The Political Forms of Modern Society: Bureaucracy, Democracy, Totalitarianism*. Edited by David Thompson. Cambridge, MA: MIT Press, 1986.

Leighton, Marian Kirsch. *Soviet Propaganda as a Foreign Policy Tool*. New York: Freedom House, 1990.

Lenin, V. I. *Polnoye sobraniie sochinenii: Pyat'desyat pervyi tom*. N.p.: Izdatel'stvo "Prospekt," 2013.

Lesch, David W. "The 1957 American-Syrian Crisis: Globalist Policy in a Regional Reality." In *The Middle East and the United States: A Historical and Political Reassessment*, edited by David W. Lesch, 4th ed., 133–56. Boulder, CO: Westview Press, 2007.

———. *Syria and the United States: Eisenhower's Cold War in the Middle East*. Boulder, CO: Westview Press, 1992.

Little, Douglas. *American Orientalism: The United States and the Middle East since 1945*. Chapel Hill: University of North Carolina Press, 2009.

———. "A Puppet in Search of a Puppeteer? The United States, King Hussein, and Jordan, 1953–1970." *International History Review* 17, no. 3 (1995): 512–44.

Love, Kennett. *Suez: The Twice-Fought War; A History*. New York: McGraw-Hill, 1969.

Lovell, Stephen. *Russia in the Microphone Age: A History of Soviet Radio, 1919–1970*. Oxford Studies in Modern European History. Oxford: Oxford University Press, 2015.

Lucas, W. Scott. *Divided We Stand: Britain, the US and the Suez Crisis*. London: Sceptre, 1996.

Lucas, W. Scott, and C J. Morris. "A Very British Crusade: The Information Research Department and the Origins of the Cold War." In *British Intelligence, Strategy and the Cold War*, edited by Richard J. Aldrich. London: Routledge, 1992.

Lynn, Denise M. *Where Is Juliet Stuart Poyntz? Gender, Spycraft, and Anti-Stalinism in the Early Cold War.* Amherst: University of Massachusetts Press, 2021.

Maatouk, Tamara. "On the Heels of 1967: Chahine, Cinema, and Emotional Response(s) to the Defeat." *International Journal of Middle East Studies* 55, no. 1 (February 2023): 25–42.

Madfai, Madiha Rashid al. *Jordan, the United States and the Middle East Peace Process, 1974–1991.* Cambridge: Cambridge University Press, 1993. Magnúsdóttir, Rósa. *Enemy Number One: The United States of America in Soviet Ideology and Propaganda, 1945–1959.* New York: Oxford University Press, 2018.

Marklund, Andreas. "The Manly Sacrifice: Martial Manliness and Patriotic Martyrdom in Nordic Propaganda during the Great Northern War." *Gender & History* 25, no. 1 (April 2013): 150–69.

Marshall, George. "The Marshall Plan Speech." Harvard University, June 5, 1947. www.marshallfoundation.org/the-marshall-plan/speech/.

Marx, Karl. *Capital: A Critique of Political Economy.* Vol. 1. Seattle: CreateSpace Independent Publishing Platform, 2010.

Mattar, Philip. "The Mufti of Jerusalem and the Politics of Palestine." *Middle East Journal* 42, no. 2 (1988): 227–40.

McAlister, Melani. *Epic Encounters: Culture, Media, and U.S. Interests in the Middle East since 1945.* Berkeley: University of California Press, 2005.

McCauley, Brian. "Hungary and Suez, 1956: The Limits of Soviet and American Power." *Journal of Contemporary History* 16, no. 4 (1981): 777–800.

McDowall, David. *Palestine and Israel: The Uprising and Beyond.* Berkeley: University of California Press, 1991.

McKittrick, Katherine, ed. *Sylvia Wynter: On Being Human as Praxis.* Durham, NC: Duke University Press, 2015.

McLaughlin, Greg, and Stephen Baker. *The Propaganda of Peace: The Role of Media and Culture in the Northern Ireland Peace Process.* Bristol: Intellect Books, 2010.

McNamara, Robert. *Britain, Nasser and the Balance of Power in the Middle East, 1952–1977: From the Egyptian Revolution to the Six Day War.* London: Routledge, 2019.

McNicholas, Anthony. "Sharq Al-Adna: Covert British Radio and the Development of Arab Broadcasting." *Middle East Journal of Culture and Communication* 13, no. 3 (November 27, 2020): 237–55.

Metzgar, Emily T. "Public Diplomacy, Smith-Mundt and the American Public." *Communication Law and Policy* 17, no. 1 (December 1, 2012): 67–101.

Miller, Rory. *Britain, Palestine and Empire: The Mandate Years.* London: Routledge, 2016.

Morris, Benny. *The Birth of the Palestinian Refugee Problem, 1947–49.* Cambridge: Cambridge University Press, 1989.

Musleh-Motut, Nawal. "The Development of Pan-Arab Broadcasting under Authoritarian Regimes: A Comparison of Sawt Al-Arab ('Voice of the Arabs') and Al Jazeera News Channel." Master's thesis, Simon Fraser University, 2006.

Nagorski, Zygmunt. "Soviet International Propaganda: Its Role, Effectiveness, and Future." *Annals of the American Academy of Political and Social Science* 398 (1971): 130–39.

Ninkovich, Frank A. *The Diplomacy of Ideas: U.S. Foreign Policy and Cultural Relations, 1938–1950*. Cambridge: Cambridge University Press, 1981.

———. *U.S. Information Policy and Cultural Diplomacy*. New York: Foreign Policy Association, 1996.

Omran, A. R., and F. Roudi. "The Middle East Population Puzzle." *Population Bulletin* 48, no. 1 (July 1993): 1–40.

Oren, Michael B. *Six Days of War: June 1967 and the Making of the Modern Middle East*. New York: Presidio Press, 2003.

———. "A Winter of Discontent: Britain's Crisis in Jordan, December 1955–March 1956." *International Journal of Middle East Studies* 22, no. 2 (1990): 171–84.

Osgood, Kenneth Alan. *Total Cold War: Eisenhower's Secret Propaganda Battle at Home and Abroad*. Lawrence: University Press of Kansas, 2006.

Ovendale, Ritchie. *Britain, the United States, and the Transfer of Power in the Middle East, 1945–1962*. London: Leicester University Press, 1996.

Partner, Peter. *Arab Voices: The BBC Arabic Service, 1938–1988*. London: British Broadcasting Corp., 1988.

Peacock, Margaret. *Innocent Weapons: The Soviet and American Politics of Childhood in the Cold War*. New Cold War History. Chapel Hill: University of North Carolina Press, 2014.

Penslar, Derek Jonathan. "Transmitting Jewish Culture: Radio in Israel." *Jewish Social Studies* 10, no. 1 (2003): 1–29.

Pirsein, Robert William. *The Voice of America: A History of the International Broadcasting Activities of the United States Government, 1940–1962*. Dissertations in Broadcasting. New York: Arno Press, 1979.

Pnina, Lahav. "The Suez Crisis of 1956 and Its Aftermath: A Comparative Study of Constitutions, Use of Force, Diplomacy and International Relations." *Boston University Law Review* 95 (2015): 1297–1354.

Podeh, Elie. "The Drift towards Neutrality: Egyptian Foreign Policy during the Early Nasserist Era, 1952–55." *Middle Eastern Studies*, December 6, 2006.

———. "The Perils of Ambiguity: The United States and the Baghdad Pact." In *The Middle East and the United States*, edited by David Lesch, 93–108. Boulder, CO: Westview Press, 2007.

———. *The Quest for Hegemony in the Arab World: The Struggle over the Baghdad Pact*. New York: Brill, 2022.

———. "The Struggle over Arab Hegemony after the Suez Crisis." *Middle Eastern Studies* 29, no. 1 (January 1, 1993): 91–110.

Podeh, Elie, and Onn Winckler, eds. *Rethinking Nasserism: Revolution and Historical Memory in Modern Egypt*. Gainesville: University Press of Florida, 2004.

Popper, Karl. "The Conspiracy Theory of Society." In *Conspiracy Theories: The Philosophical Debate*, edited by David Coady, 13–16. London: Routledge, 2019.

Potter, Simon. *Broadcasting Empire: The BBC and the British World, 1922–1970*. Oxford: Oxford University Press, 2012.

Quṭb, Sayyid. *This Religion of Islam*. Ishaat-e-Islam Trust. Delhi: Markazi Maktaba Islami, 1974.

Raleigh, Donald. "Languages of Power: How the Saratov Bolsheviks Imagined Their Enemies." *Slavic Review* 57, no. 2 (1998): 320–49.

Rawnsley, Gary D. "Cold War Radio in Crisis: The BBC Overseas Services, the Suez Crisis and the 1956 Hungarian . . . ." *Historical Journal of Film, Radio & Television* 16, no. 2 (June 1996): 197.

———, ed. *Cold-War Propaganda in the 1950s*. Houndmills, Basingstoke: Palgrave Macmillan, 1999.

———. "Overt and Covert: The Voice of Britain and Black Radio Broadcasting in the Suez Crisis, 1956." *Intelligence and National Security* 11, no. 3 (July 1, 1996): 497–522.

———. *Radio Diplomacy and Propaganda: The BBC and VOA in International Politics, 1956–64*. Studies in Diplomacy. New York: St. Martin's Press, 1996.

Riley, Barry. "The Marshall Plan Era." In *The Political History of American Food Aid: An Uneasy Benevolence*, edited by Barry Riley, 54–94. New York: Oxford University Press, 2017.

Roberts, Nicholas E. "Re-Remembering the Mandate: Historiographical Debates and Revisionist History in the Study of British Palestine." *History Compass* 9, no. 3 (2011): 215–30.

Ro'i, Yaacov, and Boris Morozov. *The Soviet Union and the June 1967 Six Day War*. Washington, DC: Woodrow Wilson Center Press; Stanford, CA: Stanford University Press, 2008.

Rolston, Bill. "When Everywhere Is Karbala: Murals, Martyrdom and Propaganda in Iran." *Memory Studies* 13, no. 1 (February 1, 2020): 3–23.

Rose, Clive. *The Soviet Propaganda Network: A Directory of Organisations Serving Soviet Foreign Policy*. London: Pinter Publishers, 1988.

Roth-Ey, Kristin. *Moscow Prime Time: How the Soviet Union Built the Media Empire That Lost the Cultural Cold War*. Ithaca, NY: Cornell University Press, 2011.

Rugh, William A. *Arab Mass Media: Newspapers, Radio, and Television in Arab Politics*. Westport, CT: Praeger, 2004.

Said, Ahmed. *Harb al'iidhaeat Alsiriyati . . . . 'abwab Jahanam, 1967*. Cairo: Maspiro, 2017.

———. "Huna Sawt al-Arab." *Albawwabat niuz*, May 5, 2018.

Said, Edward W. *Peace and Its Discontents: Essays on Palestine in the Middle East Peace Process*. New York: Knopf Doubleday, 2012.

Samuel, Edwin. *A Lifetime in Jerusalem: The Memoirs of the Second Viscount Samuel*. New York: Routledge, 1970.

Saunders, Frances Stonor. *The Cultural Cold War: The CIA and the World of Arts and Letters*. New York: New Press, 2000.

Scott, James C. *Domination and the Arts of Resistance: Hidden Transcripts*. New Haven, CT: Yale University Press, 1992.

Selim, Gehan. "Instituting Order: The Limitations of Nasser's Post-Colonial Planning Visions for Cairo in the Case of the Indigenous Quarter of Bulaq (1952–1970)." *Planning Perspectives* 29, no. 1 (January 2, 2014): 67–89.

Shaw, Tony. *Eden, Suez, and the Mass Media: Propaganda and Persuasion during the Suez Crisis*. London: I. B. Tauris, 1996.

———. "The Information Research Department of the British Foreign Office and the Korean War, 1950–53." *Journal of Contemporary History* 34, no. 2 (April 1, 1999): 263–81.

———. "Martyrs, Miracles, and Martians: Religion and Cold War Cinematic Propaganda in the 1950s." *Journal of Cold War Studies* 4, no. 2 (2002): 3–22.

Shepherd, Naomi. *Ploughing Sand: British Rule in Palestine, 1917–1948*. New Brunswick, NJ: Rutgers University Press, 2000.

Sherel', Aleksandr Arkad'yevich. *Audiokul'tura XX veka: Istoriia, esteticheskiie zakonomernosti, osobennosti vliianiia na auditoriiu*. Moscow: Progress-Traditsiya, 2004.

Shlaim, Avi. *Collusion across the Jordan: King Abdullah, the Zionist Movement and the Partition of Palestine*. Oxford: Clarendon Press, 1989.

———. *War and Peace in the Middle East: A Critique of American Policy*. New York: Whittle Books, 1994.

Simson, H. J. *British Rule, and Rebellion*. Salisbury, NC: Documentary Publications, 1977. First published 1937.

Sloterdijk, Peter, and Andreas Huyssen. *Critique of Cynical Reason*. Minneapolis: University of Minnesota Press, 1988.

Smith, Lyn. "Covert British Propaganda: The Information Research Department, 1947–77." *Millennium: Journal of International Studies* 9, no. 1 (1980): 68.

Smolansky, O. M. "Moscow and the Suez Crisis, 1956: A Reappraisal." *Political Science Quarterly* 80, no. 4 (1965): 581–605.

Smolkin, Victoria. *A Sacred Space Is Never Empty: A History of Soviet Atheism*. Woodstock, Oxfordshire: Princeton University Press, 2018.

Snyder, Alvin A. *Warriors of Disinformation: American Propaganda, Soviet Lies, and the Winning of the Cold War; An Insider's Account*. New York: Arcade Publishing, 1995.

Stanton, Andrea L. "Part of Imperial Communications." *Media History* 19, no. 4 (November 1, 2013): 421–35.

———. "Situating Radio in the Soundscape of Mandate Palestine." *Jerusalem Quarterly*, no. 86 (Summer 2021): 97–116.

———. *This Is Jerusalem Calling: State Radio in Mandate Palestine*. Austin: University of Texas Press, 2013.

———. "Who Heard What When: Learning from Radio Broadcasting Hours and Programs in Jerusalem." *International Journal of Middle East Studies* 48, no. 1 (February 2016): 141–45.

Stevens, Georgiana G. "Arab Neutralism and Bandung." *Middle East Journal* 11, no. 2 (1957): 139–52.

Stoyanovsky, Jacob. *The Mandate for Palestine: A Contribution to the Theory and Practice of International Mandates*. Westport, CT: Hyperion Press, 1979. First published 1928.

"The Strategy of Soviet Propaganda." In *Proceedings of the Academy of Political Sciences*, 214. New York: Columbia University, 1951.

Suri, Jeremi. *Power and Protest: Global Revolution and the Rise of Detente*. Cambridge, MA: Harvard University Press, 2003.

Suyuti. *Al-Budur al-Safira Fi 'ulum al-Akhira*. Edited by Abu 'Abdallah M. al-Shafi'i. Beirut: Dar al-Kutub, 1996.

Swarc, Alan. "Illegal Immigration to Palestine 1945–1948: The French Connection." PhD diss., University College London, 2006.

Takeyh, R. *The Origins of the Eisenhower Doctrine: The US, Britain and Nasser's Egypt, 1953–57*. Houndmills, Basingstoke: Palgrave Macmillan, 2000.

Tal, David. "Israel's Road to the 1956 War." *International Journal of Middle East Studies* 28, no. 1 (1996): 59–81.

Taubman, William. *Khrushchev: The Man and His Era*. New York: W. W. Norton, 2004.

Tessler, Mark. *A History of the Israeli-Palestinian Conflict*. 2nd ed. Bloomington: Indiana University Press, 2009.

Thiong'o, Ngugi wa. *Decolonising the Mind: The Politics of Language in African Literature*. Oxford: James Currey/Heinemann, 1986.

Torfing, Jacob. *New Theories of Discourse: Laclau, Mouffe and Zizek*. Toronto: Wiley-Blackwell, 1999.

Tunzelmann, Alex von. *Blood and Sand: Suez, Hungary, and Eisenhower's Campaign for Peace*. New York: Harper, 2016.

Utting, Kate. "The Strategic Information Campaign: Lessons from the British Experience in Palestine, 1945–1948." *Contemporary Security Policy* 28, no. 1 (April 1, 2007): 42–62.

Varble, Derek. *The Suez Crisis 1956*. Oxford: Osprey Publishing, 2003.

Vaughan, James. "'A Certain Idea of Britain': British Cultural Diplomacy in the Middle East, 1945–57." *Contemporary British History* 19, no. 2 (June 1, 2005): 151–68.

———. "'Cloak without Dagger': How the Information Research Department Fought Britain's Cold War in the Middle East, 1948–56." *Cold War History* 4, no. 3 (April 1, 2004): 56–84.

———. *The Failure of American and British Propaganda in the Middle East, 1945–1957: Unconquerable Minds*. Houndmills, Basingstoke: Palgrave Macmillan, 2005.

———. "Propaganda by Proxy? Britain, America, and Arab Radio Broadcasting, 1953–1957." *Historical Journal of Film, Radio & Television* 22, no. 2 (June 2002): 157–72.

Vaughan, James R. "The BBC's External Services and the Middle East before the Suez Crisis." *Historical Journal of Film, Radio & Television* 28, no. 4 (October 2008): 499–514.

———. "'A Certain Idea of Britain': British Cultural Diplomacy in the Middle East, 1945–57." *Contemporary British History* 19, no. 2 (2005): 151–68.

Vélez, Federico. "From the Suez to the Panama Canal and Beyond: Gamal Abdel Nasser's Influence in Latin America." *Varia Historia* 31 (April 2015): 163–91.

Von Eschen, Penny. *Race against Empire.* Ithaca, NY: Cornell University Press, 1997.

———. *Satchmo Blows Up the World: Jazz Ambassadors Play the Cold War.* Cambridge, MA: Harvard University Press, 2004.

Wæver, Ole. "Identity, Communities and Foreign Policy: Discourse Analysis as Foreign Policy Theory." In *European Integration and National Identity*, 20–49. London: Routledge, 2001.

Wagnleitner, Reinhold. *Coca-Colonization and the Cold War: The Cultural Mission of the United States in Austria after the Second World War.* Chapel Hill: University of North Carolina Press, 1994.

Wark, Wesley K. "Coming in from the Cold: British Propaganda and Red Army Defectors, 1945–1952." *International History Review* 9, no. 1 (1987): 50.

Warner, Geoffrey. "The United States and the Suez Crisis." *International Affairs (Royal Institute of International Affairs 1944–)* 67, no. 2 (1991): 303–17.

Waterbury, J. *The Egypt of Nasser and Sadat: The Political Economy of two Regimes.* Princeton, NJ: Princeton University Press, 1992.

Waterfield, Gordon. "Suez and the Role of Broadcasting." *Listener* 76, no. 1970 (December 29, 1966): 947–49.

Wedeen, Lisa. "Acting 'As If': Symbolic Politics and Social Control in Syria." *Comparative Studies in Society and History* 40, no. 3 (1998): 503–23.

Westad, Odd Arne. *The Global Cold War: Third World Interventions and the Making of Our Times.* New York: Cambridge University Press, 2005.

Wilford, Hugh. *America's Great Game: The CIA's Secret Arabists and the Shaping of the Modern Middle East.* New York: Basic Books, 2013.

———. "The Information Research Department: Britain's Secret Cold War Weapon Revealed." *Review of International Studies* 24, no. 3 (1998): 353–69.

Woertz, Eckart. "The Food Weapon: Geopolitics in the Middle East." In *Oil for Food: The Global Food Crisis and the Middle East*, edited by Eckart Woertz, 106–39. Oxford: Oxford University Press, 2013.

Wood, David, and Robert Bernasconi, eds. *Derrida and Differance.* Evanston, IL: Northwestern University Press, 1988.

Wright, Richard, Amritjit Singh, and Gunnar Myrdal. *The Color Curtain: A Report on the Bandung Conference.* Jackson: University Press of Mississippi, 1995.

Yaqub, Salim. *Containing Arab Nationalism: The Eisenhower Doctrine and the Middle East.* Chapel Hill: University of North Carolina Press, 2004.

Yurchak, Alexei. *Everything Was Forever, Until It Was No More: The Last Soviet Generation.* Princeton, NJ: Princeton University Press, 2005.

Zartman, I. William, ed. *Peacemaking in International Conflict: Methods and Techniques.* Washington, DC: United States Institute of Peace, 2007.

Žižek, Slavoj. *For They Know Not What They Do: Enjoyment as a Political Factor.* London: Verso, 2002.

Zurayk, Constantine. *Ma'na al-Nakba Mujaddadan* [The meaning of the Nakhba Anew]. Beirut: Dar al-'Ilm lil-Malayyin, 1967.

INDEX

Abaza, Fekry, 120
Abdulaziz, Saud bin, 197
Abdullah, King of Jordan, 38
Abou Far Al-Ghafari (Abu Dharr al-Ghifari), 31
Aburish, Said K., 169
acceptable Arabism, 168–169
Acre Central prison, 55
Aden, 183
AFL-CIO union, 102–104, 103*fig*
Africa: Radio Moscow broadcasts in, 122, 136, 157–158, 199; Sharq al-Adna broadcasts in, 122, 136; Soviet intervention in, reports of, 113; Transmission X broadcasts in, 170; US cultural exchange programs with, 109; USIA handing of the "liberation issue," 108–109; US used as foil for Britain's failure in Suez, 160–161. *See also* North Africa
Aggression at Port Said (film), 165–166
agriculture: BBC broadcasts about dangers of land redistribution, 120; British broadcasts promoting the Baghdad Pact, 124–125; Cold War promises and propaganda efforts, 22–23; food as propaganda weapon, 87–88, 89*fig*, 90; Nasser's land redistribution policies, 87; tractors as a symbol of modernity and national power, 87–88, 89*fig*; Voice of the Arabs promotion of Nasser and, 62
aid programs: food as key weapon, 87–88; Radio Moscow, vision of peaceful life from Soviet gifts, 90–92; Radio Moscow on US and British aid programs, 85–87; Radio Moscow's *Mister Johnson in Trouble*, 85–87; Soviet Union promises of aid, 82; tractors as symbol of modernity and national power, 88, 89*fig*; US Cold War strategy and, 98–99; VOA anti-Soviet propaganda about, 107–108. *See also* development, Western promises of; modernization
Akkad, Abbas Mahmoud El, 120
Al-Ahram, 63, 195, 200, 210
Al Akhbar, 145
al-Arzuzi, Zaki, 76
al-Badr, Muhammad, 182
Al-Ba'ath, 200
Albania, 94
al-Din, Ahmed Baha', 192
Algeria: *Aggression at Port Said* film, funding for, 166; anti-colonial violence in, 126, 132, 155; Nasser's opposition to France's rule of Algeria, 132; Radio Cairo broadcasts in, 61; Radio Moscow's anti-Western messages, 174, 177
al-Hadidi, Salah al-Din, 186–187
al-Hakim, Abd, 196
al-Hakim, Tawfiq, 192
al-Husri, Sari, 76
al-Husseini, Amin, 38
al-Husseini, Jamal, 49
Ali, Ahmed Rashad, 59, 69
al-Ilah, 'Abd, 178
Al-Jumhuriyah, 200
Al-Kuwatly, Shukri, 38

al-Lam'a, Raif Abu, 60
Al Misri, 106
Al-Nasir, Jamal Abd, 172
al-Rifai, Samir, 113
Al-Said, Nuri, 63, 160, 163, 178
al-Urabi, Abd, 172
American Movietone newsreels, 138
Amir, Abd al-Hakim, 142
anaphora, use in message, 67
Andrews, Chapman, 129
Anglo-Iranian Oil Company, 110
Angola, 126
animal imagery, use of, 71–72, 185
anti-Western nationalism, 117–118; after
    Suez war, 162–164; Nasser and accept-
    able Arabism, 168–169; Soviet use of
    Suez war for anti-Western propaganda,
    156–158, 160; Suez Crisis, preparations
    for war, 136–145; Syrian coup attempt,
    messaging about, 176–177; on Voice of
    the Arabs (Sawt al Arab), 162–163
Arab, messages about meaning of, 189–190
Arab Cold War, 4
Arab Higher Committee for Palestine, 37,
    38, 40, 41, 51
Arabian Nights, 69
Arabic Anecdotes and American Novelties,
    VOA, 102
Arab-Israeli conflict: language limitations
    and, 8–9; radicalizing damage of, 128–
    129, 259n12; Radio Moscow broadcasts
    about, 81–82; Voice of America broad-
    casts about, 98
Arab League: response to partition of
    Palestine, 51; threats to withhold oil,
    45–46; UNSCOP visit to Palestine,
    coverage of, 36, 38, 41; use of radio to
    promote vision of revolutionary Egypt,
    60–61
Arab League Charter, 38
Arab nationalism: Anwar Sadat's effort to
    eradicate, 204; Arab broadcasters and,
    38; Baghdad Pact and, 124–127; British
    belief of a connection between national-
    ism and Soviet communism, 123–124,
    141; British radio broadcasts, 22–23,
    94–95, 117–118, 128–129; Cold War,
    radio narratives and, 9–11; Eisenhower

administration policies on, 176; histori-
    cal narratives and meanings of peace and
    democracy, 83–85; light and illumina-
    tion imagery, use of, 73; martyr imagery,
    use of, 70–71; music, use of on Radio
    Cairo, 69–70; narratives tying Cold
    War to the cause of Arab nationalism,
    63; Nasser, public disillusionment with,
    194; Nasser's promises and promotion
    of, 1, 7, 135; radio, role in generating
    consensus for or against nationalism,
    3–5, 7, 8–10; Radio Moscow, adaptation
    to rise of Arab nationalism, 131, 174–175,
    183; Radio Moscow on Arab nationalism
    as socialist, 31, 32, 113–115; Sharq al-Adna
    narratives of, 75; Suez Crisis, conse-
    quences of, 164; Suez Crisis, prepara-
    tions for war, 136–145; Suez Crisis the
    collapse of Britain's hegemony in Middle
    East, 158–159; Voice of America (VOA)
    broadcasts, 113, 176; Voice of the Arab
    Nation broadcasts, 188–189; Voice of the
    Arabs and Radio Cairo broadcasts,
    57–60, 62–63, 76–77. *See also*
    pan-Arabism
Arab Palestinians. *See* Palestinians
Arab Palestinian state, 12; British radio
    narratives on, 18
Arabs in America, VOA, 102
Arab Workers Congress, 104–105
archives for study, 5–6, xiii–xiv; BBC
    archives, 6, 22, 43, 47, 50–51, 55, 101;
    British National Archives, 171–172;
    government archives, 6, 55; Maspero
    archive, 60; Radio Moscow archives, 6,
    29, 43, 55; Russian Federation/Soviet
    archives, 43, 47, 158; Suez Crisis, war
    broadcast archives, 206–212; Voice of
    America (VOA), 6; Voice of the Arabs, 6
Arendt, Hannah, 213–214
arms sales. *See* weapons
aspirational master narratives, 8–9
Aswan Dam project, 62, 82, 107, 113, 124,
    132, 136, 138, 203
Atlee, Clement, 46
at-Tamimin, Sad Jabr, 187
audiosphere: accusations of lying as
    common trope, 88–89, 130; agriculture

Chiang Kai-shek, 107
Chichester, Francis, 202
children: BBC, children's programming on,
118; child victim and warrior imagery,
use of, 42–43, 71, 107, 157, 201–202;
Exodus (ship), children suffering on,
42–44; Radio Moscow criticism of US
segregated schools, 182; Soviet propaganda about a good life, 25–26, 91, 92;
Transmission X, anti-communism
broadcasts, 170; UNSCOP delegation
visits of, 40; US propaganda about a
good life, 78–79, 105–106; violence
against during Jewish assaults on Palestinian villages, 55; Voice of the Arabs,
children's programming, 61
China, 113
Christianity, 14, 29–32, 40, 44
Churchill, Winston, 153
civil rights movement, 81, 109–110, 173, 182,
199–200, 218
Cold War: aspirational master narratives,
8–9; British anti-communist narratives,
17–23, 32–33, 117–124; child victim and
warrior imagery, use of, 71; communism
as scapegoat for the decline of British
influence in Middle East, 128–129;
Eisenhower Doctrine, 81, 162–164, 171,
174–175; Information Research Department (IRD), British Foreign Service
messaging and, 118–130; Iraqi Revolution, messaging about, 178; light and
illumination imagery, use of, 73–74;
narratives tying Cold War to the cause
of Arab nationalism, 63; Palestine
partition, media coverage of, 46–51;
peace, rhetoric of, 78–80; politics of
representation, shaping of, 5; post-
WWII Middle East spheres of influence, 12; radio, role of, 3–5; shared
scaffolding of meaning and signification, 217–219; Soviet and Egyptian
relations, breakdown of, 187–189; Soviet
anti-Western narratives, 26–28, 174–
175; Soviet narratives about happiness
and progress, 24–33; Soviet use of Suez
war for anti-Western propaganda,
156–158; Suez Crisis, postwar

approaches to Middle East, 165–169;
"The Goals of American Foreign Policy," USIA, 114*fig*, 115–116; Transmission X, anti-communist messages of,
170–171; US intervention in Lebanon,
179–180; US propaganda programs,
98–102; VOA's promotion of positive
images of America, 173; workers, narratives about, 102–104, 103*fig*; Yemen war
and, 182–183. *See also* capitalism; communism; peace, rhetoric of; socialism
colonialism: Ahmed Said, critiques of
imperialism and colonial West, 63,
67–69, 73, 77, 82, 83, 150, 163, 184; *Al
Ahram* and the language of anti-
imperialism, 63; anti-British sentiment
and, 17; BBC narratives of anti-
colonialism as road to communism, 96;
British efforts in defense of its colonial
interests, 8, 18, 25, 117; British radio
pro-Western programming, 3, 19–21,
20*fig*, 117–118; British withdrawal from
Palestine, legacy of, 54; French colonies,
anti-colonial violence in, 126; historical
narrative, Ahmed Said's use of, 68–69;
light and illumination imagery, anti-
colonial rhetoric and, 73; Nasser's view
of Baghdad Pact as veiled colonialism,
132; neocolonialism, 7, 69, 97, 178; peace
narratives used in defense and in opposition to colonialism, 3–4, 25–26, 32,
79–83, 91–92, 96–97, 105, 130, 182; radio
as tool of empire, 13; Radio Cairo, as
center for anti-colonialism and Arab
nationalism, 57, 68–69, 77; Radio
Moscow, on Soviet commitment to end
colonial tyranny, 129–130; Radio Moscow's anti-Western/anti-colonial messages, 3, 29, 30–32, 59, 174–175; shared
scaffolding of meaning and significance,
217–218; spheres of influence in post-
WWII Middle East, 12–14; UNSCOP
visit to Palestine, radio coverage of,
39–44; US assumption of role as colonial antagonist, 194, 196; US efforts in
defense of colonial interests, 8; USIA
contrast of Western colonialism and
Russian imperialism, 107; USIA

colonialism (*continued*)
 handling of "liberation issue," 108–109;
 Voice of the Arabs critiques of imperialism and colonial West, 59, 62–63, 74,
 76, 167, 196–197. *See also* imperialism
Colonial Office, United Kingdom, 140
Columbia, 134
Cominform, 80–81
communism: anti-British sentiment and, 17;
 avoidance of ideological language,
 104–105; British anti-communist programming, 120; British belief of a connection between Arab nationalism and,
 123–124; British discussions of Islamic
 history and anti-communist messages,
 120; conflicting narratives and over-
 lapping interests, 180; Eisenhower
 Doctrine, 171; George Orwell's anti-
 communist efforts, 121–122; historical
 narratives and meanings of peace and
 democracy, 83–85; Islam as weak bulwark against communism, 141; light and
 illumination imagery, use of, 73–74;
 peace, rhetoric of, 78–80; as scapegoat
 for the decline of British influence in
 Middle East, 128–129; Soviet and Egyptian relations, breakdown of, 187–189;
 Transmission X, anti-communist messages of, 170–171; Viktor Kravchenko's
 autobiography, *I Chose Freedom,* 120–
 121; VOA's depiction of Soviet life,
 93–94. *See also* Cold War; socialism
Communist Words Contradict Facts, 122
Congo, 113, 182, 204
conjecture, discursive power of, 217
Connor, Cyril, 16–17, 18, 24, 28, 52, 225n18
consumerism as the "good life," 99
Cuba, 182
Cyprus, 142, 150
Czechoslovakia: Egypt, arms deal with, 66,
 83, 113, 132, 137, 203, 254n56; Egypt,
 trade with, 115; Egypt, use of Russian
 jets, 149; Jewish Agency, arms sales to,
 54; labor strikes in, 94; Soviet training
 of Egyptian officers in, 129–130

The Daily Mail, 136
Daily Mirror, 184

Daily Telegraph, 161
Dayr Yassin, 55
Declaration of Washington, 108
decolonization: radio, role of, 3–5; Suez
 Crisis, effects of, 163. *See also* colonialism; imperialism
de Gaulle, Charles, 213
democracy: Arab population rejection of
 promises of democracy, 194, 218; audiosphere, repetitive language on, 4; BBC
 broadcasts about, 21, 83–84, 96, 159, 161;
 Kennedy's reinvigoration of US propaganda program, 173–174; Nasser's 1962
 speech about, 187–188; Radio Moscow
 broadcasts about, 83–84, 92, 96;
 UNSCOP partition decision, 44; US,
 Jim Crow America and, 109–110; Voice
 of America (VOA) as defender of, 11;
 Voice of America (VOA) broadcasts
 about, 83–84, 92, 106–107, 173–174,
 178–179
Denmark, 134
development, Western promises of: acceptable Arabism and, 168–169; Arab population rejection of, 194; Kennedy's
 reinvigoration of US propaganda
 program, 173–174; Suez Crisis, consequences of, 164; Suez Crisis, preparations for war, 134–135. *See also*
 modernization
discursive power of conjuncture, 217
dog imagery, use of, 71–72, 198
domino theory, 180
Don Basin, 175
Dove of Peace, 94*fig,* 95*fig*
Dulles, Allen, 180
Dulles, John Foster: London Conference
 and, 139; Suez Crisis, preparations for
 war, 132–133, 138–139, 141, 144–145;
 Suez Crisis, war over, 147–148
Duranty, Walter, 213

East Germany, 94
echoic irony, 65–67
Echo of the News, VOA, 102
economic well-being, peace rhetoric and,
 78–80
economy of the gift, 26, 79–80, 117, 135

Eden, Anthony, 108; House of Commons speech about Suez war, 148, 153; Suez Crisis, preparations for war, 132–133, 134, 138, 140; Suez Crisis, war over, 147–148; support for Israel, 153

Education and Exchange Act, US (1948), 100

Egypt, 35; acceptable Arabism and, 168–169; as Arab League member, 38; Baghdad Pact and, 124–127; bombing of Egyptian airfields, 152; China, diplomatic relations with, 113; Czech arms deal, 66, 83, 113, 132, 137, 203, 254n56; economic upheaval in, 168; Eisenhower Doctrine, effects of, 171; historical narratives and meanings of peace and democracy, 83–85; Jordan, five-year defensive pact with, 205–206; Ministry of National Guidance, 60; Nasser's crackdown on communists and socialists, 163, 167; Nasser's promotion of pan-Arab nationalism, 167–168; peace, rhetoric of, 79–80; post-WWII population boom, 90–91; pro-Palestine rhetoric of, 39; radio archives, 6; Revolutionary Command Council, 60; rewriting of Palestine's history in case of partition, 39; Sévres Protocol (1956) and, 133; Six-Day War, excerpts of broadcast transcripts, 206–213; Six-Day War (1967), lead up to, 191–193; Soviet and Egyptian relations, breakdown of, 187–189; Soviet arms sales to, 129–130; Soviet influence in, 113–115; Soviet support of post Suez Crisis, 166–169; Soviet training of Egyptian military officers, 129–130; Suez Canal, nationalization of, 132–135; Suez Crisis, consequences of, 163; Suez Crisis, war over, 146–164; Syrian coup attempt, messaging about, 175–176; television in, 61; Yemen war, support for, 182–183, 186–187. See also Nasser, Gamal Abd al; Radio Cairo; Voice of the Arabs (Sawt al Arab)

"Egypt, the Grave of her Invaders," (Voice of the Arabs program), 68

Egyptian Air Force, 149–150

Egyptian Broadcasting Service (EBS): creation of, 60; monitoring of foreign broadcasts, 61; USIA, early ties to, 113

Egyptian Home Service, 45

Egyptian Revolution, Ahmed Said's use of historical narrative, 68–69

Eisenhower, Dwight, 89*fig,* 92, 94, 98, 101, 107–108; Mossadeq coup, message to Iran, 110–111; Plan 8, 173–174; on racism in US, 109; Suez Crisis, postwar approach to Middle East, 167–169; Suez Crisis, preparations for war, 132–134, 138–139, 142, 144; Suez Crisis, war over, 147–148, 152

Eisenhower Doctrine, 81, 131, 162–164, 171, 174–175, 179–180, 203

El Hodeibi, Hassan, 106

Emirate of Sharjah, 185

"Escape from Tyranny" (Knode), 93

Eshkol, Levi, 203

Es-Said, Nuri, 39

ethnic cleansing, 55

Exodus, 41–44

Faisal, King of Iraq, 144, 178

"Faith or Fear" (Faulkner), 93–94

Falastin, 17

Faulkner, William, 93

feminism: Radio Moscow and state feminism, 91–92; traditional images of women, use of, 92

Fergusson, Bernard, 149, 153–154

Ferris, Jesse, 188

Fisher, Nigel, 184

food as propaganda weapon, 87–88; food shortages in Middle East, 90–91; "Goals of American Foreign Policy," food security and, 114*fig,* 115; Soviet shipments of food to Middle East, 82; Transmission X, description of food riots in Cuba, 170; Voice of America broadcast of food shortages in Soviet Union, 93, 94

Food for Peace program, 87

Foot, Hugh, 201

Foreign Broadcast Information Service (FBIS), 6, 43, 101

France: Algeria, unrest in, 132, 155; anticolonial violence against, 126; Eisenhower Doctrine, effects of, 171; London Conference, 139; Radio Moscow's

France (*continued*)
    anti-Western messages, 174; Sévres Protocol (1956), 133; Suez Crisis, war over, 146–164
Franzén, Johan, 189–190
freedom, promises of: Arab population rejection of, 194; BBC, anti-Soviet messages, 96, 147; *I Chose Freedom* (Kravchenko), 120–121; loss of faith in, 10, 190, 194, 218; Nasser's language of freedom to construct a police state, 217–218; peace narratives and, 96, 98; price of freedom, imagery of, 165, 185; Radio Moscow, anti-US messages, 27, 175; religion, freedom of, 106–107, 173; shared scaffolding of meaning and signification, 217–219; Suez Crisis, preparations for war, 134–135, 153; Suez Crisis, war broadcasts and, 155, 207; US Cold War propaganda, 100–101, 105–106, 109–111, 120–121, 173–174, 179; US intervention in Lebanon, 179; Voice of America (VOA) as defender of freedom, 11, 92, 93–94, 161–162, 173, 179; Voice of Justice broadcasts, 172; Voice of the Arabs, Arab nationalism and promises of freedom, 66–68, 76, 77, 127, 182–183
Freedom Riders, 109–110
Front de Libération Nationale (FLN), 126, 132
Fussell, Paul, 192

Gaitskill, Hugh, 148, 153, 155
Galilee, 55
Gaza Strip, 70; Sévres Protocol (1956) and Israeli invasion of Gaza, 133; Six-Day War (1967), broadcast excerpts from, 206; Six-Day War (1967), lead up to, 191–193; Suez Crisis and, 152; UNSCOP site visits, 40
General Electric Company, 125
gifts: BBC broadcasts, 117, 228n65; economy of the gift, 26, 74, 79–80, 115–116, 117, 135, 195; Egyptian state gifts, Nasser's promises of, 62; Egypt's refusal of US gifts, 195; PBS broadcasts, 117; Radio Cairo broadcast messages, 96; Radio Moscow's anti-western

broadcasts, 85, 90; Sharq al-Adna broadcast messages, 96, 117; Soviet gifts, 26, 74, 90, 168; Voice of America broadcast messages, 96, 112; Western cultural gifts, 13, 21, 228n65; Western gifts, promise of, 13, 74, 96, 99, 115–116, 117, 168. *See also* modernization
"Glimpse at the Soviet Navy" (BBC), 122–123
Glubb, John, 71–72, 127–128
"The Goals of American Foreign Policy," USIA, 114*fig*, 115–116
God, light as symbol for, 73
Goebbels, Joseph, 72
Golan Heights, Six-Day War (1967) and, 191–193
Grand Mosque, Mecca, 125
Great Britain. *See* British Mandate for Palestine; United Kingdom
Great October Socialist Revolution, 200
Grossman, Vasily, 72
Gulf of Aqaba, 195, 197, 203, 207

Haboker, 36
HaGalal, 19
Haganah: in Ahmed Said broadcast, 65; *Exodus* ship and, 41–43; Kol Israel (The Voice of Israel), 54; Semiramis Hotel bombing, 55
Haganah Radio, 55
Haifa, 40, 42, 55
Haifa Bay, 150
happiness, as propaganda tool, 24–25, 79, 99; BBC broadcasts, 32–33; PBS broadcasts, 32–33; Radio Moscow broadcasts, 13, 25, 102, 104, 105, 122, 155; Sharq al-Adna broadcasts, 122; Voice of America (VOA) broadcasts, 98, 99, 102–105, 103*fig*
Hare, Raymond, 61
Hashemites, 61, 168, 177, 178
Hassan, Abdel Rahman, 120
Haykal, Muhammad, 63, 187, 195
Health Program (VOA), 102
historical narratives, use of, 82, 83–84; Ahmed Said's use of, 68–69, 77, 83, 137–138, 199; BBC and IRD broadcasts, 120; meanings of peace and democracy

and, 83–85; Nasser's use of, 62, 198, 199; Radio Moscow broadcasts, 30–32, 82, 83, 122, 199; Six-Day War as watershed moment in Middle East, 215; USIA's ahistorical narratives of race in America, 109; Voice of America (VOA) broadcasts, 83

Hitler, Adolf, 213

Holocaust, 12, 31, 37, 42, 43–44, 225n20

Holy Land, 40, 50, 52, 71

holy war, religious rhetoric and iconography, 205

housing shortages, 90–91

human rights: "The Goals of American Foreign Policy," USIA, 114*fig*, 115–116

Hungary, 94; consequences of Suez Crisis, 163, 164; Soviet aggression in, 78, 110, 133, 146–147, 155, 157–158

Hussein, King of Jordan, 205–206; firing of communist government leaders, 174–175; Western allies, mending broken ties with, 213

ICE (Information Coordination Executive), 140

I Chose Freedom (Kravchenko), 120–121

"I Escaped to Speak for the Enslaved" (*Life*), 93

"I Learned Communism the Hard Way" (Ruedemann), 93

"Imagine, O Arabs," as phrase of solidarity with listeners, 66–67

imperialism: Algeria, protests against French imperialism, 174, 177; Ali Shariati on the power of Islam to overthrow imperialism, 32; Anwar Sadat on arms sales as imperialist motivations, 74–75; Arab radio stations anti-imperialism messages, 35, 39, 59, 62, 63, 65, 66, 68–69, 72, 162, 177, 185, 187, 188–189; audiosphere, competing propaganda about imperialism, 180; Baghdad Pact, Arab listener impressions of, 125–126; BBC efforts to train listeners to ignore Soviet anti-imperialism messages, 120, 122, 123; BBC on Soviet peace campaign messages, 94, 96; historical narrative, Ahmed Said's use of, 68–69, 83; IRD on

Arab nationalism's obsession with Western imperialism, 128–129; nationalization of Suez Canal as erasing last vestiges of imperialism, 135, 137–138, 139, 141–142; oil as integral for sloughing off imperialism, 74; Radio Moscow, Soviet Peace campaign messages, 96–97; Radio Moscow broadcasts on history of imperialism, 30, 48, 59; Six-Day War, anti-imperialism messaging around, 191, 196, 199, 200, 204, 206, 210; Soviet citizen's ability to critique imperialism, 157; Soviet Union's anti-imperialism propaganda, 39, 82–83, 92, 94, 96, 113, 166; Voice of America (VOA), on Egyptian anti-imperialism as procommunist, 162; Voice of America (VOA) on Soviet imperialism, 107; Voice of America (VOA) on Soviet peace campaign messages, 92. *See also* colonialism

Information Coordination Executive (ICE), 140

Information Research Department (IRD), United Kingdom, 181*fig*; British embassy complaints about dull programming, 125; communism as scapegoat for the decline of British influence in Middle East, 128–129; discussions of Islamic history and anti-communist messages, 120; feedback loops in broadcast messages, 129–130; formation and growth of, 57, 118; Iraqi Revolution, messaging about, 178; Radio Cairo, use of classical music as message to IRD, 70; radio dramas of anti-communist publications, 120–122; Radio Moscow, matching the messaging of, 122–123, 130; Sharq al-Adna programming, shaping of, 118–119, 122; Suez Crisis, preparations for war, 140; Syrian coup attempt, messaging about, 175–176; Transmission X, creation of, 170–171; Voice of Britain, rebranding of after Suez Crisis, 169–170; Voice of Britain, renaming of Sharq al Adna as, 148–149. *See also* British Broadcasting Corporation (BBC); Sharq al-Adna

International Monetary Fund (IMF), 134

broadcasts, 22, 41, 48, 50; *Exodus,* 41–44; *Haboker* newspaper reports, 36; Hitler's "Big Lie" about, 214; Holocaust and, 12, 31, 37, 42, 43–44, 225n20; immigration, 19, 35–37, 41–44, 48; Jewish assaults on Palestinian villages, 54–55; Jews in Palestine, 17, 19; *Palestine Post* newspaper reports, 17; PBS broadcasts, 21, 52; Radio Beirut broadcasts, 36, 41, 46; Radio Moscow broadcasts, 26, 36, 40–41, 54; Shar al-Adna broadcasts, 47–48; Soviet radio struggles with discussing religious topics, 29–32; Truman's support of, 38, 46–47; UN partition vote, 49–51. *See also* Kol Israel (The Voice of Israel); United Nations Special Committee on Palestine (UNSCOP)

Joffre, Joseph, 205

John Deere tractors, 88, 89*fig*

Johnson, Lyndon, 195, 202, 203–204, 213

Johnston, Alexander, 169

Jordan, 113; as Arab League member, 38; Baghdad Pact, possible membership and withdrawal from, 113, 124–125; Baghdad Pact, riots of possible membership in, 126–127, 132; British training of Jordanian pilots, 130; consequences of Suez Crisis, 163; Eisenhower Doctrine, effects of, 171; John Glubb, expulsion of, 71–72; King Hussein's firing of communist government leaders, 174–175; King Hussein's five-year defensive pact with Nasser, 205–206; Six-Day War, excerpts of broadcast transcripts, 206–213; Six-Day War (1967), lead up to, 191–193; Syrian coup attempt, messaging about, 175–176; Voice of America in, 161

Judaism: Soviet radio struggles with discussing religious topics, 29–32. *See also* Israel; Jewish population; Zionism

Kamel, Mahmoud, 121

Kaverin, Sergei, 28–29

Keating, Leslie, 52, 53

Keating, Rex, 14, 15*fig*, 18–19, 36, 37, 46, 52–54, 148

Kennan, George, 100

Kennedy, John F., 173–174

Kenya, 113, 126, 149, 154

Keynesian economics, 78–79, 104

Khaled, Laila, 194

Khalidi, Hussain, 37, 38

Khallaf Bey, Abdel Wahab, 120

Khan Yunis, 133

Khrushchev, Nikita: Anti-Religion Decree, 106; consequences of Suez Crisis, 163; on détente with Egypt and Israel, 89; fall of, 188; Suez Crisis, postwar approach to Middle East, 167–169; Suez Crisis, response to, 133, 134; Syrian coup attempt, response to, 175–176; Virgin Lands project, 87; Yemen war, support for, 182–183

King, Joe, 138

King, Martin Luther, Jr., 109–110

Kirk, George, 176

Kirkpatrick, Ivone, 16–17, 24, 28, 148, 225n18

Knode, Donald, 93

Knop, Werner, 93

Kol Israel (The Voice of Israel), 54; Six-Day War, excerpts of broadcast transcripts, 206–213; on Soviet support Egypt, 130; Suez Crisis, preparations for war, 134–136, 143; Suez Crisis, war coverage, 147, 150, 206–208, 210

Kollontai, Alexandra, 92

Kol Yerushalayim, 16

Kravchenko, Viktor, 120–121

Krupskaia, Nadezhda, 92

Kwon, Heonik, 46–47

Kyle, Keith, 60

labor unions, 102–104, 103*fig*

Laclau, Ernesto, 77

land reform: BBC anti-communist messages, 120; British anti-communist messages, 120; Nasser, land redistribution policies, 87, 113

language, power and limitations of, 3, 4–5, 7–9, 10, 11, 28; acceptable Arabism, language of, 168–169; Arabic "radio language," 57, 64, 77; Arab nationalism, language of, 59, 131, 177, 193–194, 205; Arab revolution, language of, 33, 58, 60,

language (*continued*)
63; "Big Lie," use of, 214–215; brinksmanship, language of, 116, 172; Cold
War, language of, 56, 77; ideological
language, 104–105; martyrs, language
of, 70; occupier, language of, 36; power,
language of, 217; Radioyazik (radio
language), 28–29; religious language,
204–205; shared scaffolding of meaning
and significance, 217–219; Soviet official
state language, 28–29. *See also* peace,
rhetoric of
Larson, Arthur, 161–162
leaflet drops by Royal Air Force, 149, 154
Lebanon, 35, 253n33; as Arab League member, 38, 61; Baghdad Pact, 58, 125, 162;
consequences of Suez Crisis, 163; Eisenhower Doctrine, effects of, 162, 171; PBS
broadcasts, 16, 36; Six-Day War (1967),
broadcast excerpts, 209; Soviet cultural
exchanges with, 124; Suez Crisis and,
163; Syrian coup attempt, messaging
about, 175–176; US intervention in 1958,
11, 178–180; Voice of America (VOA)
broadcasts, 113, 162, 178–180. *See also*
Radio Beirut
Lennox-Boyd, Allan, 149
liberation movements: BBC broadcasts,
126, 172; Ben-Gurion and the liberation
of Jews in Palestine, 19; CIA concerns
about, 126; France, anti-colonial violence and, 126, 132; Nasser, Suez Canal
nationalization as liberation movement,
137; Nasser's promise of liberation
under Arab nationalism, 1, 132, 167–168,
191–192; Radio Cairo broadcasts, 126,
172; Radio Moscow broadcasts, 26,
28–29, 82, 91–92, 166, 172, 177; Radio
Moscow coverage of Suez Crisis, 136,
157–158; religious rhetoric in, 205;
Six-Day War (1967), broadcasts during,
206; Six-Day War (1967), effects of, 194,
214, 218; Soviet support of, 4, 8, 13, 26,
182; United Arab Republic (UAR) and,
177, 185; US as foil for Britain's failure
in Suez, 160–161; USIA's approach to
"liberation issue," 108–109, 173; Voice
of America (VOA) broadcasts, 126, 172,

173; Voice of the Arabs broadcasts, 59,
72, 77, 126, 167, 172, 177
Lie, Trygve Halvdan, 49, 50
Lieberman, Avigdor, 44
Life, 93
light and illumination imagery, use of,
72–73; Grand Mosque in Mecca, light-
ing of, 125; in Suez Crisis messaging,
137–138
Lloyd, Selwyn, 153
London Conference, 139, 140, 141, 161
Love, Kennett, 156
Lucy, Autherine, 81
Lumumba, Patrice, 182

Mahfouz, Naguib, 192
Makhus, Ibrahim, 196–197
Malcolm X, 199
Malenkov, Georgy, 89*fig*
Mandate for Palestine. *See* British Mandate
for Palestine
Mao Tse-tung, 107
Mardam, Jamil, 36, 41
Marks, Leonard, 101–102
Marshall, George, 36, 100, 179, 262n63
Marshall Plan, 88, 89*fig*, 98, 179, 262n63
martyr imagery, use of, 70–71
Maspero archive, 60
mass demonstrations, meaning of for
participants, 157–158
Maudling, Reginald, 184
Mau Mau, 126
Mazni, Abdel Kader El, 120
McAlister, Melani, 5, 217
McCarthy, Joseph, 101–102
Mecca, Grand Mosque, 125
meter, use in messages, 67
Middle East: post-WWII population
boom, 90–91; US and UK action in
search of oil, 110–112; Voice of America
broadcast signal, 101–102
Middle East News agency, 162–163
militarization, stories about, 122–123
minha, 62–63
Ministry of Defense, United Kingdom, 140
Ministry of National Guidance, Egypt, 60
Ministry of the Heavy Machine Industry,
Soviet Union, 157

Nicholson, Godfrey, 184
"No Relaxation of Defense" (BBC), 122–123
North Africa: American tractor as savior of civilization propaganda, 88; anti-colonial messaging in, 69; anti-colonial violence in, 126; Bandung Conference, pro-African independence themes, 76; missing radio transcripts for African audiences, 47; post-WWII population boom, 90–91; Radio Beirut broadcasts, 46; Radio Moscow broadcasts, 24, 122, 199; Sharq al-Adna broadcasts, 118, 122, 136; Transmission X broadcasts, 170; US Cold War policies in, 100, 101; US cultural exchange programs with, 109; USIA handling of the "liberation issue," 108–109; US used as foil for Britain's failure in Suez, 160–161; Voice of America broadcasts, 100, 102, 113
North Atlantic Treaty Organization (NATO), 134
"Notorious Defense" (Bunni), 90
Nyardi, Nicholas, 93

oil, 45–46; radio narratives of oil as a weapon, 74; Suez Crisis, embargo response to, 134; US and UK actions in Middle East in search of oil, 110–112
Orientalism, 8–9, 13, 38; British excuses for failed messaging to Arab audiences, 161; legacy of British withdrawal from Palestine, 54; musical Orientalism, 69; politics of representation, shaping of, 5; US policymaking, influence of, 46–47
Orwell, George, 121–122
Owen Falls Dam, 124

Pakistan, 58, 124, 133, 137, 162
Palestine: British withdrawal from, 23, 34–35, 51–54; historical narrative, Ahmed Said's use of, 68–69; partition of, media coverage, 44–51; post-WWII Middle East, spheres of influence in, 12–14; Rex Keating on, 14; Soviet anti-colonial narratives about, 30–31; UNSCOP visit to, Arab radio coverage of, 36–44; as useful tool of Arab

propaganda, 187; violence after partition, 54–56; Voice of the Arabs "Who has Set Up Israel?" broadcast, 65. *See also* British Mandate for Palestine; Palestinians
Palestine Corner, 76–77
Palestine Post, 17
Palestine tragedy (1947), 68–69
Palestinian Broadcasting Service (PBS), 3, 16, 20*fig*, 25, 29, 32–33, 117; anti-communist narratives on British radio, 17–23; on Arab threats to withhold oil, 46; closing of, 51–54; *Exodus* broadcasts about, 42, 43; Palestine partition, media coverage of, 44, 47–48, 50; pro-Zionist programming on, 18–19, 37, 55; Rex Keating on, 14–15, 15*fig*, 36, 37; UNSCOP visit to Palestine, coverage of, 36, 37
Palestinian Mandate. *See* British Mandate for Palestine
Palestinians: fight for independence, 12; newspapers of, 16–17; pan-Arab radio narratives and, 76–77; PBS broadcasts to, 15, 16–18; Six-Day War (1967), lead up to, 191–193; United Nations partition, displaced populations and, 54–56; violence following partition, 55. *See also* Palestine
Panama, 139
pan-Arabism, 4, 8, 35, 56, 63, 191; acceptable Arabism, 168–169; *Aggression at Port Said* (film), 165; Arab population rejection of promises, 182, 185–186, 192, 194, 215; British broadcasters and Baghdad Pact, 124–127; Cold War narratives and, 117, 123, 176; Nasser's promotion of, 1, 8, 58, 167–168, 177, 186, 193, 194, 215; Radio Moscow broadcasts, 29, 31, 81, 92, 143, 144; Six-Day War, pan-Arab rhetoric on radio during, 193–194; Six-Day War and the failure of expectations, 193, 214–215; Soviet and Egyptian relations, breakdown of, 187–189; Soviet narratives of socialism and, 13, 31; Suez Crisis, consequences of, 10, 164; Syrian coup attempt, messaging about, 176–177; United Arab Republic (UAR), creation

Radio Algiers, 209

Radio Amman, 206, 207, 211

Radio Baku, 24

Radio Beirut, 2, 3, 35; Palestine partition, media coverage of, 45–51; UNSCOP visit to Palestine, coverage of, 36–44

Radio Cairo, 2, 3, 10, 35; accusations of lying about peace, 88–90; Ahmad Shawkat programs, 68–69; Ahmed Rashad Ali programs, 69; anti-Western narratives, 27; Baghdad Pact, opposition to, 126–127; Bandung Conference coverage, 76; British bombing of, 154–156; broadcast range and daily schedule, 61; child victim and warrior imagery, use of, 71; Cold War narratives on, 3–5; historical narratives on, 68–69; Iraqi Revolution, messaging about, 178; music broadcasts on, 69–70; Palestine partition, media coverage of, 45–51; as parent station for Voice of the Arabs, 57; as primary conduit for vision of revolutionary Egypt, 60–61; pro-Soviet Union messaging, 180; Royal Air Force (RAF) bombing of, 154–155; Six-Day War, broadcasts before the war, 196–198, 205–206; Six-Day War, excerpts of broadcast transcripts, 206–213; Suez Canal, nationalizing of, 135; Suez Crisis, preparations for war, 144; Suez Crisis, war coverage, 149–150, 153; UNSCOP visit to Palestine, coverage of, 36–44. *See also* Voice of the Arabs (Sawt al Arab)

Radio Damascus, 2, 3, 35, 129–130, 156; Palestine partition, media coverage of, 45–51; Six-Day War, broadcasts before the war, 196, 198–199, 200, 205–206; Six-Day War, excerpts of broadcast transcripts, 208–213; Suez Crisis, preparations for war, 134–135; UNSCOP visit to Palestine, coverage of, 36–44

Radio Free Europe/Radio Liberty, 113

Radio Jerusalem, 2, 204

Radio Jordan, 54

Radio Morocco, 37

Radio Moscow, 2, 3, 9–10, 11, 32–33, 149–150, 207–213; accusations of lying about peace, 88–90; *Aggression at Port Said* film, response to, 166; anti-Western narratives, 26–28, 174–175; Arab broadcasts of traditional women's roles, 92; on Arab nationalism, 113–115; Arab peace programming on, 81; avoidance of ideological language, 104–105; British radio matching with competing narratives, 122–123; claims to commitment to the truth, 27–29; feedback loops in broadcast messages, 129–130; freedom of religion, weaponization of, 106–107; historical narratives, use of, 82; on hypocrisy of Lyndon Johnson's calls for peace, 203–204; Iraqi Revolution, messaging about, 178; London Conference, messaging about, 139; messages that Soviet Union was only true ally of Arabs, 200–201; *Mister Johnson in Trouble* broadcast, 85–87; Mossadeq coup, coverage of, 111–112; music broadcasts on, 69; narratives of revolution and class conflict, 13; Palestine partition, media coverage of, 47–51, 54, 55; peace, rhetoric of, 78–80, 90–92, 96–97; peace as a vision against capitalist and imperialist threats, 81–83; *The Peace of an Uzbeck Mother* broadcast, 91; "Peace Offensive," 57; on racism and racial violence in US, 109–110; Six-Day War, broadcasts before the war, 198–202; Six-Day War, coverage of, 194; on Soviet commitment to end colonial tyranny, 129–130; state controlled narratives of happiness and progress, 23–32; state feminism, 91–92; struggles with discussing religion, 29–32; Suez Crisis, postwar coverage of, 166; Suez Crisis, preparations for war, 82–83, 134–139, 143, 144–145; Suez Crisis, war coverage, 150, 155, 156–158, 160; Syrian coup attempt, messaging about, 175–176; UNSCOP visit to Palestine, coverage of, 36, 39–44; Voice of the Arabs use of Radio Moscow themes and language, 59; workers, Cold War narratives about, 104–105

Radio Paris, 134–135, 150

Radio Peace and Progress, 24

communism as scapegoat for decline of
British influence in Middle East, 128–
129; dog imagery, use of, 72; Egypt,
influence in, 113–115, 167, 168–169;
Hungary, aggression in, 146–147, 155,
157–158; light and illumination imagery,
use of, 73–74; Palestine, ambiguous
policy toward, 38; Palestine and the
Middle East, viewed as emerging market, 12–14; Palestine partition, media
coverage of, 46; *The Peace of an Uzbek
Mother,* on Radio Moscow, 91; post-
WWII population boom, 90–91;
propaganda spending estimates, 93;
radio archives, 6; radio broadcast range
and daily schedule, 61; religion, struggles with discussing, 29–32; revolutionary rhetoric, 198–199; Six-Day War,
broadcasts of, 198–202, 205–206; Soviet
and Egyptian relations, breakdown of,
187–189; Stalinist purges and the rewriting of history, 122; state controlled
narratives of happiness and progress,
23–32; Suez Crisis, consequences of,
163–164; Suez Crisis, support for Egypt,
132–134; Suez war, mass demonstrations
against in Russia, 156–157; Suez war, use
as anti-Western propaganda, 156–158;
Syrian coup attempt, messaging about,
175–176; tractors as symbol of modernity and national power, 88, 89*fig*;
training of Egyptian military officers,
129–130; Viktor Kravchenko's autobiography, *I Chose Freedom,* 120–121; Virgin
Lands project, 87; Voice of America
(VOA), response to Soviet Peace Campaign, 93–94; Voice of the Arabs
ambiguous message about the Soviets,
75–76; Voice of the Arabs radio, Soviet
view of, 58–60; World Peace Campaign,
80–81; Yemen war, support for, 182–183,
186–187. *See also* Radio Baku; Radio
Moscow; Radio Peace and Progress;
Radio Tashkent; Radio Yerevan
Stalin, Joseph, 84*fig*; anti-religion policies,
30; BBC broadcasts, 121; death of, 80;
Iran, Soviet troops in, 18; performances
of appreciation toward Stalin, 26;

popular mobilization to annihilate spies
and agents, 198–199; public attestations
of citizen solidarity, 156; radio, state
control of, 24, 28; revolutionary rhetoric
and Stalinist show trials, 198–199;
Sharq al-Adna broadcasts, 122; show
trials, 72, 198–199; Voice of America
broadcasts, 106, 108
Stalinist Terror, 28, 121
Standard Oil of California, 110
Stanton, Andrea, 5
state feminism, 91–92
State House of Radio Broadcasting and
Sound Recording, Moscow, 23–24
Stern, 55
Stevenson, Ralph, 119
Straits of Tiran, 132
Sudan, 132
Suez, 150
Suez Canal Company, 82–83, 132–135
Suez Canal Crisis (1956), 5, 10, 70, 81,
132–135; consequences of, 163–164;
nationalization of canal, 82–83; postwar blame for propaganda failures,
159–164; preparations for war, 135–145;
rewriting of history, 197; war over,
146–164
Syria, 35; as Arab League member, 38;
British and US backed coup attempt,
175–176; CIA coup plans, 132; Eisenhower Doctrine, effects of, 171; Palestine partition, media coverage of, 45;
Six-Day War, broadcasts before the war,
200; Six-Day War, excerpts of broadcast
transcripts, 206–213; Six-Day War
(1967), lead up to, 191–193; US coup
attempt, 87. *See also* Radio Damascus
Syrian Broadcasting Organization, 35. *See
also* Radio Beirut
Syrian Communist Party, 87

Talal, Hussein bin, 127
Tanganyika, 126
TASS, 162–163, 201
television, in Egypt, 61
Tewfik, Mohammed Ali, 120
Texas Oil, 110
Teymour Bey, Mahmoud, 121

"This Is Your Enemy," Said broadcast, 66
Thompson, George, 213
Thomson, George, 184
Tiberias, 55
Tolstoy, Leo, 97
tractors, 86–88, 89fig, 91
Trafalgar Square, 155
Transjordan, 18, 44–45
Transmission X, 170–171
Tripartite Declaration, 160
Truman, Harry S., 26, 38, 46, 47, 101, 109,
    173–174
Truman Doctrine, 98
truth: "Big Lie," use of through history,
    214; British and Soviet claims to com-
    mitment to the truth, 27–29; lack of
    belief in radio propaganda, 7–8; post-
    truth world, 11; Truman's, Campaign of
    Truth, 101, 173–174
Tudeh Party, 111–112
Tunisia, 126
Turkey, 48, 58, 124–127, 162, 174, 186

UAR. See United Arab Republic (UAR)
Uganda, 126
unions, labor, 102–104, 103fig
United Arab Emirates, 185; Voice of
    America broadcasts, 203
United Arab Republic (UAR), 8, 168;
    creation of, 176–177; delegation to
    London 1965, 183–185; Nasser's speech
    to UAR Air Force Advanced Com-
    mand, 197; Six-Day War, broadcasts
    before the war, 196, 203; Six-Day War,
    excerpts of broadcast transcripts,
    206–213; Syria, withdrawal from, 182,
    186, 193; Voice of the Arabs anti-
    Western messaging, 163, 185–186. See
    also pan-Arabism
United Kingdom: acceptable Arabism and,
    168–169; Aggression at Port Said film,
    response to, 165–166; anti-Arab nation-
    alism messages from, 117–118; anti-
    communist messages from, 17–23, 57,
    117–124; Baghdad Pact, 58, 124–127;
    British radio stations in Middle East,
    14–23, 15fig, 20fig; British training of
    Jordanian pilots, 130; Central Treaty

Organization (CENTO), 178; child
    victim and warrior imagery, use of, 71;
    Cold War, radio narratives and, 3–5,
    9–11; dog imagery, use of, 71–72; Egypt,
    influence in, 168–169; Eisenhower
    Doctrine, effects of, 171; historical
    narrative, Ahmed Said's use of, 68–69;
    Information Research Department
    (IRD), 57; Israel as both manipulator
    and puppet, radio narratives of, 75;
    legacy of colonialism in Palestine, 54;
    London Conference, 139, 140, 141, 161;
    Middle East actions in search of oil,
    110–112; Palestine, withdrawal from, 23,
    34–35, 51–54; peace, rhetoric of, 78–80,
    94–97; psychological warfare, Informa-
    tion Coordination Executive (ICE)
    and, 140; radio archives, 6; Radio
    Moscow's anti-Western messages, 85,
    174; Sévres Protocol (1956), 133–134, 158;
    Six-Day War, broadcasts before the war,
    201–202; Six-Day War, excerpts of
    broadcast transcripts, 206–213; Suez
    Canal, Nasser's nationalization of,
    82–83, 132–145; Suez Crisis, British
    propaganda failures during, 159–161;
    Suez Crisis, consequences of, 164; Suez
    Crisis, tensions with United States over,
    160–161; Suez Crisis, war over, 146–164;
    Syrian coup attempt, 175–176; view of
    Palestine and the Middle East as emerg-
    ing market, 12–14; view of Voice of the
    Arabs radio, 58–60; Voice of the Arabs
    use of echoic irony against British
    claims, 65–67; in Voice of the Arabs
    "Who has Set Up Israel?" broadcast, 65;
    Yemen war of 1962, 186–187. See also
    British Broadcasting Corporation
    (BBC); British Mandate for Palestine;
    Information Research Department
    (IRD), United Kingdom; Near East
    Arabic Broadcasting Station (NEABS);
    Palestinian Broadcasting Service (PBS)
United Nations: Israel, creation of state
    (1948), 82; Security Council failed
    resolution before Six-Day War, 201; Suez
    Crisis, as test of United Nations, 143–
    144; Suez Crisis, preparations for war

response, 133–134, 140, 142, 143–144; Suez Crisis, response to war over, 147, 150

United Nations Special Committee on Palestine (UNSCOP), 9; British withdrawal from Palestine, 34–35; partition decision and vote, 44–51; visit to Palestine, radio coverage of, 36–44

United States: acceptable Arabism and, 168–169; *Aggression at Port Said* film, response to, 165–166; Central Treaty Organization (CENTO), 178; child victim and warrior imagery, use of, 71; civil rights movement, 81, 109–110, 173, 182, 199–200, 218; Cold War, radio narratives and, 3–5, 9–11, 98–99; Declaration of Washington, 108; Education and Exchange Act (1948), 100; Egypt, influence in, 168–169; Food for Peace program, 87; "The Goals of American Foreign Policy," 114*fig*, 115–116; Kennedy's reinvigoration of US propaganda program, 173–174; Lebanon, 1958 intervention in, 178–179; light and illumination imagery, use of, 73–74; Middle East actions in search of oil, 110–112; peace, rhetoric of, 78–80, 83–85, 92–97; Point IV development program, 87; propaganda programs, growth of, 100–102; propaganda spending estimates, 93; radio archives, 6; radio broadcast range and daily schedule, 61; Radio Moscow on peace as a vision against US interventions, 81–83; Radio Moscow propaganda about US aid programs, 85–87; Six-Day War, broadcasts before the war, 199–202, 205–206; Six-Day War, excerpts of broadcast transcripts, 206–213; Suez Crisis, preparations for war, 132–135, 138–139; Suez Crisis, tensions with Britain and France, 160–161; Suez Crisis, war over, 146–164; Syrian coup attempt, 87, 175–176; tractors as symbol of modernity and national power, 88, 89*fig*; view of Voice of the Arabs radio, 58–60. *See also* Voice of America (VOA)

United States Foreign Broadcast Information Service (FBIS), 6, 43, 101

United States Information Agency (USIA), 9–10, 57; broadcast expansion after Suez war, 161–164; creation of, 98–99, 101; Egyptian Broadcasting Service, early ties to, 113; Eisenhower Doctrine, effects of, 171; freedom of religion, weaponization of, 106–107; "The Goals of American Foreign Policy," 114*fig*, 115–116; growth of Middle East programming in late 1950s, 178–181; Iraqi Revolution, messaging about, 178; Kennedy's reinvigoration of US propaganda program, 173–174; "liberation issue," handling of, 108–109; Mossadeq coup, fallout from, 112–113; Mossadeq coup, lack of coverage on, 110–111; Office of Research and Intelligence, 162–163; Palestine partition, media coverage of, 46–47; promotion of kinder, gentler image of capitalism, 104; racism and racial violence in US, coverage of, 109–110; Six-Day War, broadcasts before the war, 202–204; Suez Crisis, preparations for war, 138–139; Syrian coup attempt, messaging about, 175–176; use of single Arab as example of life in America, 105–106. *See also* Voice of America (VOA)

United States Senate Foreign Relations Committee, 100

University Forum, VOA, 102

Urabi Pasha, Ahmad, 172

U.S. News Review, 115

Uzbekistan, 90–91

Vaughan, James, 5, 118

Vietnam, 137, 176, 180, 195, 200, 202, 204

Virgin Lands project, 87

Voice of America (VOA), 2, 9–11, 57, 207–213; accusations of lying about peace, 88–90, 92–97; American promise of happiness and peace, 102–105, 103*fig*; *Arabic Anecdotes and American Novelties*, 102; *Arabs in America*, 102; Arabs unwillingness to listen to broadcasts, 180, 182; avoidance of ideological language, 105; Baghdad Pact, failed messaging efforts, 126–128; Campaign of Truth, 101; early goals of, 99–100;

Founded in 1893,
UNIVERSITY OF CALIFORNIA PRESS
publishes bold, progressive books and journals
on topics in the arts, humanities, social sciences,
and natural sciences—with a focus on social
justice issues—that inspire thought and action
among readers worldwide.

The UC PRESS FOUNDATION
raises funds to uphold the press's vital role
as an independent, nonprofit publisher, and
receives philanthropic support from a wide
range of individuals and institutions—and from
committed readers like you. To learn more, visit
ucpress.edu/supportus.

www.ingramcontent.com/pod-product-compliance
Lightning Source LLC
Chambersburg PA
CBHW020824270326
41928CB00006B/434